INTERNATIONAL LAW AND INTERNATIONAL RELATIONS

This volume examines the opportunities for, and initiates work in, interdisciplinary research between the fields of international law (IL) and international relations (IR), two disciplines that have, for much of the post WWII era, engaged relatively little with one another. With contributions from IL and IR scholars as well as policy practitioners, the book's unique approach is that it is organized not only around practical case studies, but around four discrete policy challenges: responses to terrorism after September 11, 2001, controlling the flow of small arms and light weapons, addressing the demands of internally displaced persons, and responding to the call for international criminal accountability.

The contributions thus demonstrate a number of contemporary trends that are often ill-addressed by scholars of either field including the increased importance of non-state actors and the ramifications of state weakness and state illegitimacy. They also shed light upon the ways in which policymakers operate at the intersections of law and politics in the international sphere, notwithstanding the gap between the two domains highlighted by scholars. Ultimately the book analyses how policymakers can draw upon scholars to address concrete policy issues, but also how, in return, scholars can learn from the approaches of policymakers. Such interdisciplinary and policy-relevant work is meant to help develop a more concrete research agenda for the growing work linking international law and international relations.

This book will be of great interest to all students of international law, international relations and governance.

Thomas J. Biersteker is Henry R. Luce Professor of Transnational Organizations at the Watson Institute for International Studies and Department of Political Science at Brown University. **Peter J. Spiro** is Charles R. Weiner Professor of Law, Temple University, James E. Beasley School of Law. He is a former State Department and White House official. **Chandra Lekha Sriram** is Professor of Human Rights at the University of East London School of Law and Director of the Centre on Human Rights in Conflict. **Veronica Raffo** is a consultant for the World Bank in the Poverty Reduction and Economic Management Network, in the Latin America and Caribbean Region, and was previously Program Coordinator of the Global Security and Cooperation Program of the SSRC.

CONTEMPORARY SECURITY STUDIES

NATO'S SECRET ARMIES
Operation Gladio and terrorism in Western Europe
Daniele Ganser

THE US, NATO AND MILITARY BURDEN-SHARING
Peter Kent Forster and Stephen J. Cimbala

RUSSIAN GOVERNANCE IN THE TWENTY-FIRST CENTURY
Geo-strategy, geopolitics and new governance
Irina Isakova

THE FOREIGN OFFICE AND FINLAND 1938–1940
Diplomatic sideshow
Craig Gerrard

RETHINKING THE NATURE OF WAR
Edited by Isabelle Duyvesteyn and Jan Angstrom

PERCEPTION AND REALITY IN THE MODERN YUGOSLAV CONFLICT
Myth, falsehood and deceit 1991–1995
Brendan O'Shea

THE POLITICAL ECONOMY OF PEACEBUILDING IN POST-DAYTON BOSNIA
Tim Donais

THE DISTRACTED EAGLE
The rift between America and Old Europe
Peter H. Merkl

THE IRAQ WAR
European perspectives on politics, strategy, and operations
Edited by Jan Hallenberg and Håkan Karlsson

STRATEGIC CONTEST
Weapons proliferation and war in the greater Middle East
Richard L. Russell

PROPAGANDA, THE PRESS AND CONFLICT
The Gulf War and Kosovo
David R. Willcox

MISSILE DEFENCE
International, regional and national implications
Edited by Bertel Heurlin and Sten Rynning

GLOBALISING JUSTICE FOR MASS ATROCITIES
A revolution in accountability
Chandra Lekha Sriram

ETHNIC CONFLICT AND TERRORISM
The origins and dynamics of civil wars
Joseph L. Soeters

GLOBALISATION AND THE FUTURE OF TERRORISM
Patterns and predictions
Brynjar Lia

NUCLEAR WEAPONS AND STRATEGY
The evolution of American nuclear policy
Stephen J. Cimbala

NASSER AND THE MISSILE AGE IN THE MIDDLE EAST
Owen L. Sirrs

WAR AS RISK MANAGEMENT
Strategy and conflict in an age of globalised risks
Yee-Kuang Heng

MILITARY NANOTECHNOLOGY
Potential applications and preventive arms control
Jurgen Altmann

NATO AND WEAPONS OF MASS DESTRUCTION
Regional alliance, global threats
Eric R. Terzuolo

EUROPEANISATION OF NATIONAL SECURITY IDENTITY
The EU and the changing security identities of the Nordic states
Pernille Rieker

INTERNATIONAL CONFLICT PREVENTION AND PEACE-BUILDING
Sustaining the peace in post conflict societies
Edited by T. David Mason and James D. Meernik

CONTROLLING THE WEAPONS OF WAR
Politics, persuasion, and the prohibition of inhumanity
Brian Rappert

CHANGING TRANSATLANTIC SECURITY RELATIONS
Do the US, the EU and Russia form a new strategic triangle?
Edited by Jan Hallenberg and Håkan Karlsson

THEORITICAL ROOTS OF US FOREIGN POLICY
Machiavelli and American unilateralism
Thomas M. Kane

CORPORATE SOLDIERS AND INTERNATIONAL SECURITY
The rise of private military companies
Christopher Kinsey

TRANSFORMING EUROPEAN MILITARIES
Coalition operations and the technology gap
Gordon Adams and Guy Ben-Ari

GLOBALIZATION AND CONFLICT
National security in a 'new' strategic era
Edited by Robert G. Patman

MILITARY FORCES IN 21ST CENTURY PEACE OPERATIONS
No job for a soldier?
James V. Arbuckle

THE POLITICAL ROAD TO WAR WITH IRAQ
Bush, 9/11 and the drive to overthrow Saddam
Nick Ritchie and Paul Rogers

BOSNIAN SECURITY AFTER DAYTON
New perspectives
Edited by Michael A. Innes

KENNEDY, JOHNSON AND NATO
Britain, America and the dynamics of alliance, 1962–68
Andrew Priest

SMALL ARMS AND SECURITY
New emerging international norms
Denise Garcia

THE UNITED STATES AND EUROPE
Beyond the neo-conservative divide?
Edited by John Baylis and Jon Roper

RUSSIA, NATO AND COOPERATIVE SECURITY
Bridging the gap
Lionel Ponsard

INTERNATIONAL LAW AND INTERNATIONAL RELATIONS
Bridging theory and practice
Edited by Thomas J. Biersteker, Peter J. Spiro, Chandra Lekha Sriram, and Veronica Raffo

INTERNATIONAL LAW AND INTERNATIONAL RELATIONS

Bridging theory and practice

Edited by Thomas J. Biersteker, Peter J. Spiro, Chandra Lekha Sriram, and Veronica Raffo

SSRC

Routledge
Taylor & Francis Group
LONDON AND NEW YORK

First published 2007
by Routledge
2 Park Square, Milton Park, Abingdon, Oxon OX14 4RN

Simultaneously published in the USA and Canada
by Routledge
270 Madison Ave, New York, NY 10016

Routledge is an imprint of the Taylor & Francis Group, an informa business

Typeset in Times by Wearset Ltd, Boldon, Tyne and Wear
Printed and bound in Great Britain by TJI Digital, Padstow, Cornwall

British Library Cataloguing in Publication Data
A catalogue record for this book is available from the British Library

Library of Congress Cataloging in Publication Data
A catalog record for this book has been requested

ISBN10: 0-415-40076-7 (hbk)
ISBN10: 0-203-96676-7 (ebk)

ISBN13: 978-0-415-40076-3 (hbk)
ISBN13: 978-0-203-96676-1 (ebk)

CONTENTS

NOTES ON CONTRIBUTORS

Kenneth W. Abbott is Professor of Law, Willard H. Pedrick Distinguished Research Scholar, and Professor of Global Studies at Arizona State University.

Fiona B. Adamson is Assistant Professor of International Relations and Director of the Program in International Public Policy at University College London.

Thomas J. Biersteker is Henry R. Luce Professor of Transnational Organizations at Brown University. He was the director of the Watson Institute for International Studies at Brown University from 1994 to 2006.

Clarence J. Dias is President of the International Center for Law in Development.

Francis M. Deng served in the United Nations as Special Representative of the Secretary-General on Internally Displaced Persons from 1993 to 2004. He is currently codirector of the Brookings Institution–Johns Hopkins School of Advanced International Studies (SAIS) Project on Internal Displacement; Research Professor of International Politics, Law, and Society at SAIS; and founder of the SAIS Center for Displacement Studies.

Martha Finnemore is Professor of Political Science and International Affairs at George Washington University's Elliott School of International Affairs.

Harold Hongju Koh is Dean and Gerard C. and Bernice Latrobe Smith Professor of International Law, Yale Law School; and was Assistant Secretary of State for Democracy, Human Rights, and Labor, 1998–2001.

Ellen L. Lutz, Cultural Survival's Executive Director, formerly served as the Executive Director of the Center for Human Rights and Conflict Resolution at Tufts University's Fletcher School. From 1989 to 1994 she was the California Director for Human Rights Watch.

Youssef Mahmoud is currently the UNDP Resident Representative and UN Resident Coordinator in Guyana. Prior to this assignment and for a period of eight years, he was the Director of the Africa II Division, in the UN Department of Political Affairs.

Madeline Morris is Professor of Law at Duke University and Director of the Duke/Geneva Institute in Transnational Law. She has served as Senior Legal Counsel, Office of the Prosecutor, Special Court for Sierra Leone.

Robert Muggah is the project manager of the Small Arms Survey in Geneva; he has worked on postconflict recovery and reconstruction issues with multilateral and bilateral agencies in over a dozen countries.

Mary Ellen O'Connell is the Robert and Marion Short Chair in Law, Notre Dame Law School.

Diane F. Orentlicher is Professor of International Law and Codirector of the Center for Human Rights and Humanitarian Law at American University's Washington College of Law. In 2004–5 she served as the United Nations Independent Expert on combating impunity.

Veronica Raffo is a consultant for the World Bank in the Poverty Reduction and Economic Management Network, in the Latin America and Caribbean Region, and was previously Program Coordinator of the Global Security and Cooperation Program of the Social Science Research Council in Washington, DC.

William Reno is Associate Professor of Political Science at the Center for Comparative International Studies, Northwestern University, Evanston, Illinois.

Leila Nadya Sadat is Henry H. Oberschelp Professor of Law, Washington University School of Law, St. Louis.

Gerry Simpson is Reader in Public International Law at the London School of Economics and Senior Fellow at the University of Melbourne. He was a legal adviser to the Australian government on the International Criminal Court.

Peter J. Spiro is Charles R. Weiner Professor of Law, Temple University, James E. Beasley School of Law.

Chandra Lekha Sriram is Professor of Human Rights at the University of East London School of Law and Director of the Center on Human Rights in Conflict.

Curtis A. Ward is currently a consultant to *Security Council Report*. In 2000–1, he served on the UN Security Council as Deputy Permanent Representative of Jamaica to the United Nations. He has also served as an independent expert and adviser to the UN Security Council's Counter-Terrorism Committee and its liaison with regional and international organizations.

Nicholas Wheeler is Professor in the Department of International Politics at the University of Wales, Aberystwyth.

FOREWORD

When one regards the real world of global, national, and local efforts to achieve peace, equality, and prosperity, it is apparent that the way people conduct politics relies very significantly on values and norms that they believe and act upon. Such a palpable human context is often lost in academic renderings of politics, which increasingly rely on sterile formulas of behavior or quanta of manipulatable data. This sterility seems also to render much social science alien to the choices of policymakers, civil society actors, and others in the day-to-day arena of political action. It has substituted a narrow band of explanatory power for relevancy.

At the same time, international law and theory also seem disconnected from daily experience, irrelevant in a world still dominated by state actors and transnational forces, an antiquated trope of diplomats. This perception is reinforced by leaders of hegemonic powers who regard the supposed restraints imposed by international law as an annoyance to be blocked at every inconvenient turn, rather than as an opportunity to solve global problems through collective action.

This volume and a series of four workshops were convened by the Social Science Research Council to try something a little different that would address the sterility or remoteness of the disciplines and applicability of international relations (IR) and international law (IL). Begun in the summer of 2001 by Ben Rawlence of the Program on Global Security and Cooperation, the project convened leading academics from both fields, men and women with real-world experience and a demonstrated capacity for inter-disciplinarity, a hallmark of the SSRC. In its simplest formulation, the project mission was to explore how norms were manifested through law. As Rawlence recalled to me recently, "Bringing legal perspectives to bear on conventional IR ways of understanding international problems would, it was hoped, promote a better understanding of how law worked to influence outcomes and thus to reinvigorate arguments within IR that law mattered. And flowing from that is that [empirical] scholarship mattered in helping to shape laws and the perspectives of law makers."

We adopted a case-study approach, and sought out complexity and relevance in these cases. The four that were adopted, and guided by the exceptional skill of Veronica Raffo, were the attempt to enact international legal restrictions on the flow of small arms and light weapons; the ways the international community would deal with terrorism; the treatment of tens of millions of internally displaced persons worldwide; and international criminal accountability. To some extent, these choices were driven by opportunity and headlines, but those are not necessarily poor criteria. We wanted to demonstrate relevance by engaging issues of terrorism and the culpability of criminal regimes. In examining the legal status of internally displaced persons (IDPs), we had the unusual advantage of Ambassador Frances Deng's participation. He, more than anyone, had been responsible for creating and trying to implement norms as the UN Secretary-General's Representative on IDPs. We took on the small arms issue first, in part because it was receiving little attention from American policymakers (who oversee the world's largest export system), had a sizable and sophisticated community of researchers and activists, but was highly problematic with respect to solutions through international law.

The SSRC program always stressed the significance of social science research as a problem-solving enterprise, problems that afflict people the world over. Bringing these publicly spirited scholars together with practitioners – among them activists, judges, and government officials – was intentional, both to enrich the data scholars require and to provide a space and context for practitioners to reflect and learn. This project, perhaps more than any other, seemed to succeed in this way remarkably well.

As usual, there are many to thank for this at SSRC and elsewhere. These include the dozens of workshop participants, some of whose work is presented here. We are grateful as well to the foresight and generosity of our donor, the William and Flora Hewlett Foundation, and its program head, Melanie Greenberg. Intellectual work such as this is among the most satisfying one can pursue – it is both exciting as a complex puzzle and worthwhile because it can lead to enlightened action. We certainly know it met the first expectation, and hope it will fulfill the second one as well.

John Tirman
Cambridge, Massachusetts
August 2006

ACKNOWLEDGMENTS

This volume developed out of a research project sponsored by the Program on Global Security and Cooperation at the Social Science Research Council (SSRC), New York. We are thankful to John Tirman and Ben Rawlence, Program Director and Program Coordinator respectively at the SSRC, who designed the original structure of the project in July 2001. The project was further developed with the intellectual input of a "core group" of scholars that was convened by the SSRC to provide advice and guidance for the project. The members of this group were: Kenneth Abbott, Arizona State University; Thomas Biersteker, Brown University; Clarence Dias, United Nations; Martha Finnemore, George Washington University; Harold Koh, Yale University Law School; Sally Falk Moore, Harvard University; Anne-Marie Slaughter, Princeton University; Peter Spiro, University of Georgia Law School; Chandra Lekha Sriram, University of East London; and Nicholas Wheeler, University of Wales, Aberystwyth. Our thanks go to them as well, for their insightful advice and active engagement throughout the life of this project. The project received financial support from a grant from The William and Flora Hewlett Foundation, for which we are grateful.

The project took the form of a workshop series on different policy areas: Small Arms and Light Weapons Proliferation (workshop held in February 2002); Terrorism (workshop held in November 2002); Internally Displaced Persons (workshop held in June 2003); and International Criminal Accountability (workshop held in November 2003). Many of the chapters in this book are expanded versions of the papers presented at these meetings. We would like to thank all the speakers and participants at these workshops for their thought-provoking presentations, engaged discussions, and insightful analysis.

We take this opportunity to recognize the intellectual, editorial, and administrative support of the staff at the Program on Global Security and Cooperation at the SSRC, whose prodding, skills, and efficiency were absolutely essential to this project: John Tirman, Itty Abraham, Petra Ticha, Maggie Schuppert, Karim Youssef, Thodleen Dessources, and Sion Dayson. A special thank you to all of them.

Finally, we thank our editor Andrew Humphrys at Routledge, for his interest in and support for this volume.

1

INTRODUCTION

International law and international politics – old divides, new developments

Veronica Raffo, Chandra Lekha Sriram, Peter Spiro, and Thomas Biersteker

Introduction: law and politics after the Cold War

Since the end of the Cold War, the international political terrain has altered significantly. We no longer live in a world of discrete national communities, but rather in a world of increasing economic, political, and cultural interdependence, where the trajectories of countries are heavily enmeshed with each other, and where the very nature of everyday processes links people together across borders in multiple ways. Globalization, understood as a multidimensional phenomenon, has put pressure on polities everywhere, gradually circumscribing and delimiting political power.[1] The operation of these transnational social forces has had a profound effect on both the functioning and the conceptualization of international law and international politics.

The end of the Cold War heralded the end of a bipolar world in which law was subjugated to the imperatives of superpower spheres of influence. Pressures from below, such as from nongovernmental organizations (NGOs), and "global civil society," have brought the rights agenda to the fore, calling into question the absolute and unfettered sovereignty of the nation-state over its citizens.[2] With the perceived transformation of state sovereignty as the basis for power politics, the structure of international relations has changed: issues that transcend or disrupt traditional state interests, such as arms flows, human rights, terrorism, migration and displacement of populations, international finance, and the increasingly legalized nature of relations at the multilateral level, have risen to prominence. In this process, international law has increasingly embraced a broader variety of actors, overturning the exclusive position of the state and buttressing the role of suprastate, substate, and nonstate actors.

To study these emerging governance phenomena and questions of codification and enforceability of international law, new approaches to research are needed that can link macrosystemic-level analysis with detailed fieldwork.

Locating the nexus of different types of authority and power, and then further analyzing the drivers of social and legal processes within a web of overlapping political and legal jurisdictions, is a task that requires a multidisciplinary approach.

We intend this volume as an initial effort toward building such a knowledge base, and seek to contribute to a deeper understanding of how international law can be adapted to today's security challenges. The contributors not only examine the opportunities for interdisciplinary collaboration between the fields of international law (IL) and international relations (IR), but also initiate a research agenda, build an empirical base, and offer a multidisciplinary approach designed to provide concrete answers to real-world problems of governance, engaging both the theory and the practice of global security.

Genesis of the project

In July 2001 the Global Security and Cooperation program of the Social Science Research Council (SSRC) convened highly recognized scholars in IR and IL for a planning meeting for a new research project.[3] This SSRC initiative was aimed at forging collaboration between the fields of international law and international relations, both in theory and in practice, in order to address contemporary global security challenges. The project concentrated upon three central questions: (1) To what extent are international norms manifested through law? (2) In what ways can methodological and theoretical collaboration between the fields of IR and IL be fostered? (3) In what ways can social science research be mobilized effectively to enhance our knowledge about the utility of international norms through law?

The project drew on the expertise of a core group of scholars,[4] who chose a case-study approach to go beyond abstract meta-theoretical discussion of the relationship between IL and IR and concentrate on fresh approaches to urgent problems of international security and governance. The goal was the production of new knowledge as well as bridging the gap between relevant scholars and on-the-ground practitioners in a systematic and innovative way. The core group also identified several policy challenges crucial to the achievement of a sustainable global peace, challenges that require new research and new ways of applying research and scholarship. The four policy areas selected by the group were small arms and light weapons (workshop held in February 2002), terrorism (workshop held in November 2002), internally displaced persons (IDPs) (workshop held in June 2003), and international criminal accountability (workshop held in November 2003). This volume is organized into distinct sections that engage these specific policy challenges, in the order in which the workshops devoted to them occurred.

The purpose of the workshops was to examine these policy problems through the lenses of different legal and social science methods in order to illuminate how law and political processes intersect to influence the possibilities for international cooperation. By examining specific challenges in international politics through crosscutting theoretical frames, this project sought first to generalize about the cases and contribute to theory-building on the structure and efficacy of international mechanisms for regulating transnational governance issues; and second, to apply these theoretical insights in the service of case-specific policy problems and provide practitioners with empirical research on which to base negotiations or advocacy efforts. The workshops thus were aimed at clarifying the variables at play in each case in order to assist those practitioners who are committed to enhancing global security by the application of norms through law. The evidence of the politico-legal process at work in international affairs contributed, simultaneously, to an ongoing examination of the theoretical and methodological habits of the scholarly disciplines of law and international relations.

In order to foster greater interaction between practitioner experience and more theoretical approaches, the workshops were structured in such a way that each panel would feature practitioners (including policymakers working for governmental agencies as well as international organizations, and also NGO activists) and scholars from different disciplines.

In discussions at the workshops, the advantage of approaching these policy problems from the intersection of IL and IR became evident. On the one hand, IL as a discipline has suffered from overreliance on legal cases involving states without paying due attention to case studies (a new method for IL) rather than cases seeking adjudication, or without paying due attention to nonstate actors, who are increasingly the greatest perpetrators and victims of violence and conflict. On the other hand, IR has focused mainly on power and state-to-state relations, leaving out considerations of justice, nonstate actors, sustainable peace, international crime, and violence and its means. When these considerations cross international borders, as they increasingly do, neither traditional IR nor IL – taken alone – is sufficient.

This volume is intended to bridge the analytic and methodological shortcomings of both fields while also drawing on their respective strengths. Through case studies concerning some of the most pressing problems facing the world today, the distinguished contributors to this volume seek to ground discussions of norms, justice, peace, violence, and conflict in relation to the real world and thereby move beyond the existing limits of both disciplines.

International law and international relations: defining the gap, bridging the gap

The fields of international law and international relations have become increasingly intertwined in recent years, beginning to reverse a long tradition of viewing them as separate arenas. For several decades, this tradition was reinforced by the development of the academic disciplines of both international relations and international law.[5]

The dominance of the realist, and later, neorealist school of thought in international relations in the post-World War II era was perhaps the most significant reason for the divide between international law and international relations, as the realist school tended to promote the argument that law was largely derivative of international power politics. Political realists argued that law was epiphenomenal in the international sphere, and that it was generally ignored when contrary to state interests; it was a tool of the strong used to impose constraints on the weak, or something that states agreed to abide by only as long as it supported their own interests – and happily violated when it ceased to do so. This built upon the realists' traditional claims that the international system is one of anarchy, that the primary units are states, and that states pursue self-interest and survival.

Surely, the realists argued, it was clear that law could not constrain the external behavior of nations in any serious way; only the use of force was respected. If realists were correct that states were rational, unitary actors concerned with their own survival, then they would be loath to enter into agreements that in any way constrained their ability to act. Even if they were to make such agreements, they would do so only when it was in their own interest, and would feel quite free to abrogate them should their interests change. Law, and by extension international institutions, were therefore ineffectual and "epiphenomenal."[6] Major international law texts were dropped from the required reading lists for international relations students in leading research-oriented departments.

The skepticism of realism was compounded by skepticism from within legal or jurisprudential study, specifically by positivists who, following a tradition deriving from John Austin, argued that international law could not properly be law because it lacked the requisites. The positivists argued that as sovereign states were the highest authority in global society, it was by definition impossible to place limitations or authorities above them. As a result, international law could not function like domestic law: there might be some elements of international law that resembled domestic law, such as primary and secondary rules, and even adjudicatory bodies, but there was no apparatus for enforcement, no global police force.[7]

Of course, these challenges did not go unanswered, and there are a host of arguments that have been put forward for the role and relevance of law in contemporary international politics. Arguments for bridging the gap between international law and international relations have grown since the late 1980s and early 1990s. Further, the divide was less pronounced in the United Kingdom, where the importance of law in international relations was emphasized by adherents of the "English School."[8] At the same time, some groups of IR scholars – liberal institutionalists, social constructivists, and those who discuss legalization in international life – have begun to move past debates about the relevance or status of international law, to queries or arguments about *how* it functions in international life.

While the IR–IL divide was not just a peculiarly American phenomenon, it was most visible in the United States. Scholars of the English School embraced the role of law, rules, and norms in international society, often proudly proclaiming themselves to be working in a "Grotian tradition," referring to Hugo Grotius, a seventeenth-century scholar who is often referred to as the "father of international law."[9] These scholars argued that even though international politics was anarchic, lacking a unitary hierarchical structure, this did not mean that rules and indeed law could not govern state behavior. They argued rather that international society was an anarchical society, but a *society* nonetheless, a carefully regulated one.[10]

Liberal institutionalists' arguments vary, but they combine key elements of liberalism with elements of institutionalism. They argue for the importance of institutions and cooperation in the international system – far from being anarchic, they argue, international order is maintained and rule-governed. This may be the case, in large part, for self-interested reasons: states create institutions that facilitate activities in which they wish to engage, such as trade, or ease the risks of risky negotiations, such as those over arms control. These theorists argue that because institutions or regimes facilitate transparency, reduce transactions costs, and reduce the risks of cheating, states will create rules and abide by them. Many also argue that, once created, institutions develop an identity and power of their own, constraining state behavior even where states may wish to deviate from agreed rules. Path dependency ensures that institutions are easier to maintain than they are to create. Liberal institutionalists may further argue that liberal states that adhere to the rule of law at home will be more likely to promote rule-governed behavior internationally, and to create and abide by international legal regimes.[11]

Constructivists, too, have embraced the role of law and norms in international politics. They reject the realist claim that anarchy in the sense of the absence of a unitary ruler in international relations means that behavior cannot be ordered. As Alexander Wendt put it, anarchy is what states make of it, and they can construct social interactions and institutions that are orderly. Norms have an impact upon state actors, shaping their identity and interests, and thus shaping their behavior. The account of normative development that they offer often reads very much like that of the emergence and shaping of international law, particularly customary law. By this account, norms may emerge initially through the efforts of a few norm entrepreneurs. Over time, these entrepreneurs are able to convince actors to adhere to their norms, and at some point, when a sufficient number have adopted a norm, a tipping point is reached and it becomes embedded. Central to this account is the nature of actors' belief systems: actors change behavior because they believe it to be in their interest, or consistent with their identity, to do so. Norms, and indeed law, are then not cynical fictions as realists might suggest, but rather create real limits on state behavior.[12]

Finally, emergent work devoted to the so-called legalization of international politics focuses less on debates about whether or not international law is important in international politics and more on explaining how legalized institutional arrangements come to be. They use state interests and preferences to help explain why states choose to develop regimes that appear to constrain them. Such legalization can be harder or softer, and its creation is driven by state interests. States will strategically choose harder or softer law according to their needs. Harder law has the advantage of reducing transaction costs, strengthening credible commitments, and resolving problems of incomplete contracting and later interpretive disputes. Softer law has lower contracting costs and lower sovereignty costs, facilitating compromise and allowing the possibility of coping with uncertainty.[13]

International lawyers have been saying for years that "law matters" in international affairs; now, current events are proving them right and IR scholars are taking note. Myriad books and articles have been devoted to the subject, seeking to identify the gap between international law and international relations, and arguing that it must be bridged, since roughly the end of the Cold War.[14] Some work has devoted attention to the insights that can be derived from the engagement between IR and IL for specific challenges, such as that of responding to mass atrocities.[15] But more remains to be done.

For analysts taking law seriously, the question now becomes: How do we take the theoretical engagement between the two fields and use it to interpret and explain aspects of contemporary international politics? Further, how can these analyses be made relevant to policymakers seeking to craft solutions to policy challenges at the intersection of international law and politics? And how can both IL and IR gain from the insights of practitioners? Many practitioners are already simultaneously engaged in integrating concepts from both international law and international relations into their daily work and have little time for meta-theoretical musings about how the two can be better integrated in the abstract.

International law, international relations, policy practitioners, and the state

Each of the three different communities (international law scholars, international relations scholars, and policy practitioners) engaged in conversations in the four sections that compose this volume (small arms and light weapons, terrorism, internally displaced people, and international criminal accountability) has a distinct relationship to the state. As already discussed, most mainstream international relations scholars are explicitly or implicitly state-centric in their orientation and analysis. The same is true of many scholars of international law, which has long privileged the law of states. Practitioners, including those represented in this volume, are often either former state officials or representatives of nongovernmental organizations who define their mission in opposition to state policies. For all three, whether they respect or abhor the state, securing a change in state policy is often their primary goal or best indicator of success.

Yet the state construct itself has become increasingly problematic in recent years. The state faces challenges both from above and from below. The Westphalian state ideal – that neat convergence of an unchallenged (sovereign) location of final authority over a people with an unproblematic identity residing within a clearly demarcated territorial boundary – is a rare achievement, if it ever even existed.[16]

A key challenge from above is the emergence of institutions within which states voluntarily bind themselves, such as the International Criminal Court (ICC) (discussed in this volume) and the United Nations (UN). The UN Security Council has increasingly invoked Chapter VII of the UN Charter in resolutions passed since the end of the Cold War, making its resolutions binding on *all* member states. In particular, the UN's frequent invocation of Chapter VII in its counterterrorism resolutions since September 11, 2001, has led to complaints from some member states of a growing "democratic deficit" in the UN system.

The codification of new norms, such as the "responsibility to protect," poses a different kind of challenge to the Westphalian state ideal from above. The idea that all states have a responsibility to protect populations located within their territorial space (and if they do not or are unable to do so, that others implicitly have a right to intervene) constitutes a significant redefinition of the operational meaning of state sovereignty. It is a direct descendent of the Nuremburg trials, the Universal Declaration of Human Rights, the Genocide Convention, and the Helsinki accords. There will inevitably be violations of this emergent norm, but the codification of the idea in the 2005 UN summit declaration is a significant normative challenge to the Westphalian state ideal.

Challenges to the state from below include the emergence of both relatively benign institutions, such as the growth of institutions of global civil society, and less benign elements, such as groups engaged in transnational terrorism. Further, in some places the institutions of the state have virtually ceased to exist (in the so-called failed or collapsed states of sub-Saharan Africa, such as Somalia, Sierra Leone, or Liberia).

As a result of these challenges from below, nonstate (often private) actors increasingly play authoritative roles in international affairs, roles ranging from market-based standard-setting organizations to transnational networks engaged in acts of terrorism.[17] Whether they invoke market authority, the authority of expertise, or the authority that comes from the provision of subnational security (sometimes by warlords), substate actors variously operate below the radar of the state, challenge centralized state legitimacy, and increasingly provide alternatives to the unachieved Westphalian state ideal.

The four sections that compose the bulk of this volume address these different challenges from above and below the state and are indicative of the new kinds of problems facing the world in the twenty-first century. However normatively appealing the unrealized Westphalian state ideal, a growing number of actors and analysts are beginning to see the state as a problem, not as the sole source of effective solutions.

This poses both normative and methodological challenges for international law and international relations scholarship. Individuals and corporate entities are increasingly becoming central agents in international affairs, quite independent of their relationship to the state. The agency of individuals before international legal (and quasi-legal) institutions has become an issue for both IL and IR: they can, for example, trigger internal reviews of World Bank projects or challenge their designations on UN sanctions lists. These developments do not eliminate the importance of the state in international law and international relations. Rather, a state-centered focus, taken alone, is increasingly inadequate for a growing number of important issues in international affairs.

This realization has been reached simultaneously by international law scholars, international relations scholars, and policy practitioners. It has been our hope in the various workshops that are summarized in this volume, that by bringing together IL scholars, IR scholars, and policy practitioners, we might be able to generate some new insights and go beyond the core realization that IL, IR, and policy practitioners have already reached independently. By grounding the conversation in four different empirical contemporary global security issues, we have attempted to go beyond general calls for greater collaboration among the three communities and to explore the connections between them that might emerge out of common concern.

The task, however, is simple. International law scholars share a body of international legal case knowledge that often seems arcane and exclusionary to IR scholars and policy practitioners. IR scholars are often caught up in metatheoretical debates and epistemological arguments of their own. IR scholars' concern with research design and methods of analysis may seem equally arcane to IL scholars and policy practitioners. At the same time, the advocacy of some practitioners is sometimes off-putting to IL and IR scholars who seek "objectivity."

There are challenges in combining practitioner observations and normative commitments to outcomes with theoretical generality and analytical commitments on the part of both IR and IL, just as there are questions of how practitioner knowledge can be incorporated into social science and legal understanding, and how those bodies of theory can assist practitioners on the ground. We have not addressed all of these issues in the volume, but we have at least begun the conversation.

Organization of the volume

This volume seeks to contribute to the growing literature on the linkages between international law and international relations in two novel ways. First, it brings into the discussion policy practitioners, who regularly operate in the arenas of both law and politics, and whose concerns offer new insights into the relationship between law and politics in the "real" world. Second, it seeks to deepen our understanding of the interplay of law and politics by focusing upon four discrete clusters of policy challenges: the spread of small arms and light weapons, the threat of and responses to terrorism, the protection of internally displaced persons, and the demand for international criminal accountability.

These four policy challenges were chosen as subjects of inquiry, initially for the policy workshops and then for this volume, for several reasons. First, each represents a pressing contemporary policy problem. Second, the policy approach to each has been more or less legalized, or is in the process of becoming more legalized. Third, each represents an arena in which state interests, and thus international politics, are clearly implicated. Fourth, these four areas represent very different types of challenge: terrorism may pose a direct security threat to states, as may the spread of small arms, and may be viewed as "hard" politics, while international criminal accountability and protection for IDPs represent "softer" responses to humanitarian concerns. In examining each of these challenges and the responses to date, we see clearly the interplay of law and power relations in policymaking.

The volume has been structured into four sections, each devoted to one of these four policy challenges, with an additional section of three chapters drawing out insights and conclusions. Each section analyzes emerging international processes and institutions from the comparative perspectives of both international law and international relations, and introduces the perspectives of policy practitioners. The structure of the sections themselves replicates the structure of the policy workshop at which the essays that would become this book were presented, in that each section includes the contributions of scholars from different disciplines as well as contributions of practitioners, including policymakers working for governmental agencies and international organizations, as well as NGO activists.

Small arms and light weapons

The chapters in Part I of the volume each deal in different ways with the challenge of responding to a transborder and substate problem with traditional methods of arms control, which are often state-centric and focused upon regulating supply rather than demand. Clear divisions emerge among the contributors about the ramifications of this challenge. While Harold Koh seeks to identify potential international regulatory and legal responses, and is relatively optimistic, Will Reno suggests that the current approaches are overly deferential to the state, failing to recognize the many situations in which armed groups may have control, and even a degree of legitimacy, in a given locale. This disagreement has real ramifications for the regulation of small arms, but also for how we think about the place of law in international relations. Certainly, to the degree that we continue to understand international law as something that can only be created by states, found in sources identified by Article 38 of the Statute of the International Court of Justice (ICJ), the result will be attempts to encourage states to regulate arms flows domestically, or attempts to prevent arms flows by placing constraints such as sanctions upon states. Responses are thus state-driven and state-centric, replicating the "black box" conception of the state promoted by simple versions of structural realism. Certainly, there have been increased international attempts to curb flows of arms to groups – the 1993 sanctions and arms embargoes imposed upon Angolan rebels under UN Security Council Resolution 864 were the first of their kind. Sanctions on groups rather than states have become more common since, and the responses to terrorist financing in Security Council Resolution 1373, taken up in other chapters of this volume, demonstrate the recognition by states that there is a need to respond legally to nonstate actors directly. The problem is potentially more complex than this, however – in failed states or repressive and genocidal or "democidal" states, armed groups might represent more legitimate forces than does the officially recognized state. They may provide some measure of basic services, including security, and be viewed by the population in a territorial control as a necessary evil or even as legitimate. In such contexts, Reno suggests, regulatory responses that preference the state may potentially do harm by stemming the flow of weapons to groups. However, the legal regimes developed to date do not, and perhaps cannot, differentiate among more or less legitimate armed groups or states. Here the insights of constructivism or other IR theories, perhaps in tandem with the insights of Thomas Franck on sources of legitimacy in international law, might potentially help us to think about more nuanced responses.[18] This is perhaps a key insight of a recent volume on the place of law in international politics edited by Christian Reus-Smit.[19] Constructivism may help us analyze the place of law in international politics, suggesting that it is more than simply a result of political contestation, but also has a feedback effect, shaping politics. As such, law is part of a complex interplay of factors, and helps to shape understandings about norms of appropriate behavior, and legitimacy.[20] This appears to be the case in two of the contributions on small arms, with Reno mounting a serious challenge to the constraints placed upon legitimate actors and possessors of small arms, and the apparent exclusion of certain armed groups. This is a more radical claim than that of Robert Muggah, who nevertheless also challenges the state-centric model, and is antithetical to some of the strong arguments that Koh makes for the role of law in constraining the flow of small arms.

Muggah argues that legal and regulatory responses to the flow of small arms and light weapons currently focus only upon the supply of small arms, not the sources of demand, or the effects of small arms. This appears to be partly an artifact of the epistemic community addressing these arms flows, many of whom were previously active in more conventional arms control.[21] Conventional arms controllers emphasize supply-focused and state-centered regulatory mechanisms. Their focus is thus excessively state-centric, and is unable to appreciate why communities, groups, and individuals seek to acquire weapons to combat radical insecurity in "failed" or "failing" states. This problem is compounded by the fact that states continue to be the primary actors negotiating international agreements, further hampering regulatory efforts that might take account of the role of nonstate groups, both NGO and armed, and individuals, in developing new norms and law surrounding small arms and light weapons.[22]

Koh, writing as both an academic and a practitioner, places great emphasis upon the importance of regulatory responses. Indeed, he emphasizes the need for academics to recognize the practical challenges faced by practitioners in addressing the flow of small arms, and the need for practitioners to be better informed by some of the theoretical work of academics. He argues not for a blind optimism or faith in regulations, but for a constructive and informed use of transnational legal processes. It is through the spread of norms and transnational regulation that problems that seem insuperable at first glance, he argues, might actually be tackled successfully. He argues, following constructivist work demonstrating the spread of human rights norms, that the spread of norms, practice, and regulation, vertically and horizontally, may help limit the spread and use of small arms.[23] The spread of such norms may also support regulatory regimes that are ultimately more flexible than the state-centric ones depicted and critiqued by Reno and Muggah.

Terrorism

The chapters in Part II of this volume examine law and politics in the wake of the terrorist attacks of September 11, 2001. Mary Ellen O'Connell and coauthors Gerry Simpson and Nicholas J. Wheeler consider the twinned dynamics of the US invasion of Iraq and the global war on terrorism. Simpson and Wheeler propose alternative conceptions of the invasion itself within and outside international legal frameworks. O'Connell highlights the George W. Bush administration's attempted use of international law as a weapon against perceived adversaries. In each analysis, the contributors argue that US actions have been lawless within an international legal model, although both analyses also conclude that any attempt by the Bush administration to legalize or legitimize its actions has failed. By contrast, both Fiona Adamson and Curtis Ward highlight the importance of nonstate actors and international organizations in any effort to systematize developments relating to terrorism. Ward challenges statist IR conceptions of global security issues in describing major innovations in UN efforts against terrorism, while Adamson challenges traditional assumptions of both IR and IL by offering a transnational political conception of terrorism. All four chapters in this section point to the growing role of international law and institutions in international relations, even in an area implicating core security concerns.

Simpson and Wheeler seek to explain the 2003 US invasion of Iraq in ways that take account of the action in international law terms. Treating the invasion as inconsistent with current international legal doctrine, the authors suggest three possible explanations for it. First, the Bush administration may have been seeking to challenge norms about self-defense, seeking to broaden the possibilities for anticipatory, or "preemptive," self-defense. This attempt clearly failed, as few international actors showed any inclination to accept the implicit and occasionally explicit proposal to transform the law defining acceptable use of force. Alternatively, the US invasion may have been an assertion of sovereign exceptionalism in which the United States perceives itself as above the law. Finally, and most provocatively, Simpson and Wheeler suggest that the United States may have been claiming a legalized hegemony, a right of self-defense available *only* to the United States, which would directly challenge entrenched legal conceptions of sovereign equality, but might also resolve the contradiction between empire and law. Simpson and Wheeler's analysis allows for the integration of realist IR conceptions of power with the presence of a meaningful international legal framework.

O'Connell also examines the apparent use by the Bush administration of international law as a weapon of international politics. Here the subject is *jus in bello* rather than *jus ad bellum*, that is, the laws of conduct in war as opposed to the laws relating to the initiation of war. O'Connell casts the administration's "war" discourse as a tool for claiming the considerable discretion afforded to belligerents in their treatment of enemy actors. This discretion is largely unavailable in peacetime, even in response to criminal behavior, which terrorism was most commonly designated as prior to the events of September 11, 2001. As O'Connell explains, war has its privileges. But the United States has denied duties attendant to belligerency as well (most notably with respect to the treatment of detainees), thus attempting to establish a legal asymmetry. Here her analysis resonates with Simpson and Wheeler's discussion of legalized hegemony. O'Connell further suggests that the United States will face material consequences for its violations of the laws of war.

Where O'Connell and Simpson and Wheeler see the legal justifications offered as perversions of the law, Adamson and Ward address the challenge terrorism poses to our conceptions of international relations. Adamson highlights the inability of dominant IR paradigms to account for nonstate actors such as terrorist networks. Realists view nonstate actors as irrelevant or as state proxies, which when translated into policy requires identifying a state sponsor of such groups. While more open to accounting for nonstate influence, liberal IR theory likewise largely frames such influence in a state-ordered system. Where nonstate actors are destabilizing, the liberal response is a regulatory one. Adamson instead offers a "political mobilization" view of violent nonstate actors. Terrorism is thus an element in transnational constituency building. Thus the appropriate response to terrorist activities is at least in part proactively political, delegitimizing violent activity and addressing underlying political movements represented by terrorist groups. This response is both institutional and legal.

Ward, a former ambassador of Jamaica to the United Nations, offers in his commentary a distinct practitioner perspective on terrorism and the IR–IL divide. His analysis is informed in significant part by his time on the Security Council, on which Jamaica was a nonpermanent member following the terrorist attacks on the United States in 2001. Ward is highly skeptical of the realist approach he sees reflected in much of US unilateralism since these attacks. US actions, such as the invasion of Iraq, he argues, are not merely illegal, but are also, in part as a consequence of that illegality, ineffective or counterproductive. He argues rather that multilateral responses, such as those taken by the Security Council, have a greater chance of success.

Taken together, these chapters offer fresh insights into the challenges posed by contemporary terrorism and responses to it for academics and policymakers alike. A clear message is that an analysis of the problem from a purely state-centric perspective is insufficient: nonstate actors, be they substate actors or international organizations, play a central role. Simultaneously, the putative contradiction between law and power in the international system, and indeed the general realist rejection of the place of law in IR, is open to challenge. It thus is important to understand in a more nuanced fashion the ways in which the powerful seek to legitimize or legalize their activities, as well as the ways in which they may seek to recast law in pursuit of their own interests.

Internally displaced persons

The chapters in Part III of this volume address the problem of internally displaced persons – that is, persons forced to flee their homes for such reasons as armed conflict, situations of generalized violence, violations of human rights, or natural or human-made disasters, but who remain within the borders of their own countries. In this section, Francis Deng, Special Representative of the UN Secretary-General (SRSG) for internally displaced persons, explains norm development through the lens of the Guiding Principles on Internal Displacement, enriching the analysis from a combined practitioner and academic perspective. Deng describes the process by which the Guiding Principles were developed, the reasoning behind the recourse to "soft law," and the reception the principles received at the international, regional, and national levels, and reflects on their current and potential impact as a nascent international normative framework. While arguing that it seems highly unlikely that the process started in 1998 with the formulation of the Guiding Principles could be reversed, Deng acknowledges that their long-term success as a normative instrument – in terms of both acceptance by states as well as visible effects on the ground – is not yet ensured. Looking back on his ten-year experience as SRSG, Deng concludes that it is possible to invigorate or create new norms at the international level, and to do so relatively quickly.

Kenneth Abbott's response to Deng examines privately (as opposed to state) generated soft law in international governance. Abbott compares the development of the Guiding Principles to other cases of privately generated soft law, in the broader framework of "legalization."[24] Abbott points out that the Guiding Principles resemble other soft law instruments, but argues that what makes the Guiding Principles a particularly interesting instance of international norm creation is the fact that, unlike other soft law instruments adopted by representatives of states, they were drafted and finalized primarily by private experts. Abbott suggests that, by affording particular types of actors (such as NGOs and other nonstate activists, international organization officials, and weaker states) greater access and influence on outcomes, private soft law processes may have unique political advantages. Abbott also demonstrates how Deng's account of the legal drafting by norm entrepreneurs fits into the process of "strategic social construction"[25] whereby apparently technical and neutral work arises from a political agenda.[26] Abbott also engages with the questions of legitimacy and authority raised by other contributors in this volume from a different perspective, by discussing the strategies used by norm entrepreneurs involved in the dynamics of private soft law creation. Abbott concludes by emphasizing that, since the Guiding Principles are a "work in progress" (still in the stage of norm dissemination and adoption, following the "life cycle" stages proposed by Finnemore and Sikkink),[27] their future poses a test for normative theories of international relations.

The dialogue between Deng and Abbott also demonstrates the value of interactions between academics and practitioners, and in particular the rich opportunities for collaboration. In responding to Deng's hypotheses and statements, Abbott not only brings Deng's observations into the framework of his well-developed theory, but also gives feedback to Deng regarding the strengths and weaknesses of the strategies that Deng designed. The dialogue crystallizes key concerns of the project: the need to combine practitioner experience and commitment with theoretical and analytical insights from both IR and IL; the possibility of incorporating practitioner knowledge into social science and legal understanding; and the potential for these bodies of theory to inform practitioners on the ground.

International criminal accountability

The chapters in Part IV of this volume take divergent positions on both the theory and practice of international criminal accountability. Leila Nadya Sadat, Madeline Morris, and Diane Orentlicher each offer academic/practitioner perspectives on the complexities of jurisdiction in the imposition of international criminal accountability, as does Ellen Lutz in her commentary. Jurisdiction is contentious in this arena because it is of necessity extraterritorial: international courts or domestic courts prosecute crimes occurring in faraway locales, where domestic courts are usually unwilling or unable to pursue such cases.[28] Extraterritorial exercise of jurisdiction clearly challenges certain state-centric aspects of both realism in IR theory, and traditional international law. For each, the state sovereignty dictates other states largely cannot or should not judge the internal behavior of state actors. To do so would interfere in "matters which are essentially within the domestic jurisdiction of any state."[29]

There is thus great controversy over the appropriate reach of jurisdiction, in particular the jurisdiction of the International Criminal Court. There has in particular been dispute over the potential for extension of the court's reach to some citizens of nonstate parties. While the court largely cannot judge acts by citizens of nonstate parties, it can do so if they act upon the territory of state parties. It is this facet that has raised US concerns about the vulnerability of its military and civilian workers abroad, triggering controversial responses.[30]

As Sadat explains, however, it was not inevitable that ICC jurisdiction would depend upon the offender's nationality. Early discussions suggested that jurisdiction could rest solely upon a state having delegated territorial jurisdiction, or even that nationality ought not be a bar if the UN General Assembly believed a person had committed "international crimes." Sadat argues that the traditional limits upon extraterritorial jurisdiction placed upon states do not extend to international courts, because while states are in a horizontal legal relationship to each other, international courts are positioned vertically above states. Thus tribunals do not merely receive their legal powers through delegation by states; rather, states are a creation of international law, and domestic and international legal systems thus exist in a "symbiotic" relationship to one another. This interpretation clearly cuts at the core of realist objections – that international law is at most a convenient fiction created by states, or is a construct of their own rational interests – and at traditional international law emphasizing consent.[31]

Morris emphatically rejects this interpretation, arguing that the underlying dilemma is between the need to pursue crimes that perpetrator regimes will refuse to, and an international system "premised on the sovereign equality of states." It is the respect for sovereign equality, clearest in the continued respect for state and official immunity, that led the International Court of Justice to condemn Belgium's exercise of universal jurisdiction over the Democratic Republic of Congo's foreign minister, who was protected by state immunity. Thus domestic courts, at least, cannot challenge such immunity. But the ICJ suggested that while domestic courts could not do so, international courts might be allowed to, and here Morris suggests that the dicta might have gone too far, implying that the ICC might be allowed to reject immunity claims even by officials of nonstate parties. She argues that the ICC has jurisdiction precisely because a territorial state has delegated its jurisdiction to the Court, and thus if the state must recognize immunity, then so too does the ICC. These concerns are consistent with Morris's suggestions elsewhere that ICC jurisdiction over citizens of nonstate parties is undemocratic.[32]

Orentlicher challenges Morris's interpretation, although she recognizes the same conundrum: true accountability for serious crimes requires piercing the veil of sovereignty, yet international law respects sovereignty. She recognizes that the evolution of what she refers to as "transnational legal development and processes" is a challenge to traditional consent-based conceptions of lawmaking. She rejects the suggestion that judges in general are any less accountable than political branches of government, and further that decisions abroad may undermine domestic pacts in postconflict societies. She argues that transnational proceedings are part of a broader process of norm development, shaping and constituting the values of domestic and international law. This interpretation, which draws heavily upon the constructivist perspective in IR theory, thus rejects a state-centric or consent-based understanding of the development and enforcement of international criminal law.

The chapter by Chandra Lekha Sriram and Youssef Mahmoud is distinct in that it uses the prism of one case, the Special Court for Sierra Leone (SCSL), as a window on IR theory debates about international accountability. It is framed as both a response to and an elaboration upon realist challenges to the utility of prosecutions. Realists such as Jack Snyder and Leslie Vinjamuri reject constructivist arguments like the one elaborated by Orentlicher above.[33] These realists argue that the primary concern after armed conflict or domestic repression ought not be accountability, but rather stability and the restoration of security and the rule of law. Sriram and Mahmoud consider several IR theory approaches to the problem of postconflict justice, constructivism, liberalism, and realism. While they concur in part with the realist perspective, they argue that it is not sufficiently fine-grained. It worries only in the most general terms about the potential of postconflict justice to provoke further conflict, but does not take seriously the needs of postconflict security, including the restructuring of institutions and disarmament, demobilization, and reintegration processes. Through a close examination of these needs in the context of the SCSL, they demonstrate how such countries may require more detailed policy responses than IR theory can inform.

Lutz offers a vigorous commentary from an academically grounded, and advocacy-oriented, perspective. She reminds us that disagreement continues among academics and policymakers alike regarding the appropriate extent of extraterritorial jurisdiction, and debates about the legitimacy and efficacy of international criminal accountability, we have simultaneously seen the inexorable expansion of both. This has been made possible in part through the norm-changing efforts of leading practitioners who, she notes, sought to work creatively with the law and helped to shape a reality that might have been unthinkable just a decade ago, in reality in which former rights abusers may no longer find safe haven from accountability.

Key conclusions

The three chapters in Part V offer distinct insights regarding the intersections of the disciplines of international law and international relations, but also about the place of law in contemporary international politics. The chapter by Peter Spiro addresses a central issue that emerged repeatedly throughout the project, although it was not an original focus of inquiry: the attitude of the US towards international law. He sketches out a possible alternative to the current US unilateralism and skepticism about international law, drawing upon international relations theory. He offers a theory of liberal transnationalism, arguing that international law will be incorporated progressively by the US not because it is good to do so, but rather because rational institutional action compels it. This fusion of liberal and constructivist insights offers a challenge to contemporary realist explanations for US behavior, and insights for international lawyers interested in greater US incorporation of international law domestically. The chapter by Martha Finnemore offers a constructivist interpretation of the chapters in the volume, emphasizing the dynamics of change in international law and politics, the importance of social context, and the role of nonstate actors. The final concluding chapter, by Clarence Dias, offers a legal practitioner and activist perspective on the international law and international relations divide. He, like Finnemore, emphasizes the importance of norms in international politics and law, and illustrates the role of norms in shaping both through the examples of small arms and terrorism addressed in the volume. The concluding contributions, taken together, offer not only robust arguments for the importance of international law, but also offer further guidance to increase its role in contemporary international politics.

Insights from the volume: new perspectives on old divides

A close examination of our four key policy challenges – small arms and light weapons, terrorism, internally displaced people, and international criminal accountability – reveals a number of crosscutting themes, emerging not only within the individual sections of the volume, but also across them. These include the primacy of the state, and specific challenges to it, the sources of legitimacy and authority in the international system, the evolution of norms in theory and practice, and the relationship between practitioners and academics, whether expert in international law or international relations.

The state

The state is the central player in international law and international relations. It has traditionally been the author and sole subject of international law, with individuals unable to represent themselves on the international stage, but only to be represented by their own states. The state has also often been treated as the principal object of study of international relations: traditional realist theory viewed states as the only unit of analysis. Substate actors, whether individuals, NGOs, or domestic policy processes, have not therefore been central in either academic discipline. Policymaking has both shaped and reflected this divide, with states of central concern in multilateral negotiations, or in international organizations such as the United Nations.

Yet as the contributions to the volume clearly demonstrate, this vision of the world is flawed. It fails first and foremost to take account of a host of nonstate actors, whether terrorist groups, individuals responsible for, or victims of, violations of international criminal law, or persons such as IDPs who have no state to speak for them. It fails also to take account of transnational processes such as the transborder flow of small arms and light weapons. Each of these sets of actors and dynamics presents distinct policy challenges that purely state-oriented responses cannot address. Traditional conceptions of international law and international relations are ill equipped to deal with failed or failing states. When the central unit of analysis is displaced, and the nonstate actors and processes are ignored, the result is not only weak analysis, but also a limited range of practical responses. Thus, for example, the IL, IR, and policy response to terrorist threats has been to focus on alleged state sponsors even while declaring a war upon an act or tactic. Regulatory responses have been state-driven, with an emphasis on the use of force against specific state territory, or on compelling states to monitor and regulate groups upon their territories, or on encouraging states to join existing legal regimes. They have been notably ill-suited to responding to the groups themselves. Similarly, a state-centered focus on the state in controlling arms flows potentially makes two errors: first, of assuming that states can control such flows, and second, of assuming that the state is the only legitimate possessor of arms or provider of security. Where states are failed or failing, these assumptions are clearly insufficient.

Sources of legitimacy and authority

A second insight emerges from the final point above: while states are assumed to be the legitimate repositories of legal or political authority, they may not always be. This is a fundamental challenge to the Weberian conception of a state as the actor with the monopoly of the legitimate use of force in a given territory.[34] In many instances the state is incapable of or uninterested in providing security to all in its territory. This is a fundamental feature of the terrorist threat. Simultaneously, the state may not be viewed by those in its territory as legitimate, and thus they may seek to protect themselves with "illegal" weapons, or may seek the protection of nonstate authorities. States may also lose legitimacy where, through the commission of heinous acts by their own officials, or through failure to control violence by individuals, serious crimes in international law are committed. Prosecution of state officials for such acts is certainly an infringement upon traditional state sovereignty, justified on the grounds that such acts are of "international" concern. But to the degree that states continue to be viewed as the only legitimate creators of international law, it may be difficult to pursue their officials. However, an alternative argument might suggest that states derive their legitimacy democratically, thus permitting us to view some acts as illegitimate and to sanction them. Interestingly, the reliance upon democratic legitimacy may militate in favor of accountability, as just noted, but may also form the basis for a rejection of some activities of bodies like the ICC. It is the specter of "unrepresentative" foreign judges passing judgment upon Americans that forms the core of the "democratic deficit" objection to the ICC and other international regimes.

Norm development

Norms as such have no specific value in *traditional* international law or international relations theory. Customary international law may have emerged from the development of norms, but this evolution is not the subject of study: what is of the greatest importance is state practice, and state belief that such practice is legally obligatory. Some IR theory, particularly realism and institutionalism, has little place for norms, or the purveyors of norms, typically individuals and NGOs. Norms are merely aspirational, marginal to the real decisions taken by states based upon calculations of interests. As discussed earlier, constructivists take norms more seriously, describing in detail their proponents and evolution. And practitioners are regularly norm developers, whether consciously or not.

As the policy problems in this volume illustrate, many of the increasingly legalized responses to contemporary issues such as the plight of IDPs or the demand for international criminal accountability have their roots in norms, not extant law or political demands. So, for example, it has been a norm entrepreneur, Francis Deng, who has taken a leading role in the development of norms to guide state behavior with the Guiding Principles on Internal Displacement. Similarly, the movement for an international criminal court was initially spurred by a transnational collective of NGOs and advocates who were able to promote the "norm" of accountability to states who previously deemed many acts designated as criminal to be essentially within their domestic authority. The norm has yet to become universally accepted in either instance, but traditional IL or IR theories, save perhaps for constructivism, have difficulty explaining the degree to which they have developed, as have agreements like the ICC treaty, without an account of norms and their (usually nonstate) proponents. While the persistent expectation is that policy actors are only state actors, this is increasingly not the case. Policymaking can be shaped not only by nonstate actors, but also by engagement with academics.

Practitioners and academics

From its inception, this project focused upon international law and international relations scholars as the central actors, and sought to engage with policymakers to cast light on specific policy problems. In other words, the academic debate was to be informed by policymaker insights, but the reverse was not taken into consideration. However, the workshops themselves, the policy developments described in the chapters, and the direct engagement of policymakers and academics with each other, as coauthors or as authors of the chapters, fundamentally altered this expectation. Many of the academics involved in creating this volume were also policy practitioners – several of the authors in the section on international criminal accountability were involved in the movement for an international criminal court, or have been consultants for governmental or intergovernmental bodies. Also interesting is the way in which policymakers, many of whom have an academic background, explicitly draw upon key theoretical paradigms in IR or IL. For example, Francis Deng's account of the development of the Guiding Principles on Internal Displacement illustrates his own use of the concepts of norms in the academic literature, and reflects too his thoughtful adoption of insights from the feedback offered by Ken Abbott in his commentary. The centrality of policymakers not only as providers of information or objects of study, but also as active and critical consumers of academic literature on key issues, as well as producers of such literature, became vividly apparent during the development of the volume, transforming a bilateral engagement between two disciplines into an engaged dialogue among three perspectives.

Conclusion: moving the debate forward

This volume emerged from a project that sought not only to consolidate the lessons from a generation of scholarship on the gaps and linkages between international law and international relations scholarship, but also to move the debate forward.[35] Thus the volume focuses upon four contemporary policy challenges, in order to glean insights into the differential concerns and prescriptions of scholars from distinct disciplines. Not surprisingly, the central importance of the state, and the dangers of state-centric analyses, are recurrent themes in most chapters. The specific policy chapters further allow this volume, like the policy workshops that preceded it, to engage not only with academics from the two disciplines, but also with practitioners trained in either or both. Their contributions cast significant light upon the ways in which policymakers function at the intersection of law and politics, and often seek to craft solutions to policy problems in ways integrating legal and political analysis, and dealing with or working around the problematic role of the state. This may entail closer collaboration with some nonstate actors, recognition of threats that other nonstate actors may pose, or cooperation through supranational institutions. The academic debate over the relationship between international law and international relations has much to learn from the ways in which policymakers navigate the divide regularly. Similarly, as some of the engagements in the volume demonstrate, policymakers can learn and adapt their analyses, informed by the academic debate. In this way, it may be the case that each of the "three communities" might strengthen its own methods and analyses, and engage further with the other communities. This volume is but a first step in what is hoped will be a productive discussion.

Notes

1 David Held *et al.*, *Global Transformations: Politics, Economics, and Culture* (Cambridge: Polity Press, 1999). See also Daniele Archibugi, David Held, and Martin Kohler, eds, *Reimagining Political Community: Studies in Cosmopolitan Democracy*

(Cambridge: Polity Press, 1999); David Held, *Democracy and the Global Order: From the Modern State to Cosmopolitan Governance* (Cambridge: Polity Press, 1995); Charles Beitz, *Political Theory and International Relations* (Princeton: Princeton University Press, 1979/1999).

2 Mary Kaldor, "Transnational Civil Society," in Tim Dunne and Nicholas Wheeler, eds, *Human Rights in Global Politics* (Cambridge: Cambridge University Press, 1999); Richard Falk, *On Humane Governance* (Cambridge: Polity Press, 1995), pp. 195–213.

3 For a full description of the research project, see www.ssrc.org/programs/gsc/gsc_activities/il_ir.page.

4 Kenneth Abbott, Arizona State University; Thomas Biersteker, Brown University; Clarence Dias, United Nations; Martha Finnemore, George Washington University; Harold Koh, Yale University Law School; Sally Falk Moore, Harvard University; Anne-Marie Slaughter, Princeton University; Peter Spiro, University of Georgia Law School; Chandra Lekha Sriram, University of East London School of Law; and Nicholas Wheeler, University of Wales, Aberystwyth.

5 Friedrich V. Kratochwil, "How Do Norms Matter?" in Michael Byers, ed., *The Role of Law in International Politics: Essays in International Law and International Relations* (Oxford: Oxford University Press, 2000), pp. 35–68.

6 See Anne-Marie Slaughter Burley, "International Law and International Relations Theory: A Dual Agenda," *American Journal of International Law* vol. 87, no. 2 (April 1993), pp. 205–39; E. H. Carr, *The Twenty Years' Crisis: An Introduction to the Study of International Relations* (London: Palgrave Macmillan, 2001); Kenneth Waltz, *Theory of International Politics* (New York: McGraw-Hill, 1979).

7 John Austin, *The Province of Jurisprudence Determined* (Cambridge: Cambridge University Press, 1995), lecture 5; H. L. A. Hart, *The Concept of Law* (Oxford: Clarendon Press, 1961); compare Hans Kelsen, *Principles of International Law* (New York: Rinehart, 1952).

8 Hedley Bull, *The Anarchical Society: A Study of Order in World Politics* (London: Palgrave Macmillan, 1971).

9 See Hugo Grotius, *The Right of War and Peace*, 3 vols (Indianapolis, IN: Liberty Fund, 2005).

10 Bull, *Anarchical Society*; Martin Wight, *International Theory: The Three Traditions* (London: Holmes and Meier, 1992).

11 Robert O. Keohane, *After Hegemony: Cooperation and Discord in the World Political Economy* (Princeton: Princeton University Press, 1995); Abram Chayes and Antonia Handler Chayes, *The New Sovereignty: Compliance with International Regulatory Agreements* (Cambridge: Harvard University Press, 1998); Robert Keohane and Lisa Martin, "The Promise of Institutionalist Theory," *International Security* vol. 20, no. 1 (Summer 1995), pp. 39–51.

12 Martha Finnemore and Kathryn Sikkink, "International Norm Dynamics and Political Change," *International Organization* vol. 52, no. 4 (Autumn 1998), pp. 887–917; Alexander Wendt, "Anarchy Is What States Make of It: The Social Construction of Power Politics," *International Organization* vol. 46, no. 2 (Spring 1991), pp. 391–425; Alexander Wendt, *Social Theory of International Politics* (Cambridge: Cambridge University Press, 1999).

13 See *International Organization* vol. 54, no. 3 (Summer 2000), a special issue devoted to "legalization and world politics," edited by Judith Goldstein, Miles Kahler, Robert O. Keohane, and Anne-Marie Slaughter.

14 Slaughter Burley, "International Law and International Relations Theory"; Kenneth W. Abbott, "Modern International Relations Theory: A Prospectus for International Lawyers," *Yale Journal of International Law* vol. 14, no. 2 (Summer 1989),

pp. 335–411; Michael Byers, ed., *The Role of Law in International Politics: Essays in International Relations and International Law* (Oxford: Oxford University Press, 2001); Christian Reus-Smit, ed., *The Politics of International Law* (Cambridge: Cambridge University Press, 2004).

15 Kenneth W. Abbott, "International Relations Theory, International Law, and the Regime Governing Atrocities in Internal Conflicts," *American Journal of International Law* vol. 93 (April 1999), pp. 361–79.

16 Stephen Krasner, *Sovereignty: Organized Hypocrisy* (Princeton: Princeton University Press, 1999).

17 Rodney Hall and Thomas Biersteker, eds, *The Emergence of Private Authority in Global Governance* (Cambridge: Cambridge University Press, 2002).

18 Wendt, *Social Theory of International Politics;* Thomas Franck, *The Power of Legitimacy Among Nations* (Oxford: Oxford University Press, 1990).

19 Reus-Smit, *Politics of International Law.* See also Chandra Lekha Sriram, "Book Review: *The Limits of International Law* and *The Politics of International Law,*" *APSR-Perspectives on Politics* vol. 3, no. 3 (September 2005), pp. 686–8.

20 Reus-Smit, *Politics of International Law*, p. 5.

21 See, for example, Peter Haas, "Introduction: Epistemic Communities and International Policy Coordination," *International Organization* vol. 46, no. 2 (Winter 1992), pp. 1–35; and the other articles on epistemic communities in this special issue of *International Organization.* See also Dana B. Eyre and Mark C. Suchman, "Status, Norms, and the Proliferation of Conventional Weapons: An Institutional Theory Approach," in Peter J. Katzenstein, ed., *The Culture of National Security: Norms and Identity in World Politics* (New York: Columbia University Press, 1996), pp. 79–113.

22 See, for example, Richard Price, "Emerging Customary Norms and Anti-Personnel Landmines," in Reus-Smit, *Politics of International Law*, pp. 106–30.

23 Ellen Lutz and Kathryn Sikkink, "The Justice Cascade: The Evolution and Impact of Foreign Human Rights Trials in Latin America," *Chicago Journal of International Law* vol. 2 (Spring 2001), pp. 1–33.

24 See Kenneth W. Abbott, Robert O. Keohane, Andrew Moravcsik, Anne-Marie Slaughter, and Duncan Snidal, "The Concept of Legalization," *International Organization* vol. 54 (2000), pp. 401–19; Special Issue, "Legalization and World Politics," *International Organization* vol. 54, no. 3 (2000), reprinted as Judith L. Goldstein, Miles Kahler, Robert O. Keohane, and Anne-Marie Slaughter, eds, *Legalization and World Politics* (Cambridge, MA: MIT Press, 2001).

25 Martha Finnemore and Kathryn Sikkink, "International Norm Dynamics and Political Change," *International Organization* vol. 52 (1998), pp. 910–11.

26 Abbott, "Privately Generated Soft Law in International Governance," Chapter 10 in this volume.

27 Finnemore and Sikkink, "International Norm Dynamics and Political Change."

28 Brad Roth and Chandra Lekha Sriram, "Externalization of Justice: What Does It Mean and What is at Stake?" *Finnish Yearbook of International Law* vol. 12 (2001), pp. 2–6; Chandra Sriram, *Globalizing of Justice for Mass Atrocities: A Revolution in Accountability* (London: Routledge, 2005).

29 *UN Charter*, Art. 2(7).

30 *American Servicemembers' Protection Act*, 22 U.S.C. 7241.

31 Stephen D. Krasner, *Sovereignty: Organized Hypocrisy* (Princeton: Princeton University Press, 1999); Jack L. Goldsmith and Eric A. Posner, *The Limits of International Law* (New York: Oxford University Press, 2004).

32 Madeline Morris, "The Disturbing Democratic Deficit of the ICC," *Finnish Yearbook of International Law* vol. 12 (2001).

33 Jack Snyder and Leslie Vinjamuri, "Trials and Errors: Principle and Pragmatism in

Strategies of International Justice," *International Security* vol. 28, no. 3 (Winter 2003–4), pp. 5–44.

34 Max Weber, "'Politik als Beruf," *Gesammelte Politische Schriften* (Munich, 1921), pp. 396–450 (lecture).

35 Anne-Marie Slaughter, Andrew Tulumello, and Stephan Wood, "International Law and International Relations Theory: A New Generation of Interdisciplinary Scholarship," *American Journal of International Law* vol. 92, no. 3 (July 1998), pp. 367–97.

Part I

SMALL ARMS AND LIGHT WEAPONS

2

MOVING FORWARD?

Assessing normative and legal progress in dealing with small arms

Robert Muggah

Introduction

Small arms and light weapons, while traditional weapons of war, present relatively new challenges for international law. Over the past decade there has been considerable normative and practical attention devoted to their control and regulation. The bulk of diplomatic and multilateral activity, however, has been directed toward regulating the "supply" of illegal arms – preventing their illicit manufacture, stockpiling, transfer, and trade. Comparatively little attention has been devoted to understanding, much less responding to, their "direct and indirect effects." Even less concern has been registered about "demand" – the motivations and means that drive the acquisition and ownership of such weapons in situations of war or peace. This is in large part because the development of norms and regulation was initially driven by an arms control community more familiar with supply-focused and state-centered regulatory mechanisms. This paradigm is less useful in understanding the demand for small arms in unstable states and internal conflicts, and thus the regulatory responses are inadequate. While the prominence of traditional disarmament paradigms is one problem, so too is political will: many states resist attempts to examine the sources, including their own predations and weaknesses, that drive demand for small arms. And as states continue to be the relevant actors in negotiating international agreements, regulatory efforts have been hampered. However, these obstacles notwithstanding, nongovernmental organizations (NGOs) and other nonstate actors have been sources of norm development emphasizing concerns about the effects of small arms and the sources of demand that could increasingly become enshrined in legal agreements.

This chapter contends that current international, regional, and national approaches to small arms control are narrowly conceived. Even though a norm associated with the control of illegal small arms supplies appears to be evolving at the international and regional levels, it may be only partially effective. Small arms control requires a broader framework – a holistic and integrated conceptualization of the issue. In addition to strengthening norms associated with the supply of small arms, a more sophisticated grasp of both "effects" and "demand" reduction is essential if effective regulation is to be developed and enforced. Though regulatory mechanisms associated with effects and demand reduction are virtually absent in international law, practical interventions that focus on these latter two aspects of the small arms issue at the regional and national levels are quietly emerging.

This chapter provides a general overview of the discourse and debates on small arms control from supply and demand perspectives. Divided into four sections, it briefly reviews the contemporary discourse on small arms control from the early 1990s onward. It then turns to a number of key issues associated with the production, stockpiling, and trade of weapons, and the effect of and demand for weapons. The last two sections reflect on some of the recent normative developments, and their effects, associated with controlling the supply and demand for small arms.

Ultimately, the responsibility for elaborating normative and practical instruments to regulate small arms, as with nuclear, chemical, or biological weapons, has traditionally been the preserve of the disarmament community. As this chapter demonstrates, the focus of current international activity – particularly state-led efforts – has consistently been directed toward regulating the illegal supply and trade of such weapons. Casting the problem as one of "illicit" and "criminal" activity arises from traditional biases within the arms control and law enforcement communities. They also appeal to governments that are loath to consider the political dimensions of the small arms trade in political forums. Action has been further complicated by the absence of universally binding norms or standards to regulate the possession or use of small arms and light weapons. The issue continues to be cast to large extent in vague terms associated with regional security or international peace and security.

There is a growing debate in the disarmament community about whether or not a "norm" on small arms is emerging. Though contested in the international relations literature, norms can guide or prescribe state behavior.[1] Described by some international relations scholars as a "a standard of appropriate behaviour for actors within a given identity,"[2] norms have also been referred to as a shared assessment of what is right, statements of what states and other actors "should do" and not necessarily descriptions of how they behave.[3] Treaty and custom are the two principal sources of international law and may also derive from and demonstrate the existence of norms. But the critical test of a "functioning" norm lies in the consequences of a clear breach.

The evolution of the small arms discourse

The debate on small arms, until comparatively recently, focused primarily on the regulation of their supply to states, nonstate actors, and to a lesser extent, civilians. Part of this could be attributed to the bias of disarmament experts and negotiators: policymakers and technical specialists lacked a detailed understanding of the full scale or dimensions of the small arms issue. But other reasons for this one-dimensional approach are structural and historical. The 1970s and 1980s were not conducive to a spirit of multilateral transparency on conventional arms. Moreover, in a strategic environment dominated by the costs and benefits of nuclear and biological weapons, small arms were seen as inconsequential, a marginal or "soft" issue. Research was confined to a small group of scholars, investigative researchers, and peace activists. From the beginning, the focus was almost entirely on the United States, North American and European exports, and to a lesser extent, civilian possession.[4]

As such, attention was directed primarily toward various points on the supply chain: from production and manufacturing, holdings and stockpiles, and exports and imports, to trafficking and commercial distribution. As the importance attached to the issue grew, a UN Panel of Experts was appointed in 1997 and again in 1999 to revisit the issue of small arms and to recommend ways of regulating the production and illegal trade of such weapons. The success of the Ottawa Process to Ban Anti-Personnel Landmines also generated enthusiasm among certain diplomats and activists of the possibilities for further constraining the trade in small arms and light weapons, and the associated political dividends that might result.

By the late 1990s, a sizable literature on the dynamics of the small arms trade – including its legal, gray, and black dimensions – had quickly emerged.[5] Because disarmament and security experts provided most of its intellectual sources and analyses, they transferred supply-side orthodoxies from conventional discourse.[6] As the following sections make clear, multilateral and regional activities have subsequently focused on devising (nonlegally binding) mechanisms to curb the illegal manufacture, stockpiling, brokering, and trade of small arms. Though difficult to measure, a general norm associated with the containment of illegal arms flows appears to have quietly evolved at the international, regional, and national levels.

Until very recently, however, comparatively little attention has been paid to either the short- to medium-term effects of small arms, or what drives their demand in the first place. While multilateral action on small arms is arguably driven by the threat they pose to order, stability, development, and human rights, the specific causal or dependent relationships between arms availability and their impacts are rarely analyzed or understood in detail. Further, the factors that drive acquisition by states, nonstate actors, and civilians are seldom analyzed and often dismissed by disarmament experts as too complex to treat within the rubric of arms control.[7]

While the UN, its member states, and nongovernmental organizations have regularly denounced the "destabilizing effects" of unregulated weapons availability, their threat to international security, and the implications of poverty, inequality, and ethnic tension for weapons accumulation, the debate remains simplistic.[8] Alternatively, empirical research focusing on the effects of small arms or the factors driving particular types of armed violence adopted too narrow a criminological, epidemiological, and ballistics-oriented perspective at the expense of a broader, more systemic conceptualization of effects.[9] While early research may have been of value from a domestic American perspective, it seldom extended beyond this context.

Research and action on the effects of and demand for small arms grew rapidly in the latter half of the 1990s. Social scientists and practitioners, together with enlightened policymakers and donors, broadened the debate – drawing attention to the wide range of direct and indirect effects of small arms as well as the motivations and means (independent variables) that condition demand.[10] Since the beginning of the twenty-first century, the conceptualization of small arms control has expanded, with public health, development, humanitarianism, international humanitarian, and human rights law and other disciplines brought to bear.[11]

The emergence of a genuinely interdisciplinary debate has facilitated a subtle change in approach to understanding and therefore responding to small arms. While there has been incipient norm development emphasizing containing the supply of small arms, there has also developed a broader approach that seeks to address "perpetrators and victims" as well as the "weapon." This approach has facilitated a reframing of the issue beyond the supply-oriented view.[12] However, work emphasizing the effects of and demands for small arms is still nascent. Despite literally thousands of small-scale interventions seeking to address the effects and demand for small arms at the local level – from violence reduction projects in Brazil and Kenya's shantytowns to arms amnesties in Kosovo and Haiti – these efforts have not engendered genuine normative shifts emphasizing either effects or demand reduction.

Considering the supply, effects, and demand for small arms

As a result of the growing interest in regulating the small arms trade, much is now known about their manufacture, stockpile, brokering, and trade. For example, it is now estimated that the global stockpile already tops 650 million units, and production continues. Global production of both military-style and commercial small arms, including handguns, assault rifles, and rocket-propelled grenade launchers, is estimated at 7.5 million units annually. Despite the myth that only Western countries produce and export weapons, over 1,250 companies in more than 90 countries are involved in some aspect of arms production.

The distribution of weapons is also better understood. Small arms are widely distributed within the civilian population. Armed forces are estimated to possess over 40 percent of small arms globally, while police hold little more than 3 percent. By contrast, civilians are estimated to legally hold more than 55 percent of global stockpiles. The rest, less than 1 percent, are divided between insurgent groups and private security companies – those that, together with the state, arguably contribute most to persistent insecurity in war-affected countries. Given these diverse holding patterns, the tenuous regulatory infrastructure directed reservedly at state stockpiles is especially disconcerting. Indeed, regulation of the security services, including paramilitaries, is weak in developed and developing countries alike. Equally troubling, legislation and enforcement over civilian holdings is inadequate or nonexistent in most states.

The global trade in small arms is modest in comparison to the global trade in conventional arms. The total estimated value of the legal trade in small arms is less than $4 billion per year – a mere 10 percent of the global trade in conventional weapons.[13] The largest exporters are the United States, Italy, Belgium, Germany, Russia, Brazil, and China, while dominant importers include the United States, Saudi Arabia, Cyprus, Japan, South Korea, Germany, and Canada. Though the importance of the trade as a proportion of gross domestic product varies from region to region, there appears to be a decline in overall legal production due to declining state demand. The scale and distribution of the *illegal* trade is still exceedingly difficult to measure, though valued by the Small Arms Survey at less than $2 billion annually.[14]

Much more difficult to measure are the direct and indirect effects of small arms (see Table 2.1). With 90 percent of internal conflicts occurring in developing countries – states with the weakest surveillance and monitoring capabilities – it is difficult to report with accuracy the number of fatal and nonfatal injuries

Table 2.1 Framing the direct and indirect effects of small arms

Direct and indirect effects	*Examples of indicators*
Mortality and injury	Firearm death Firearm injuries Psychological trauma
Public health costs	Lost productivity Costs of treatment and rehabilitation
Criminality	Rates of firearm-related homicide Aggravated assault Armed robbery Insurance premiums Private security firms
Humanitarian impacts	Rates of forced displacement Access to basic needs Firearm-related fatalities and injuries of relief personnel Militarized refugee camps Operational and security costs
Underdevelopment	Access to and quality of social services Trends in foreign direct investment Social capital and cultural networks

sustained by combatants or civilians. According to best estimates, there are at least 300,000 fatal firearm-related injuries per year during wartime – the majority of these in Africa and South Asia – and at least two to three times as many nonfatal injuries.[15] At least 200,000 additional men, women, and children are killed by small arms each year as a result of armed criminality, domestic violence, and suicide. Rates of firearm homicide are highest in Latin America and the Caribbean – some five times the global average.[16] Over half of the world's firearm suicides are registered in North America and Western Europe. Though the relationship between firearm accessibility and overall levels of violence remains difficult to prove, it is clear that small arms facilitate armed violence and ratchet up the long-term effects.[17]

The far-reaching social and economic costs of small arms misuse in terms of fatal and nonfatal injuries, while rarely discussed in disarmament circles, undermine opportunities and productivity of poor communities. Scarce household resources are being devoted to the treatment and care of the victims of violence, as well as to informal and unregulated forms of "security provision" – such as paramilitarism and vigilantism. Small arms availability and misuse in the conflict and postconflict context is strongly associated with the increasing lethality of criminality, forced migration, the deterioration of investment and trade, and the obstruction of aid delivery and assistance.[18] Both directly and indirectly then, small arms misuse erodes the quality and quantity of humanitarian assistance and development.

The demand for small arms and light weapons can be conceived as having at least three dimensions: demand by the defense and security sectors, demand by nonstate groups, and micro-level demand by individuals.[19] While the sources of state-level demand remain somewhat unclear, it is certainly conditioned by a number of independent variables: defense policies, procurement and budgetary constraints, civilian control of the defense sector, force structures and mobilization strategies, and historical precedents.[20] On the other hand, there is also demand from nonstate actors during ongoing conflicts. This includes arming before and during the outbreak of violence, sustaining stocks during cease-fires, and the use of weapons as a bargaining tool during the postconflict period. Here, demand is conditioned by, inter alia, available resources and rents, command and control structures, and formal and informal alliances and networks between actors. Demand at the group and individual levels is influenced by a combination of real and relative prices, and by resources and preferences[21] held by consumers.[22]

Development of norms and regulations to control supply

The UN Programme of Action (United Nations General Assembly [UNGA], 2001), is the primary normative/regulatory mechanism for controlling the supply of small arms at the international level.[23] The program is the centerpiece of small arms control given "the central role such documents play in the creation and dissemination of new norms."[24] Its goals were to "frame" future debates on the nature of the problem – even as it excluded specific dimensions – and to serve as a baseline for promoting the development of international and national norms on the issue. The action program emphasizes the importance of strengthening and developing norms and measures on the control of small arms at the global, regional, and national levels.[25] But it is not legally binding, giving rise to questions regarding its utility to guide multilateral interventions. Moreover, the Small Arms Survey has observed that "it may be a fundamental first step, it is not a collection of norms on its own."[26]

Can the UN Programme of Action establish a general norm? Optimists argue that it has instrumental value: the UN Secretary-General suggested, for example, that it is "essential in building norms" and that it gives concrete expression to norms.[27] Pessimists argue that it carries little weight, is devoid of legitimacy, and will do little to contribute to normative development on small arms control.[28] Whether or not state positions on any aspects of small arms and light weapons have changed as a result of participation in the multilateral process is a source of considerable debate. Ultimately, determining the action program's relative influence on norm development is difficult: though it undoubtedly reflects existing practice for many states, it has clearly prompted action by others seeking to comport with international standards.

There are a number of areas where the UN Programme of Action has arguably informed state behavior and practice. It has underlined the standards associated with state transfers of small arms to areas where their availability might lead to or exacerbate violations of established international laws. Its nuanced attention to discrete aspects of the "small arms issue" – from brokering[29] to marking and tracing[30] – may also indicate incipient norm development. With more than half of all countries participating in the development of the action program claiming to have taken concrete steps to respond to the terms laid out therein, it is clear that it influences state behavior (see Table 2.2). But there are also areas left out by the program due to fixed negotiating positions of

Table 2.2 State reporting on the UN Programme of Action (2003)

Region	*Total states*	*2002*		*2003*	
		Reports	*% of region*	*Reports*	*% of region*
Africa	52	3	6	23	44
Americas	35	3	9	18	51
Asia	29	2	7	12	41
Europe	48	7	15	37	71
Middle East	14	0	0	10	71
Oceania	14	1	7	3	21
Total	192	16	8	103	54

Source: Small Arms Survey, *Rights at Risk* (Oxford: Oxford University Press, 2004).

particular states.[31] Civil society also played an instrumental role in influencing norm development though lobbying at the national level and through support for the reporting of action among less developed states[32] and submission of model conventions on arms brokering and international arms transfers.

But the elaboration of other regulatory mechanisms has also contributed to norm development around supply-side arms control. The UN Firearms Protocol is also a key treaty that regulates various aspects of small arms at the international level. Negotiated as part of the UN Convention Against Transnational Organized Crime in 2001, it is the first legally binding instrument concerning small arms at the global level.[33] It nevertheless adopts a more narrow approach to the problem of illicit firearms manufacturing and trafficking than does the UN Programme of Action. The Firearms Protocol elaborates a range of provisions for marking and tracing, the licensing of transfers, and the criminalization of specific conduct in order to tighten controls over transfers and suppress illegal activity. While the scope of the UN Programme of Action is much broader than that of the Firearms Protocol, these two instruments constitute the core guidelines for regulating small arms.

There has been considerably more rapid progress in addressing the small arms issue at the regional level. The development of regional and national supply-side legislation appears to have emerged partly in response to international activity on the issue, including the UN Programme of Action and the Firearms Protocol.[34] Agreements range from the Convention Against Illicit Firearms Manufacture and Trafficking (Organization of American States [OAS], 1997), the Document on Small Arms (Organization for Security and Cooperation in Europe [OSCE], 2000), and the Code of Conduct on Arms Exports (European Union [EU], 1998), to the Firearms Protocol (South African Defense Community [SADC], 2000), the Bamako Declaration (Organization of African Unity [OAU], 2000), and the Nairobi Declaration on Small Arms (2001) – all of which appear to be reinforcing international, regional, and national efforts to regulate the supply of small arms. Though not all are legally binding, regional efforts in Europe and the Americas appear to focus on information sharing and norms on transparency – particularly through the use of national export reports.[35] In Africa, while the Bamako Declaration was important in establishing language for the UN Programme of Action, agreed in 2001, the SADC Protocol represents a more concrete innovation for which legally binding and monitoring and enforcement mechanisms are being developed. For the rest of the continent, and indeed in South and Southeast Asia and the Pacific, politically binding interventions appear to be the norm. Though common approaches appear to be emerging, it is difficult to determine whether a regional norm (or a cluster of regional norms) exists.

National laws associated with small arms control are also rapidly being articulated, strengthened, and reviewed. But many of these adaptations are undertaken voluntarily and independent of the provisions of the UN Programme of Action, the Firearms Protocol, or the regional instruments highlighted above.

Though existing international law can transcend national law when weapons are used to violate human rights, it tends not to address small arms per se, but focus on specific (proscribed) acts. States nevertheless maintain ultimate control over domestic regulation. However, there is a range of international instruments addressing the use of small arms by national authorities. One example is the Code of Conduct for Law Enforcement Officials, adopted by the UNGA in 1979. In addition to calling for respect for human rights, the code (Article 3) indicates limits to use of force by law enforcement officials. This basic obligation is bolstered by the Basic Principles on the Use of Force and Firearms by Law Enforcement Officials, elaborated by the UNGA in 1990.[36]

International instruments not directly related to small arms have also been invoked to constrain international, regional, and national arms transfers. There are few legally binding international restrictions on the right of states to transfer arms (with the exception of weapons of mass destruction). Rather, states have preferred to sign nonbinding mechanisms, emphasizing their right to self-defense, often in a regional context. Arms embargoes imposed by the United Nations Security Council, which are binding on UN member states, constitute the most important set of international regulatory mechanisms. International law also proscribes the use of specific weapons.[37] The principal sources of international humanitarian law that relate to small arms are the St. Petersburg Declaration of 1868, the Hague Conventions of 1999, the four Geneva Conventions of 1949, and two additional protocols of 1977. But soft law associated with regulating the "transfer" of weapons is also influential in certain circumstances. The transferring state can sometimes incur "secondary or derivative responsibility for violations of international law committed by a recipient state or nonstate actor."[38] Relevant international law in this context includes prohibitions on use of force; prohibitions on interference in the international affairs of another state, prohibitions on provision of assistance to terrorists, international humanitarian law, international human rights law, and the prohibition of genocide.

Effects and demand-side normative development

Not surprisingly, there are few normative instruments designed to mitigate the effects of small arms or that focus on demand reduction. In fact, even basic acknowledgment of effects-reduction is notably absent from substantive sections of the UN Programme of Action, the Firearms Protocol, or other small arms-specific regulatory mechanisms. While some lip service is paid to the consequences of excessive accumulations of small arms, the discourse remains focused on controlling supply. The preamble to the UN Programme of Action, for example, describes the consequences of the "excessive accumulation and uncontrolled spread" of small arms and notes a host of negative consequences linked to proliferation, but does not note the negative effects upon human rights.

While no global or integrated instrument exists for small arms per se, a cluster of existing norms associated with human rights, violence against women, and responsible policing might be harnessed to ensure effects and demand reduction. For example, the Universal Declaration of Human Rights contains a range of provisions directly relevant to the preservation of "life, liberty and security of person . . . and prevention of cruel, inhuman and degrading treatment or punishment."[39] Though not legally binding, the Universal Declaration is commonly held to form part of customary international law, which is legally binding.[40] Other mechanisms, such as the UN Declaration on the Elimination of Violence Against Women (1993), UN Security Council Resolution 1325, on women, peace, and security, and the policing protocols cited above, also emphasize the importance of responsible practice among law enforcement officers.

These norms are also reinforced by the growing consensus among international humanitarian and development agencies of the importance of responding to the effects of, and demand for, small arms. International agencies such as the International Committee of the Red Cross, the World Health Organization, Human Rights Watch, and others engaged in the formal debate on small arms have reinforced the importance of effects- and demand-based response.[41] Because the "humanitarian perspective" emphasizes the practice and consequences of warfare (as opposed to technical aspects associated with marking, tracing, and export controls), this perspective may enable consensus in an otherwise politicized debate among gun advocates, defense ministries, and the disarmament community. For example, the recognition of explicitly effects-based concerns impels producer states to account for the lawful or illicit transfer of weaponry to regimes violating the basic human rights of civilians. Where weapons are already transferred, this approach would require states to reorient their attention to protecting former combatants and civilians who face arms-related violence on a daily basis.[42] While civil society activity on the small arms issue has proven influential at the multilateral level, NGO influence in the negotiations of the UN Global Conference on Illicit Trade in Small Arms and Light Weapons of 2001 and the preparation of the action program, for example, were perhaps most important at the national level. Nongovernmental actors proved perhaps more adept at setting agendas rather than achieving discrete outcomes.

Despite the direct and indirect influence of NGOs in influencing state practice, there is still relatively little attention given to demand in the UN's action program. Normative commitments to demand reduction are only nominally recognized in the preamble. For example, in paragraph 7, states are characterized as noting their concern for the "close link between terrorism, organized crime, trafficking in drugs and precious minerals and the illicit trade in small arms and light weapons," and stressing "the urgency of international efforts and co-operation aimed at combating this trade simultaneously from both a supply and demand perspective." Moreover, in paragraph 4 of the preamble, it is noted that states are "concerned by the implications that poverty and underdevelopment may have for the illicit trade in small arms and light weapons."[43] The listing of these variables (e.g. terrorism, organized crime, drugs and exploitable resources, poverty, underdevelopment) indicates a degree of recognition, albeit ambiguous, of the linkages between demand and small arms trade and misuse. The preamble of course has no legally binding effects.

As Ernie Regehr has observed: "The current [action program] ... is tellingly short on direct references to demand or demand reduction, perhaps an indirect acknowledgement that any demand reduction strategy presents daunting challenges."[44] Civil society actors have repeatedly stressed the need to develop a holistic agenda to small arms and light weapons control in order to give shape to an incipient norm on "effects" and "demand" reduction.

Paradoxically, even as the UN Programme of Action fails to articulate a coherent description of the effects of and demand for small arms, it lays out a number of indirect approaches to redressing them. The UN's action program emphasizes disarmament, demobilization, and reintegration (DDR) of former combatants, the special needs and vulnerabilities of children, the importance of "promoting dialogue and a culture of peace by encouraging ... education and public awareness programmes," the need to make "greater efforts to address problems related to human and sustainable development," and "security sector reform."[45] All of these are recognized as "practical" interventions to reduce the effects of and demand for small arms by practitioners on the ground.

In fact, despite the considerable weaknesses associated with diplomatic and normative approaches to effects and demand reduction, a set of practical interventions has already been launched. Many of these are not directly concerned with or derived from international arms control and disarmament communities, but rather emerge from other sectors. Development agencies, including the United Nations Development Programme (UNDP), the United Nations Children's Fund (UNICEF), the World Health Organization (WHO), World Vision, and Oxfam–Great Britain, among others, have begun to explore behavioral and attitudinal aspects associated with small arms acquisition and possession. These agencies and NGOs, comprising "epistemic communities," have begun to reframe the issue, exert national and international influence, and engage in a combination of lobbying and practical interventions.

Nongovernmental organizations, UN agencies, and governments throughout the developed and developing world are currently carrying out concrete efforts to reduce the threat and misuse of small arms. The International Action Network on Small Arms (IANSA), for example, includes at least 500 nongovernmental partners in over 100 countries. Regional networks seeking to promote awareness and advocacy on the issue have emerged in South Asia, Latin America, and West Africa. Operational arms of the United Nations, specifically the UNDP, UNICEF, the United Nations High Commissioner for Refugees (UNHCR), and the International Organization for Migration (IOM), have also undertaken a range of comprehensive interventions to reduce armed violence. The World Bank has initiated no less than 14 DDR initiatives since 2000, while the UNDP has begun as many as 45 weapons reduction projects over the same period.[46] Actions include the strengthening of regional and national arms control norms and legislation, the reduction of children's exposure to armed violence through demobilization and reintegration programs, the demilitarization and policing of camps for refugees and internally displaced persons, the implementation of national and regional DDR programs for former combatants, and the administration of weapons for development programs. A number of developed-country governments, such as those of the United States, the United Kingdom, and Germany, have begun to fund the strengthening of export and import legislation (in both supplying and receiving countries), the reform of security sectors, and the collection and destruction of weapons out of their state department, defense ministry, and overseas development assistance (ODA) budgets.[47]

Conclusion

There are grounds for cautious optimism on the evolving norms surrounding small arms control. Since its emergence in the early 1990s, the debate has advanced in at least two ways. First, the issue itself is attracting increasing levels of attention from multiple constituencies. The discussion of small arms is now a regular feature of country statements in UN forums.[48] Second, discussions have become increasingly nuanced, with a focus on specific language and commitments. Not only have discrete issues such as tracing and brokering been addressed, but the relationship between small arms and issues such as human security, crime, and development are increasingly emphasized.[49]

The definition of small arms problems in precise terms – even if primarily in relation to regulating "supplies" – is perhaps an early stage of norm development. But the extent to which commitment is seen desirable or "right and appropriate" remains to be seen. Language emphasizing practical action remains sparse. Though some emphasis on the shared responsibility of all states is highlighted in the UN Programme of Action, attention remains focused on supply-side policies – export controls and the provision of bilateral assistance. Even so, the UN's action program will be central to norm determination and norm development at the international level in the coming years.

A gap persists between state commitment and practice. Despite the aforementioned norms associated with supply-side regulation, transparency on small arms production, holdings, and transfers remains a massive lacuna, making it difficult to demonstrate the extent to which states adhere to such commitments. What is more, conformity with norms is difficult to monitor. For some states, the UN's action program reflects the status quo, while for others it remains difficult to tell whether they are interested in compliance at all. Though a general commitment to action exists, and many states appear to endorse political (though not legal) norms requiring them to prevent and eradicate the illegal trade, attention remains focused on the supply-side approach. Moreover, the general norm remains to be translated into specific action at the global, regional, and national levels. It may also be too early to tell.[50]

The framing of the small arms issue has from the beginning privileged a supply-side dimension, both because of state dominance in the process and because of the particular approaches favored by traditional arms controllers. For a variety of reasons, some political and others institutional, the elaboration of norms associated with reducing the effects of small arms and comprehensively tackling demand has been slow to develop. But in this case, practice is leading process, and norms are being developed well in advance of any formal regulatory efforts. Concrete interventions are taking place at the national level. NGOs continue to influence domestic agendas, and international and national agencies are adopting practical approaches to tackling demand. UN member states have an opportunity to redress this inconsistency when the action program is reopened for negotiation in 2006. Future norm development and regulatory efforts might then focus upon direct and indirect effects of small arms, and their persistent demand rather than solely their supply.

Notes

1 See, for example, Robert Axelrod, "An Evolutionary Approach to Norms," *American Political Science Review* vol. 80, no. 4 (December 1986), pp. 1095–111; Friedrich Kratochwil, *Rules, Norms, and Decisions: On the Conditions of Practical and Legal Reasoning in International Relations and Domestic Affairs* (Cambridge: Cambridge University Press, 1989).
2 See, for example, Martha Finnemore and Kathryn Sikkink, "International Norm Dynamics and Political Change," *International Organization* vol. 52, no. 4 (1998), p. 98.
3 See, for example, Edward Laurence and Rachel Stohl, "Making Global Public Policy: The Case of Small Arms and Light Weapons," *Occasional Paper* 7 (Geneva: Small Arms Survey, 2002), p. 36.
4 See, for example, Andrew Sampson, *The Arms Bazaar* (New York: Viking Press, 1977); Albert Pierre, *The Global Politics of Arms Sales* (Princeton: Princeton University Press, 1982); Joseph Smalldone, "U.S. Commercial Arms Exports: Policy, Process, and Patterns," *Defence Institute of Security Training Management Journal* vol. 10, no. 3 (1988), pp. 61–83; Edward Laurence "Political Implications of Illegal Arms Exports from the United States," *Political Science Quarterly* vol. 107, no. 3 (1992), pp. 109–40; Nathalie Goldring, *Research Sources on the International Trade in Light Weapons* (London: BASIC, 1995).
5 See, for example, Small Arms Survey, *Profiling the Problem* (Oxford: Oxford University Press, 2001).
6 Small Arms Survey, *Profiling the Problem* (Oxford: Oxford University Press, 2001), and subsequent annual reports each year accord a chapter to each of the themes identified in Table 2.1.
7 See, for example, Ron Smith and Ali Tasiran, "The Demand for Arms Imports," *Journal of Peace Research* vol. 42, no. 2 (2005), pp. 167–81.
8 See, for example, UN General Assembly, "Illicit Trade in Small Arms and Light Weapons in All Its Aspects," Resolution 56/24 (December 24, 2001); United Nations, *Report of the Panel of Governmental Experts on Small Arms*, UN Doc. A/52/298 (August 1999); United Nations, *Report of the Panel of Governmental Experts on Small Arms*, UN Doc. A/52/298 (August 1997).
9 See, for example, Small Arms Survey, *Profiling the Problem*; Robin Coupland, "The Effects of Weapons: Defining Superfluous Injury and Unnecessary Suffering," *Medicine and Global Survival* vol. 3, no. 1 (1996), available online at www.ippnw.org/MGS/V3Coupland.html; Georg Scharf, "The Effects of Mortar Bombs and Similar Weapons in Limited Conflict," *Background Paper for the Medical Profession and the*

Effects of Weapons (Geneva: International Committee of the Red Cross, 1996); Phil Cook, "The Effects of Gun Availability on Robbery and Robbery Murder," in Robert Haveman and Bruce Zellner, eds, *Policy Studies Annual* (Beverly Hills, CA: Sage, 1979).

10 See, for example, David Hemenway, Tomoko Shinoda-Tagawa, and Matthew Miller, "Firearm Availability and Female Homicide Victimization Rates Among 25 Populous High-Income Countries," *Journal of the American Medical Women's Association* vol. 57, no. 2 (2002), pp. 100–4; Phil Cook, *Gun Violence: the Real Costs* (Oxford: Oxford University Press, 2000); Centre for Disease Control (CDC), "Rates of Homicide, Suicide, and Firearm-Related Death Among Children: 26 Industrialised Countries," *Morbidity and Mortality Weekly Report* no. 46 (1996) available online at www.cdc.gov/mmwr/; Etienne Krug, Keith Powell, and Linda Dahlberg, "Firearm-Related Deaths in the United States and 25 Other High- and Upper-Middle-Income Countries," *International Journal of Epidemiology* vol. 27 (1998), pp. 214–21.

11 See, for example, World Health Organization (WHO), *World Report on Violence and Health* (Geneva: Oxford University Press, 2002); International Committee of the Red Cross (ICRC), *Arms Availability and the Situation of Civilians in Armed Conflict* (Geneva: ICRC, 1999); Keith Krause, "Multilateral Diplomacy, Norm Building, and UN Conferences: The Case of Small Arms and Light Weapons," *Global Governance* vol. 8, no. 2 (2002), pp. 247–63; Robert Muggah and Peter Batchelor, *Development Held Hostage: The Socio-Economic Impacts of Small Arms Availability and Misuse* (New York: United Nations Development Programme, 2004); Robert Muggah with Martin Griffiths, "Reconsidering the Tools of War," *Network Paper* 39 (London: Overseas Development Institute, 2002).

12 Krause, "Multilateral Diplomacy, Norm Building, and UN Conferences."

13 Consult, for example, Small Arms Survey, *Rights at Risk* (Oxford: Oxford University Press, 2004); Stockholm International Peace Research Institute (SIPRI), *SIPRI Yearbook: Armaments, Disarmament, and International Security* (Oxford: Oxford University Press, 2002).

14 Small Arms Survey, *Profiling the Problem*, p. 168.

15 See, for example, Krug, Powell, and Dahlberg, "Firearm-Related Deaths."

16 See Small Arms Survey, *Rights at Risk*, p. 174.

17 Small Arms Survey, *Development Denied* (Oxford: Oxford University Press, 2003).

18 See, for example, Robert Muggah, "No Magic Bullet: A Critical Perspective on DDR and Weapons Reduction in Post-Conflict Contexts," *Journal of Contemporary Security Policy* (2005).

19 See David Atwood and Robert Muggah, "Disaggregating Demand for Small Arms and Light Weapons," in Centre for Humanitarian Dialogue, *Putting People First* (Geneva: Centre for Humanitarian Dialogue, 2005).

20 See, for example, Dylan Hendrickson and Andrzej Karkoszka, "The Challenges of Security Sector Reform," in *Stockholm International Peace Research Institute* (Oxford: Oxford University Press, 2002), pp. 175–202; Ron Smith and Ali Tasiran, "The Demand for Arms Imports," *Journal of Peace Research* vol. 42, no. 2 (2005), pp. 167–81.

21 See, for example, Atwood and Muggah, "Disaggregating Demand for Small Arms and Light Weapons."

22 See John Sislen and Fred Pearson, *Arms and Ethnic Conflict* (New York: Rowman and Littlefield, 2001); Robert Muggah and Jurgen Brauer, "Diagnosing Demand: An Economic Framework to Assessing the Demand for Small Arms," *Discussion Paper* 50 (University of Cape Town: School of Economics and Management, 2004); Robert Muggah, "Diagnosing Demand: Assessing Motivations and Means for Small Arms in

Solomon Islands and Papua New Guinea," *Occasional Paper* 15 (Canberra: Australian National University, 2004).

23 The UN Programme of Action to Prevent, Combat, and Eradicate the Illicit Trade in Small Arms and Light Weapons in All Its Aspects was adopted by consensus in 2001. It is a soft law instrument and not legally binding.

24 See, for example, Krause, "Multilateral Diplomacy, Norm Building, and UN Conferences."

25 The UN Programme of Action states that it should ensure concrete commitments regarding development of measures to prevent illegal manufacturing and trafficking in small arms and light weapons (para. 1.22).

26 Small Arms Survey, *Development Denied*, p. 247.

27 Krause, "Multilateral Diplomacy, Norm Building, and UN Conferences."

28 See, for example, Human Rights Watch, "UN: Programme of Inaction on Small Arms," *Human Rights News*, July 19, 2001; Aaron Karp, "Laudable Failure: The UN Small Arms Conference," *SAIS Review* vol. 22, no. 1 (Winter–Spring 2002), pp. 177–93.

29 See, for example, Fund for Peace, *Model Convention on the Registration of Arms Brokers and the Suppression of Unlicensed Arms Brokering* (2001), available online at www.fundforpeace.org.

30 Pursuant to a provision in the UN action program, the UN Group of Governmental Experts on Tracing Illicit Small Arms and Light Weapons was established in 2002 with the purpose of examining the feasibility of an international marking and tracing instrument.

31 See, for example, Laurence and Stohl, "Making Global Public Policy"; Krause, "Multilateral Diplomacy, Norm Building, and UN Conferences."

32 In 2003, the UN Development Programme and the UN Department for Disarmament Affairs launched a project to strengthen the capacity of states to report on their implementation of the UN Programme of Action. See www.undp.org/bcpr/smallarms/poa.htm.

33 The Firearms Protocol was adopted by the General Assembly in 2001. By the end of 2002, 52 states had signed on, with three ratifications.

34 For example, prior to the UN Programme of Action in 2001, more than 50 high-level seminars and conferences took place in the three years preceding the UN conference where the program was agreed. See Krause, "Multilateral Diplomacy, Norm Building, and UN Conferences."

35 In 1997, the Council of the European Union agreed on its Programme for Preventing and Combating Illicit Trafficking in Conventional Arms. By 1998 it had developed a code of conduct on arms exports and agreed on a joint action. See Krause, "Multilateral Diplomacy, Norm Building, and UN Conferences."

36 The principles note that force and firearms are to be used only as a last resort (Principle 4), and then only with restraint and in proportion to the objective being pursued (Principle 5a). States are also required to "ensure that arbitrary or abusive use of force and firearms by law enforcement officials is punished as a criminal offence under the law" (Principle 7).

37 The 1997 Convention on Anti-Personnel Landmines is the most well known.

38 Emanuella Gillard, "What's Legal? What's Illegal?" in Lora Lumpe, ed., *Running Guns: The Global Black Market in Small Arms* (London: Zed Books, 2000), p. 30.

39 Barbara Frey, "Human Rights and Small Arms," *UNHCHR Sub-Commission on the Promotion and Protection of Human Rights Mandated by Resolution 2001/120* (2002).

40 Many of the Universal Declaration's provisions have been incorporated in legally binding form into human rights treaties.

41 Krause, "Multilateral Diplomacy, Norm Building, and UN Conferences."
42 Such perspectives draw on Article 1 of the Geneva Conventions (1949) and Protocols (1977).
43 See, for example, Atwood and Muggah, "Disaggregating Demand for Small Arms and Light Weapons."
44 See Ernie Regehr, "Reducing the Demand for Small Arms and Light Weapons: Priorities for the International Community," *Working Paper* 04-2 (Waterloo: Project Ploughshares, 2004), p. 9.
45 Ibid.
46 See, for example, Muggah, "No Magic Bullet."
47 See, for example, www.dfid.gov.uk/pubs/files/salw_briefing.pdf; www.gtz.de/small-arms.
48 Small Arms Survey, *Development Denied*, p. 227.
49 Small Arms Survey, *Development Denied.*
50 Krause, "Multilateral Diplomacy, Norm Building, and UN Conferences," p. 248.

3

SMALL ARMS, VIOLENCE, AND THE COURSE OF CONFLICTS

William Reno

Introduction

Contemporary insurgencies continue to be relegated by academics and policymakers to the category of mere criminal activity; as a result, the responses are largely those of regulation and law enforcement. Many insurgent groups or rebels both engage in predatory behavior and are responsible for massive violations of human rights. Scrambles for diamonds shaped the character of warfare in Sierra Leone, Liberia, and Angola in the 1990s, and international responses seek to address predatory behavior. Protocols such as those arising from the Kimberley Process seek to regulate the trade in these "blood diamonds."[1] Equally important are efforts to regulate the trade in the small arms, the portable, easily tradable, and cheap weapons that rebels often buy with these looted resources. This phenomenon created the impetus for the United Nations Global Conference on Illicit Trade in Small Arms and Light Weapons, which was held in 2001.[2] While these responses are important, the emphasis upon the criminality of the groups and the emphasis upon regulatory and law enforcement responses has inherent limitations, particularly as international responses remain state-centric and biased toward state sovereignty.

In practical terms, these measures target the nonstate armed groups that fight against state regimes and that are responsible for many human rights violations. This is especially true where state institutions have become weak and militias and rebel armies have proliferated. These measures also are grounded in a regulatory framework that takes for granted the state system as it is presently constituted. Article 11 of the 2001 UN protocol on small arms, for example, acknowledges the right to self-determination of all peoples,[3] but goes on to state that this is not meant to encourage action undermining the territorial integrity or political unity of states acting in conformity with this right. That is, the use of small arms for the purposes of a rebellion that would alter or break apart member states of the UN is not legitimate, at least not in global terms. Whether intended or not, framing regulation in this manner further criminalizes the exercise of violence on the part of nonstate groups in broad international diplomatic terms. It also puts a powerful tool in the hands of state officials who face threats from armed groups within their countries, allowing them to seek support from the international community and criminalize the activities of their domestic opponents.

This regulatory effort reinforces a deeply conservative bias toward present state-centrism in the international system. Much as the Congress of Vienna in 1815 sought to contain violent and disruptive French republicanism, current regulation of nonstate violence seeks to target the threat that nonstate armed groups pose to failing and collapsing states. The framers of the Congress of Vienna ignored the aspirations of many people, and within several decades nationalist groups jeopardized this arrangement. Likewise, many of those who use illicitly obtained small arms imagine themselves to be fighting for the legitimate destinies of their own communities. A few succeed in using illicit transfers of arms to create zones of control that a significant number of people within those areas regard as a legitimate order.

This is not to say that global efforts to regulate the trade in natural resources and small arms in conflicts relieve state officials from their obligations to respect human rights. Moreover, many rebels and insurgents are extremely violent and prey upon and undermine the communities in and around which they operate. But do all nonstate armed groups use small arms and other resources of violence in similar ways or produce the same results? The economies of both northern and southern Somalia rely on overseas remittances, and small arms are widely available, yet patterns of violence are very different in the two zones. Congo's western diamond-mining district is more peaceful than mining areas in the east. These and other counterintuitive examples rarely turn up in analyses of conflict, resources, and small arms. These groups do not control internationally recognized sovereign states and therefore they and their behavior often are relegated to the category of illicit and clandestine activity. Variations in the outcomes of such conflicts, especially in similar circumstances, challenge the proposition that readily available small arms always fuel conflicts and promote predatory behavior. The history of state building is replete with examples of coercive groups that created order. I address this prospect below through the lens of the social organization of violence, rather than treating small arms and violence as separate causal factors. Instead, I examine who possesses the capacity to exercise violence, and how their relations with other groups in their societies shape their behavior. One implication of this approach is that it leaves open the possibility that access to small arms *for some groups under certain circumstances* may promote order and help control predatory violence. This argument is important for policymakers. It suggests that while limiting small arms flows to most nonstate groups may mitigate violence and promote order, in some contexts such limitations may exacerbate violence and promote the fragmentation of armed groups.

In this chapter I provide a framework to explain relations between conflict and resources, including small arms. I argue that high degrees of predatory violence are linked to patronage-based political systems. These political strategies produce distinctive social contexts in which key state officials support violent commerce and other rent-seeking activities. Official authority is not based upon conventional notions of legitimacy or administration through bureaucratic institutions. Instead, political cliques control markets, especially in natural resources, to manipulate others' access to economic opportunities to enhance their power. Those officials and their associates exploit these opportunities from behind the façade of sovereign statehood. This strategy rests upon eliminating autonomous economic opportunities, which also means limiting the autonomy of other social groups outside this political network.

Two key observations emerge from this analysis. First, state collapse often is a consequence of a political strategy in which the exercise of coercion shapes the violence that accompanies subsequent conflicts. Coercive authority structures, *not* a political void, produce particularly violent conflicts among competing armed groups. Second, local politico-economic structures shape relationships among political authority, resources, and coercion differently.

Local social structures and violent conflict

The idea that small arms inevitably promote conflict assumes that participants in conflicts pursue opportunities for personal advancement. Paul Collier's and Anke Hoeffler's "looting model of rebellion" suggests that "opportunities are more important in explaining conflict than are motives." Small arms are a key ingredient in shaping the opportunity structures of combatants. Their easy availability means that individuals and small groups are free to loot, since central agencies face difficulty in controlling this proliferation of cheap weapons. Collier and Hoeffler's analysis of 78 large civil conflicts between 1960 and 1999 confirms that the availability of natural resources plays a major role in conflict and guns play an important role in securing them. [4] These arms also give their holders the capacity to participate in lucrative global criminal networks.[5] Many policymakers have made this conclusion a central feature of their understandings of the causes and possible remedies for ongoing conflicts.[6] Access to criminal networks is said to bolster the viability of these insurgents as they attract more members, and to give them an interest in continuing conflict for further financial gain.

For example, John Hirsch, the US ambassador to Sierra Leone at the height of that country's 1991–2002 war, wrote of the leader of the Revolutionary United Front (RUF) insurgents: "Documents taken from Sankoh's residence revealed . . . he was continuing to systematically exploit the country's diamonds for his personal benefit,"[7] which included trips to South Africa to buy guns.[8] It is apparent in this case that the availability of small arms contributed to violent predation. Moreover, the wide availability of small arms can empower people with particular types of social capital.[9] The head of the National Patriotic Front of Liberia (NPFL), Charles Taylor, became a successful leader on the basis of his skills as a violent entrepreneur. Taylor was more efficient at obtaining loot to buy guns and attract followers, while his patient and studious rival, Elmer Johnson, undertook the arduous task of trying to raise a politically cohesive insurgent army, only to be killed, apparently on Taylor's orders.

While opportunity is an important element shaping insurgents' behavior, it does not explain all behavior. Indeed, ambiguities about individual predation and group solidarities may reflect the variations in how violence and existing social structures interact. A security dilemma may arise in which the arming by some may be viewed as defensive or offensive. Those who choose to respond with defensive armaments might find that their actions are then interpreted as aggressive.[10] Social structures such as ethnic solidarities can play a major role in how weapons are used. The legitimacy, adaptability, and relationship of these social structures to prewar state authority will have important bearing on whether local community leaders can discipline young men with guns.

Changeable and contingent individual motives may not matter that much in determining "root causes" of conflicts. More important is the role that these changing social relationships can play in encouraging or even compelling some people to use guns to provide public goods such as order for communities while others in similar material circumstances prey upon local people and turn on their associates. Why do some groups use guns to solve problems of cooperation and to provide order? Mancur Olson and Robert Bates observed that predators who protect groups that otherwise could withhold resources succeed in the long run when compared with unrestrained predators. Here, short-term individual aggrandizement and long-term community cooperation are compatible and intertwined motivations.[11] But different outcomes reflect the capabilities of and contexts in which social groups pursue their interests.

These varied social relationships appear in recent conflicts. By September 2001, for example, Afghanistan's Taliban rulers had cut opium production to just 4 percent of the previous year's quota, giving up an income of $100 million, even as they fought rivals for control of the country.[12] That the Taliban forwent immediate gains in the face of military pressure indicated that it could command followers and control individuals' predatory impulses, including its own. This was an impressive feat, given the weakness of formal state institutions and the autonomy of local warlords. The Taliban was a very different organization than Sierra Leone's predatory RUF or Liberia's NPFL, even though all operated in factionalized societies with ample clan and regional bases for mobilization. All had access to major clandestine economic opportunities and to global sources of small arms, but the Taliban integrated self-interest into a framework that also provided a type of public good.

Likewise, Burma's government uses income from drug trafficking, a resource implicated in predation in many other conflicts, to pacify insurgent groups and incorporate them into a centrally organized state. This mirrors a historical pattern in which central authorities recruit predators to control peripheral areas and impose order.[13] These and other examples illustrate the importance of relationships among formal and informal authorities, fighters, and resources such as small arms. Groups that successfully control followers discipline those members, and in turn shape members' motivations. This phenomenon suggests an underlying factor that conventional investigations of motives, or an exclusive focus on small arms as causes of illegitimate violence, may obscure. Young men who mined diamonds in one part of Sierra Leone did use guns to prey upon local communities, while others in similar circumstances joined home guard units to protect local communities. Clan-based northern Somalia is much more peaceful than clan-based southern Somalia. Young men from Dagestan and the Ingush Autonomous Republic do not join their Chechen neighbors in battle. Individual motivations matter less than the social structures into which individuals were recruited and in which they are disciplined.

Coercion, violence, and collapsing states

The UN's Resolution 1514 of 1960, the Declaration on the Granting of Independence to Colonial Countries and Peoples, ensures global recognition of sovereignty of former colonies regardless of "inadequacy of political, economic, social or educational preparedness," or of internal administrative coherence or capabilities.[14] This guarantee of global recognition of sovereignty created what Robert Jackson called "quasi-states" with governments "deficient in the political will, institutional authority, and organized power to protect human rights or provide socio-economic welfare."[15] Opposition groups might thus hijack effective state agencies and launch their own bids for power.[16] More than two-thirds of African countries have experienced violent transitions of government, despite recent political reforms.[17] Elections played important roles in sparking violence in Congo-Brazzaville, Nigeria, Tanzania, Guinea-Bissau, and Côte d'Ivoire. Rulers facing such threats preemptively disrupt power bases of potential competitors, even if this means undermining institutions. Thus rulers replaced bureaucracies with sprawling patronage networks under their personal control. This also hindered the development of autonomous nonstate social organizations, as patronage networks moved into commercial, religious, and youth politics and other realms.

Rulers who weakened their own states found an alternative means to exercise power through dominating the distribution of economic opportunities. At first this involved manipulating economic regulations and distributing state assets to political allies, including people who could mobilize force on behalf of the regime. The predictable result was that formal economies and state revenues shrank. Then politicians extended their economic activities to clandestine markets. State power, backed by private militias, remained viable in this context, since the capacity to declare activities illegal, then sell exemption from prosecution, enabled political favorites to accumulate wealth while giving the political boss the means to punish opponents. A striking feature of states such as Congo, Sierra Leone, Liberia, and Nigeria is the extent to which control of clandestine markets and their integration into political patronage networks replaced state administration as means of dominating people.

Rulers use coercion and violence, but also corruption, to manage their relations with other social groups. One can see major differences in the social organization of corruption in East Asia, compared with Africa. To offer but one example, Transparency International's corruption perceptions index for 2003 shows Kenya and Indonesia tied for 122nd place, indicating that business people regard both as quite corrupt. Yet Indonesia's economy per capita grew 2.3 percent each year from 1991 to 2002, compared with Kenya's 0.9 percent annual contraction.[18] Why does economic growth accompany corruption in East Asia? Perhaps "crony capitalists" and rulers share benefits from strong state institutions and rising state capacity to control societal resources. Together they use informal relationships to distribute economic opportunities on the basis of political loyalties.[19] This relationship resembles Charles Tilly's analysis of state building as a racketeering enterprise in which victims gain some leverage over predatory rulers.[20] Greedy rulers can promote the long-term prosperity of their "victims" to increase resources available to all. But if close associates pose the greatest coup threat, they become dangerous, basic social consensus fails, and short-term considerations dominate. In this context small arms really do spur individual predation.

In most very weak and collapsing states, patronage relationships lack broad long-term reciprocity. This is reflected in the political economies of these states. In Zimbabwe, Kenya, Côte d'Ivoire, and Namibia, rulers damaged their societies' relatively bright economic prospects and greatly diminished their own access to resources. Why choose this path? Rulers in these states destroyed their formal economies to eliminate potential challenges to their power. Patronage in collapsing states is a zero-sum affair, keeping beneficiaries insecure as a means of disciplining them. Impoverishment reinforces the exclusivity of this relationship, equipping the ruler with a capacity to sell selective exemption from the harm that the ruler's own choices have created.

Regimes based upon this particular patronage organization fail in large part to satisfy Thomas Hobbes's basic definition of government as an organization that provides nonexclusionary public goods to a defined community.[21] Asserting an exclusive right to exercise violence in order to provide public goods such as order is an essential political foundation of government. This idea of governance informed European international law up to the late nineteenth century.[22] It continues to find resonance in indigenous notions of governance in places where local people consider their globally recognized state officials to be the main predators and sources of disorder. This standard in principle tolerates heterogeneity of internal political arrangements so long as they provide at least basic public goods to communities, regardless of the political or social forms these authorities assume.

This principle distinguishes governance from a racketeer's use of violence. A racketeer creates disorder so as to charge individuals for exemption from the harm that befalls those who do not pay. Unlike a tax collector's boss, the racketeer does not provide order to all. Effective racketeers are especially violent and destructive. This prevents rival gangs or enterprising associates from claiming some of the racketeer's victims as their own clients and ensures that no would-be clients provide their own group security as a public good. The racketeer imposes general insecurity precisely to turn his provision of security into a private good and to force the undecided to seek his protection simply to survive.[23]

Likewise, many rulers of collapsed states make citizens poorer and less secure. They control as much economic opportunity as possible, including clandestine economies, which enables them to sell access to individuals. Those able to find a niche in this system often are those who are experts in especially predatory uses of violence. They trade these skills for access to commercial networks that the ruler dominates, to join what essentially is a violent private commercial syndicate. From this perspective, what distinguishes governments from racketeers is how violence is organized relative to members of the group and how violence is used in relation to members of the wider community, not international diplomatic conventions concerning legal recognition.

In most collapsing states, violence, political power, and commerce are fused in a system that is defined in terms of the private interests of its members. For example, UN investigators estimated that commercial transactions under Charles Taylor's personal control, mostly in diamonds and timbers, were about five times larger than Liberia's official budget in 2001 and exceeded domestic revenue collection that year by 25 times.[24] Likewise, Zimbabwe's president maintains an economically disastrous fixed exchange rate for the benefit of a political clique. With access to a national bank, official documents, and passports that foreign governments accept as legitimate, the president's associates are the country's largest clandestine economy operators. Meanwhile, the country's economy contracted by 19 percent in 2002–3 and threatened the stability of southern Africa.[25] Violence in these cases grows out of distinctive political economies and social contexts. I argue below that these factors shape the variation in the behavior of armed groups, and examine the role that small arms play in this process.

Coercion, greed, and public goods

A perspective that associates sovereign authority with the capacity to control a society, and provide that society's members with at least minimal public goods such as order, may have difficulty treating some contemporary governments as truly sovereign.[26] Yet, this approach would have little difficulty accepting insurgents that provide stability and security for particular communities as governments. Those who fail to accomplish these tasks would be considered to have lost their sovereignty and their actions would be considered illegitimate. This approach stands in opposition to aspects of the analysis of the impact of small arms proliferation on local order in the work of Harold Koh, former US assistant secretary of state for democracy, human rights, and labor, 1998–2001: "The pervasive presence of guns perpetuates a culture of societal violence." Given this situation, writes Koh, "what hope is there for democracy and civil society?"[27] Obviously guns play a key role in violence where it does occur. But an international law perspective that does not extend legitimacy to organizations that use guns to establish order and provide other public goods, regardless of their diplomatic status, does not acknowledge armed groups that begin to behave much like recognized sovereign states. This is true even when local people regard existing sovereign states as a major cause of disorder in their everyday lives, and armed groups equipped with "clandestine" weapons as protectors of law and order.

This paradox appears in the absence of a mechanism to extinguish Somalia's sovereignty today, as some 40 militias contend for power in the southern two-thirds of the country, which has lacked a central administration since 1991.[28] The relatively peaceful self-styled Republic of Somaliland to the north has built a stable political order that taxes and regulates commerce. Its leadership had reined in local warlords and militias by the mid-1990s and now provides citizens with levels of personal security beyond that in many recognized states. Its government submits evidence of its capacity and willingness to provide these public goods, yet it is not recognized as a sovereign state in the international system.[29] People in southern Sudan may have good reason to regard former insurgents of the Sudan People's Liberation Army (SPLA) as defenders against predations from the north, even if some SPLA members preyed upon southerners. Yet all are or were nonstate armed groups in international law and all engage in the illicit transfer of small arms.

Violence alone is not a clear indication of the nature of the groups that exercise it or of their relations with local society. The UN-mandated Special Court in Sierra Leone indicted Chief Sam Hinga Norman, the head of an ethnic militia, the Civil Defense Forces (CDF), for well-documented human rights abuses. But this prosecution drew local criticism. Protesters argued that Hinga Norman had protected civilians against the rebels and helped force the rebels to negotiate.[30] They approved of the fact that CDF fighters battled elements of the government's army that had joined RUF fighters in their "Operation No Living Thing" attack on the capital in 1999.[31] As the indictment was made public in 2003, the militia's second-in-command offered to assist the official army's efforts to stem incursions of Liberian fighters, encouraging the popular perception that the CDF was better able to protect the country from foreign threats than the government army.[32]

Different uses of resources and violence among armed groups reflect the social institutions shaping the range of opportunities available to armed actors. These institutions can include clan and ethnic associations, bureaucratic remnants of collapsing state agencies, clandestine business arrangements, and diasporas. Outcomes depend on whether or not those who control access to resources and weapons, including clandestine channels, enjoy local legitimacy, and whether or not they can withhold resources in exchange for compliance. The relationship of these groups to state power in the prewar period plays a crucial role in determining whether or not they can later exercise this type of social control, and the degree to which they promote public goods. Outside resources, such as foreign aid and military assistance, and their impact on these local structures of control, will affect whether guns and clandestine resources are used to promote order or disorder and predation. These social factors allow one to distinguish between violence in the pursuit of a private association's exclusionary interests and the provision of public goods. What is relevant is particular communities' perception of the legitimacy of violence. Resources, including clandestine and illicit rackets – and even small arms – may then be factors in preserving or creating order.

These observations should inform outside intervention in cases of state collapse. It may be a bad idea *in some instances* to block clandestine trades, even in weapons, for example. Sanctioning certain armed actors might reduce short-term violence, but also could strengthen more predatory groups if the targets of sanctions provided order. International actors often ignore informal local authorities who lack the apparatus that outsiders usually associate with authority, yet they may exercise social control over resources. In southwestern Nigeria, for example, elderly ladies who regulate urban markets play key financial roles in organizing and controlling urban vigilantes.[33]

Variations in social contexts of armed groups drive the variable nature of violence. In Somalia, President Siad Barre (1969–91) built a political network based on distributing parts of the formal and even the clandestine economy to strongmen whom he thought he could trust. Suspicious of his own state's institutions, he financed this alliance through skimming foreign aid and manipulating creditor-mandated land tenure reforms to distribute land to his political allies. These allies tended to deploy private militias made up of otherwise unemployed youth, and were thus insulated from the social consequences of their predations because they were reliant only upon the president's favor. They were thus able to construct something more like a violent private commercial syndicate than a government. Some presidential clients recognized that they could attract their own followers if they allowed such followers to prey upon unpopular locals, mobilizing grievances as they looted. The president recognized that such a social relationship with local people would create an autonomous power base for his clients, so he punished those who pursued this strategy.

Those excluded from the president's political networks could not benefit from his predatory strategy. Some were on the wrong side of old political battles, or drew presidential suspicion because of their kinship ties. Political marginalization forced them to organize their own clandestine economic activities outside "official" illicit activities. Unable to secure presidential protection, local strongmen, especially in the area that later became the Republic of Somaliland, had to turn to kinship networks for protection and local elders to guarantee and adjudicate business agreements. Clan-based credit systems, which had long existed as informal commercial networks that handled overseas remittances, now were integrated more tightly into this defensive arrangement. This enabled local businessmen and elders who tapped into the earnings of overseas Somali workers to exercise some leverage over militia leaders.

By the time general conflict broke out in the north in 1988, enterprising figures that under other circumstances might have become predatory found that they could not finance their militias through predation of local communities without suffering negative consequences. They remained reliant on overseas remittances to finance their militias. To do this they had to make their peace with local elders who ran these informal networks. Elders also recognized that outsider youth would offer enterprising politicians an independent following beyond elders' control. Therefore they made life very difficult for outsider youth.[34] Ties to elders restrained the young men. The elders were part of the glue that bound those who exercised coercion to those who enjoyed deep-rooted legitimacy in local communities. The US decision to impose sanctions against these informal financial networks as "illicit" financial institutions in 2002 as part of the "war against terror" drew immediate protest from these areas. Local leaders pointed out that these measures risked undermining what security and order had been created in the wake of Somalia's collapse by weakening the social reciprocity between those who controlled resources and those who had the means to exercise violence.[35]

In fact, enterprising militia leaders did loot local communities in February 1992 when Abdirahmaan Ali Tuur led a force to sack the port city of Berbera. Tuur used this loot to arm men and claim a seat at negotiations organized by the UN and Egyptian government. This incident convinced northern authorities of the need to restrict UN political involvement in their territory and ban local participation in peace talks, lest this disrupt their social control over resources, and thus their control over violence. This fractious effect of outside mediation appears in Mogadishu too. Militias proliferated again in 2001–2 as negotiations offered the prospect of an external audience and externally guaranteed sovereign state and the chance to obtain wealth and power without popular legitimacy or the use of socially accepted methods. UN investigators reported "some leading businessmen have outflanked militia leaders from their own clans and have started buying the backing of individual militia fighters."[36] This they attributed to "part of the competition between Somali groups in advance of the anticipated conference of concerned parties in Nairobi under the auspices of IGAD (Intergovernmental Authority on Development) peace negotiations."[37]

Somalia's situation highlights the consequences of external approaches that treat armed groups in a uniform fashion and that privilege strategies to rebuild *states* at the expense of *organizations* more adept at providing order. This dynamic also appeared in Sierra Leone in the late 1990s. Military setbacks forced the RUF into peace negotiations in 1998–9. The peace agreement included Foday Sankoh, the RUF's primary organizer of diamonds-for-arms transactions in a coalitional government – as head of an agency administering Sierra Leone's diamond resources! Sankoh used his new office to sell diamonds abroad, without having to rely upon intermediaries who demanded hefty risk premiums when dealing with him as a rebel leader. A year later, the RUF took several hundred UN peacekeepers hostage, creating a crisis that ended when British forces intervened and coordinated with the CDF militia to rescue the hostages and fight the RUF and renegades from the government army.[38] International efforts to engage the RUF and the government of Sierra Leone did not account for how local people decided what was legitimate authority and how this indigenous idea might extend to the CDF militia.

Nonetheless, CDF militias, which arguably had a measure of legitimacy and offered a modest degree of security to communities, also engaged in clandestine diamond mining. The militia's organizers came from among the local elite who had been relatively marginalized in prewar politics. They too had to rely on local customary practices – here, mobilization of young men's initiation societies – to fend off attacks from armed gangs that capital-based politicians sponsored. The local elite also organized young men to mine diamonds, just as corrupt politicians in the capital did. Thus the wartime armed group developed in a context that integrated locally legitimate practices for controlling youth with the use of armed gangs to protect the community from predatory outsiders. When war came to CDF-dominated areas, young men from the same social groups from which the RUF drew recruits were more likely to join the CDF to protect their communities instead. This wartime behavior built on the reciprocal obligations of local strongmen and miners to guarantee each other's security. While the international community regarded the activities of both as illicit, their social relationship also helped to create order.

Sierra Leone demonstrates how clandestine economies can be integral components of strategies to control violence and create order as a public good in a context where an incumbent government is organized more like a predatory private business syndicate. It also shows the difficulties of international engagement of these groups within the existing framework of states. When Nigerian and British expeditionary forces moved CDF units outside their home areas to fight RUF rebels, these units split into factions, looted, and became more general abusers of human rights. This was due in part to their removal from the mechanisms of social control that bound them to the communities they protected.

This example also shows the difficulties of applying uniform judgments about the exercise of coercion to armed groups, regardless of social context. For example, Nigerian and British forces assisted CDF units fighting the RUF into 2001.[39] In 1998, after RUF and renegade elements of the army had captured the capital, officials in London, the British ambassador to Sierra Leone, and the West African expeditionary force cooperated with the CDF to import small arms in contravention of a UN embargo to expel rebels from the city.[40] The urgency of bringing order to the country overrode concerns about uniform adherence to human rights norms, the regulation of small arms imports, or concerns about fighters' motivations, a tendency also common among foreign armies in Afghanistan, Iraq, and elsewhere that seek indigenous allies that can claim local legitimacy and provide order at a low cost.

Once Sierra Leone's war ended and the temporary alliance with outside forces dissolved, the UN-sponsored Special Court issued indictments for Chief Sam Hinga Norman, the former CDF national coordinator and minister of internal affairs, and two of his associates, including the head of the initiation society that had become the core disciplining agency of the CDF. David Crane, speaking for the prosecution in the Court, insisted that the case must focus on the alleged crimes, not politics.[41] But politics cannot be barred from the court of public opinion, a considerable portion of which regarded the CDF as a last line of defense against people who had come to kill civilians. In a more perfect world, the government would have carried out this task, but instead a substantial element of government forces had joined with the RUF. Moreover, at least one member of the UN Security Council had earlier relied on the CDF to help fight the RUF.

Other contexts illustrate the variable relations between armed groups and the resources and coercion that support or undermine the provision of public goods. The Ingush Autonomous Republic of Russia's former president Ruslan Aushev also used clandestine economic channels and informal social institutions to control predation without building a strong state apparatus. He confronted Islamist internationalists from neighboring Chechnya, who recruited local young men and helped them kidnap people to finance their group and to challenge local secular nationalists. Many Ingush people regarded these Islamists as bandits, and tried to retaliate against families of local fighters who collaborated in their activities. Aushev expelled Arab "guests" and asked for the consent of village elders to close new mosques that outsiders had built. Mosques were dismantled, and then rebuilt with local labor. He asked families of kidnapping victims to forgive local fighters, and help find them jobs in the many rackets that found their way to Aushev's land-locked republic, which officially became a tax-free "offshore economic zone." This arrangement appears to have helped keep at bay predation by young men who could have easily taken advantage of the region's material opportunities. Most households in this region have substantial private arsenals, offering ample opportunities to prey on others, but the region's order remains a remarkable contrast to that of neighboring Chechnya.[42] Such mobilization of patriarchal ethnic customs against the threat of militancy challenges many conventional ideas about small arms control, and is not easily generalized. Nonetheless, these strategies share the common feature of establishing order on the basis of shared bonds of social reciprocity that are used to discipline predatory motives.

Dealing with complexity

It is evident that small arms and greed motivate people. But focusing on motivations of individuals without consideration of social factors does not tell us where sustained order comes from, since logically it never should arise. Otherwise one has to import the tricky assumption of false consciousness to explain away inconvenient cooperation. It is harder, though more interesting and productive, to explain variation in conflicts and the formation and maintenance of large-scale political organizations through a closer contextual examination of socio-economic relations. For example, high levels of corruption may occur alongside a government's provision of the basic public good of growing prosperity. Of course, economists are not insensitive to the importance of social structures. Andrei Schleifer and Robert Vishny, and Susan Rose-Ackerman and Jacqueline Coolidge, for example, place political institutions and social interactions at the center of their analyses of corruption. Rose-Ackerman even concludes that increased greed may reduce probabilities of conflict, at least temporarily, provided it is coupled with a political strategy that centralizes the distribution of patronage where formal institutional structures lack capacity and popular legitimacy.[43]

Explaining these variations requires an analytical framework that can adapt to contextual variation. It has to account, for example, for why armed groups sometimes are predatory and sometimes not, and sometimes in different ways, or why corruption takes different forms, regardless of how armed groups got their guns. The alternative is to define illicit behavior in the same way and assume that armed groups all will use resources such as small arms with the same motivations and in the same manner. This can lead to dramatic mismatches between personal motivations and outcomes, as for example when a focus on Saddam Hussein's personal intentions and actions based on faulty assumptions, and valid information derived from available evidence, obscured a much more complicated situation. Real life shows how the tendency to assimilate new data into preexisting flawed frameworks may grow, as "the more ambiguous the information, the more confident the actor is of the validity of his image, and the greater his commitment to the established view."[44]

Conclusion: implications for small arms regulation and the international relations–international law discourse

In the realm of international law and diplomacy, existing states are the primary interlocutors. For great powers this arrangement minimizes potentially disruptive border wars and the rise of new groups who might have ideas about how to order local authority that are at odds with other international norms. For regimes in very weak states this strips some of their domestic challengers of the hope of gaining international recognition. The global effort to regulate the trade in small arms takes place in this context. It denies other groups of outside formal recognition for their state-building efforts to control the exercise of coercion and use that control for the benefit of local communities. In practical terms, this means that processes that would have been lauded as state-building successes in historical terms now face formidable new obstacles in the international arena.

Therefore, while the regulatory effort to control small arms trafficking helps to limit the flow of weapons to predatory groups, it also freezes in place political arrangements that some communities consider to be unjust and at odds with what they consider to be their proper political destinies.

The stakes of this contradiction for regulation of small arms are great. If international law is applied against the interests of insurgents whom local people believe are their legitimate rulers, then they may come to see international law as a threat to their political aspirations. This is not to say that regulating the flow of small arms is a bad thing. Instead, the argument here is that armed groups may use weapons for all sorts of different purposes. Many are predators and are deeply resented, and regulation will be appreciated. A minority of them may enjoy legitimacy because they control their members and use weapons to oppose tyrannies that the international community lacks either the political will or the capacity to oppose. Therefore, regulating the flow of small arms is a deeply political action, a fact that the current regulatory regime shows little evidence of recognizing.

Notes

1 Kimberley Process, *Interlaken Declaration on the Kimberley Process Certification Scheme for Rough Diamonds* (November 5, 2002), available online at www.kimberleyprocess.com:8080/site/www_docs/plenary_meetings9/interlaken_declaration.pdf.

2 United Nations, *Report of the United Nations Conference on the Illicit Trade in Small Arms and Light Weapons in All Its Aspects* (July 9–20, 2001), available online at http://disarmament.un.org/cab/smallarms.

3 Ibid., Art. 11.

4 Paul Collier and Anke Hoeffler, "Greed and Grievance in Civil War," *Policy Research Working Paper* (Washington, DC: World Bank, 2001), quotes from p. 2.

5 Paul Collier and Nicholas Sambanis, eds, Special Issue, *Conflict Resolution: Understanding Civil Wars* vol. 46, no. 1 (February 2002).

6 United Nations, *Report of the United Nations Conference on the Illicit Trade in Small Arms and Light Weapons in All Its Aspects*; expert panel reports on the commerce in arms and natural resources in conflicts in Sierra Leone, Liberia, Congo, Angola, and Somalia.

7 John Hirsch, *Sierra Leone: Diamonds and the Struggle for Democracy* (Boulder: Lynne Rienner, 2001), p. 89.

8 United Nations, *Third Report of the Secretary-General on the United Nations Mission in Sierra Leone* (2000), para. 7.

9 The World Bank maintains a website on social capital, including research on its impact on conflict and development, available online at http://lnweb18.worldbank.org/essd/sdvext.nsf/09bydocname/socialcapital.

10 Jack Snyder and Robert Jervis, "Civil War and the Security Dilemma," in Barbara Walter and Jack Snyder, eds, *Civil Wars, Insecurity, and Intervention* (New York: Columbia University Press, 1999), pp. 15–37.

11 Mancur Olson, *Power and Prosperity* (New York: Basic Books, 2000); Robert Bates, *Prosperity and Violence: The Political Economy of Development* (New York: W. W. Norton, 2001).

12 UN Drug Control Program, *Afghanistan Annual Opium Poppy Survey 2001* (Islamabad, 2001), pp. iii, 11.

13 See Jake Sherman, "Burma: Lessons from the Cease-Fires," in Karen Ballentine and Jake Sherman, eds, *The Political Economy of Armed Conflict: Beyond Greed and Grievance* (Boulder: Lynne Rienner, 2003), pp. 225–55; Karen Barkey, *Bandits and Bureaucrats: The Ottoman Route to State Centralization* (Ithaca: Cornell University Press, 1994).
14 United Nations, "Declaration on the Granting of Independence to Colonial Countries and Peoples," Resolution 1514 (December 14, 1960), Art. 3, available online at www.un.org/depts/dpi/decolonization/declaration.htm.
15 Robert Jackson, *Quasi-States: Sovereignty, International Relations, and the Third World* (New York: Cambridge University Press, 1990), p. 21.
16 Joel Migdal, *Strong Societies and Weak States* (Princeton: Princeton University Press, 1988), pp. 139–41.
17 Patrick McGowan, "African Military Coups d'État, 1956–2001: Frequency, Trends, and Distribution," *Journal of Modern African Studies* vol. 41, no. 3 (2004), pp. 339–70.
18 Transparency International corruption index, available online at www.transparency.org/cpi/2003/cpi2003.en.html; human development index, UN Development Programme, *Human Development Report 2003* (New York, 2003); per capita growth, World Bank, *World Development Report 2003* (New York: Oxford University Press, 2003).
19 David Kang, *Crony Capitalism: Corruption and Development in South Korea and the Philippines* (New York: Cambridge University Press, 2002).
20 Charles Tilly, "War Making and State Making as Organized Crime," in Peter B. Evans, Dietrich Rueschemeyer, and Theda Skocpol, eds, *Bringing the State Back In* (New York: Cambridge University Press, 1985), pp. 169–91.
21 Thomas Hobbes, *Leviathan* (New York: Oxford University Press, 1996), pp. 82–95.
22 "De Facto Government," *Digest of the Published Opinions of the Attorneys-General and the Leading Decisions of the Federal Courts with Reference to International Law Treaties, and Kindred Subjects* (Washington, DC: US Government Printing Office, 1877), pp. 78–81.
23 Diego Gambetta, *The Sicilian Mafia* (Cambridge: Harvard University Press, 1993).
24 Compare International Monetary Fund, *Liberia: Staff Report for the 2001 Article IV Consultation and Overdue Financial Obligations to the Fund* (Washington, DC, February 11, 2002), paras 35, 56; United Nations, *Report of the Panel of Experts Appointed Pursuant to Security Council Resolution 1395 (2002), Paragraph 4, in Relation to Liberia* (April 2002), pp. 23–34.
25 John Robertson, "The Zimbabwean Economy: The Current Position and the Way Forward," in Brian Kagoro, John Makumbe, John Robertson, Patrick Bond, Edward Lahiff, and Richard Cornwell, eds, *Zimbabwe's Turmoil: Problems and Prospects* (Pretoria: Institute for Strategic Studies, 2004), pp. 24–6.
26 Tom Farer, "Problems of an International Law of Intervention," *Stanford Journal of International Studies* vol. 3 (1968), pp. 20–6.
27 Harold Hongju Koh, "Lecture: A World Drowning in Guns," *Fordham Law Review* vol. 71 (2003), p. 2340.
28 UN Security Council, *Report of the Panel of Experts on Somalia Pursuant to Security Council Resolution 1425 (2002)* (March 25, 2003), paras 23, 25.
29 Republic of Somaliland, *Submission on Statehood and Recognition of the Republic of Somaliland* (Hargeisa, 1996).
30 Augustine Beecher, "A Tale of Two Betrayals," *Standard Times* (Freetown), May 27, 2003, p. 3.
31 Commonwealth Human Rights Initiative, *In Pursuit of Justice: A Report on the Judiciary in Sierra Leone* (Freetown, 2002), p. 28.

32 International Crisis Group, *Sierra Leone: The State of Security and Governance* (Freetown, September 5, 2003), p. 13.

33 Observations from my field research of the O'odua People's Congress in Lagos and Ibadan, Nigeria, 2000 and 2003.

34 Gerard Prunier, "A Candid View of the Somali National Front," *Horn of Africa Bulletin* (1991), p. 109.

35 International Crisis Group, "Somalia: Continuation of War by Other Means?" (Nairobi, December 21, 2004), p. 31.

36 UN Security Council, *Report of the Team of Experts Appointed Pursuant to Security Council Resolution 1407 (2002), Paragraph 1, Concerning Somalia* (New York, July 3, 2002), para. 32.

37 Ibid., para. 28.

38 United Nations, *Tenth Report of the Secretary-General on the United Nations Mission in Sierra Leone* (New York, June 25, 2001), para.16.

39 My observation, Daru Headquarters, Kailahun District, Sierra Leone, May–June 2001; UN Security Council, Resolution 1315 (2000), available online at www.specialcourt.org/documents/backgrounddocs/scres1315e.pdf.

40 United Kingdom, House of Commons, *Select Committee on Foreign Affairs Second Report: Sierra Leone* (London: Her Majesty's Stationery Office, August 21, 1999).

41 Special Court for Sierra Leone, *Prosecutor of the Special Court* v. *Sam Hinga Norman, Moinina Fofana, Allieu Kondewa*, Case no. SCSL-04-14-T, "Opening Statements for the Prosecution, Presentation by Mr. Crane," (June 3, 2004), p. 12, lines 23–5.

42 Georgi Derluguian, "From Afghanistan to Ingushetia," unpublished manuscript, on file with author. This also is the source of information in the preceding paragraph.

43 Andrei Schliefer and Robert Vishny, "Corruption," *Quarterly Journal of Economics* vol. 108 (August 1993), pp. 599–617; Susan Rose-Ackerman and Jacqueline Coolidge, "Kleptocracy and Reform in African Regimes," in Bornwell Chikulo and Kempe Ronald Hope, eds, *Corruption and Development in Africa: Lessons from Country Case Studies* (New York: St. Martin's Press, 2000), pp. 57–86.

44 Robert Jervis, *Perception and Misperception in International Politics* (Princeton: Princeton University Press, 1976), p. 195.

4

COMMENTARY: A WORLD DROWNING IN GUNS

Harold Hongju Koh

Introduction

This chapter discusses a familiar subject in unfamiliar settings. The subject is gun control; the settings are such cities as Freetown, Sierra Leone; Pristina, Kosovo; Medellín, Colombia; Kabul, Afghanistan; Port-au-Prince, Haiti; and Mogadishu, Somalia. In every continent, in every city on the planet, there are more guns than we could ever use. At the dawn of the twenty-first century, we live in a world drowning in guns. Why is this so and what should we do about it?

The solution lies in the answer to three questions: First, how big is the world's gun problem and how did it come about? Second, what can and should we – as responsible lawyers, scholars, and human rights activists – do about this huge and growing global problem? Third, what kind of global gun control regime could we and should we try to build?

The problem

Today there are an estimated 639 million documented small arms in the world. That is more than one for every twelve men, women, and children on the face of the earth. Significantly, all sources concede that this estimate undercounts the actual number by tens of millions. It does not include, for example, the millions of undocumented, privately held guns in such major countries as China, India, Pakistan, or France.[1]

This chapter focuses on a category known as "small arms and light weapons," a category generally understood to encompass weapons that possess three characteristics. First, an ordinary person can carry them. They are transportable by individual human beings, and thus are so-called man- or woman-portable. Second, they are capable of delivering lethal force. Third, they are primarily designed for military use, and so exclude recreational weapons.

While no universally accepted legal terminology exists, considerable agreement has begun to emerge that the term "small arms" includes, at a minimum, handguns, revolvers, pistols, automatic rifles, carbines, shotguns, and machine guns. "Light weapons," which are usually heavier, larger, and designed to be hand-carried by teams of people, include grenade launchers, light mortars, shoulder-fired missiles, rocket launchers, artillery guns, anti-aircraft weapons, antitank guns, and related ammunition.[2]

What characteristics distinguish this class of small arms and light weapons? First, they are *portable*, easily concealed, and easily used. Unlike complex weapon systems, these systems require little or no maintenance, logistics, support, or training. Throughout the developing world, small arms are regularly carried by teenagers and children. Indeed, for all the worldwide effort that has been expended to reduce the flagrant use of child soldiers in armed conflict,[3] the availability of small arms contributes as much to the global proliferation of child soldiers as any governmental policy.[4]

Second, small arms are not just portable, they are *cheap*: cheap to make and cheap to buy. The most famous example is the AK-47, the famous Kalashnikov assault rifle, of which some 70–100 million are believed to exist worldwide.[5] In southern Africa, AK-47s can be bought for as little as $15, the same price as a bag of maize.[6] The AK-47 is the "rifle of choice" for guerrilla movements. An AK-47 even appears on the Mozambican national flag.[7] In 2003 the *Washington Post* reported that, on the eve of the US attack on Iraq, anywhere from one million to seven million Iraqi civilians were armed with AK-47s in anticipation of the coming war.[8] An AK-47 possesses only nine moving parts, and thus is relatively simple to handle and reproduce.[9] A growing number of countries have achieved self-sufficiency in the indigenous production and manufacture of small arms and related ammunition, and many of those countries are even apparently starting to export small arms.[10]

Third, small arms and light weapons are shockingly *durable*. Because they have minimal maintenance requirements, small weapons can remain operational for up to 20 years. Usable small arms can still be found that date back more than half a century to World War II. For that reason alone, small arms users are far less likely to destroy their weapons than they are simply to trade them in for better, more modern weapons. I saw this with my own eyes while visiting a so-called militia disarmament center on the border of West and East Timor in late 1999.[11]

Fourth, small arms are *tradable*. Guns that are sold legally often wind up in illegal hands. Their fungibility, their portability, their small size, and their widespread availability make them an alternative black-market global currency for transnational terrorists. Large shipments can pass undetected across national borders and travel huge distances.

Fifth, because of these attributes – portability, price, durability, and availability – small arms dramatically fuel and inflame armed conflicts.[12] The Deputy Secretary-General of the UN, Louise Fréchette, reported that small arms were the only weapons used in 46 of the 49 wars conducted since 1990.[13] Three million civilians – almost the equivalent of the population of Ireland – have been killed by small arms since 1990.[14] Yet the costs of these weapons run far deeper than just the mortality, injury, and psychological trauma of people who are shot: further costs include public health and lost productivity, increased crime and insecurity, humanitarian costs, and the undermining of development.[15] There are also increased threats to regional security, peacekeeping costs, threats to peacekeepers and humanitarian relief workers, and security costs to counteract the use of these weapons.[16]

Sixth, until recently this flood of guns has gone almost entirely unregulated. Until the past decade, there has been no systematic focus on small arms. The task of regulating small arms has been complicated by many factors. First, a lack of knowledge, which follows from the fact that less than half of the exporting countries publish, or even maintain, data on their small arms exports. Second, the nature of the weapons themselves makes them difficult to track. Third, the large number of producing companies and countries and the black and gray markets for such goods make both controlling supplies and distinguishing licit from illicit trade difficult. Fourth, nearly all such weapons have some legal uses for police work, military purposes, and the like. Fifth and finally, human rights and civil liberties arguments are often made in favor of individuals' rights to possess such weapons under domestic law.[17]

Given this complex mix of problems, it would be easy simply to say that this is one of the world's problems we cannot solve. Indeed, I must confess that this was my own reaction when I first encountered this issue as US assistant secretary of state for human rights. But during my time in office, two things changed my mind.

First, when I visited places like Colombia, Kosovo, Sierra Leone, and East Timor, I saw that the very promiscuous presence of guns chokes civil society. I perceived, viscerally, that guns kill civil society. The pervasive presence of guns perpetuates a culture of societal violence. People simply do not want to invest money in places where everyone carries guns. Why should people trust ballots when somebody else will trust the rule of the gun?

The second event that deeply affected me was meeting with Oscar Arias Sanchez, the former president of Costa Rica, the winner of the Nobel Peace Prize. During what I expected would be a friendly meeting, he turned to me, provocatively, and said, "If you are from the US Government and you care about human rights, why don't you stop the flow of guns into Latin America?"[18] I answered, "Well, it is difficult," and gave some of the reasons that I have just given to you. He said to me angrily, "Don't we have enough guns? If the US really cares about human rights, why don't you do something about the guns?"

Since that day, his words have weighed upon me. I have to admit that he was right. If we really care about human rights, we have to do something about the guns. But what, precisely, should we do? How do we develop and establish a global system of effective controls on small arms and light weapons?

The approach

When I was in government, what most bothered me was the gap between ideas and influence. As a professor I suspected, and as an official I confirmed, a sad paradox: usually, in the world of policymaking, *those with ideas have no influence and those with influence have no ideas.* Even decisionmakers who seek an innovative solution to a problem often have no time to consult the academic literature, and when they do, they find the literature so abstract or impenetrable that it cannot be applied to the problem at hand. But if that is generally true, how do we bridge the gap in this case and move from ideas to influence?

I have elsewhere sought to explain why nations do and do not obey international law. The key to understanding whether nations will obey international law, I have argued, is *transnational legal process*: the process by which public and private actors – namely, nation-states, corporations, international organizations, nongovernmental organizations – interact in a variety of forums to make, interpret, enforce, and ultimately internalize rules of international law.[19] Those seeking to create and embed certain human rights principles into international and domestic law should promote transnational *interactions*, that generate legal *interpretations*, that can in turn be *internalized* into the domestic law of even skeptical nation-states.

Applying this approach to developing a global regulatory solution for small arms and light weapons, a five-stage process might emerge:

- First, knowledge – understanding the nature of the global problem.
- Second, networks – the creation of NGO and civil society networks to start to build a regime to address the problem.[20]
- Third, developing norms and recruiting committed individuals who are willing to promote those norms and to speak out against the practice.
- Fourth, "horizontal process," a shorthand term for legal process that occurs at an intergovernmental level. This horizontal process can transpire either at a formal intergovernmental level or at informal state-to-state gatherings.[21]
- The fifth and final step I call "vertical process," the process whereby rules negotiated among governments at a horizontal, intergovernmental level are internalized into the domestic statutes, executive practice, and judicial systems of those participating nations.

That, in a nutshell, is how, in my view, international law becomes law that people actually obey: by moving from knowledge, to networks, to norms, to horizontal process, to vertical process. But if these are the steps toward global regime building, how far have we actually proceeded up this ladder with regard to the global regulation of small arms and light weapons?

Let's start with the question of knowledge: Why did we know so little about the small arms problem until the past decade?[22] The short answer is that during the Cold War, a huge global arms trade existed, but most of it involved conventional weapons of a very large size.[23] At the same time, a very large small arms trade was also occurring, but like a hill hidden under the floodwaters, it was dwarfed and overshadowed by this huge trade in larger conventional arms. After the Cold War, both the supply and the demand side of the large arms trade diminished. At the same time, some of the major producers of small arms, like Russia and other countries of the former Soviet Union, continued to manufacture AK-47s at their old levels, creating a dramatic oversupply. So as conventional arms sales started to drop, suddenly the extent of the ongoing small arms trade became more visible. By the early 1990s a massive oversupply emerged.

Only two global regimes existed for dealing with these problems. First, the UN Register of Conventional Arms,[24] which does not record the number of small arms. Second, the so-called Wassenaar Arrangement, a club of 33 exporting states that agree to consult on voluntary transfers of arms, but that functions opaquely, with no formal clout and little enforcement power.[25]

But in 1993, academic articles started to appear about the small arms trade, and academic conferences began to spotlight the topic and seek UN action.[26] Research nongovermental organizations (NGOs) in several supplying countries also took up this issue – including the Arms Division of Human Rights Watch, the Bonn International Center for Conversion, the British American Security Information Council (BASIC), International Alert, and the Institute for Security Studies in South Africa. Activist NGOs began to get involved as well. The international gun control lobby soon linked up with the domestic gun control lobbies in leading countries.[27]

And then, as with the landmines treaty, transnational norm entrepreneurs entered the picture and started to create action networks. One of the leaders of this movement was Oscar Arias, who gathered 18 Nobel Prize winners to create an international code of conduct with regard to arms transfers.[28] Finally, transnational activists developed their own network, the International Action Network on Small Arms (IANSA), a group of over 300 NGOs.[29]

As I have argued elsewhere, networks can achieve only so much by exerting outside pressure. To be genuinely effective, they need sympathetic people, inside the horizontal intergovernmental process, who can harness their pressure and champion their cause. Into this picture finally entered a norm sponsor, the Secretary-General of the United Nations, who in his 1995 "Call to Action" encouraged the international community to turn its focus on what he called the weapons "that are actually killing people in the hundreds of thousands."[30] The current UN Secretary-General heightened that commitment in his *We the Peoples* report, when he called for a worldwide effort to prevent war by, inter alia, reducing the "illicit transfers of weapons, money, or natural resources" that help fuel ethnic and territorial conflicts.[31]

Critically important was the conceptual move that converted small arms from a back-burner arms control issue into a pressing human rights and development issue. Early on, Southern countries rejected external interference with their access to small arms, arguing that as they could not develop nuclear weapons they ought to have access to other weaponry. But once the United Nations and NGOs in these countries made the factual case that the prevalence of small arms was a direct cause of the destruction of economic, human rights, and rule of law structures, key leaders within these countries acquired an incentive to discuss a global regulatory process.

These negotiations gave rise to the negotiation and conclusion of regional and global measures at the intergovernmental level. In 1997 the United States and 27 other Western Hemisphere nations concluded the Inter-American Convention Against the Illicit Manufacturing of and Trafficking in Firearms, the first international agreement designed to prevent, combat, and eradicate illicit trafficking in firearms, ammunition, and explosives.[32] This Organization of American States (OAS) convention gave impetus to the United Nations Protocol Against the Illicit Manufacturing of and Trafficking in Firearms, Their Parts and Components, and Ammunition, supplementing the United Nations Convention Against Transnational Organized Crime, which was designed to build upon and globalize the standards incorporated in the regional OAS convention.[33] In 1998 the 15 EU nations entered into a political commitment to frame a code of conduct to govern small transfers.[34] Later that year, 21 nations met in Oslo, Norway, for the first intergovernmental small arms conference. The final Oslo document, "Elements of a Common Understanding," called for global support of 11 ongoing international regulatory efforts. Shortly thereafter, about 90 countries plus numerous NGOs met in Brussels for a conference on "sustainable disarmament for sustainable development."[35] At about the same time, 16 member states of the Economic Community of West African States (ECOWAS) declared a three-year renewable moratorium on the production, import, and export of light weapons in the West African region.[36] At the December 1999 United States–European Union summit in Washington, DC, a statement of "common principles on small arms and light weapons" was issued pledging to observe the "highest standards of restraint" in their small arms export policies.[37]

These conferences, followed by a series of UN resolutions, created the impetus for the first United Nations Global Conference on Illicit Trade in Small Arms and Light Weapons, which finally took place in July 2001. The conference marked the George W. Bush administration's first engagement with this issue. There were some hopeful signs: a consensus UN program of action was finally developed, which enumerated the humanitarian and socio-developmental consequences associated both with illicit weapons trade and with weapons accumulation.[38] Some global norms were articulated to guide the actions not just of states, but also of intergovernmental organizations, NGOs, and individual experts in addressing the problems of small arms proliferation, availability, and misuse. The participants made halting commitments to implementing regulatory measures at national, regional, and global levels. But the norms discussed were not binding, and the norms themselves were underdeveloped. No legally binding measures were adopted, no statements were made regarding transparency or civilian possession of firearms, and the role of nonstate actors both in creating and curing the problem was not clearly elaborated. Most troubling, all discussion still took place within an arms control, rather than a human rights, framework, giving participating states too much freedom to place these issues on the back burner, while citing other more pressing priorities.[39]

The most memorable speech at the UN conference was delivered by the US undersecretary for arms control, John Bolton, who declared what became quickly known in the small arms trade as "Bolton's Do Nots." After saying that the United States supported restraints on light weapons, he qualified that support by declaring: "[1] We do not support measures that would constrain legal trade.... [2] [We] do not support the promotion of international advocacy.... [3] [W]e do not support measures limiting trade in SA/LW [small arms and light weapons] solely to governments.... [4] [T]he United States will not support a mandatory Review Conference," and – most amazing to a student of US constitutional law – "[5] "[T]he United States will not join consensus on a final document that contains measures abrogating the Constitutional right to bear arms."[40] This final don't was unnecessary and provocative, as the conference documents did not propose to alter legal gun ownership or national gun possession laws.[41]

Senator Dianne Feinstein quickly challenged Undersecretary Bolton's view, pointing out that the Second Amendment had never been used to overturn any US federal gun law, much less a treaty, and was even less a treaty negotiating position.[42] Thus the United States could easily engage the treaty-negotiating process without committing itself to a regime that would affront legitimate Second Amendment concerns. The 2001 UN conference represented a dramatic missed opportunity, both for the emerging transnational legal process of global small arms regulation and for the United States as a potential leader of that process.[43]

Thinking about a solution

If the past decade has now produced both knowledge and a network, this leaves open three questions: First, what norms should we now develop? Second, what "horizontal process" should we use to develop and internationalize those norms? Third, how should we envision a complementary "vertical process," whereby the global norms that emerge from the horizontal process can become internalized into domestic legal systems?

Norms and horizontal process

The successful global landmines campaign teaches important lessons. The challenge is how best to generate a law-declaring forum and to foster an interpretive community capable of announcing and clarifying a clear set of norms.

Here, the US government initially chose to pursue its multilateral objectives through UN-sponsored efforts conducted via the so-called Geneva Process. In May 1996 the Review Conference for the United Nations Convention on

Conventional Weapons ("Conventional Weapons Conference") developed a revised Protocol II to the 1980 convention.[44] The 61-member UN Conference on Disarmament, based in Geneva, began considering limitations on the use of landmines in late 1996. The US government preferred the Geneva approach to others, because as participants in this process, major exporters and users of mines, such as Russia and China, would be bound by the outcome of the Conventional Weapons Conference.[45] But the Conventional Weapons Conference, run on a consensus model, broke down when the Mexican government objected to the consideration of the landmine issue in the Geneva forum.[46] Frustrated with what they perceived to be a lack of progress toward a total ban through the UN-sponsored efforts, NGOs and a number of mid-sized countries switched course and created a new law-declaring forum, outside established organizational structures, the Ottawa Process.[47] As Jody Williams of the International Coalition to Ban Landmines put it in her Nobel Peace Prize acceptance speech: "[W]e invited them to a meeting and they actually came."[48] Canadian foreign minister Lloyd Axworthy emerged as a leading governmental norm entrepreneur.[49] Once the Ottawa Process was fully engaged, it was only a matter of time before the flat-ban convention on landmines ultimately emerged.

Only time will tell whether the small arms negotiations will come to fruition in the UN conference or in an alternative setting. At this point, either the nascent Oslo Process or the private–public Brussels Process may yet overtake the UN conference framework. Moreover, the Nobel Peace Laureates' Initiative, headed by Oscar Arias, has drafted a set of principles to govern arms transfers that goes much further than do the statements of the UN Global Conference on Illicit Trade in Small Arms and Light Weapons. An interpretive community has begun to form, comprising both governmental and nongovernmental entities, that in turn has begun actively to debate the contours of the norms at issue.

The norms developed in this horizontal setting should be bright-line norms. One of the major accomplishments of the landmines convention was to focus on a clear, bright-line legal rule that people could understand, the so-called flat ban.[50] But the regulation of small arms presents a far more difficult problem, for we are a long way from persuading governments to accept a flat ban on the trade of *legal* arms. So what kind of enforceable norms can be developed? To be viable, a global regime should incorporate at least three elements.

First, a marking and tracing regime must be implemented. Most governments mark their weapons, but the United States and its allies, major suppliers of small arms, do not trace their newly manufactured weapons in any consistent way.[51] One of the most significant outcomes of the UN conference was the establishment of a UN committee to develop a regime that could in turn develop international rules for collating and making available all global marking and tracing information. The UN register of conventional arms could be modified so countries could be required to submit information about their small arms production. In addition, a number of countries have proposed complementary regional registers that would explicitly enumerate small arms in specific countries.[52] In due course, a marking and tracing norm could be embedded in a treaty: Article VI of the Inter-American Convention Against the Illicit Manufacturing of and Trafficking in Firearms, for example, calls for marking at the time of manufacture, importation, and confiscation of firearms, grenades, and other covered weapons, and Articles XI and XIII further require various forms of record-keeping and information exchange.[53]

Second, transparency and monitoring of these processes by international NGOs is critical.[54] The Helsinki Final Act and the creation of an international NGO network to monitor its "human dimension" provisions demonstrated the power of international NGO monitoring as a way of promoting governmental compliance with inconvenient norms.[55]

Here, the most pertinent recent example may be the unexpected rise of the global anticorruption movement. We have seen a rapidly expanding global good-governance movement, marked by the enactment of US and other national foreign corrupt practices laws,[56] an Organization for Economic Cooperation and Development antibribery convention,[57] and perhaps most significant, Transparency International[58] – a transnational network of NGOs.[59] What made the global anticorruption movement successful, and a model that could be followed here, was that it forged a transnational network of private and public entities, including multinational corporations, dedicated both to self-regulation and to the monitoring of rogue actors.

Third and most important, the horizontal process should produce a "transfer ban" that would prevent legal arms from being transferred either to illicit users or to recognized human rights violators.[60] Although this would not be easy to do, under US domestic arms law there already exist restrictions on making transfers or licenses to certain gross violators of human rights who have been so certified.[61] There is an array of methods by which small arms are diverted from legal to illegal markets, including falsification of documents, diversion from surplus, illegal resale, purchases by surrogates, and illegal sales by dealers and brokers.[62] Each of these forms of illegal transfer needs to be separately targeted, and the UN Programme of Action singles out some 25 local measures that could be taken to do so.[63]

Vertical process: internalization

The greatest challenge we face in this process is to create a legal framework that combines a treaty framework built around clear norms with concrete domestic obligations. The UN Global Conference on Illicit Trade in Small Arms and Light Weapons laid out a list of measures to be implemented by nation-states at the national level, ranging from enacting laws regulating small arms production to preventing the use of small arms against children in armed conflict.[64]

Yet as important as specific domestic legal regulatory enactments is the broader strategy for internalization of the emerging global norms.[65] If a norm against illicit transfers can be internationalized through the emerging horizontal process described above, by what techniques can we further promote the legal, political, and social internalization of that emerging international norm into domestic legal systems?

Here the Inter-American Convention Against the Illicit Manufacturing of and Trafficking in Firearms provides the best model. This OAS convention, inter alia, requires each state to establish a national firearms control system and a register of manufacturers, traders, importers, and exporters of these commodities; to establish a national body to interact with other regional states and a regional organization advisory committee; to standardize national laws and procedures with member states of regional organizations; and to control borders and ports effectively. Other key provisions include an obligation for an effective licensing or authorization system for the import, export, and in-transit movement of firearms;[66] an obligation to mark firearms indelibly at the time of manufacture and import to help track the sources of illicit guns; and an obligation for states to criminalize the illicit manufacturing of and illicit trafficking in firearms.

These national approaches should be supplemented with a private–public network that expressly targets arms brokering and financial transfers. Here too, a useful transnational legal process model has emerged in the area of conflict diamonds. The Kimberley Process has brought together countries and companies to negotiate the terms of a diamond control regime that would track every diamond export, import, and re-export transaction through monitoring, audited chains of custody, criminal penalties, tamper-proof packaging, and standardized record-keeping. Thankfully, the United States, the world's largest importer of diamond jewelry, has accepted the Kimberley Process's proposed documentation and record-keeping requirements.[67]

Other potential enforcers of the norms of the small arms regime include corporate actors, who should be enlisted in the internal monitoring of private security companies that they employ. In Guatemala, for example, the Chamber of Industry reports that private security companies employ more than twice as many security agents as the number of civilian police officers in that country.[68] In recent years, a number of innovative human rights partnerships have arisen among governments, businesses, and civil society that have sought to internalize human rights obedience into corporate behavior by suggesting minimum corporate standards for human rights performance in the day-to-day conduct of large multinational corporations.[69] During my time at the US State Department, we applied this approach to work with corporations, other governments, and the NGO community to develop principles for improving human rights performance in the oil, mining, and energy sectors. The objective of these principles was to provide companies with practical guidance on how to prevent human rights violations in dangerous environments. These principles could easily be extended and globalized to include as corporate security requirements the monitoring of small arms held and used in the corporations' name abroad by private security agents.[70]

Yet another factor contributing to the ease of illicit arms transfers in the Western Hemisphere has been the presence of financial and tax havens throughout the Caribbean that facilitate money laundering, which in turn supports arms brokering and large-scale weapons trade. Article XII of the OAS convention[71] borrows from the information disclosure provisions of international tax treaties and usefully stipulates that states parties should exchange information on "techniques, practices, and legislation to combat money laundering related to illicit manufacturing of and trafficking in firearms."[72]

More fundamentally, however, to effectuate fully the goals of the small arms regime, the United States must focus on supply-side solutions and destination controls. Through bilateral and multilateral diplomacy, the US government should start a process of promoting exchanges and destroying existing small weapons caches.[73] One promising precedent occurred in September 2000, when US, Albanian, Norwegian, and German diplomats signed a memorandum of understanding on the destruction of over 130,000 small arms and light weapons in Albania.[74]

These weapons destruction measures, however, must be combined with supply-side control measures within the United States. The United States manufactures and sells some $463 million in light weapons annually.[75] In 1998 it exported its light weapons to 124 countries, in five of which those weapons were later used against US and UN soldiers.[76] Reasonable domestic supply-side solutions would include new export control statutes imposing strict and administrable destination controls.[77] To address this concern, in 1996, US president Bill Clinton signed arms-brokering legislation that amended the Arms Export Control Act to give the State Department greater authority to monitor and regulate the activities of arms brokers.[78] Key provisions included requirements that all brokers must register with the State Department, must receive State Department authorization for their brokering activities, and must submit annual reports describing such activities. The United States is currently working to promote adoption of similar laws by other nations by incorporating such a provision into the international crime protocol being negotiated in Vienna. Perhaps the strongest mode of internalization of supply-side controls would come through an enhanced search for technological solutions. One particularly intriguing idea is the promoting production of smart or "perishable ammunition" – for example, AK-47 bullets that would degrade and become unusable over time.

US legal scholars are not mere bystanders in this exercise. They can promote norm internalization through the analysis and development of legal and policy arguments regarding international gun controls. Three areas come to mind. The first is the thorough constitutional research on the Second Amendment that has been invoked by NGOs to reject efforts by John Bolton and others to apply the Second Amendment argument extraterritorially.[79] The second is the interdisciplinary research by Ian Ayres and John Donohue rejecting the empirical hypothesis that more guns produce less crime in US society.[80] Some international relations specialists have extrapolated from the "more guns, less crime" hypothesis to suggest that arms control efforts in heavily armed "warlord states" would be similarly counterproductive, claiming that heavily armed societies – for example, Ingushetia and Somaliland – exhibit a lower level of conflict because the near-universal possession of guns deters all carriers.[81] The Ayres–Donohue research effectively counters this conclusion with massive empirical evidence that demonstrates that, if anything, in most of the jurisdictions sampled (at least in the United States), more guns have been associated with more, rather than less, crime. Third, legal scholars can identify new norms that might target some of the most egregious examples of small arms abuse. One possible avenue might be to focus on the criminalization per se, under international criminal law and complementary domestic law, of such acts as bringing small arms into refugee camps.[82]

Conclusion

In short, we have a problem: a world drowning in guns. What should we do about it? We have knowledge, we have networks, and we have an emerging horizontal process to generate norms. We now need to use those emerging norms to create an international framework, and then internalize those norms in US domestic law, while at the same time pursuing supply-side solutions and harmonizing the national approach of the United States with the approaches of other countries.

This may seem like a fantasy. To fan the belief that a global solution may be possible, Americans in particular need to think about what role our government will play. In the history of the human rights movement, the United States has been exceptional in many ways, but it has been most exceptional, I believe, in its global *leadership* role in human rights. If anything, it is our job, as human rights activists and academics, to urge the United States to follow the better angels of its own national nature.[83] There is no reason on earth why our children and our children's children should grow up in a world drowning in guns.

Acknowledgments

This chapter is adapted from the Robert L. Levine Distinguished Lecture, delivered on April 2, 2002, at the Fordham University School of Law in New York City, and later published as Harold Hongju Koh, A *World Drowning in Guns*, Fordham Law Review vol. 71 (2003), p. 2340. The lecture grew out of thoughts inspired by the Social Science Research Council (SSRC) Workshop on Law and International Relations sponsored by the Program on Global Security and Cooperation of February 2002 in Washington, DC. I am grateful to John Tirman, Tom Biersteker, Ben Rawlence, and the other participants in that workshop for their illuminating papers and presentations on the relationship between international law and small arms proliferation. I am also grateful to Danielle Morris, Jessica Sebeok, and Steve Vladeck of Yale Law School for splendid research assistance, and to my many friends at Fordham for their gracious hospitality during my visit.

Notes

1 Small Arms Survey, *Counting the Human Costs* (Oxford: Oxford University Press, 2002). Updated information is available online at www.smallarmssurvey.org.

2 See the website of the UN Department for Disarmament Affairs, at http://disarmament.un.org/cab/register.html.

3 See, for example, David Weissbrodt *et al.*, *International Human Rights: Law, Policy, and Process*, 3rd edn. (Cincinnati, OH: Anderson Publishing, 2001), pp. 38–83.

4 See, for example, Human Rights Watch, "My Gun Was As Tall As Me: Child Soldiers in Burma" (October 2002), available online at www.hrw.org/reports/2002/burma.

5 See Small Arms Survey, *Profiling the Problem* (Oxford: Oxford University Press, 2001), available online at www.smallarmssurvey.org/yearbook2001/chapter_2.pdf. See generally, Michael Klare, "The Kalashnikov Age," *Bulletin of Atomic Science*, January–February 1999, available online at www.bullatomsci.org/issues/1999/jf99/jf99klare.html.

6 Small Arms Survey, *Profiling the Problem*. See also Richard Norton-Taylor, "Small Arms Trade: When Will U.K. Bite the Bullet on Gun Traffic?" *Guardian* (London), July 11, 2001, p. 15.

7 See the Mozambique flag online at http://encarta.msn.com/encnet/refpages/refmedia.aspx?refid=461533911.

8 See Rajiv Chandrasekaran, "Iraq Arms Civilians As Second Line of Defense Against U.S.," *Washington Post Foreign Service*, February 4, 2003, p. A1.

9 "A World Drowning in Guns."

10 See Klare, "The Kalashnikov Age."

11 See Harold Hongju Koh (US assistant secretary of state for democracy, human rights, and labor), "On-the-Record Briefing on Recent Trip to Indonesia" (October 12, 1999), available online at www.state.gov/www/policy_remarks/1999/991012_koh_indonesia.html.

12 See Patrick Brogan, *World Conflicts: A Comprehensive Guide to World Strife since 1945* (Lanham, MD: Scarecrow Press, 1998), p. 644. See International Information Programs, "Can Small Arms and Light Weapons Be Controlled?" (June 2, 2001), available online at http://usinfo.state.gov/topical/pol/arms/stories/01060243.htm.

13 United Nations, "Deputy Secretary-General Calls for 'Strongest Possible' Action Programme from Small Arms Conference," press release (September 7, 2001), available online at www.un.org/news/press/docs/2001/dsgsm137.doc.htm.

14 Human Rights Watch, "Major New Campaign Launched Against Small Arms Proliferation," press release (May 11, 1999), available online at www.hrw.org/press/1999/may/iansa.htm. Graduate Institute of International Studies, "Small Arms Survey 2001 Executive Summary," available online at www.smallarmssurvey.org/yearbook2001/sas2001exec_en.pdf.

15 See, for example, Human Rights Watch, "Liberian Refugees in Guinea: Refoulement, Militarization of Camps and Other Protection Concerns" (November 2002), available online at www.hrw.org/reports/2002/guinea. See also Lawyers Committee for Human Rights, "Refugees, Rebels, and the Quest for Justice," available online at www.lchr.org/refugees/reports/ref_rebels_intro.pdf.

16 Robert Muggah and Peter Batchelor, "Development Held Hostage: Assessing the Effects of Small Arms on Human Development: A Preliminary Study of the Socio-Economic Impacts and Development Linkages of Small Arms Proliferation, Availability, and Use" (United Nations Development Programme, April 2002), available online at www.undp.org/erd/smallarms/docs/development_held_hostage.pdf.

17 The Second Amendment states: "A well regulated Militia, being necessary to the security of a free State, the right of the people to keep and bear Arms, shall not be

infringed." See generally, Natalie J. Goldring, "The NRA Goes Global," *Bulletin of Atomic Science* vol. 55 (January–February 1999), available online at www.bullatomsci.org/issues/1999/jf99/jf99goldring.html. Compare the website of the Second Amendment Sisters, at www.sas-aim.org/stand/un.html.

18 Indeed, this is the core objective of the Oscar Arias Foundation. Information available online at www.arias.or.cr/Eindice.htm.

19 See the following by Harold Hongju Koh: "The 1998 Frankel Lecture: Bringing International Law Home," *Houston Law Review* vol. 35 (1998), p. 623; "The 'Haiti Paradigm' in United States Human Rights Policy," *Yale Law Journal* vol. 103 (1994), pp. 2391–2; "How Is International Human Rights Law Enforced?" *Indiana Law Journal* vol. 74 (1999), p. 1397; "Transnational Legal Process," *Nebraska Law Review* vol. 75 (1996), p. 181; "Transnational Public Law Litigation," *Yale Law Journal* vol. 100 (1991), pp. 2347, 2358–75; "Why Do Nations Obey International Law?" *Yale Law Journal* vol. 106 (1997), p. 2599.

20 See, for example, Margaret Keck and Kathryn Sikkink, *Activists Beyond Borders: Advocacy Networks in International Politics* (Ithaca: Cornell University Press, 1998); Annelise Riles, *The Network Inside Out* (Ann Arbor: University of Michigan Press, 2000). See also Jackie Smith *et al.*, eds, *Transnational Social Movements and Global Politics: Solidarity Beyond the State* (Syracuse, NY: Syracuse University Press, 1997).

21 Ibid., pp. 649–51.

22 In understanding this question, I am greatly indebted to Edward J. Laurence of Monterey Institute of International Studies for his excellent unpublished paper, "The History of the Global Effort to Regulate Small Arms," presented at SSRC Small Arms Workshop, Washington, DC (February 2002).

23 See Edward J. Laurence, *The International Arms Trade* (New York: Lexington Books, 1992).

24 See the website of the UN Register of Conventional Weapons, at http://disarmament.un.org/cab/register.html.

25 See online document index at www.wassenaar.org/docs.

26 See Jeffrey Boutwell *et al.*, eds, *Lethal Commerce: The Global Trade in Small Arms and Light Weapons* (Cambridge, MA: American Academy of Arts and Sciences, 1995); See Swadesh Rana, *Small Arms and Intra-State Conflicts* (Geneva: United Nations Institute for Disarmament Research, 1995); Aaron Karp, "Small Arms Control: The Need for Coordination," *Disarmament Forum* vol. 2 (2000), p. 5.

27 See the website of the Brady Center, at www.bradycampaign.org/facts/index.asp.

28 See the website of the Commission of Nobel Peace Laureates' Initiative to Control Arms Transfer, at www.arias.or.cr/eindice.htm.

29 See the IANSA website, at http://www.iansa.org.

30 United Nations, *Supplement to An Agenda for Peace: Position Paper of the Secretary-General on the Occasion of the Fiftieth Anniversary of the United Nations*, U.N. Doc. A/50/60–S/1995/1 (January 3, 1995), available online at www.un.org/docs/sg/agsupp.html.

31 Kofi A. Annan, "We the Peoples: The Role of the United Nations in the 21st Century," available online at www.un.org/millennium/sg/report.

32 See *Inter-American Convention Against the Illicit Manufacturing of and Trafficking in Firearms, Ammunition, Explosives, and Other Related Materials* (November 1997) (signed by the United States and 28 other OAS member states), available online at www.iansa.org/documents/regional/reg5.htm.

33 See UN General Assembly, Resolution 55/255, UN GAOR, 55th Sess. (2001), available online at http://untreaty.un.org/english/treatyevent2002/texts/english/firearms_11.pdf.

34 See *EU Joint Action of 17 December 1998, 1999/34* (1999) (adopted by the Council on the basis of Article J.3 of the Treaty on the European Union's Contribution to combating the destabilizing accumulation and spread of small arms and light weapons), available online at www.iansa.org/documents/regional/eujoint.pdf.

35 See Oslo Meeting on Small Arms, *An International Agenda on Small Arms and Light Weapons: Elements of a Common Understanding* (July 13–14, 1998), available online at www.iansa.org/documents/regional/2000/jan_00/oslomeeting.htm. See also Sustainable Disarmament for Sustainable Development, *The Brussels Call for Action* (October 13, 1998), available online at www.unesco.org/cpp/uk/declarations/brussels.pdf.

36 The United Nations African Institute for the Prevention of Crime and the Treatment of Offenders has begun to survey the small arms legislation, regulations, and law enforcement capacities of various African countries.

37 See *US–EU Statement of Common Principles on Small Arms and Light Weapons* (December 17, 1999), available online at www.iansa.org/documents/regional/dec_99/eu_statement_dec17_99pdf.pdf.

38 See United Nations, *Report of the United Nations Conference on the Illicit Trade in Small Arms and Light Weapons in All Its Aspects* (July 9–20, 2001), available online at http://disarmament.un.org/cab/smallarms.

39 See *UN Programme of Action to Prevent, Combat, and Eradicate the Illicit Trade in Small Arms and Light Weapons in All Its Aspects*, available online at http://disarmament.un.org/update/jun2001/article2.htm.

40 John R. Bolton, *Statement to the Plenary Session of the UN Conference on the Illicit Trade in Small Arms and Light Weapons in All Its Aspects* (July 9, 2001), available online at www.un.int/usa/01_104.htm.

41 Editorial, *Baltimore Sun*, July 12, 2001, p. 16A.

42 See *United States* v. *Miller*, 307 U.S.C. 174, 178 (1939); David B. Kopel, "The Supreme Court's Thirty-five Other Gun Cases: What the Supreme Court Has Said About the Second Amendment," *St. Louis University Public Law Review* vol. 18, no. 9 (1999), pp. 99, 101; Senator Dianne Feinstein, "Statement on the Bush Administration's Opposition to a UN Accord to Stem the Flow of Guns Feeding International Terrorism and Drug Wars," press release (July 10, 2001), available online at www.senate.gov/~feinstein/releases01/sarms2.htm. See Laurence H. Tribe and Akhil Reed Amar, "Well-Regulated Militias, and More," *New York Times*, October 28, 1999; Akhil Reed Amar, "The Second Amendment: A Case Study in Constitutional Interpretation," *Utah Law Review* vol. 2001 (2001), p. 889; Sanford Levinson, "The Embarrassing Second Amendment," *Yale Law Journal* vol. 99 (1989), p. 637; William Van Alstyne, "The Second Amendment and the Personal Right to Arms," *Duke Law Journal* vol. 43 (1994), p. 1236. Compare Carl T. Bogus, "The Hidden History of the Second Amendment," *University of California-Davis Law Review* vol. 31 (1998), p. 309; David C. Williams, "Civic Republicanism and the Citizen Militia: The Terrifying Second Amendment," *Yale Law Journal* vol. 101, no. 3 (1991) p. 551; David C. Williams, "The Militia Movement and Second Amendment Revolution: Conjuring with the People," *Cornell Law Review* vol. 81 (1996), p. 879.

43 See United Nations, *Report of the United Nations Conference on the Illicit Trade in Small Arms and Light Weapons in All Its Aspects* (July 9–20, 2001), available online at http://disarmament.un.org/cab/smallarms/files/aconf192_15.pdf.

44 See "Landmines: Dual Track," *The Economist* (London), January 25–31, 1997, p. 42.

45 See Frances Williams, "Momentum Grows for UN Landmine Ban Talks," *Financial Times* (London), January 22, 1997, p. 4.

46 See "Mexico Blocks Conclave on World Land-Mine Ban," *Washington Post*, June 13, 1997, p. A33.

47 See Jessica Mathews, "The New, Private Order," *Washington Post*, January 21, 1997, p. A11.
48 See Jody Williams, "Nobel Lecture" (December 10, 1997), available online at www.icbl.org/resources/jodynobel.html.
49 See Dana Priest, "Mine Decision Boosts Clinton-Military Relations," *Washington Post*, September 21, 1997, p. A22.
50 See Convention on the Prohibition of the Use, Stockpiling, Production, and Transfer of Antipersonnel Mines and on Their Destruction, available online at www.icbl.org/treaty/treatyenglish.html. See Monica Schurtman, "The International Campaign to Ban Landmines and the Ottawa Landmines Treaty: Applications to the Movement to Restrict Small Arms and Light Weapons Transfers," unpublished paper prepared for the SSRC Workshop on Law and International Relations (February 6–7, 2002).
51 See Arms Trade Resource Center, "U.S. 'Supplier of Choice' for Weapons Sales" (August 20, 2001), available online at www.worldpolicy.org/projects/arms/updates/082001.html.
52 See Small Arms Transparency and Control Regime in Africa, available online at www.unrec.org/eng/satcra.htm.
53 See UN General Assembly, *Inter-American Convention Against the Illicit Manufacturing of and Trafficking in Firerams, Ammunition, Explosives, and Other Related Materials*, 24th Special Sess. (November 13, 1997), available online at www.iansa.org/documents/regional/reg5.htm.
54 See *Small Arms and the Humanitarian Community: Developing a Strategy for Action*, Report of the Proceedings of the Nairobi Conference (November 18–20, 2001).
55 See generally, William Korey, *The Promises We Keep: Human Rights, the Helsinki Process, and American Foreign Policy* (New York: St. Martin's Press, 1993).
56 "Foreign Corrupt Practices Act," *Pub. L.* vol. 91, no. 95–213 (1997) Stat., p. 1494.
57 See OECD Convention on Combating Bribery of Foreign Public Officials in International Business Transactions, available online at www.oecd.org/pdf/m00007000/M00007323.pdf.
58 See the website of Transparency International, at www.transparency.org.
59 Examples include the Lima Declaration (1997); the Durban Commitment (1999), and the Principles to Combat Corruption in African Countries (1999). See also 10th International Anti-Corruption Conference, at www.10iacc.org/download/workshops/cs52a.pdf.
60 See Barbara Frey, "The Availability and Misuse of Small Arms and Light Weapons in the Context of Human Rights and Humanitarian Norms," unpublished paper prepared for the SSRC Workshop on Law and International Relations (February 6–7, 2002).
61 See Federation of American Scientists, Arms Sales Monitoring Project, "United States Arms Transfer Eligibility Criteria Index Page," at http://fas.org/asmp/campaigns/legislationindex.html. For website links to bills and public laws relating to arms transfers and foreign military assistance, see Federation of American Scientists, Arms Sales Monitoring Project, "Bills and Public Laws," at http://fas.org/asmp/resources/billlaws.html. See also Federation of American Scientists, Arms Sales Monitoring Project, "Government Documents," at www.fas.org/asmp/resources/govtdocs.htm. The website of the Bureau of Democracy, Human Rights, and Labor can be found at www.state.gov/g/drl.
62 See, for example, Human Rights Watch, "No Questions Asked: The Eastern Europe Arms Pipeline to Liberia" (2001), available online at www.hrw.org/backgrounder/arms/liberia1115.htm.

63 See generally, Wendy Cukier, "Combating the Illicit Trade in Small Arms and Light Weapons: Strengthening Domestic Regulations" (March 2001), available online at www.international-alert.org/pdf/pubsec/btb_brf7.pdf.

64 See http://disarmament.un.org/cab/smallarms, the website of the United Nations Conference on the Illicit Trade in Small Arms and Light Weapons in All Its Aspects (July 9–20, 2001).

65 See Koh, "The 1998 Frankel Lecture." I have argued elsewhere that international law norms can be internalized into domestic legal systems through a variety of legal, political, and social channels. See, for example, *Brief Amici Curiae of Mary Robinson et al., Lawrence* v. *Texas*, 123 S. Ct. 1512 (2003), no. 02-102. See also the following by Harold Hongju Koh: "The 2001 Richard Childress Memorial Lecture: A United States Human Rights Policy for the 21st Century," *St. Louis University Law Journal* vol. 46 (2002), p. 293; "Why America Should Ratify the Women's Rights Treaty (CEDAW)," *Case Western Reserve Journal of International Law* vol. 34 (2003), p. 258; "Paying 'Decent Respect' to World Opinion on the Death Penalty," *University of California Davis Law Review* vol. 35 (2002), p. 1085.

66 The US Bureau of Alcohol, Tobacco, and Firearms and the US Customs Service have engaged in interdiction and investigative efforts along the southwestern border of the United States, and US attorneys in that region have increased their efforts to prosecute arms traffickers caught attempting to smuggle firearms into the United States.

67 See www.treas.gov/offices/enforcement/ofac/legal/eo/diamond_eo.pdf.

68 See William Godnick, "Tackling the Illicit Trade in Small Arms and Light Weapons," unpublished paper prepared for the SSRC Workshop on Law and International Relations (February 6–7, 2002).

69 See Leon H. Sullivan, *Moving Mountains: The Principles and Purposes of Leon Sullivan* (Valley Forge, PA: Judson Press), pp. 106–12. See also UN Secretary-General Kofi Annan's Global Compact initiative (available at www.unglobalcompact.org).

70 See US Department of State, Bureau of Democracy, Human Rights, and Labor, "Voluntary Principles on Security and Human Rights," fact sheet (December 20, 2000), available online at www.state.gov/www/ global/human_rights/001220_fsdrl_principles.html. See Harold Hongju Koh (US assistant secretary of state for democracy, human rights, and labor) *et al.*, "Voluntary Principles on Security and Human Rights" (December 20, 2000), available online at www.state.gov/www/policy_remarks/2000/001220_koh_hr.html; "Contemporary Practice of the United States Relating to International Law: Voluntary Human Rights Principles for Extractive and Energy Companies," *American Journal of International Law* vol. 95 (2001), pp. 626, 636 (ed. Sean D. Murphy); Bennett Freeman *et al.*, "A New Approach to Corporate Responsibility: The Voluntary Principles on Security and Human Rights," *Hastings International and Comparative Law Review* vol. 24 (2001), p. 423.

71 *OAS Inter-American Convention,* Art. XII, available online at www.defenselink.mil/acq/acic/treaties/small/oas/oasconvention.htm.

72 *OAS Inter-American Convention,* Art. XIII (1)(e).

73 The United States has recently contributed experts and funds to destroy small arms, light weapons, and ammunition in Liberia, Haiti, and the former Yugoslavia, and has agreed with 10 nations of southeastern Europe on a program to destroy illicit arms.

74 See US Department of State, Bureau of Political-Military Affairs, "Small Arms/Light Weapons Destruction in Albania Memorandum" (September 7, 2000), available online at www.state.gov/www/global/arms/bureau_pm/smallarms/000907_albania.html.

75 See Human Rights Watch, "My Gun Was As Tall As Me."

76 See Norton-Taylor, "Small Arms Trade," p. 15.

77 US law prohibits arms and munitions retransferral of arms exported from the United

States by the recipient without prior US approval, and suspected diversions and transshipments are investigated. The United States has also implemented sanctions and embargoes established by the United Nations by prosecuting those who violate embargoes. The United States has also refused to authorize commercial or government-to-government weapons transfers to conflict areas not then subject to UN embargoes such as the Democratic Republic of Congo, Ethiopia, Eritrea, and Angola.

78 Law enforcement officials made the first seizure of munitions under the provisions of the new legislation in November 1999.

79 See notes 57–58.

80 Ian Ayres and John J. Donohue III, "Shooting Down the More Guns, Less Crime Hypothesis," *Stanford Law Review* vol. 55 (2003), p. 1193; John R. Lott Jr., *More Guns, Less Crime: Understanding Crime and Gun-Control Laws* (Chicago: University of Chicago Press, 2000).

81 William Reno, "Arms, Internal War, and the Causes of Peace," unpublished paper prepared for the SSRC Workshop on Law and International Relations (February 6–7, 2002); William Reno, "Small Arms, Violence, and the Course of Conflicts," Chapter 3 in this volume. Reno argues that the current regulatory system, in seeking to deny small arms to all nonstate actors, ignores the possibility that some of these groups may be seeking to establish order in the face of predatory, dictatorial governments. Accordingly, Reno would adjust small arms regulatory schemes to account for contextual differences in purposes among nonstate organizations. But Reno nowhere explains how such distinctions among nonstate actors would be drawn, nor why limiting small arms trade could not be combined with more effective international pressure to remove predatory regimes.

82 Kathi Austin, "Armed Refugee Camps as a Microcosm of the Link Between Arms Availability and Insecurity," unpublished paper prepared for the SSRC Workshop on Law and International Relations (February 6–7, 2002); Human Rights Watch, *Liberian Refugees in Guinea: Refoulement, Militarization of Camps and Other Protection Concerns* (November 2002), available online at www.hrw.org/reports/2002/guienea.

83 Harold Hongju Koh, "On American Exceptionalism," *Stanford Law Review* vol. 55 (2003), p. 1479.

Part II

TERRORISM

5

INTERNATIONAL TERRORISM, NONSTATE ACTORS, AND TRANSNATIONAL POLITICAL MOBILIZATION

A perspective from International Relations

Fiona B. Adamson

International terrorism as a conceptual challenge for international relations

The problem of international terrorism presents a conceptual challenge to the discipline of international relations (IR), which has traditionally been concerned with understanding conflict and cooperation among state actors, rather than the role that nonstate actors play in the international security environment. Yet international terrorism is inherently an international phenomenon that impacts overall levels of international security and international stability, and therefore falls squarely within the domain of what IR should be able to explain and understand.

In this chapter I suggest a framework for thinking analytically about international terrorism from an IR perspective. In order to do so, I argue that, rather than focusing on specific groups, particular ideologies, or even particular strategies or threats of terror and violence, the most fruitful approach for IR scholars to take is to devise a broad research agenda around the role that nonstate actors and transnational political movements play in the international security environment. Specifically, I propose that there is a common and identifiable pattern of transnational organizing and transnational strategies that nonstate political entrepreneurs adopt when mounting a violent challenge to the political status quo. This pattern of transnational political mobilization coexists with an international system of states, and has been a prevalent feature of international politics for at least the past two centuries.

Examining the international systemic-level activities of nonstate actors necessitates a shift in IR thinking away from so-called billiard ball models of the international system in which world politics is conceived of solely as interactions among unitary state actors operating within an anarchic environment.[1] Instead, such a perspective suggests the utility of viewing the international system as a single political space – a world polity in which both state and nonstate actors interact and respond to changing opportunity structures at the global level.[2] By conceiving of the international system as a world polity – a space of political contention, in addition to interstate competition – we have the starting point for analyzing international terrorism as a political phenomenon, in addition to analyzing it as a security threat. This, I argue, provides some analytical leverage for thinking about long-term systemic-level political responses to the problem of international terrorism, as opposed to relying exclusively on military and policing responses.

I begin by placing current concerns regarding international terrorism in their historical context. International terrorism is not a new feature of the international security environment, and it is useful to be reminded of this through a brief survey of past examples of transnationally linked nonstate actors who employed violence as a tool for achieving their political goals. Second, I discuss how dominant theories of international relations have dealt with the question of nonstate action in world politics – and argue that both realist and liberal paradigms have been unable to respond adequately to the challenge of international terrorism, largely because of their focus on states as the most significant actors in international relations as well as, in the case of liberalism, the inability to account adequately for the role that violence may play in the constitution of political order. Third, I discuss the advantages of employing a political mobilization framework for analyzing international terrorism, which draws on insights from the literatures on social movements and political mobilization. Finally, I conclude with a discussion of the theoretical and policy implications of such a framework, emphasizing the need to promote stronger institutional channels both within and beyond the state for nonstate actors to use to articulate political grievances. Such institutions, including strong regional court systems, provide a useful focus for a common research agenda that could be pursued by both international relations and international law scholars.

Nonstate actors, political violence, and international security

The use of strategies of violence and terror by nonstate actors and transnational political movements is not a new feature of the international security environment. For at least the past two centuries, politically motivated nonstate groups have organized transnationally as a way of mounting a challenge to the political status quo, and many of these groups have employed violence as a means of furthering their goals. The ideology employed by such groups has varied across time and place, but the transnational strategies employed share similarities. Some scholars have characterized international terrorism as emerging in historical waves, but upon closer examination it would appear that the use of political violence by transnationally networked nonstate actors has been an almost constant source of insecurity in world politics over the past two centuries – what has changed has been largely the mobilizing ideologies employed by such groups.[3]

For a historical perspective on the use of political violence by nonstate actors and transnational movements, one need only think of the multitude of political groups that mobilized transnationally during the nineteenth century, many of which used violence as a tactic with which to pursue their political goals. Such groups included anarchist and socialist groups in both Europe and North America. While most anarchists and socialists were nonviolent, these global movements also included radical and violent wings, in which members circulated pamphlets that provided instructions on such skills as bomb-making and the use of dynamite.[4]

In addition to anarchist and socialist networks, a number of nationalist movements were also organized transnationally during the late-nineteenth and early-twentieth centuries. A prominent example includes the Irish nationalist movement, which was active transnationally in the form of the Fenian groups that operated in Ireland, Great Britain, the United States, Australia, and parts of Europe.[5] A number of nationalist movements operated in the declining Hapsburg and Ottoman Empires, such as the Young Ottomans (which were organized transnationally across Europe), the Inner Macedonian Revolutionary Organization, Greek and Albanian nationalism movements, and the Young Bosnians.[6] The pattern of transnational political mobilization accompanied by violence continued throughout the twentieth century in the form of transnationally organized anti-imperial, anticolonial, and separatist nationalist movements. The Algerian nationalist movement and the Palestinian nationalist movement are two of the most prominent examples. While their ideology was nationalist, their strategies were transnational – both of these movements operated internationally and used political violence and terrorism to pursue their goals.[7] In the past decades, a wide variety of contemporary conflicts that have been categorized as "civil wars" – from Kosovo to Kashmir and from Chechnya to Northern Ireland – have involved transnationally organized nonstate actors who use strategies of violence and terror to pursue their goals.[8]

While there are certainly important differences between previous transnationally organized movements and the activities of Al-Qaida and other radicalized groups, there are also many striking similarities in terms of both their transnational dimensions and their strategic uses of violence. The primary differences are, of course, the nature of the mobilizing ideology – political Islam, as opposed to nationalist or other secular ideologies – as well as advances in technology. Contemporary transnational movements use the Internet to communicate with one another rather than circulating pamphlets, and may have access to more destructive weaponry than was available to groups operating in the past. However, there are also many historical continuities. The use of informal channels for fundraising, the circulation of political propaganda via transnational social networks, and the linking of a global ideology to transnationally organized underground networks are all features of Al-Qaida that resemble earlier transnational movements that employed tactics of terrorism.

The "new threat" posed by Al-Qaida is not necessarily an objectively novel feature of the international security environment, but is rather subjectively experienced as new to this generation of American citizens. The magnitude of the attacks of September 11, 2001, the fact that they occurred within the territorial borders of the United States and were directed at US civilians, and the fact that the United States is the declared target of Al-Qaida's activities, all magnify this subjective experience. Yet if one takes a more objective perspective on the activities of Al-Qaida, the similarities that exist between the current wave of "jihadist" terrorism and earlier waves of political violence by transnationally organized nonstate actors provide important points of comparison and together suggest a fruitful analytical lens through which to view the role played by nonstate actors and transnational movements in the international security environment – a role that has been largely ignored by mainstream international relations theory.

International relations theory and violent nonstate actors

There has been a surprisingly limited amount of theoretically informed research in IR on violent nonstate actors. This arguably stems from two factors. The first is theoretical and path-dependent, in the sense that the discipline of IR has been driven and moved forward by debates that are structured around some widely accepted starting propositions regarding what constitutes legitimate areas and methods of inquiry in IR. The most obvious starting point is the assumption of the primacy of sovereign states as the main actors in international affairs, and the treatment of states as unitary actors.[9] In many respects, this has had the effect of marginalizing questions relating to nonstate actors in the discipline. The second significant factor concerns the sociology of knowledge production, in which the research agenda of IR has historically been either consciously or unconsciously driven by US foreign policy interests; and unlike most other states in the world, the United States has been relatively untouched by international terrorism over the past half decade.[10] Only a few years ago the study of terrorism was still considered a marginal field for scholars interested in international peace and security. As one scholar noted in 2002, "a principal interest in terrorism virtually guarantees exclusion from most academic positions."[11] Even today, most of the scholarship on terrorism tends to be empirically driven, and there has been very little written on terrorism by IR scholars.[12]

Despite the relative paucity of theoretically driven research on the topic, however, it is nevertheless possible to try to use the dominant paradigms of IR to deduce some propositions about the impact of violent nonstate actors and transnational movements on the international security environment. Indeed, realist and liberal theories of IR each suggest a different type of lens through which to formulate appropriate policy responses to international terrorism. As such, it is useful to examine both realist and liberal perspectives on violent nonstate actors, as a prelude to introducing a political mobilization perspective.

The realist paradigm of international relations still holds a great deal of sway over the field of IR. Realists do not completely ignore nonstate actors. Most realists acknowledge the existence of nonstate actors – they simply argue that they are peripheral to understanding the international system and the international security environment compared with the interests and behavior of states. As Kenneth Waltz argued, "transnational movements are among the processes that go on within" the international system; they are not, however, a crucial defining feature of system structure.[13]

This means that for most realists, nonstate actors are not endowed with any independent agency or power in international politics. Power is treated as an attribute that is distributed across unitary state actors who must each prioritize their own security interests. The very structure of the system is determined by the distribution of power, which rests in state actors.[14] In this view, nonstate actors may engage in activities at the international or transnational level, but their behavior does not affect the fundamental structure of international politics. Realists, for example, would point out that the structure of the international system was unipolar both before and after September 11, 2001 – the attacks on New York and Washington, DC, did not fundamentally alter the structure of the international security environment.[15]

When realists do look explicitly at the activities and behavior of nonstate actors, they tend to view them as being mere extensions of existing configurations of state power and capabilities.[16] Nonstate actors are shaped by and respond to the institutional structures of states, but there is little acknowledgment that nonstate actors may operate independently and have goals and strategies that are autonomous from any one particular state. Similarly, there is little acknowledgment by realists that states can be shaped and restructured by the activities of nonstate actors, as well as vice versa.

The realist paradigm suggests a particular lens through which to view the problem of international terrorism: the logical responses to international terrorism, from a realist perspective, are to either refocus attention on states as the source of security threats, treat violent nonstate actors as proxies for state interests, or view nonstate actors as being "statelike."[17] Indeed, one can easily see the marks of some of these realist assumptions on the US response to the September 11 attacks on New York and Washington, DC. Even in the early days following the attacks there was a sense of disbelief among some in the policy community that nonstate actors could have been acting independently in the attacks, and at the highest level government officials were convinced that a state sponsor had to be somehow involved.[18] There was an immediate attempt to refocus attention on states, especially "rogue states," despite the lack of any significant evidence of a link between Al-Qaida and any state actor.

In addition to removing the Taliban from Afghanistan, the George W. Bush administration quickly focused attention on dangers posed by Iraq, Iran, and North Korea – none of which had any significant links with Al-Qaida. The US intervention in Iraq was justified in part by its alleged links with Al-Qaida, despite the lack of any intelligence to support such views. The overall discourse that has been employed since September 11 has been one of war and warfare – the "war on terrorism" – prioritizing the military dimensions of the post-September 11 response and conjuring up analogies with World War II and the Cold War. The overall policy response is therefore to combat terrorism as one would combat security threats emanating from states – through a *militarized response.*

In contrast to the realist view of international relations, nonstate actors have figured more prominently in liberal approaches to international politics. Liberals are much more willing to endow nonstate actors with autonomy and agency. For example, many liberals view power as being not just distributed across states, but also embedded in other entities such as international institutions and non-governmental organizations (NGOs).[19] Liberal constructivists have been active in initiating an IR research agenda on transnational networks and nonstate actors, and there is a significant body of work that examines NGOs and transnational advocacy groups as independent forces in world politics.[20] Liberal approaches to world politics tend to view power as multidimensional, with an emphasis on the "soft power" of ideas and influence, in addition to military and economic power.[21] However, in this worldview, nonstate actors have been largely assumed to play a stabilizing role in the international system. Nonstate actors are generally treated as extensions of domestic interest groups lobbying states by invoking norms or using tools of persuasion. Or, nonstate actors are treated as members of a global civil society that can contribute to international stability by performing tasks such as monitoring human rights violations and assisting in postconflict reconstruction and development.[22]

Yet there is a selection bias in liberal studies of nonstate actors. Liberals and liberal constructivists have overwhelmingly focused their attention on nonstate actors who themselves operate according to liberal principles. In other words, few liberals have examined the role played by nonstate actors who are willing to use strategies of coercion and violence to achieve their goals. Thus their overall conclusions regarding the role that nonstate actors play as a stabilizing force in the international security environment have been flawed. The full range of nonstate actors in the international system includes not just liberal NGOs such as Amnesty International and Greenpeace, but also illiberal groups willing to use violence. Liberals will be reluctant to lump these two kinds of nonstate actors together into a single framework. Thus nonstate actors who use violence also ultimately drop out of the liberal worldview of international politics, and are not treated as autonomous agents with an independent impact on international politics. This may explain why liberals tend to treat international terrorism as a "global problem" much like cross-boundary pollution or the spread of disease – the solution advocated by liberals would thus be to encourage cooperative ventures among states within the framework of international regimes and institutions as a way of facilitating a common response to the global problem of terrorism.

The liberal response is therefore likely to be a regulatory response – in other words, it will emphasize the importance of international organizations as providing multilateral forums for coordinating state responses to international terrorism. Viewed as a "global problem," the emphasis will be on encouraging interstate cooperation and coordination on such issues as terrorist financing, border control, migration, and intelligence sharing.[23] Liberals are reluctant to endow nonstate actors who employ strategies of violence with autonomy or agency, and are reluctant to examine the use of violence as a tool in protracted political struggles. International terrorism, therefore, is viewed as an agentless problem to be dealt with through mechanisms of interstate cooperation, rather than a tactic or strategy that is used by politically motivated nonstate actors and transnational movements.

A political mobilization perspective on violent nonstate actors

As opposed to the dominant realist and liberal approaches to the problem of international terrorism, I argue that a more useful way of thinking about violent nonstate actors and international security is through the lens of a *political mobilization* perspective.[24] This perspective understands international terrorism as a particular tactic or strategy that is employed within the broader context of political mobilization and contention by nonstate actors. As such, one can identify a common logic of transnational mobilization used by both violent and nonviolent nonstate actors at the level of the international system. By using strategies of transnational mobilization, relatively weak nonstate actors can consolidate spatially dispersed resources from across the international system and convert them into coherent projections of power that directly challenge the political status quo. This same basic logic of transnational political mobilization is used by both human rights groups and terrorist organizations. In both cases, nonstate actors make use of a variety of resources, including ideational and identity resources, financial and material resources, and institutional and organizational resources.

Much of the liberal constructivist writing on nonstate actors has rightly focused on the power of ideas and normative frameworks as a tool for political change. Realists have critiqued liberal constructivists for a selection bias in much of their research that leads them to focus on groups that promote liberal norms. However, research has shown that most of those who carry out acts of terrorism do not view themselves primarily as promoting violence, but rather as promoting a particular idea, identity, or ideology. Bruce Hoffman has argued that "the terrorist is fundamentally an *altruist:* he believes that he is serving a 'good' cause designed to achieve a greater good for a wider constituency – whether real or imagined – which the terrorist and his organization purport to represent . . . the terrorist is fundamentally a *violent intellectual.*"[25]

In this regard, much of the political mobilization activity associated with groups who use violence shares similarities with other forms of political mobilization. There is an attempt to create a transnational political constituency by using a politicized identity category or ideology to create transnational networks of political support. The ideology or identity category used for mobilization purposes can be distinguished from the use of violence as a tactic or strategy. The ideology of nationalism has been a common mobilizing ideology employed by nonstate actors operating transnationally; at other times, socialism, anarchism, or liberalism have been deployed. In the case of Al-Qaida and other groups, a radical version of Islamism has been used to create and politicize a transnational support base. The process of politicization involves the strategic deployment of a salient and meaningful political ideology in order to construct a transnational political movement.

Ideology alone, however, is not sufficient for building a transnational political movement. Amnesty International and Greenpeace need financial resources to promote their causes, just as "illegitimate" nonstate actors need financial resources to operate transnationally. In both cases, nonstate political entrepreneurs need to mobilize their support base or find outside sources of funding to generate the resources needed to operate. The mobilization of financial resources by Al-Qaida is not therefore unique, but rather follows a common pattern. Both licit and illicit nonstate actors rely on voluntary contributions and on recruiting skilled and unskilled labor into their movement. In addition, illicit movements – not surprisingly – rely on illicit sources of revenue, such as gray economy networks, organized crime, "taxes," and extortion.

Revolutionary organizations in the late nineteenth century, for example, successfully built up transnational constituencies that they could draw upon for financial support. One of the most prominent examples is Irish nationalist organizations, who were certainly willing to employ violence in support of the cause of Irish independence from Great Britain. Between 1916 and 1921, nearly 800,000 Irish Americans joined nationalist organizations, contributing over $10 million to Sinn Fein and the Irish Republican Army (IRA).[26] A contemporary example of transnational resource mobilization by a nationalist organization is the Liberation Tigers of Tamil Eelam of Sri Lanka, which has had an extremely effective fundraising organization. During the 1990s, its $50 million annual budget was acquired through a combination of direct donations by Tamil migrant communities, money skimmed off from the budgets of Tamil NGOs, human smuggling operations, and Tamil-run businesses.[27] A 3 percent war tax on all earnings abroad was collected by the "Homeland Calling" fund of the Kosovo Liberation Army (KLA) during the Kosovo conflict, and the Zurich-based newspaper *Voice of Kosovo* routinely appealed for donations to the KLA from the transnational diaspora of supporters.[28] These are all examples that bear strong similarities to some of the "terrorist financing" strategies used by Al-Qaida.

Transnational political movements – whether "legitimate" or "illegitimate" – need some form of organizational structure in order to operate. Groups such as the Kurdistan Workers Party (PKK), Algeria's National Liberation Front, the IRA, Hamas, and other transnationally organized nonstate political actors fall somewhere on the continuum of transnational social movements, deterritorialized proto-states, and organized networks of terror and crime. Most are not just involved in violence, but also provide a political organizational structure as well as, in many cases, social services, such as welfare, policing, education, and employment – in addition to the more intangible and status benefits of membership, identity, and existential meanings – to constituencies that are marginalized within the given political order. Contemporary political science, with its bias toward studying liberal NGOs, has largely relegated participation in nonstate organizations as belonging to the realm of "civil society," but this misses the fact that transnationally organized movements may have a geopolitical agenda, rather than simply a social or cultural agenda, and may view themselves as directly challenging the interests and identities of existing state elites.

The transnational organizational structures that are built up by nonstate actors who employ violence therefore represent both practical and conceptual challenges. Practical, in that networks of violence are often intimately intertwined with networks of services that are relied upon by marginalized constituencies. Conceptual, in that the labels "terrorist network," "social movement," or "proto-state" each only provide partial descriptions of the overall phenomenon of transnationally-organized political movements that employ violence as a strategy.

Within the broader context of transnational mobilization in the pursuit of political goals, strategies of terrorism and violence can be one component of an overall agenda that is designed to challenge the status quo. In addition to inflicting pain and damage, and weakening the existing political order, terrorism, writes Hoffman, "is designed to create power where there is none or to consolidate power where there is very little. Through the publicity generated by their violence, terrorists seek to obtain the leverage, influence and power they otherwise lack to effect political change on either a local or an international scale."[29] As a "weapon of the weak," terrorism is deployed by groups to gain media attention and visibility as the first step in gaining "name recognition" within the international community.[30] Even if acts of terrorism are universally condemned, they can stimulate media coverage of an issue and provide an opening for the more moderate organizations to ask the public to consider the legitimacy of the cause as separate from the tactics with which the cause is being promoted.[31] In this regard one must note that one of the observable outcomes of September 11, 2001, has indeed been a spotlight of media attention on the Middle East and Islam, and an opening for more moderate voices to have their grievances publicly considered and deliberated, to a much greater extent than had been possible prior to the terrorist attacks.

Conclusion: implications of a political mobilization perspective

What are the theoretical and policy implications of taking a political mobilization perspective on terrorism? I would suggest that the implications are very different from those of either a mainstream realist or a liberal perspective on international terrorism. The primary difference is the added political dimension. By viewing terrorism as a tool in a political struggle, as opposed to simply a security threat to be dealt with through military means, or a "global problem" to be regulated through interstate cooperation, a political mobilization perspective points to the combination of strategies that are needed to respond to the challenge of international terrorism. In other words, if a realist perspective suggests a *military* response to terrorism as a long-term strategy, and a liberal perspective suggests a *regulatory* response, then a political mobilization perspective suggests the need for a *political* response.

By a political response, I do not mean "political" in the sense of responding to specific demands or grievances that are articulated by nonstate actors who use strategies of violence, as has been suggested by some with regard to the specifics of US foreign policy in the Middle East. I bracket this issue for the purposes of this discussion. Rather, if terrorism is a political tool used in the context of transnational political mobilization, there is a need to both delegitimize and criminalize this political tool (which is well under way, and which liberals and realists would also be in agreement with), while simultaneously providing alternative channels for grievance articulation and claims-making by ideologically motivated nonstate actors.

This proactive political response goes beyond public diplomacy or "reaching out to moderates," and includes actively strengthening institutional frameworks that can be used by nonstate actors to articulate grievances and demands, both at the level of the state and at levels beyond the state. In a sense, this is simply an argument for strengthening opportunities for democratic participation and strengthening the rule of law at the level of the international system, in addition to promoting democratic reforms within states. The international system does not have a strong institutional infrastructure available to nonstate actors to channel political demands and grievances effectively, other than through states and the representatives of states. It could be argued that the process of "modernization" has outpaced the process of "institutionalization" at the level of the international system.[32]

If the strengthening of effective intelligence collection, coordination, policing, and surveillance is the only form of institutionalization that occurs at the global level as a long-term response to terrorism, the result will be a gross imbalance. It is useful, therefore, to at least frame the question in terms of thinking about the types of *political and legal institutions* that could be used to address this broader issue over the long term. For researchers in international relations, this means thinking outside the conceptual straightjacket imposed by "states in anarchy" and instead beginning to think in terms of the factors that create political stability at the domestic level – such as legitimacy, robustness of institutions, and avenues for democratic participation – and what such factors might look like transposed to the level of the international system.[33] For international legal theorists, this requires increased attention to the position of individuals and nonstate actors as subject/objects of international law, in addition to the traditional focus on state actors. In particular, it suggests the need to think creatively about the type of institutions that could be drawn upon by individuals to make claims and articulate grievances beyond the level of the state.

What would such institutions look like? One such example can be seen in the impact that processes of regionalization have had in Europe in providing new domestic and regional institutional channels for articulating political demands in ways that delegitimize and offer alternatives to strategies of violence as political tools for articulating grievances. One could point to the case of transnationally organized nonstate actors in Turkey, where both Kurdish political entrepreneurs and Islamist political entrepreneurs have made use of the European Court of Human Rights (ECHR) to articulate grievances and engage in claims-making against the Turkish state.[34] The ECHR has been used as a venue in which individuals can make claims against governments, thus providing an additional institutional channel for articulating grievances in the face of blocked opportunities at the domestic level. A focus on institutional development at the regional and supranational levels should be accompanied by the criminalization of violence as a tool for political change. In the example of the PKK in Turkey, an international policing action resulted in the arrest of the PKK leader. Yet it is unlikely that this alone would have mitigated Kurdish violence without an accompanying change in both the domestic and supranational political opportunities available to political entrepreneurs to pursue their demands. The lifting of many restrictions on Kurdish expression in Turkey, which has been brought about largely through the pressures Turkey has been under to undertake domestic political reforms in order to conform to the criteria for membership in the European Union, and the recent victory of the moderate Islamist Justice and Development Party, which ran on a pro-European platform, provide other examples of the moderating effect that the complex institutional developments in Europe are having.

Of course, it is valid to ask to what extent aspects of the model can be applied to other regions. But as a general model it suggests the effectiveness of strengthening supranational institutional channels, in tandem with exerting pressure for internal reform to increase the availability of domestic political channels for articulating grievances and political demands. The role that robust institutionalization can play in addressing the *political dimensions* of transnational mobilization by nonstate actors in ways that provide institutional channels and legitimate avenues for the articulation of grievances deserves closer study. This is one possible research agenda that scholars in the fields of both international relations and international law could converge on, and that could potentially generate useful insights for the formulation of long-term political responses to the challenge posed by international terrorism.

Notes

1 For the classic statement of this model, see Kenneth Waltz, *Theory of International Politics* (Reading, MA: Addison-Wesley, 1979). For a more recent variant, see Alexander Wendt, *Social Theory of International Politics* (Cambridge: Cambridge University Press, 1999).

2 For work in sociology that treats the international system as a world polity, see John Boli and George M. Thomas, eds, *Constructing World Culture: International Non-governmental Organizations Since 1875* (Stanford: Stanford University Press, 1999); John W. Meyer, "The World Polity and the Authority of the Nation-State," in A. Bergesen, ed., *Studies of the Modern World-System* (New York: Academic Press, 1980), pp. 109–37; John W. Meyer *et al.*, "World Society and the Nation-State," *American Journal of Sociology* vol. 103, no. 1 (1997), pp. 144–81; George M. Thomas *et al.*, *Institutional Structure: Constituting State, Society, and the Individual* (Beverly Hills, CA: Sage, 1987). A review of the literature, from an IR perspective, can be found in Martha Finnemore, "Norms, Culture, and World Politics: Insights from Sociology's Institutionalism," *International Organization* vol. 50, no. 2 (1996), pp. 325–47. My use of the term in this chapter diverges in some respects from usages in this literature.

3 For literature that argues that international terrorism has occurred in "waves," see David C. Rapoport, "The Fourth Wave: September 11 and the History of Terrorism," *Current History* (December 2001), pp. 419–24; Audrey Kurth Cronin, "Behind the Curve: Globalization and International Terrorism," *International Security* vol. 27, no. 3 (Winter 2002–3), pp. 30–58.

4 See Bruce Hoffman, *Inside Terrorism* (New York: Columbia University Press, 1998), pp. 18–21.

5 Leon O'Broin, *Revolutionary Underground: The Story of the Irish Republican Brotherhood, 1858–1924* (Dublin: Gill and Macmillan, 1976); Richard Vincent Comerford, *The Fenians in Context: Irish Politics and Society, 1848–82* (Dublin: Wolfhound Press, 1985); Eric Hobsbawm, *The Age of Capital, 1848–1875* (New York: Vintage, 1996), pp. 92ff.

6 M. Şükrü Hanioğlu, *The Young Turks in Opposition* (New York: Oxford University Press, 1995); Hoffman, *Inside Terrorism*, pp. 20ff.; Hobsbawm, *The Age of Capital.*

7 Hoffman, *Inside Terrorism.*

8 Mary Kaldor, *New and Old Wars: Organized Violence in a Global Era* (Stanford: Stanford University Press, 1999), refers to such conflicts as "new wars."

9 For a discussion of the treatment of states as the primary actors in world politics, see Wendt, *Social Theory of International Politics,* pp. 193–245.

10 See Steve Smith, "Paradigm Dominance in International Relations: The Development of International Relations as a Social Science," *Millennium: Journal of International Studies* vol. 16, no. 2 (1987), pp. 189–206, for a discussion along these lines.

11 Audrey Kurth Cronin, "Behind the Curve", p. 57.

12 One exception is Ken Booth and Timothy Dunne, *Worlds in Collision: Terror and the Future of Global Order* (London: Palgrave Macmillan, 2002), an edited collection of essays that contains contributions by IR theorists, among others. Since 2001, numerous scholars have produced works examining terrorism, but the majority of these do not make explicit links to debates in International Relations theory. See, for example, Robert A. Pape, *Dying to Win: The Strategic Logic of Suicide Terrorism* (New York: Columbia University Press, 2005).

13 Waltz, *Theory of International Politics*, p. 95.
14 Waltz, *Theory of International Politics*.
15 Compare, for example, the discussions of unipolarity in William C. Wohlforth, "The Stability of a Unipolar World," *International Security* vol. 24, no. 1 (Summer 1999), pp. 5–41; William C. Wohlforth, "U.S. Strategy in a Unipolar World," in G. John Ikenberry, *America Unrivaled: The Future of the Balance of Power* (Ithaca: Cornell University Press, 2002), pp. 98–118.
16 For an argument on how nonstate actors are shaped by states, see Stephen D. Krasner, "Power Politics, Institutions, and Transnational Relations," in Thomas Risse-Kappen, ed. *Bringing Transnational Relations Back In: Non-State Actors, Domestic Structures, and International Institutions* (Cambridge: Cambridge University Press, 1995).
17 In other words, realists may tend to treat international terrorist organizations as "unitary rational actors."
18 See, for example, the chronicling of events following September 11 in Bob Woodward, *Bush at War* (New York: Simon and Schuster, 2002).
19 See, for example, discussions in Robert O. Keohane, *Power and Governance in a Partially Globalized World* (London: Routledge, 2002).
20 For representative work, see Margaret Keck and Kathryn Sikkink, *Activists Beyond Borders: Transnational Advocacy Networks in International Politics* (Ithaca: Cornell University Press, 1998); Audie Klotz, *Norms in International Relations: The Struggle Against Apartheid* (Ithaca: Cornell University Press, 1995); Richard Price, "Reversing the Gun Sights: Transnational Civil Society Targets Land Mines," *International Organization* vol. 52, no. 3 (1998), pp. 613–44; Thomas Risse-Kappen, ed., *Bringing Transnational Relations Back In*.
21 See discussion in Joseph Nye, *Soft Power: The Means to Success in World Politics* (New York: PublicAffairs, 2004).
22 Keck and Sikkink, *Activists Beyond Borders*; Klotz, *Norms in International Relations;* Price, "Reversing the Gun Sights"; Jessica Mathews, "Power Shift," *Foreign Affairs* vol. 76 (January–February 1997), pp. 50–66; Paul Wapner, *Environmental Activism and World Civic Politics* (New York: State University of New York Press, 1996).
23 On global financing, see Thomas Biersteker and Peter Romaniuk, "The Return of the State? Financial Reregulation in the Pursuit of National Security After September 11," in John Tirman, ed., *The Maze of Fear: Security and Migration After 9/11* (New York: New Press, 2004), pp. 59–75.
24 Such a perspective can be found in the sociological and comparative politics literatures on political mobilization, contentious politics, social movements, and resource mobilization. For representative examples, see Charles Tilly, *From Mobilization to Revolution* (Reading, MA: Addison-Wesley, 1978); Sidney Tarrow, *Power and Movement: Social Movements and Contentious Politics* (Cambridge: Cambridge University Press, 1998); Doug McAdam *et al.*, *Dynamics of Contention* (New York: Cambridge University Press, 2001).
25 Hoffman, *Inside Terrorism,* p. 43. Emphasis in original.
26 Kerby A. Miller, "Class, Culture, and Immigrant Group Identity in the United States: The Case of Irish-American Ethnicity," in Virginia Yans-McLaughlin, ed., *Immigration Reconsidered* (New York: Oxford University Press, 1990), pp. 96–129.
27 Daniel Byman *et al.*, *Trends in Outside Support for Insurgent Movements* (Santa Monica, CA: Rand, 2001), pp. 48–9.
28 Chris Hedges, "Kosovo's Next Masters," *Foreign Affairs* vol. 78, no. 3 (May–June 1999), pp. 24–42.
29 Hoffman, *Inside Terrorism*.

30 Brigitte Nacos, *Terrorism and the Media: From the Iran Hostage Crisis to the Oklahoma City Bombing* (New York: Columbia University Press, 1994).

31 This intangible quality of legitimacy, rarely discussed by IR theorists, is what separates a terrorist from a freedom fighter, what can transform a rebel into a statesperson, an opposition movement into a regime. See Yossi Shain, *The Frontier of Loyalty: Political Exiles in the Age of the Nation-State* (Middletown, CT: Wesleyan University Press, 1989), for a discussion regarding competing claims of legitimacy by dissident exiles and governments.

32 Samuel P. Huntington, *Political Order in Changing Societies* (New Haven: Yale University Press, 1968).

33 If one scholar's assessment that the current conflict between Al-Qaida and the United States is analogous to the early stages of a "global civil war" is correct, then the use of domestic analogies for achieving international stability becomes even more salient. See Stein Tonnesson, "A Global Civil War?" *Security Dialogue* vol. 33, no. 3 (2002).

34 The Kurdish Human Rights Project in London, for example, has submitted more than 100 cases to the European Commission and European Court of Human Rights, and engages in monitoring of compliance and the effects of Court decisions on Turkish legislation and practice. See the project's website, at www.khrp.org. The Court is also being used as a venue by Islamist women for mounting a legal challenge to the Turkish banning of headscarves in universities and other public institutions.

6

CRYING WAR

Mary Ellen O'Connell

Introduction

On September 12, 2001, President George W. Bush declared a global war on terror.[1] This was stirring rhetoric at a moment of crisis. It was not, however, a correct statement as a matter of law. In the weeks and months that followed, it became clear why the administration spoke of a global war. International law permits certain actions during war that are criminal in peacetime. The administration wanted those privileges and so it made a false claim of global war. This false claim was the first step in what turned out to be a series of international law violations, violations that have denied basic human rights to thousands of individuals and have cost the United States dearly – by several measures. This chapter examines the high cost of America's post-September 11 international law violations. It first recounts a number of serious violations; it then considers what may have motivated administration officials to violate the law, and, finally, it looks at what those violations have apparently cost the United States.

The violations

The rights and duties of nation-states differ in war and peace. It follows, therefore, that international law indicates when wartime versus peacetime law applies. The Bush administration, however, in its zeal to claim wartime privileges globally, ignored the understanding of war found in international law, substituting a definition of its own. In addition, after September 11, the administration focused exclusively on wartime privileges, ignoring wartime duties. Within months of the global war declaration, the United States was committing serious international law violations. Having departed from its wartime duties in the fabricated global war, the administration displayed only limited interest in observing its duties in the real wars of Afghanistan and Iraq. The policy of claiming wartime rights everywhere and rejecting wartime duties has resulted in significant international law violations, including summary execution, unlawful detention, torture, and inhuman treatment, as well as the woeful neglect of the duties of an occupying power to preserve and protect the citizens, cultural heritage, and basic infrastructure of the occupied nation.

The false claim of war

No single treaty or rule of customary international law precisely defines war.[2] Nevertheless, it is easy enough to discover in international legal sources the factual situation that triggers wartime rights and duties. Before the adoption of the United Nations Charter in 1945, formal declarations of war were significant to the determination of whether states were involved in a de jure war. After the adoption of the Charter, "war" fell out of use as a legal term of art.[3] The Charter, in Article 2(4), prohibits all uses of force, war, and lesser actions, except in self-defense or as mandated by the Security Council. Following the adoption of the Charter, treaties relevant to war, such as the Geneva Conventions of 1949, substituted the term "armed conflict" for "war." "War" ministries became "defense" ministries. States engaging in armed conflict rarely declared war. What mattered after 1945 was actual fighting, not nineteenth-century formalities. The question of whether the law of war or peace applies came to depend on the existence of actual armed conflict, not the rhetorical or even technical invocation or declaration of war.

Armed conflict exists when two or more armed groups engage each other in significant armed hostilities. In *Prosecutor* v. *Tadić,* the International Criminal Tribunal for the Former Yugoslavia defined "armed conflict" as existing "whenever there is a resort to armed force between States or protracted armed violence between governmental authorities and organized armed groups or between such groups within a state."[4] The 1949 Geneva Conventions apply in "armed conflict" and occupation.[5] Additional Protocol II to the 1949 Conventions, applicable in noninternational armed conflicts, applies to "more than situations of internal disturbances and tensions such as riots and isolated and sporadic acts of violence." Isolated and sporadic acts of violence such as border clashes and naval incidents are not armed conflict.[6]

The intermittent nature of terrorist attacks means that they will not generally, by themselves, amount to armed conflict: "'International terrorism implies the intermittent use or threat of force against person(s) to obtain certain political objectives of international relevance from a third party.' . . . [T]he intermittent factor, which is a hallmark of terrorism, excludes it from constituting war *per se.* But . . . terrorist tactics may be adopted in war for the purpose of guerilla warfare."[7] Oscar Schachter observed in 1995 that "no State has considered itself to be legally at war in response to terrorism."[8] The official British position has been that armed conflict does not refer to the presence of ordinary crimes or terrorism.[9]

Officials in the Bush administration, however, argue that the series of intermittent attacks on the United States by Al-Qaida between 1993 and 2001 did constitute an armed conflict, and thus, they say, President Bush's declaration of a "global war on terror" on September 12 was factually correct.[10] These officials confuse armed attack with armed conflict. Yes, the United States was attacked, but until it counter-attacked, until it engaged in significant armed hostilities, there was no armed conflict. Following the 1993 attack on the World Trade Center and the attack on the USS *Cole* in Yemen in 2000, there was no counter-attack. American and Yemeni law enforcement officials treated the attacks as criminal acts. After the attack on the US embassies in Nairobi and Dar-es-Salaam, the United States did counter-attack in Sudan and Afghanistan. There was, however, no counter-counter-attack. The violent exchange was too intermittent and too short in duration to constitute armed conflict.

The series of Al-Qaida attacks on the United States are legally significant for another reason, however. While the attacks did not constitute armed conflict, they did give rise to the right of self-defense against Afghanistan. The right of self-defense is triggered if an armed attack occurs. Once the right is triggered, the victim of the attack is allowed to take offensive military force against the state responsible for the unlawful attack.[11] Because of the clandestine nature of terrorist attacks, the victim state will not always know if there is a state responsible for the attack, nor if more attacks are planned, such that self-defense is warranted. In the case of September 11, Al-Qaida had, by its own public admission, carried out the attacks; the United States made a case that Afghanistan sufficiently supported Al-Qaida so as to be legally responsible for the attacks, and because of the series of prior attacks and clear and convincing evidence of future attacks, a case for self-defense could be made.[12]

Hostilities in self-defense began with a US air offensive against Afghanistan on October 7, 2001. Those hostilities occurred in Afghanistan, not all over the world. Afghanistan became a theater of war, and the law of armed conflict applied in Afghanistan. The United States generally did not then behave as if it were in a worldwide war. There was certainly no expectation that members of the US military would become lawful targets outside the Afghan war zone. Four years after the armed conflict in Afghanistan began, the question became, "When do hostilities end?" The answer depends on the intensity of the fighting and the measure of control the government is able to exercise – in Afghanistan.

Thus, exchange and intensity are two key factors that separate terrorist attacks from armed conflict. Another is control of territory. In today's world, this means armed conflict always takes place in connection with a state. For this reason, many scholars say that nonstate actor groups cannot engage in armed conflict. To engage in significant armed hostilities, a group must control sufficient territory – it must be at least a quasi-state.[13] When the Oklahoma City bombing occurred, no one considered it an armed conflict. The same was true in Yemen, Nairobi, Kenya, Bali, Madrid, Istanbul, Saudi Arabia, Morocco, and London. The bombers held no territory in those states. The governments were in control and did not need to use their militaries to fight the bombers. The situation in Afghanistan in 2001 was different. Al-Qaida was supported by the Taliban and its military forces. The Taliban refused to end that support. The

United States and Britain then engaged the combined forces of the Taliban and Al-Qaida on the territory of Afghanistan. Thus an armed conflict with Al-Qaida was possible only because of the link between Al-Qaida and the Taliban, the de facto government of Afghanistan.

In addition to those cases where terrorist groups are linked to a state, terrorist groups may also engage in armed conflict where they take control of sufficient territory so as to challenge a government. The Abusayyef terrorist group, operating in The Philippines, is an example. The Philippine government has had to use its military to counter this group because it controls territory in The Philippines.[14] This control means that a group of terrorists is able to engage in armed conflict – a civil war. It is engaged in more than just crime. The Irish Republican Army (IRA), ETA, the Red Brigades, and the Red Army Faction never gained this type of control, and their acts remained crimes. Al-Qaida has engaged in armed conflict in Afghanistan and Iraq, but its violent actions in the rest of the world have been crimes.

Officials in the Bush administration have tried to counter the requirement of a state territory connection. They have pointed out that treaties regulating the use of armed force do not focus narrowly on states, and they argue that it is legally possible for nonstate actor groups to engage in armed conflict.[15] This argument fails to take into account the nature of armed conflict and the geographic facts of modern life. It is simply not possible to engage in armed conflict without some relationship to state territory. As the Bush administration itself likes to point out, international humanitarian law (IHL) that regulates the waging of war and occupation is not designed to apply to nonstate actor groups in control of no territory.[16] Such groups do not meet the criteria for lawful combatants. They do not wear insignia, form units under discipline, or carry weapons openly. The administration concludes from all of this that such persons are unlawful combatants because of these deficiencies. But the fact is, they are not combatants at all.[17] They are criminals. To be a combatant, one must take direct part in hostilities that amount to armed conflict.

The Bush administration's case for war also invokes the number of persons who have been killed by terrorists as an argument that terrorism today is war, not crime.[18] This observation recalls the definition of war used by many political scientists. Rather than use the understanding found in international law, one finds common reliance on the understanding developed for the Correlates of War Study. This study counts an incident as war if 1,000 violent deaths occur. The actual threshold number may vary; numbers as low as 25 are sometimes used. Determining that a situation is war based only on an arbitrary number of deaths, however, is too simplistic and results in clear anomalies. The attack on the World Trade Center is counted as an armed conflict, but the attacks on the Madrid train, the African embassies, London Transport, and others are not, owing solely to the numbers killed, even though they were carried out by the same terrorist group with the same intention and in a similar way. The international law understanding of war is much closer to the real-world understanding – war is more than a matter of numbers. War or armed conflict exists when armed groups, in control of territory, engage in intense hostilities of some duration.

Despite the common sense of the international law understanding, the Bush administration's alternative understanding of war has not been dismissed out-of-hand. This may be due to a couple of factors. First, it took some time for the international legal community to really understand that the administration was not using mere rhetoric of the "war on drugs" type. In addition, international law literature does not reflect much discussion on the difference between war and terrorism. States generally have been reluctant to acknowledge that a terrorist challenge has reached the level of armed conflict. To recognize that an armed conflict is raging on state territory is to acknowledge that the state faces a challenge so serious it can no longer be dealt with by law enforcement measures. Under international law this has not been a problem. As long as the situation is not armed conflict, the law of peace prevails. The law of peace has better protections for individual human rights, and states have typically accepted the concomitant heavier legal burden to avoid enhancing the status of terrorists from that of criminal to that of combatant. As a result, few states, if any, made false claims of war prior to September 12, 2001.[19]

In the summer of 2005, some in the Bush administration seemed to understand that they had made a strategic error in claiming to be at war with terrorism. Secretary of Defense Donald Rumsfeld stated that instead of a war, the United States was involved in a "global struggle against the enemies of freedom, the enemies of civilization."[20] General Richard Myers, chairman of the Joint Chiefs of Staff, said too that the "war on terror" would more aptly be named a "global struggle against violent extremism."[21] Myers pointed out that contemporary global conflicts require "all instruments of our national power, all instruments of the international communities' national power."[22] Stephen Hadley, the national security adviser, said that the conflict was broader than a war on terror: "It's broader than that. It's a global struggle against extremism."[23] Only a few days after administration officials began using the new line, President Bush terminated the new terminology: "Make no mistake about it, we are at war."[24] Perhaps someone in the administration realized that without a war, the United States would no longer have any legal basis for a number of its policies.

False claims of privilege

It appears the Bush administration decided to declare a global war against terrorism to get the benefits of wartime privileges – especially the rights to kill without warning and to detain without trial. Those privileges do not apply in peace. Events also show, however, that the administration's conduct of the global war has been inconsistent, contradictory, and often counterproductive.

As already mentioned, the Bush administration does not treat the whole world as a battlefield. It does not recognize members of the US military to be lawful targets wherever they are. Since September 11, members of the US military have been considered lawful targets only in the actual war zones of Afghanistan and Iraq. For the administration's targets, however, any place the administration selects could be a war zone. The same place will be a war zone for one person while it is a zone of peace for everyone else. For example, José Padilla was arrested at Chicago's O'Hare Airport and designated a combatant even though O'Hare was not a war zone for anyone else. International law accepts extending the higher human rights standards of peace in war, but it cannot tolerate the lower standards of war in peace. Even worse is the application of the lower standards in only selected cases. This ad hocism is inconsistent with the very concept of law that requires the application of rules fairly.

During an armed conflict, regular members of the armed forces who respect the law of war may not be prosecuted for the deaths they cause. This is known as the combatant's privilege, or combatant immunity. Lawful combatants have the privilege to kill enemy fighters without warning.[25] Absent an armed conflict, law enforcement officials may only use lethal force in self-defense or the defense of others in the face of an imminent threat.[26] On November 3, 2002, agents of the US Central Intelligence Agency (CIA), using an unmanned Predator drone, fired a Hellfire missile against a vehicle in remote Yemen, killing six men. One of those men was suspected of being a high-ranking Al-Qaida lieutenant.[27] Following the attack on the USS *Cole* in 2000, the United States sent agents of the Federal Bureau of Investigation (FBI) to work with Yemeni authorities to solve the case. Police techniques were used. Conditions in Yemen at the time of the Predator strike had not changed markedly from the time of the *Cole* attack. Yemen was not the scene of an armed conflict, nor had its government declared that it was unable or unwilling to deal with suspected terrorists on its territory. The United States has also used Predator drones to kill people in Pakistan.[28]

Absent an armed conflict, the full range of international human rights law applies and protects criminal suspects. Individuals may not be killed on suspicion of membership in a group. Rather, authorities must at least make the attempt to arrest a suspect and not simply execute him. It is not possible, however, to attempt to arrest someone using an unmanned drone; the strike was an extrajudicial killing, as the UN special rapporteur on the subject affirmed.[29]

The administration has also claimed the right to detain without trial. During armed conflict, combatants who fall into the hands of a party to the conflict may be detained without trial until the end of hostilities.[30] "The purpose of captivity is to exclude enemy soldiers from further military operations. Since soldiers are permitted to participate in lawful military operations, prisoners of war shall only be considered as captives detained for reasons of security, not as criminals."[31] However, detainees may be tried for law violations committed prior to capture in proceedings consistent with minimum due process.[32] Arguably, the detaining power has a duty to try persons for grave breaches of humanitarian law.[33] In the absence of an armed conflict, international human rights law prohibits detaining people for months or years without trial.[34] If authorities wish to detain someone because he or she is a criminal suspect, the person may be detained only pursuant to a fair, public, and prompt trial.[35] Suspects may not be detained indefinitely. After September 11, the United States detained hundreds and possibly thousands of prisoners as "enemy combatants," holding them without trial even though many of the individuals were not detained in hostilities.

International humanitarian law does not simply relax certain peacetime restraints. It also imposes duties on warring parties. For example, all detainees must be registered and have the right to be visited by the International Committee of the Red Cross (ICRC). Lawful combatants and civil internees are entitled to conditions of detention commensurate with the housing of the detaining power's own soldiers. Coercive interrogation is never allowed. There is no necessity exception for such interrogation. Detainees may not be transferred for the purposes of coercive interrogation or to hide them from the ICRC. All detainees must be treated humanely at all times. Apparently the Bush administration has had no interest in complying with these duties with respect to detainees in the global war on terror. It has tried to avoid compliance by arguing that even though it has detained hundreds under the detention-without-trial privilege found in international humanitarian law, broad categories of detainees have no IHL protections.[36]

The creation of the myth that some persons have no IHL protections apparently laid the foundation for the torture, coercion, and abuse of persons in US detention.[37] The prevailing view at detention centers, regardless of location, appears to be that, because the administration says terrorists are unlawful combatants, and because unlawful combatants have no IHL protections, they are entitled to no more than the president's discretionary promise of "humane treatment." The administration considers even this limp protection inapplicable in cases of "military necessity." In addition to the general administration policy that designated detainees as having no legal protections, Defense Secretary Donald Rumsfeld authorized the use of unlawful interrogation techniques at Guantanamo Bay, Cuba. These techniques include stress positions, forced grooming, nudity, the use of dogs, and physical coercion.[38] With respect to detainees in Iraq, he authorized the illegal hiding of detainees from the International Committee of the Red Cross, and their unlawful transfer. General Ricardo Sanchez, commander of US forces in Iraq, authorized the use of muzzled dogs to threaten detainees, and the use of stress positions, isolation, and sleep deprivation.[39] The CIA is using "waterboarding" at undisclosed locations.[40] The FBI at Guantanamo Bay observed numerous outrages, including chaining in the fetal position for 24 hours without relief, sexual abuse and humiliation, and burning the inside of the ear with cigarettes.[41] In Iraq and Afghanistan, dozens of detainees in US custody have died from beatings and related causes.

In addition to these failures to observe wartime duties respecting detainees, Secretary Rumsfeld dismissed America's duties as an occupying power in Iraq. First, the administration tried to deny it was an occupier, claiming instead to be a "liberator." Even when it finally dropped that pretense, it still paid no attention to the Hague Regulations, binding on the United States, that require the occupying power to maintain law and order.[42] The occupier's obligation is even greater with respect to protecting cultural property. The United States recognizes much of the 1954 Hague Convention on the Protection of Cultural Property in Time of War as binding customary international law, including Article 4(3),[43] yet in Iraq, US forces were not ordered to protect the Iraqi National Museum or other cultural heritage sites from looting, either during the invasion or during the occupation. The United States had a legal obligation to protect cultural heritage; it had no such obligation to protect the oil ministry and other places the administration chose to protect. Secretary Rumsfeld dismissed the legal obligation, however, saying the United States was not in Iraq to stop looting. As he said in his now infamous comment, "Freedom's untidy. And free people are free to make mistakes and commit crimes and do bad things."[44] The Hague Regulations, however, state unequivocally that the occupying power is not free to allow people to commit crimes. It is the duty of the occupying power to stop them.[45] The Bush administration did not even give the orders to carry out wartime duties.

The motivations

As of the summer of 2005, officials in the Bush administration had not provided detailed accounts of how the post-September 11 legal strategy was reached.[46] Nevertheless, several relevant factors are evident and worth taking into account here, regardless of what administration officials may some day say. [47] These factors include the importance of international law in international relations, the administration's interest in avoiding peacetime criminal law, and the ideology of several key lawyers involved.

Given the Bush administration's contempt for international law and international institutions, realists and neoconservatives might have expected officials to ignore international law altogether on September 12. The president might have declared that the United States would do whatever he judged necessary in response to the attacks. He did not go so far. Rather, the administration developed a legal strategy based on a declaration of war. True, the strategy conflicts in fundamental ways with international law, but surely realists and neoconservatives have wondered why the administration bothered at all in the circumstances of September 11.

Frankly, the administration had no choice. Despite what realists and neoconservatives think about international law, no government has ever dismissed international law as irrelevant. Most states, as Louis Henkin observed in the 1970s, observe most of international law most of the time.[48] And the states that observe international law most closely enjoy an elevated status in the world as a result of the normative authority they enjoy. In the United States, since the 1960s, there has been less pressure on the government to comply closely with international law (and thereby gain greater standing in the world) than in some countries. American realists have constantly undermined the importance of international law, and they have likely had some influence on foreign policy-makers. In the real world, however, as the state system is currently structured, international law is inevitable. Only those states that contemplate standing outside the world community would say international law does not matter. They would literally become outlaw states, and there are no such states in existence today.

This is the case owing to several features of international life. First, a significant proportion of the world's people understand international law to exist at some level. There is common knowledge of the United Nations, of the United Nations Charter, of the Charter's prohibition on the use of force, respect for human rights, international boundaries, and the like. World leaders have for centuries spoken of the importance of adherence to international law, and international law violators have been punished – at Nuremberg, Tokyo, The Hague, Strasbourg, and elsewhere. As a result, there is a common expectation that governments are bound by this law. Populations judge the conduct of governments on how well they respect international law. Simply to say none of this matters at the very moment the United States was seeking international cooperation in response to September 11 would have been unthinkable. The Bush administration did not do the unthinkable.

In addition to world public opinion, world governments of course have sophisticated knowledge of international law and high expectations that relations with other governments will generally conform to legal rules. Treaties and rules of customary international law are officially considered binding – without exception. For the United States to exhibit no concern for treaties or rules of customary international law would result in reevaluation of relations between the United States and other countries of the world. The United States is a party to more than 10,000 treaties.[49] For all of those to suddenly be called into question would have thrown more confusion into a moment of crisis. The Bush administration did not risk this on September 12.

Then there are lawyers inside and outside the US government who are deeply committed to international law. They understand the importance of international law as a means to a more peaceful, prosperous, and moral world order. American international lawyers and judges understand that international law is part of US law. To reject it wholesale would be an intolerable act of lawlessness. Some committed international lawyers have even compared the Bush administration's less radical policies to legal strategies developed by Adolf Hitler's lawyers in the 1930s, manipulating international law to gain its power without respecting its restraints.[50]

Bush's lawyers did not dismiss international law. They sought to exploit it. Declaring a global war on terrorism, they argued that the United States could use lethal force anywhere in the world and detain without the need of evidence beyond a reasonable doubt. The disdain for international law was apparently such that only the privileges of wartime have been evident in the policies, not the burdens. International legal protections for individuals were dismissed as not owed to the people the United States branded as terrorists. Thus the United States has taken the position consistently since September 11 that it is acting lawfully under international law. How could lawyers of any quality at all come up with such patently indefensible policies?

Already on September 12, 2001, it was evident that the Bush administration was interested in a legal strategy that would allow it to avoid the burdens of the criminal law. Lawyers arguing that the global war on terror allows the United States to treat terrorist suspects as combatants typically raise the argument that criminal law requires proof beyond a reasonable doubt, speedy trial, defense lawyers, and so on. These aspects of criminal law cannot change peace to war, although lawyers in the Bush administration argue as if they should. Ruth Wedgwood has written that treating terrorists as combatants is justifiable because they have declared war on the United States.[51] Declarations of war are irrelevant to finding armed conflict, but Wedgwood's interest is not in trying to prove that the war on terror is a real war with real combatants, but in the fact that applying national criminal law can be cumbersome. She makes it clear that the Bush administration's war on terror is about making it easy to kill, detain, and interrogate people, not about a defensible case of war or combatancy under international law.[52]

In addition to this opportunism in Bush's case for global war, the beliefs of administration lawyers also hold some clues. A number of top administration lawyers who advised on global war policy do not actually believe that international law is really law or that it can actually bind the executive branch, including John Bolton,[53] John Yoo,[54] and Jack Goldsmith.[55] In speaking to a conservative group of lawyers known as the Federalist Society in 2003, Bolton expressed a cardinal tenet of these lawyers' thinking vis-à-vis international law. He opined that the president's actions in international relations can be authorized only within US law. To consider that the president could be restrained by international law means the country would lose its independence.[56] Bolton goes further: he does not recognize international law as binding on the United States.[57] Goldsmith has written that international law can no more bind the United States than does a letter of intent or an employee handbook.[58] Yoo wrote in a memo on interrogation techniques – now known as the "Torture Memo" – that the president of the United States is not bound by customary international law because it is not part of federal law.[59] Yoo also wrote that when the president acts in his capacity as commander in chief, he may authorize any interrogation technique, including torture, despite the fact that torture violates both treaties to which the United States is party and *jus cogens* or peremptory norms of international law.[60] For these men, it was possible to tell the president with a straight face that he could do basically anything he wanted in the global war on terror and still not violate any law that mattered – to them.

Numbers of lawyers in the US State Department and in the military have indicated how they tried to explain what international law really required.[61] The advice of Yoo and the others, however, was apparently too attractive to top officials to dismiss. The fact that the legal analysis supporting this advice is risible to any mainstream international lawyer has led reporters and others to question the competence or intelligence of the Bush lawyers.[62] The explanation for the advice, however, seems to lie in their anti-international law agenda. It is an agenda highly compatible with neoconservative ideology. Both place the United States in a world of its own – a place of hegemonic dominance where it is above other states and the law of international society.

The consequences

The negative consequences of the Bush administration's unlawful legal strategy have been many and serious. Most of the negative consequences can be traced to international reaction to the prison at Guantanamo Bay, Cuba, which is a highly visible symbol of wrongdoing in the global war on terror. Other consequences are more directly attributable to the illegal invasion of Iraq and the failure strictly to apply international humanitarian law. That failure is in turn traceable to the legal strategy of the US global war on terror. The most serious negative consequence is that thousands of individuals have suffered denial of basic human rights – death, false imprisonment, torture, and abuse. In addition, the United States has lost moral authority in the world, undercutting its ability to win cooperation and press for such policies as respect for human rights. Also, the United States is facing unending legal action for its wrongdoing. These actions will tie up considerable resources and could end up costing the United States billions in compensation. Finally, the wrongs of the global war are being used to recruit ever more individuals to the cause of anti-American terror, and undermining US claims to promote human rights.[63]

Because these are legal wrongs and not just odious policies, victims will be able to bring lawsuits, and they are doing so. Criminal complaints have been filed by citizens in Chile and Germany against Secretary of Defense Donald Rumsfeld, former CIA director George Tenet, and others for the abuse of detainees in Iraq, Afghanistan, Guantanamo Bay, and at undisclosed locations.[64] Italy issued arrest warrants in June 2005 for CIA agents accused of kidnapping a man on the streets of Milan and flying him, via Germany, to Egypt, where he alleges he was tortured.[65] Civil suits have been filed for compensation for torture and abuse in the United States and elsewhere.[66] Beginning in 2002, hundreds of suits for review of detention have been filed. These actions will be ongoing in the United States and many other countries where jurisdiction is provided over torture, coercion, cruelty, and abuse regardless of where the crime was committed.[67]

Another serious cost is the widespread hatred engendered against the United States for prisoner abuse at Abu Ghraib, Guantanamo Bay, and Bagram Air Base in Afghanistan.[68] Virulent anti-American rioting broke out on news that a Koran had been desecrated at Guantanamo Bay, resulting in 17 deaths in

Pakistan and Afghanistan.[69] Abuse of detainees has been linked to increased recruiting among insurgent forces fighting in Iraq.[70] That sort of link has been seen before. When the British were using abusive measures against IRA suspects, IRA recruitment benefited.[71] When Britain ended abusive measures after a decision by the European Court of Human Rights, it reached a peace accord with Republican parties and the use of violence and support for the IRA declined. Germany and Italy provide even stronger examples of states that eliminated serious terrorism challenges, from the Red Army Faction and the Red Brigades respectively, while remaining committed to requirements of international human rights principles.

The failure to follow rules governing treatment of detainees has in all likelihood cost the United States valuable intelligence. Experienced US Army interrogators recognize that the use of coercion and abuse is unlawful and counterproductive to intelligence gathering.[72] Societies known to use torture, coercion, and abuse have not resolved their problems with terrorism. Societies that have abandoned such practices or never used them in the first place have had greater success.[73]

Societies that have had success against terrorism are also societies where governments apply national criminal law to terrorism, not law of war. The motivation for this preference is the perception that calling opponents "combatants" and declaring war against them elevates their status above that of mere criminals.[74] There is a reason that members of the IRA used hunger strikes to try to pressure the British government into recognizing them as prisoners of war. According to Christopher Greenwood, however, these groups cannot legally be termed combatants, but are mere bands of criminals.[75]

President Bush, through his policy of global war, has given a degree of legitimacy to terrorist groups opposing the United States. During a speech to soldiers at Fort Bragg, North Carolina, in the summer of 2005, to support his argument that the United States is involved in a real war with terrorism, Bush actually quoted Osama bin Laden. He not only pointed to bin Laden's belief in a global war, but also used bin Laden's terminology to describe the US undertaking: a "third world war."[76] Why would the United States want to take the position that a band of criminals was able to launch World War III? By dramatic contrast, when London Transport was bombed on July 7, 2005, Prime Minister Tony Blair would not give the terrorists the benefit of a platform. He stated briefly the facts and went on about his business, refusing to allow the bombers the satisfaction of knowing they had disrupted British life to much extent at all – let alone engaged the British in an armed conflict or a world war.[77]

Failure to respect fundamental human rights norms and fundamental principles, such as the prohibition on the use of force, have led many to see the United States as a rogue nation and to the belief that fighting such a nation is in a just cause.[78] Ironically, the 2002 US national security strategy includes violation of international law as a factor in defining rogue nations.[79]

Conclusion

The United States is not in a world of its own. It needs international moral consensus about the wrongfulness of terrorism. It needs to send the clear message that it is in the right, and that other nations would be acting morally to cooperate with it. International law has developed over centuries, reflecting real experience and consensus norms. Its processes make it possible for the international community to reflect shared moral principle, and it lays out practical steps for an orderly world. Following September 11, 2001, the United States had the sympathy and support of the world – it was so clearly the victim of an international crime. The United Nations Security Council adopted far-reaching resolutions at America's request. Then, however, when it became clear that the United States had adopted an indefensible legal policy called the "global war on terror," a shift began. The first heated criticism of US policy post-September 11 was over President Bush's executive order of November 2001. This order allowed the trial of suspected terrorists before military commissions appointed by the secretary of defense, with the power to execute upon a two-thirds vote.[80] From this extraordinary step, the Bush administration went on to establish the prison at Guantanamo Bay, to dismiss the Geneva Conventions as "quaint" and "obsolete," to use torture and abuse against detainees, to render detainees to countries that torture, to invade Iraq, and to fail to carry out occupation obligations.

The United States transformed itself within three years of September 11 – from victim of an awful crime to perpetrator of grave violations of international law. This reversal in large part owes to the administration's lawyers who promoted their own agenda over their nation's. Their concern over preservation of some abstract notion of independence cost the United States the wisdom found in international law rules and standing associated with law compliance. It was possible for them to do so in a context where international law had come to be viewed by nonlawyers as only marginally relevant to high policy.

When countries sink as low as the United States has, they typically turn back to international law. The negative consequences of the global war on terror teach once again the value, both moral and practical, of good-faith adherence to international law – real international law.[81]

Acknowledgments

With thanks for insights to Christopher Haas, and for research assistance to Phillip Campbell.

Notes

1 See the following speeches by George W. Bush: "President's Address to the Nation on the Terrorist Attacks," *Weekly Compilation of Presidential Documents* vol. 37 (September 11, 2001), p. 1301; "President's Address to a Joint Session of Congress on the United States Response to the Terrorist Attacks of September 11," *Weekly*

Compilation of Presidential Documents vol. 37 (September 20, 2001), p. 1432; "Training Camps and Taliban Military Installations in Afghanistan," *Weekly Compilation of Presidential Documents* vol. 37 (October 7, 2001), p. 1432; "President's Address Before a Joint Session of the Congress on the State of the Union," *Weekly Compilations of Presidential Documents* vol. 39 (January 28, 2003), p. 109; all available online at www.whitehouse.gov.

2 Nathaniel Berman, "Privileging Combat? Contemporary Conflict and the Legal Construction of War," *Columbia Journal of Transnational Law* vol. 43, no. 1 (2004), pp. 1-71.

3 See Mary Ellen O'Connell, "Ad Hoc War," in Horst Fischer *et al.*, eds, *Krisensicherung und Humanitarer Schutz: Crisis Management and Humanitarian Protection* (Berlin: BWV, 2004), pp. 405, 408.

4 See also *Prosecutor* v. *Tadić*, Decision on the Defense Motion for Interlocutory Appeal on Jurisdiction, no. IT-94-1 (October 2, 1995), para. 70.

5 Common Article 2 of the four Geneva Conventions provides that the conventions "shall apply to all cases of declared war or of any other armed conflict which may arise between two or more of the High Contracting Parties, even if the state of war is not recognized by one of them."

6 Christopher Greenwood, "Scope of Application of Humanitarian Law," in Dieter Fleck, ed., *The Handbook of Humanitarian Law in Armed Conflict* (New York: Oxford University Press, 1995), pp. 39, 42.

7 Ingrid Detter, *Law of War*, 2nd edn (Cambridge: Cambridge University Press, 2000), p. 25.

8 Oscar Schacter, *International Law in Theory and Practice* (Dordrecht: Martinus Nijhoff, 1991), p. 169.

9 Marco Sassoli, "Use and Abuse of the Laws of War in the 'War on Terrorism,'" *Law and Inequality* vol. 12, no. 2 (Summer 2004), p. 195, citing Reservation by the United Kingdom to Art. 1, para. 4, and Art. 96, para. 3, of Protocol I.

10 See Curtis A. Bradley and Jack L. Goldsmith, "Congressional Authorization and the War on Terrorism," *Harvard Law Review* vol. 118 (2005), pp. 2047–68; Stephan Hadley, "Remarks at the Moritz College of Law of the Ohio State University" (September 24, 2004).

11 Mary Ellen O'Connell, "Lawful Self-Defense to Terrorism," *University of Pittsburgh Law Review* vol. 63 (2002), p. 889.

12 Ibid., pp. 892–95.

13 See Alain Pellet, "No, This Is Not War," *European Journal of International Law* (October 3, 2001), available online at www.ejil.org/forum_wtc/ny-pellet.html.

14 See Mary Ellen O'Connell, "To Kill or Capture Terrorists in the Global War on Terror," *Case Western Reserve Journal of International Law* vol. 35 (2003), p. 325.

15 Bradley and Goldsmith, "Congressional Authorization," pp. 2069–70.

16 Memorandum from William J. Haynes II, General Counsel of the Department of Defense, Enemy Combatants, available online at www.cfr.org/publication.php?id= 5312.

17 See Sassoli, "Use and Abuse of the Laws of War"; Christopher Greenwood, "War, Terrorism, and International Law," in Michael Freeman, ed., *Current Legal Problems* vol. 56 (New York: Oxford University Press, 2004), pp. 505, 529.

18 Bradley and Goldsmith, "Congressional Authorization," p. 2068.

19 Mary Ellen O'Connell, "Enhancing the Status of Non-State Actors Through a Global War on Terror," *Columbia Journal of Transnational Law* vol. 43 (2005), p. 435. See also Peter Spiro, "Not War, Crimes," *FindLaw's Legal Commentary*, September 19, 2001.

20 Kim R. Holmes, "What's in a name? 'War on Terror' Out, 'Struggle Against Extrem-

ism' In," Web memo, Heritage Foundation (July 26, 2005), available online at www.heritage.org/research/nationalsecurity/wm805.cfm.

21 Sidney Blumenthal, "Selling the War: When Your Mission Is Failing, Is It Enough Simply to Rename It? Not If You Care About Credibility" (July 28, 2005), available online at www.salon.com/opinion/blumenthal/2005/07/28/war_on_terror/index.html.

22 Ibid.

23 Ibid.

24 Richard W. Stevenson, "President Makes It Clear: Phrase Is 'War on Terror,'" *New York Times*, August 4, 2005, available online at www.nytimes.com/2005/08/04/politics/04bush.html.

25 Jordan J. Paust, "The Right to Life, Human Rights Law and the Law of War," *Saskatchewan Law Review* vol. 65 (2002), pp. 411, 419, n. 46. See also Knut Ipsen, "Combatants and Non-Combatants," in Fleck, *Handbook*, p. 68.

26 Office of the UN High Commission for Human Rights, *Basic Principles on the Use of Force and Firearms by Law Enforcement Officials*, adopted by the Eighth United Nations Congress on the Prevention of Crime and the Treatment of Offenders, Havana, Cuba, August 27–September 7, 1990, available online at http://193.194.138/html/menu3/b/h_comp43.htm.

27 O'Connell, "Ad Hoc War."

28 "CIA Drone Kills Qaeda Operative," APS Diplomat News Service, May 30, 2005.

29 "Yemen/USA: Government Must Not Sanction Extra-Judicial Executions" (November 8, 2002), available online at http://web.amnesty.org/library/print/engamr511582002; UN Doc. E/CN.4/003/3, paras. 37–39. See also, Michael J. Dennis, "Human Rights in 2002: The Annual Sessions of the UN Commission on Human Rights and the Economics and Social Council," *American Journal of International Law* vol. 97, no. 17 (2003), pp. 364, 367.

30 *Geneva Convention [No. III] Relative to the Treatment of Prisoners of War* (August 12, 1949), Art. 118, 75 U.N.T.S. 135. Compare *Protocol Additional to the Geneva Conventions of 12 August 1949, and Relating to the Protection of Victims of International Armed Conflicts* (June 8, 1977), Art. 75(3).

31 Horst Fischer, "Protection of Prisoners of War," in Fleck, *Handbook*, p. 326.

32 *Prisoner's Convention*, Arts. 84, 105; *Additional Protocol I*, Art. 75.

33 *Prisoner's Convention*, Art. 129.

34 *International Covenant on Civil and Political Rights* (December 16, 1966), Art. 9(1), 999 U.N.T.S. 171.

35 Ibid., Art. 14(3)(c).

36 See Alberto Gonzales, "Decision Re Application of the Geneva Convention on Prisoners of War to the Conflict with al Qaeda and the Taliban" (January 25, 2002), reprinted in Karen J. Greenberg and Joshua L. Dratel, eds, *The Torture Papers: The Road to Abu Graib* (Cambridge: Cambridge University Press, 2005), p. 118.

37 Mary Ellen O'Connell, "Affirming the Ban on Coercive Interrogation," *Ohio State Law Journal* vol. 66 (forthcoming November 2005).

38 See Donald Rumsfeld, "Counter Resistance Techniques" (December 2, 2002), reprinted in Greenberg and Dratel, *Torture Papers*, p. 236. See also "Counter Resistance Techniques" (January 15, 2003), reprinted in Greenberg and Dratel, *Torture Papers*, p. 239; Tim Golden and Tom Van Natta Jr, "U.S. Said to Overstate Value of Guantanamo Detainees," *New York Times*, June 21, 2004, p. A5.

39 LTG Ricardo Sanchez, CJTF-7 Interrogation and Counter-Resistance Policy (September 14, 2003), available at the website of the American Civil Liberties Union, at http://action.aclu.org/torturefoia.

40 Douglas Jehl and David Johnston, "C.I.A. Expands Its Inquiry Into Interrogation Inquiry," *New York Times*, August 29, 2004, p. A10.

41 See FBI communications on unlawful interrogation techniques at Guantanamo Bay, available at the website of the American Civil Liberties Union, at http://action.aclu.org/torturefoia. See also Adam Zagorin and Michael Duffy, "Inside the Interrogation of Detainee 063," *Time*, June 20, 2005, p. 26.

42 *Convention Respecting the Laws and Customs of War on Land* (1907 Hague Convention IV) (October 18, 1907), Annex, Art. 43, 36 Stat. 2277, T.S. no. 539, 1 Bevans 631.

43 *Convention for the Protection of Cultural Property in the Event of an Armed Conflict* (1954), Art. 4(3), 249 U.N.T.S. 240.

44 Joel Brinkley, "Rumsfeld Defends Rebuilding of Iraq," *International Herald Tribune*, May 28, 2003, p. 5.

45 *Hague Convention* (1954), Art. 4(3).

46 Abram Chayes, *The Cuban Missile Crisis: International Crises and the Role of Law* (Oxford: Oxford University Press, 1974).

47 Jess Bravin, "U.S. Mishandled Prisoner Policy, Ex-Adviser Says," *Wall Street Journal*, April 5, 2005, available online at http://online.wsj.com.

48 Louis Henkin, *How Nations Behave,* 2nd edn (New York: Columbia University Press, 1979), p. 47.

49 Congressional Research Service, S. Rpt. 106-71, *Treaties and Other International Agreements: The Role of the United States Senate*, (2001), p. 39.

50 Detlev Vagts, "Hegemonic International Law," *American Journal of International Law* vol. 95 (2001), p. 843.

51 Ruth Wedgwood, "Combatants or Criminals? How Washington Should Handle Terrorists," *Foreign Affairs* (May–June 2004), available online at www.foreignaffairs.org/20040501faresponse83312/ruth-wedgwood-kenneth-roth/combatants-or-criminals-how-washington-should-handle-terrorists.html.

52 See also, Memorandum from William J. Haynes, II, General Counsel of the Department of Defense, Enemy Combatants, available online at www.cfr.org/publication.php?id= 5312; Compare Thomas Franck, "Criminals, Combatants, or What? An Examination of the Role of Law in Responding to the Threat of Terror," *American Journal of International Law* vol. 98 (2004), p. 686; Francisco Forrest Martin, "Using International Human Rights Law for Establishing a Unified Use of Force Rule in the Law of Armed Conflict," *Sasketachewan Law Review* vol. 64 (2001), p. 347.

53 Bolton was undersecretary of state for arms control and international security from 2001 to 2005.

54 Yoo was deputy assistant attorney general in the Office of Legal Counsel in the Department of Justice from 2001 to 2003.

55 Goldsmith was special counsel to the General Counsel of the Department of Defense from September 2002 through June 2003, and was assistant attorney general, Office of Legal Counsel, from October 2003 through July 2004.

56 Address by John Bolton to the Federalist Society, November 13, 2003.

57 John R. Bolton, "The Risks and Weaknesses of the International Criminal Court from America's Perspective," *Virginia Journal of International Law* vol. 41 (2000), pp. 186, 193. See also, John Bolton, "Is There Really 'Law' in International Affairs?" *Transnational Law & Contemporary Problems* vol. 10, no. 1 (Spring 2000) pp. 1-47; John Bolton, "The Global Prosecutors: Hunting War Criminals in the Name of Utopia," *Foreign Affairs* (January–February 1999), p. 157; John R. Bolton, "Clinton Meets 'International Law' in Kosovo," *Wall Street Journal*, April 5, 1999, p. A23.

58 See generally, Jack Goldsmith and Eric Posner, *The Limits of International Law* (New York: Oxford University Press, 2005).

59 John Yoo, Letter regarding the "views of our Office concerning the legality, under

international law, of interrogation methods to be used on captured al Qaeda operatives," reprinted in Greenberg and Dratel, *Torture Papers*, p. 218; "Working Group Report on Detainee Interrogations in the Global War on Terrorism: Assessment of Legal, Historical, Policy and Operational Consideration," reprinted in Greenberg and Dratel, *Torture Papers*, p. 286. (The "Torture Memo" is also known as the "Haynes Memorandum.")

60 Ibid.

61 Captain Jane Dalton remarks at the annual International Law Issues Conference at the Naval War College (June 24, 2005).

62 "U.S. Senate Judiciary Committee Holds a Hearing on the Nomination of Alberto Gonzales to be U.S. Attorney General," *Congressional Quarterly*, January 6, 2005 (FDCH Political Transcripts). See also Richard B. Bilder and Detlev F. Vagts, "Speaking Law to Power: Lawyers and Torture," *American Journal of International Law* vol. 98 (2004), p. 689.

63 Anthony Lewis, "Guantanamo's Long Shadow," *New York Times*, June 21, 2005; "China Slams U.S. Human Rights Report as Irresponsible," *Asian Political News*, April 4, 2005.

64 See the website of the Center for Constitutional Rights, at www.ccr-ny.org/v2/legal/september_11th/sept11article.asp?objid=1xiadjooqx&content=472.

65 Victor Simpson, "Arrest Warrants Ordered in Italy for 13 CIA Agents," *Columbus Dispatch*, June 25, 2005, p. A3.

66 For details of cases brought on behalf of torture victims against US officials and private contracting firms, see www.humanrightsfirst.org/us_law/etn/lawsuit/statements/lit-posner-030105.htm and www.ccr-ny.org/v2/reports/report.asp?objid=cbct36qkps&content=401. See also David Shucosky, "Russian Released from Guantanamo Sues US for Alleged Abuses," *Jurist*, June 28, 2005, available online at http://jurist.law.pit/edu/paperchase/2005/06/russian-released-from-guantanamo-sues.php; Danielle Knight, "Outsourcing a Real Nasty Job," *USNews.com*, May 23, 2005, p. 34

67 See James Thuo Gathii, "Torture, Extraterritoriality, Terrorism, and International Law," *Albany Law Review* vol. 67, no. 2 (December 2003), p. 335.

68 See, for example, "Treatment of Detainees Fuels Hatred of America," *The Republican*, June 15, 2005, p. A08. See also Organization for Security and Cooperation in Europe (OSCE), Report on Guantanamo, July 2005, available online at www.oscepa.org/admin/getbinary.asp?FileID=1066.

69 See Paul Watson and Halima Kazem, "Karzai to Seek Control Over Afghan Prisoners," *Philadelphia Inquirer*, May 21, 2005, p. A03.

70 See Dana Priest, "Iraq New Terror Breeding Ground," *Washington Post*, January 13, 2005, available online at www.truthout.org/docs_05/011505z.shtml.

71 Michael P. O'Connor and Celia M. Rumann, "Into the Fire: How to Avoid Getting Burned by the Same Mistakes Made Fighting Terrorism in Northern Ireland," *Cardozo Law Review* vol. 24, no. 4 (2003), pp. 1657, 1701–2.

72 "Declaration of Peter Bauer Filed in Support of Plaintiffs' Motion for Preliminary Injunction Against CACI International," para. 9, *Saleh* v. *Titan*, Case no. 04 CV 1143 R (NLS) (S.D. Cal. 2004). See also "Declaration of Marney Mason Filed in Support of Plaintiffs' Motion for Preliminary Injunction Against CACI International," available online at www.ccr-ny.org/v2/legal/september_11th/docs/CACI_Injunction0904.pdf. See also Jeremy Waldron, "Torture and Positive Law: Jurisprudence for the White House," available online at www.columbia.edu/cu/law/fed-soc/otherfiles/waldron.pdf, pp. 38–9, citing, in particular, Henry Shue, "Torture," *Philosophy and Public Affairs* vol. 7 (1978), p. 124.

73 O'Connor and Rumann, "Into the Fire," pp. 1657, 1683.

74 Christopher Greenwood, "War, Terrorism, and International Law," *Current Legal Problems* vol. 56 (February 2004), pp. 505, 529.
75 Ibid.
76 David E. Sanger, "Bush Declares Sacrifice in Iraq to Be 'Worth It,'" *New York Times*, June 29, 2005, p. A1.
77 John Tierney, "When Fear Stalks, Tune Out," *New York Times*, July 9, 2005, p. A29.
78 Phillippe Sands, *Lawless World: America and the Making and Breaking of Global Rules* (New York: Viking Books, 2005).
79 *The National Security Strategy of the United States* (September 2002), available online at www.whitehouse.gov/nsc/nss.html.
80 See Harold Hongju Koh, "The Case Against Military Commissions," *American Journal of International Law* vol. 96 (2002), p. 337.
81 Scott Shepard, "Rove Won't Apologize for Remark," *Atlanta Journal-Constitution*, June 24, 2005, p. C3.

7

PREEMPTION AND EXCEPTION

International law and the revolutionary power

Gerry Simpson and Nicholas J. Wheeler

Introduction

In a landmark speech to the US Military Academy at West Point on June 1, 2002, President George W. Bush declared that the United States could not rely on a strategy of deterrence for its security in a post-September 11 world. Instead, he asserted America's right to strike first in combating the peril posed by terrorist networks and "rogue states" armed with weapons of mass destruction (WMD).[1] No American government had ever advanced such a justification for the use of force, and it has profound implications for the existing international legal framework regulating the recourse to violence. The decision by the United States, in conjunction with its British and Australian allies, to overthrow the regime of Saddam Hussein in March 2003 has been viewed by many as the first test of the so-called Bush Doctrine. But in the eyes of the majority of states in international society, the new strategy poses a fundamental challenge to the principles underpinning the UN Charter.

This chapter takes as its concrete concern the immediate substantive question as to whether the Bush administration is seeking to create a new legal basis for the use of force that would be available to all states. Or alternatively, whether the new US policy attempts to carve out an amendment to the existing legal rules that only applies to America, or indeed, whether the United States is seeking to move outside the legal framework altogether by excepting itself from these rules. But some preliminary questions arise, too. And these go to the very heart of the inquiries pursued in this volume. We suggest that there are three matters that need to be addressed as a prelude to any consideration of the specific question of current US policy.

First, how should we study international politics? Or to put this question more pointedly, what is the benefit of studying preemption and the Iraq crisis from the vantage points provided by the disciplines of international relations (IR) and international law (IL)? What are "the theoretical and methodological habits" of the two disciplines?[2] What new habits, good and bad, might be picked up doing cross-disciplinary work?

Second, are we to approach this period in world politics as novel or unprecedented? Or does it simply reproduce relations found in previous eras? This question is of course significant, because it has implications for the initial methodological and theoretical question. New experience may require new thinking, but on the other hand, existing theoretical orientations or normative projects may be perfectly adequate if the underlying structures of international order have remained stable. In this chapter we suggest that while the United States may be a revolutionary power, its capacity to impose new political and juridical relations is limited.

Third, and finally, how are we to approach the question of sovereignty? Sovereignty, in its many guises, has insinuated itself into a position of centrality in the practice and study of the international order. A typical account of the two fields, and one that recalls our first methodological and theoretical concern, might suggest that IR and IL are two disciplines divided by differing conceptions of sovereignty, with at least some IR viewing sovereignty as essentially a prelegal phenomenon (capable of being constrained by legal norms but apt, at times, to bypass these norms), and IL conceiving of sovereignty as constituted by a framework of legal norms.[3] This distinction returns us to the substantive questions forming the core of our analysis here: Does the Bush administration's preemption doctrine seek to effect a transformation of current understandings of sovereignty either by curtailing the sovereign immunities of states subject to action under the doctrine or, more dramatically, by reconfiguring the application of international legal norms within a radically asymmetrical pattern of unequal sovereignty? Or does it seek to go even further by relying on the idea of a sovereignty which is external to the law altogether – an exception to the legal framework, induced by a state of emergency brought into existence by the sovereign itself.

This chapter, then, is about the Bush Doctrine and international society. It explains the doctrine as a consequence of the status of the United States as a revolutionary power, defined as one that cannot be reassured by existing multilateral structures. Given this overarching assumption, we frame the doctrine in terms of three key questions, concerning interdisciplinarity, novelty, and sovereignty, before going on to assess three possible understandings or conceptualizations of the doctrine (as "global lawmaking," "legalized hegemony," or "sovereign exceptionalism"). Ultimately, we argue that the resistance to the doctrine on the part of key constituencies in international society must lead to the conclusion that any attempt at global lawmaking has failed. This leaves two possibilities. Either the United States is attempting to bring into existence a new legal order in which asymmetrical norms arise in relation to the use of force in self-defense, or the United States believes itself to be a sovereign exempt from certain normative structures altogether (at least during certain self-defined moments of emergency). These initiatives, then, pose a serious challenge to IL assumptions about equal sovereignty, and they posit a world so transformed that the old structures must be superseded. And finally, they demand that we reconsider the relationship between two disciplines that have been in intermittent conversation for just over half a century: public international law and international relations.

The dual agenda revisited

We begin by considering the broader interdisciplinary questions of method and theory. Robert Jackson compared public international lawyers and scholars of IR in the following terms:

> Lawyers, as I understand them, seek knowledge of the rules that constitute particular legal orders and their validity. . . . The main point is to establish with as much certainty as possible what the law is in particular domains in order to give instruction to the legal student or practitioner . . . Political scientists are interested in rules not to determine their current legal status but to ascertain the extent to which they shape political life.[4]

This image of lawyering has been compounded by criticisms from outside and inside the discipline. Lawyers, it is said, are obsessed with case law to the detriment of a broader understanding of international politics.[5] Indeed, if there is a single methodological habit that appears to distinguish the two fields of IL and IR, it is the centrality accorded by lawyers to judicial decisions. So, the critics aver, in engaging with the debates around the Iraq war, lawyers are too inclined to consider legal precedents (e.g. the *Caroline*, justifying anticipatory self-defense) or judicial decisions (e.g. *Nicaragua*, distinguishing use of force from armed attack, and *Oil Platforms*, setting out standards of proportionality and necessity to be applied to force).[6] The self-image of IR, in contrast, is one of a discipline grounded in the real world of missiles, interests, choices, structures, and occasionally norms (broadly understood to include much more than mere "rules"). Associated with this is a tacit distinction between "ought" and "is": international law is perceived as normative (testing the Iraq intervention against preexisting legal standards) while IR is analytic (working out what Iraq tells us about the current direction of the international order). Or to put it yet another way, IL is backward-looking (how does this intervention measure up to what has come previously?) and IR has its eyes on the future (what does the intervention presage for the international system?).

This image, though, requires some complicating. It is true that international lawyers fetishize the jurisprudence of international courts – especially the International Court of Justice (ICJ) – but this is combined with awareness on the part of most international lawyers and diplomats of the Court's position on the margins of not just political but *legal* practice. Of course, there are "practicing" lawyers who appear at the ICJ and who probably do regard the Court as the central lawmaking institution in the system, but they are in a minority.[7] Indeed, what is little appreciated on the outside is that IL's constituent instruments themselves subordinate case law to other higher sources of law. Article 38 of the Statute of the International Court of Justice, regarded as an authoritative description of the sources of law, enjoins the ICJ itself to apply treaties, customary *practice*, and general principles of law first before applying other subsidiary sources such as academic writing and *judicial decisions*. Alongside this, there has been a long-running retreat from formal accounts of lawmaking to a more sociologically grounded approach to lawyering, whether this be Michael Reisman calling for an approach to legal analysis that takes in "incidents" rather than rules or Richard Falk demanding the study of cosmopolitan values or just about everyone decrying the state-based or textual approach to law.[8]

Meanwhile, IR has moved towards law from the other direction. The study of state interests remains central to the enterprise, but the last decade has witnessed a growing interest in how rules, norms, and principles condition the pursuit of interests. Moreover, with the development of constructivism in IR, the idea that interests are given and unchanging has been challenged by the claim that state identities and interests are constituted by norms, and that as these change in international society, new possibilities open up for action that were previously excluded. Scholars applying constructivist ideas empirically have shown how changing norms are pushing international society in a more solidarist direction, and a central aspect of this is recognition of the centrality and importance of international law.[9]

What is curious about the Iraq war is the way in which these trends diverged and converged. Some IR scholars concentrated their attention on legal institutions. After all, the UN Security Council was critical to the way the crisis played out, and the interpretation of its resolutions became a factor in the battle to assert legitimacy. Lawyers, meanwhile, began asking what the intervention might mean for both the international legal and the political order. There was a shift to pragmatism, and the old formalism of cases and rules was jettisoned in favor of a more responsive and flexible legal order.[10] But there were divergences too. Some lawyers escaped into formalism, or a return to rules. There were calls for the UN Charter to be interpreted strictly and without reference to a possibly transformed strategic environment; there were technical debates about how to interpret Security Council resolutions (were the rules of interpretation found in the Vienna Convention on the Law of Treaties relevant?); and there were arguments about proportionality and necessity, and the meaning to be attributed to the specific fact matrix in the *Caroline* case. And while this was occurring, there was a fresh bout of skepticism on the IR side about whether international law actually mattered at all. Realists seemed to have their intuitions confirmed in the Iraq crisis – the "coalition of the willing" had invaded Iraq without worrying too deeply about the illegality of its action. In this chapter we cannot hope adequately to pursue each of these threads, but we lay out what we see as the possible responses to law and intervention in Iraq.

The Bush Doctrine: responding to the new threat from the coupling of global terrorism and WMD

Since September 11, 2001, the United States has faced a situation in which, for all its awesome firepower, it remains vulnerable to attack by hidden terrorist networks possessing WMD.[11] Washington's nightmare scenario is that groups like Al-Qaida will acquire or develop these weapons, and the Bush Doctrine is the administration's response to this novel danger. In his speech at West Point, the president highlighted the limits of traditional deterrent strategies in meeting this new danger: "Deterrence – the promise of massive retaliation against nations – means nothing against shadowy terrorist networks with no nation or citizens to defend."[12] What is controversial, and deeply problematic, is the administration's claim that the only effective way to meet this challenge is to remove those governments – by diplomatic or military means – that are viewed as potential conduits of WMD to the terrorists.

Bush's identification of Iraq, Iran, and North Korea as specific sponsors of terrorism in his January 2002 State of the Union address would have been more persuasive if evidence of direct links between these states and Al-Qaida had been adduced. Rather, what motivated the administration was the conviction that such links either must exist – however covertly – given the "evil" nature of these regimes, or would develop in the future. Benjamin R. Barber captures the way in which the war on terror became focused on state actors against whom there was no direct evidence of culpability for the attacks against the United States on September 11. He writes that the new

> Doctrine is designed to apply to known terrorist perpetrators who have committed aggressive and destructive acts but whose location and origins remain uncertain; it has been applied however, to states whose location is known and identity obvious even though their connection to actual aggression is far less certain.[13]

Barber's contention overlooks how far the Bush administration has identified a specific threat emanating from those governments – armed with or developing WMD – that it has labeled "rogue states." Even without the link to global terrorism, Bush and his advisers believe that the very nature of these regimes poses a fundamental threat to both America's values and its security. Given the administration's prognosis that both rogue states and terrorist groups are beyond deterrence, the only effective strategy is to ensure that the danger posed by these entities does not materialize in the first place.

In his 2002 State of the Union address, Bush had warned that "I will not wait on events while dangers gather. I will not stand by as peril draws closer and closer. The United States of America will not permit the world's most dangerous regimes to threaten us with the world's most destructive weapons."[14] This commitment to taking the offensive against America's enemies was center-stage in the 2002 US national security strategy (NSS), made public in September of that year: "*To forestall or prevent* such hostile acts by our adversaries, the United States will, if necessary, act pre-emptively."[15] It is argued in the NSS that the existing legal right of self-defense rests "on the existence of an imminent threat – most often a visible mobilization of armies, navies, and air forces preparing to attack."[16] The strategy calls for a broadening of "the concept of imminent threat to the capabilities and objectives of today's adversaries."[17] The argument is that groups like Al-Qaida armed with WMD could kill millions of civilians from secret bases, and without warning. Given that the location of the rogue states is known, it might be thought that the administration would be prepared to rely on deterrence in meeting the threat they pose. However, the NSS considers that these states could also attack the United States covertly, employing the most destructive weapons known to humankind. The strategy document alleges that given the enormous costs of inaction in the face of such terrifying weapons, there is a "compelling" need to "take anticipatory action to defend ourselves, *even if uncertainty remains as to the time and place of the enemy's attack.*"[18] This formulation of the legal right to self-defense is very different from the restrictive criteria established by the *Caroline* case, and represents a new American policy of preventive war. The latter is one that is fought with a view to warding off a potential danger before it materializes into a specific intention to attack.

The logic of the Bush Doctrine is that it could justify actions taken anywhere, on a spectrum spanning the restrictive criteria of the *Caroline* case on the one hand, to full-blown preventive war on the other. It represents a fundamental assault on the principle of sovereignty, because through it the administration put others on notice that the United States reserved the right to intervene against those "regimes with a history of aggression [that] pursue weapons of mass destruction."[19] Two fundamental questions are raised by this analysis of the Bush Doctrine: First, is the administration seeking to establish a new right of anticipatory action that would, potentially, be available to all states? And second, who should decide when this doctrine is to be applied? Three possible responses to these questions have dominated the legal and political debate surrounding the Bush Doctrine. These responses have serious implications for the way we might choose to understand the relationship between IR and IL, and they raise important questions about the way we understand the meaning of sovereignty in the international legal order.

The first response is that the Bush administration is engaged in lawmaking within the bounds of the sovereign equality regime under international law. The second and especially the third response fundamentally challenge the existing regime of international law. The former views the Bush Doctrine as an example of legalized hegemony whereby the great power(s) brings into existence an asymmetrical constitutional or legal order in which it enjoys a series of immunities and privileges not exercisable by other states. The third response is that the United States sees itself as a "global sovereign" entitled to exempt itself from the ordinary legal rules.

Legitimating preventive war: unilateral and collective responses

The first reading of the Bush Doctrine views it as an exercise in international lawmaking. The United States is seeking agreement to a fundamentally different interpretation of the meaning of imminent threat that would permit a general right of anticipatory action against rogue states and terrorist groups developing or seeking WMD. To achieve such a far-reaching modification of the existing legal framework would require the support, or at least acquiescence, of the vast majority of states. As the World Court put it in its *Nicaragua* decision: "Reliance by a State on a novel right or an unprecedented exception to the principle might, if shared in principle by other states, tend towards a modification of customary international law."[20] Instead, with the exceptions of Israel, India, Australia, and Russia, most governments have rejected the arguments coming out of Washington for changing the law on self-defense.[21] The UK attorney-general, for example, stated in the House of Lords in April 2004 that preemptive self-defense had no place in international law.[22] States worry that giving others the discretion to use force when they judge that a threat is an imminent one fundamentally undermines the restraints against the use of force built into the UN Charter. One further adverse consequence of the United States being identified with a policy of preemption is that it significantly reduces its diplomatic leverage in counseling restraint in cases where governments are deliberating over the merits of launching an anticipatory attack.[23]

The case of India and Pakistan provides a very good illustration of the dangers here. India's belief that Pakistan is complicit in terrorist attacks against Indian forces in Kashmir might lead it to attack the bases of Islamic extremists inside Pakistan, leading to a war that has the potential to go nuclear. The worry is that in a future crisis between the two countries, such as erupted in 2001–2 over Kashmir, "a U.S. policy of preemption may provide hawks in India the added ammunition they need to justify a strike against Pakistan in the eyes of their fellow Indian decision-makers."[24] Anxieties about the dangers of legitimating a doctrine of preemptive/preventive war were widely expressed by governments in September 2003 at the 58th UN General Assembly. These concerns were eloquently expressed in Kofi Annan's own speech to the General Assembly when he registered his deep unease with a policy that "represents a fundamental challenge to the principles on which, however imperfectly, world peace and stability have rested for the last fifty eight years. . . . If it were to be adopted, it could set precedents that resulted in a proliferation of the unilateral and lawless use of force."[25]

Although the US-led invasion of Iraq is widely viewed as the first test of the Bush Doctrine, it is often overlooked that the United States did not principally rely on this justification in making the legal case for war.[26] It is true that, led by the president, key officials within the administration often invoked a self-defense rationale in justifying war. However, an explicit legal claim on these grounds was never formally employed to defend the action, with the United States relying, like the United Kingdom and Australia (its principal partners in the coalition), on the claim that the war was justified under existing Security Council resolutions.[27] The fact that the United States did not explicitly raise a new legal claim to justify the Iraq war undermines the contention that Washington was seeking to change the law, since, as noted above, any modification of the existing legal rules, or interpretations of those rules, depends upon states justifying their actions in these terms. This can be contrasted with the position of UK prime minister Tony Blair, who has been explicitly calling for the rejection of a Westphalian legacy shielding outlaw states (defined as those who both massively abuse human rights at home and develop WMD) from the threat or exercise of intervention.[28]

Opposition to the idea of changing the international lawbook to permit a unilateral right of preventive war was mixed with a growing realization that the UN system of collective security had to be capable of responding to the new threat posed by the coupling of global terrorism and WMD. In his 2003 speech to the General Assembly, Secretary-General Annan had invited the membership to empathize with the fears that make some states feel "uniquely vulnerable since it is those concerns that drive them to take unilateral action."[29] He did not mention the United States by name, but his message was clear: a key challenge facing the UN was to persuade Washington that the vulnerabilities driving the Bush Doctrine could be effectively addressed through collective action. To advance this goal, the Secretary-General set up a High-Level Panel (HLP) on "threats, challenges, and change." The remit of the 16-member panel, comprising former state leaders and diplomats, was to investigate the broad spectrum of threats and challenges facing the UN in the twenty-first century. The group's report, *A More Secure World: Our Shared Responsibility*, was delivered to Annan in December 2004.

The HLP's radical prescription for meeting the challenge of the Bush Doctrine, without succumbing to the ills of unilateralism, was for the Security Council to extend its Chapter VII powers to encompass the preventive use of force. But the UN panel was emphatic that such a legal right should not be exercisable by individual states. Mindful of the deep divisions in the Council over the legitimacy of using force preventively against Iraq, the panel made the following recommendation:

> If there are good arguments for preventive military action, with good evidence to support them, they should be put to the Security Council, which can authorize such action if it chooses to. If it does not so choose, there will be, by definition, time to pursue other strategies, including persuasion, negotiation, deterrence and containment – and to visit again the military option.
>
> For those impatient with such a response, the answer must be that, in a world full of perceived potential threats, the risk to the global order and

> the norm of non-intervention on which it continues to be based is simply too great for the legality of unilateral preventive action, as distinct from collectively endorsed action, to be accepted. Allowing one to so act is to allow all.[30]

To assist the Council in its deliberations, the panel proposed adopting the following five criteria of legitimacy in deciding whether to authorise the use of force: seriousness of threat, proper purpose, last resort, proportional means, and balance of consequences. These five guidelines closely mirror those set out in the 2001 report, *The Responsibility to Protect*, produced by the Canadian-sponsored International Commission on Intervention and State Sovereignty. But even if it proves possible to secure a consensus at the UN on these substantive criteria, which derive heavily from traditional just-war thinking, the HLP ignores the troubling issue of what should happen if the Council fails to agree that the criteria have been met in a particular case.

The HLP considers that if a consensus cannot be secured in the Council over whether to use force preventively, there is "time" to pursue other strategies, such as diplomacy and deterrence. This was certainly the view of most states on the Security Council when confronted with US and UK requests for authority to use force against Iraq in 2002–3. Led by France and Russia, the majority position in the Council was that Iraq's development of WMD did not constitute a threat that warranted forcible regime change. It was agreed that Iraq was in violation of a raft of Security Council resolutions demanding disarmament of its WMD that dated back to 1991. However, rather than employ the military instrument to neutralize this threat, most members looked to Hans Blix, and his team of UN weapons inspectors, to contain the danger. Under Resolution 1441, adopted unanimously on November 8, 2002, Blix was required to report back to the Council on whether Iraq was in "material breach" of said resolution, which had given Iraq "a final opportunity to comply" with its disarmament obligations under successive Council resolutions.[31] Had Blix in his reports to the Council on January 27, February 14, and March 7, 2003, found incontrovertible evidence of Iraq's development of WMD, this would have significantly changed the dynamics in the Council in favor of a new UN resolution authorizing the use of force. Instead, it was evident that had the United States and United Kingdom (and Spain and Bulgaria, which supported the Anglo-American position) tabled such a resolution, this would have failed to secure the necessary nine votes, leaving aside the issue as to whether France and Russia would have vetoed it. But the majority view in the Council that the diplomatic track had not been sufficiently tested ran up against the bedrock US position that this could not be relied upon to disarm Iraq effectively.

The Bush administration was convinced that the regime of Saddam Hussein clearly met its criteria for justifying preventive military action, namely a history of aggression, support for terrorism, and brutal treatment of its citizens. The logic of "regime profiling" of this kind is that there can be no lasting accommodation between the United States and regimes like Iraq's that seek to develop

WMD. Against this background, it becomes evident that, from Washington's perspective, the Security Council's commitment to disarming Iraq through the route of UN weapons inspectors was fatally flawed. The UN route relied on the premise that the United States could accept Saddam remaining in power, provided that his military ambitions were effectively halted. However, those guiding American policy believed that UN inspections offered no long-term guarantee against Iraq developing nuclear weapons. Blix might have highlighted in his reports the need for the Council to put in place a long-term system for verifying that Iraq was not developing WMD. But this aspiration could not overcome the deep-seated suspicion that members of the administration felt toward the UN as a guardian of US security in a post-September 11 world.[32] If this mind-set continues to guide policymaking in the second Bush administration, the prospects for achieving a consensus in the Security Council on how to handle future proliferation threats will be slim indeed. But if the Council is divided over using force in future cases of this kind, those unilateralists in Washington who are not reassured by UN talk of collective security will argue that the only route to US security lies in the exercise of American military preponderance.

America as the exceptional hegemon

The new administration had put the world on notice before the attacks on September 11, 2001, that it would privilege American values and interests over fidelity to the rules of multilateral bodies.[33] What changed after the attacks was the belief that America confronted a state of emergency that could only end when the threat from global terrorism had been finally eradicated. In his foreword to the NSS, Bush had declared that "the war against terrorists of global reach is a global enterprise of uncertain duration."[34] What defines this emergency is the administration's belief that the existing international legal framework is inadequate to meet the new threat, and the concomitant claim that the world should recognize the indispensable need for American power in meeting it.

This raises a question related to our second overarching theme of novelty. We reject the view professed by Washington that the current transformations are structurally unprecedented, and that America is a uniquely imperilled great power. Is the United States really more vulnerable today than it was during the Cold War, when Soviet missiles could have wiped out millions of Americans in less than 30 minutes? We also dismiss the proposition that great powers have never before attempted a usurpation of international legal authority, or that the extent of US power makes it a unique danger to international order. But what we do accept is that the Bush administration has been behaving like a "revolutionary power" in its response to September 11.[35] The defining feature of a revolutionary power, as Henry Kissinger argued in his classic *A World Restored*, is not that a state feels insecure – since this condition is endemic to a system of sovereign states – "*but that nothing can reassure it.*"[36] As a consequence, it seeks the will-o-the-wisp of absolute security, but this can only produce insecurity for all. Pierre Hassner has chillingly pointed out that since "there will always be some terrorists and some weapons of mass destruction . . . the only end in sight to such a [quest] would be total . . . control by the United States."[37] But the revolutionary aspirations of the American Republic run up against the constraining tendencies of the international legal order, and this tension can be seen in relation to the question of whether the United States should be granted exceptional rights or a form of extralegal sovereign exceptionalism.

The Bush administration has not expressly formulated a legal claim that it should be granted exceptional rights in relation to the use of force, but the administration looks to the rest of the world to recognize that the United States should be exempted from playing by the established rules. This raises a profound question for the relationship between IR and IL. By seeming to rewrite the rules of sovereignty, the United States challenges sacred concepts in international law. IR scholars have long accepted the asymmetries in power and capacity among states, and indeed the differences in rights and privileges exercisable by some states as a result.[38] By contrast, international lawyers have been committed to the preservation of sovereign equality. For lawyers, states possess equal rights and duties (they may have quite varying capacities in relation to enforcement of these rights and duties), and these are universalizable.[39] The Bush Doctrine, we suggest, presents a challenge to this vision of law. Not only does it expand the right of self-defense, but there is also an underlying implication that this right might itself be enjoyed asymmetrically. The outer parameters of the right to self-defense thus reconfigured become exercisable *as a matter of law* only by the United States (and perhaps its allies).

This idea of legalized hegemony (the exception in law) can be contrasted with the idea of a sovereignty that is *external* to law. This notion has been much explored in contemporary political and social theory.[40] Here is not the place to engage in great detail with this idea, but there is no doubt that arguments for the existence of extralegal justification need to be taken seriously by those who seek to understand US motivations. It may be that the United States, or elements within the Bush administration, seek not a change in the law (applicable to all) nor even an asymmetrical application of legal norms (and neither global law reform nor legalized hegemony has gained widespread acceptance by the international community) but instead, and more radically, the (re)establishment of a zone of sovereign decision (exercisable in states of emergency) somewhere beyond the law altogether. There are traces of this view in the powerful sovereign libertarianism of some neoconservative voices in Washington, and it is already present in the attempt to create spaces outside the sphere of international human rights law (Guantanamo Bay) and subject to exclusive executive emergency discretion.[41]

However, the more America tries to defend the Bush Doctrine by appealing to exceptionalist arguments, the more it will be robbed of international legitimacy. The architects of the NSS exhibit a curious naiveté about power in failing to understand that it cannot last unless it is grounded in a wider consensus about norms and values that goes beyond calculations of narrow military capabilities.[42] Intriguingly, the normally opposed schools of classical realism and liberal internationalism have made common cause in critiquing the administration for its dismissive attitude to international law and international institutions.[43] The US experience in Iraq has provided an important and salutary lesson in the high political costs that attend unilateral actions that lack international legitimacy. These costs have manifested themselves in a number of ways, but one of the most obvious is that the United States has found few partners prepared to bear the burden of the occupation in terms of treasure and lives. This has increased the costs of the operation for US taxpayers, and sapped the will of the American public for future adventurism of this kind.

The second Bush administration stands at a crossroads, and Iran is likely to be the test case of whether it has given up fantasies of legalized hegemony or "sovereign exceptionalism" and returned to international law.[44] At the time of writing, the United States is supporting the diplomatic efforts to secure Iran's compliance with its international obligations under the Nuclear Nonproliferation Treaty, led by the European Union troika of the United Kingdom, France, and Germany. Iran does not pose an imminent nuclear threat to the United States or its allies (including Israel). But there are voices within the administration who believe that given the domestic nature of the Iranian regime, it will, like Iraq, be able to subvert international monitoring of its nuclear ambitions, and rapidly move to a full-blown weapons capability. This neoconservative and radical nationalist grouping within the administration was not reassured by the multilateral route over Iraq, and it remains deeply suspicious that it can work in defanging Iran's capabilities. Moreover, it has let it be known that if Israel, which is fearful of a nuclear-armed Iran, does not take the law into its own hands by launching an "Osirak II," the United States might have to take such action itself.[45] America is too overstretched to even begin to contemplate regime change in Tehran, but air strikes against Iranian nuclear facilities remain a possible though risky option.

The political costs of a unilateral preventive strike would be considerable, and it is most likely that Washington would first seek Security Council approval for economic sanctions against Iran. But even if the Council would support this coercive step, how much time is the United States prepared to give sanctions in changing Iranian behavior? From the perspective of the hard-liners in the administration, delay only brings nearer the day when Iran becomes a fully fledged nuclear weapons state. But if Washington decides in the months and years ahead to use force against Iran, would this have the support of the Security Council? Or would the deep divisions that opened up between the permanent members over military action against Iraq once again produce paralysis in the Council? The UN's High-Level Panel report is aimed, crucially, at bringing Washington back into the UN fold, but this aspiration rests on the premise that the United

States can be reassured by the possibility of collective action under Chapter VII of the Charter. Unfortunately, what the report is silent on is what happens if there is disagreement in the Council over the preventive use of force. And if there is a lack of consensus in the Council on how to deal with Iran, the issue of war or peace will turn on whether the Bush administration believes that the dangers of a nuclear-armed Iran sufficiently outweigh the considerable political costs of being seen to abandon international law yet again.

Conclusion

In assessing the moral, legal, political, and strategic issues raised by the Bush Doctrine, it is important to bear in mind that it is open to three fundamentally different interpretations. On the one hand, the new US policy of "anticipatory action" can be conceived as an attempt to alter the UN Charter based rules governing the use of force. Such a legal change, if widely accepted in international society, would represent a radical shift in the legitimate bases for using force. The Charter was aimed at severely restricting the recourse to war on the part of individual states. The Bush Doctrine seeks to relax these restraints by issuing a general license for intervention in cases where a state judges that others are developing WMD that will pose a future threat to its very existence. It does not require the existence of an imminent threat to be triggered and it does not depend upon the authority of the Security Council.

The disagreement over Iraq turned on the question of whether it constituted such a threat to regional and global security so as to justify regime change in Baghdad. What worries the Bush administration after September 11, 2001, is not the 99 percent certainty that "rogue states" armed with WMD would be deterred from threatening US interests or aiding terrorists – but the 1 percent uncertainty that this might happen. It is the elimination of this type of risk that drives current US policy. Yet the United States will never be able to build an international consensus around this proposition, because it sanctions going to war against hypothetical dangers that have not yet materialized. The administration would reply that the costs of delaying action in such cases are too high to risk. But if other states were to employ the same logic, the principles of sovereignty and nonintervention upon which the existing international order rests would come crashing down.

Given that the administration is well aware of this, it must be laying claim to special rights that it wishes to deny to others. We have suggested two readings of this, both of which locate the Bush Doctrine in terms of American exceptionalism. Far from seeking to change the general rules on the use of force, America seeks to exempt itself from these (through one of the two forms of exceptionalism we have discussed), while simultaneously claiming a special right to intervene to protect itself from the dangers of global terrorism. In any one of these manifestations, it is evident that the Bush Doctrine represents (though to different degrees) an assault on the principles of the UN Charter. This is rooted in the related conviction that this is a novel situation, and that America, uniquely threatened after September 11, has a responsibility to use its position of military superiority to promote a world safe for democratic values (even where this requires other states to forfeit their sovereign rights). These developments, in turn, suggest two possible futures for the IR–IL conversation. In the first, after a decade or so of multilateralism, of institutional proliferation, of legalization, and of cross-disciplinary ardor, we might be looking at a freezing of relations. This is possible if IR scholarship seeks to locate Bush II in an already existing language of spheres of influence and sovereign exceptionalism (and hegemony) while lawyers resist acknowledgment of norms intended to be enjoyed and applied unequally and retreat into doctrinal purism or critique. In the second future, there is less hubris on both sides. International lawyers finally recognize the ways in which inequality and "the exception" are found in the very origins of their field, while IR scholars begin (and in some cases continue) to acknowledge the distinctiveness (not just another regime), power (not just material), and constituting power (circumscribing how we speak and understand) of law. Needless to say, we hope that this chapter will stimulate the latter research agenda.

Acknowledgments

This chapter draws on an earlier paper first presented by Wheeler as "The Bush Doctrine: The Responsibilities of Sovereignty or a Revolutionary Challenge to the Principles of International Order," SSRC Workshop on International Law and Terrorism, Washington, DC, November 14–15, 2002, and subsequently published as "The Bush Doctrine: American Exceptionalism in a Revolutionary Age," Asian Perspective vol. 27 no. 3 (2003), pp. 183–216. In putting together this article, we would like to thank Cian O'Driscoll and Alistair Finlan for their comments on earlier versions, and Peter Spiro for his helpful suggestions in how to develop the argument.

Notes

1 "Remarks by the President at the 2002 Graduation Exercise of the United States Military Academy" (June 1, 2002), available online at www.whitehouse.gov/news/releases/2002.../20020601-3.htm.
2 See project description at www.ssrc.org.
3 There are obvious exceptions to this, largely realist, account of the role of legal normativity.
4 Robert Jackson, *Quasi-States: Sovereignty, International Relations, and the Third World* (Cambridge: Cambridge University Press, 1990), p. 3.
5 Michael Reisman and Andrew R. Willard, eds, *International Incidents: The Law That Counts in World Politics* (Princeton: Princeton University Press, 1988).
6 *The Caroline Case* (1837), 29 Brit & For St Papers 1137; "Military and Paramilitary Activities In and Against Nicaragua" (*Nicaragua* v. *United States of America*), 1986 I.C.J. Reports 14 (June 27, 1986); "Oil Platforms" (*Islamic Republic of Iran* v. *United States of America*), 2003 I.C.J. Reports (November 6, 2003).

7 Thomas Franck, *Power of Legitimacy Among Nations* (Oxford: Oxford University Press 1990); Richard Falk, *Revitalising International Law* (Ames: Iowa State University Press, 1989); Robert McCorquodale, "An Inclusive International Legal System," *Leiden Journal of International Law* vol. 17, no. 3 (September 2004), pp. 477–504.
8 Reisman and Willard, *International Incidents.*
9 See, for example, Christian Reus-Smit, *The Politics of International Law* (Cambridge: Cambridge University Press, 2004); Martha Finnemore, *The Purpose of Intervention: Changing Purposes of the Use of Force* (Cornell: Cornell University Press, 2004); Nicholas J. Wheeler, *Saving Strangers: Humanitarian Intervention in International Society* (Oxford: Oxford University Press, 2000).
10 Abraham Sofaer, "On the Necessity of Preemption," *European Journal of International Law* vol. 14, no. 2 (2003), pp. 209–26. For a discussion, see Gerry Simpson, *Great Powers and Outlaw States* (New York: Cambridge University Press, 2004).
11 David Rieff, "Hope Is Not Enough," *Prospect*, October 2003, p. 32.
12 "Remarks by the President."
13 Benjamin R. Barber, *Fear's Empire: War, Terrorism, and Democracy* (New York: Norton, 2003), p. 105.
14 George W. Bush, "State of the Union Address," January 29, 2002, available online at www.whitehouse.gov/news/releases/2002/01/20020129-11.html.
15 "The National Security Strategy of the United States of America" (September 2002), available online at www.whitehouse.gov/nsc/nss.html. Emphasis added.
16 Ibid. Even *this* reading of the law on self-defense is not uncontroversial. It was used, for example, as a justification for the Israeli action in 1967, but international lawyers remained divided on the legality of such action. In recent years the balance has swung in favor of a restrictive form of anticipatory self-defense.
17 "National Security Strategy of the United States."
18 Ibid. Emphasis added.
19 Richard Haass, "Existing Rights, Evolving Responsibilities," remarks by Ambassador Haass to the School of Foreign Service and the Mortara Centre for International Studies, Georgetown University, Washington, DC, January 15, 2003.
20 "Military and Paramilitary Activities In and Against Nicaragua," para. 207.
21 Michael Byers, *War Law* (London: Atlantic Books, 2005).
22 Lord Goldsmith, "House of Lords Debate" (April 21, 2004), cols. 369–77, available online at www.publications.parliament.uk/pa/ld200304/ldhansrd/vo040421/text/40421-07.htm#40421-07_spmin0.
23 Michael E. O'Hanlon, Susan E. Rice, and James B. Steinberg, "The National Security Strategy and Preemption," Policy Brief 113 (Washington, DC: Brookings Institution, December 2002), p. 7.
24 Ibid.
25 Kofi A. Annan, "Speech to the General Assembly" (September 23, 2003), reprinted in *New York Times*, September 23, 2003.
26 Letter dated March 20, 2003, to the Security Council President from US Ambassador Negroponte, available online at www.un.int/usa/03iraqltr0320.htm.
27 Ibid. See also, for the UK position: "Iraq: Legal Basis for the Use of Force" (March 17, 2003), House of Commons Foreign Affairs Committee, *House of Lords Hansard,* written answers (March 17, 2003), col. wal, available online at www.fco.gov.uk; "Memorandum of Advice on the Use of Force Against Iraq" (March 18, 2003), provided by the Australian Attorney General's Department and the Department of Foreign Affairs and Trade.
28 "Speech by the Prime Minister" (March 4, 2003), available online at http://politics.guardian.co.uk/iraq/story/0,12956,1162991,00.html.
29 Annan, "Speech to the General Assembly."

30 "A More Secure World: Our Shared Responsibility," in United Nations, *Report of the Secretary-General's High-Level Panel on Threats, Challenges, and Change* (2004), p. 63.
31 UN Security Council, Resolution 1441 (November 8, 2002).
32 Lawrence F. Kaplan and William Kristol, *The War over Iraq: Saddam's Tyranny and America's Mission* (San Francisco: Encounter Books, 2003), pp. 91–4.
33 Condoleezza Rice, "Promoting the National Interest," *Foreign Affairs* vol. 79, no. 1 (January–February 2000), pp. 45-62.
34 "National Security Strategy of the United States."
35 David C. Hendrickson, "Toward Universal Empire: The Dangerous Quest for Absolute Security," *World Policy Journal* (Fall 2002), p. 9
36 Kissinger argues that "Only absolute security – the neutralization of the opponent – is considered a sufficient guarantee, and thus the desire of one power for absolute security means absolute insecurity for all the others." Henry Kissinger, *A World Restored: The Politics of Conservatism in a Revolutionary Era* (London: Victor Gollancz, 1977), p. 2.
37 Pierre Hassner, "Friendly Questions to America the Powerful," *National Interest* (Fall 2002), available online at www.inthenationalinterest.com/Articles/Vol1Issue13/Vol1Issue13Hassner.html.
38 Hedley Bull, *The Anarchical Society* (London: Macmillan, 1977), pp. 200–33.
39 We might contrast here the workings of an international legal order periodically receptive to legalized hegemony and the theorizing about that order by international lawyers in which these practices are obscured or elided. This tension is explored in much greater detail in Simpson, *Great Powers and Outlaw States.*
40 Giorgio Agamben, *State of Exception*, translated by Kevin Attell (Chicago: University of Chicago Press, 2005); Carl Schmitt, *The Concept of the Political*, translation, introduction, and notes by George Schwab (Chicago: University of Chicago Press, 1996).
41 See, incidentally, *Abbasi* v. *Secretary of State for Defence, Abbasi* v. *Secretary of State for Commonwealth and Foreign Affairs,* para. 64, available online at www.courtservice.gov.uk/judgmentsfiles/j1354/abassi_judgment.htm
42 An excellent criticism of the Bush Administration's understanding of power is developed in Christian Reus-Smit, *American Power and World Order* (Cambridge: Polity Press, 2004).
43 On the classical realist side, there is David Hendrickson's comment that "the more powerful the state, the more important that it submit to widely held norms and consensual methods." Hendrikson, "Towards Universal Empire," p. 4. Compare this to G. John Ikenberry's argument that "[u]nchecked U.S. power, shorn of legitimacy and disentangled from the postwar norms and institutions of the international order, will usher in a more hostile international system, making it far harder to achieve American interests." G. John Ikenberry, "America's Imperial Ambition," *Foreign Affairs* vol. 81, no. 5 (September–October 2002), p. 58.
44 Robert Tucker and David Hendrickson, "The Sources of American Legitimacy," *Foreign Affairs* vol. 83, no. 6 (November–December 2004), pp. 28–9.
45 Rowan Scarborough, "Israel Pushes U.S. on Iran Nuke Solution," *Washington Post,* February 21, 2005, available online at http://washingtontimes.com/national/20050221-123842-3048r.htm; Paul Harris and Jason Burke, "Flirting with Armageddon: Welcome to a New Arms Race," *Observer*, February 20, 2005.

8

COMMENTARY: CONVERGENCE OF INTERNATIONAL LAW AND INTERNATIONAL RELATIONS IN COMBATING INTERNATIONAL TERRORISM

The role of the United Nations

Curtis A. Ward

Introduction

Perhaps no event or series of events in modern history has done more to disturb the balance in the relationship between international law and international politics than the tragic events of September 11, 2001. However, the debate over the primacy of law in international relations should have long been settled. The advancement of peaceful relations and coexistence of states, which in practice is the essence of international relations, could not be sustained over any extended period of time without internationally recognized rules. As J. L. Brierly aptly noted, "international law is performing a useful and indeed a necessary function in international life enabling states to carry on their day-to-day intercourse along orderly and predictable lines."[1]

In this chapter I will discuss the role of the UN Security Council before and after September 11, 2001, in its efforts to create an international legal regime to address terrorism, from the vantage point of my personal engagement over the past six years in the efforts of the Security Council and its subsidiary organs. Responding to terrorism necessarily requires legal and political responses, yet as I discuss, both scholarly and policy responses have been flawed, due in large part to flawed international relations analysis that cannot adequately address nonstate actors and threats. I ascribe further failures of analysis and policy to the dominance of realist interpretations and prescriptions, which have led to a rejection of multilateralism and international law by (at least) one state. I would advocate approaches both scholarly and practical that, drawing on liberal institutionalism, emphasize multilateral responses and the central role of law in international politics. The moderate successes of the UN Security Council in responding to terrorism may offer some guidance, and I turn to them before considering some of the flawed responses to terrorism.

An increasingly active Council after the Cold War

The UN Security Council, emerging from decades of Cold War malaise, began in earnest to deal seriously with internal and international threats to peace, including terrorism. Prior to September 11, the Council had already significantly expanded its role in the maintenance of international peace and security generally. It charted a new course in its legislative and enforcement authority – in particular, responding to the atrocities flowing from conflicts, including intrastate conflicts, many of which were spawned during the Cold War and which exploded at its demise. The Council's new legislative activism was aimed at state and nonstate actors alike, including measures taken under Chapter VII of the UN Charter to impose targeted sanctions on parties to intrastate conflicts, and measures against terrorists and terrorist groups.[2]

The Council's response to the conflicts in the former Yugoslavia and Rwanda included the establishment of international criminal tribunals – the International Criminal Tribunal for Yugoslavia (ICTY)[3] and the International Criminal Tribunal for Rwanda (ICTR)[4] – each having jurisdiction over crimes defined by each respective statute. Creation of such international criminal tribunals would not have been possible during the Cold War, and was only made possible through a convergence of the prudent exercise of international relations between the permanent members of the Security Council within the prerogatives of UN Charter-based international law.

The Security Council and terrorism before September 11, 2001

The Council began to engage with the issue of terrorism seriously in 1999, primarily as a response to Osama bin Laden and Al-Qaida, and to the attacks on US embassies in Dar-es-Salaam, Tanzania, and in Nairobi, Kenya, in August 1998, which were ascribed to him. The Security Council adopted two antiterrorism resolutions in quick succession – Resolution 1267 on October 15, 1999,[5] and Resolution 1269 on October 19, 1999.[6] Resolution 1267 imposed an asset freeze on the Taliban for harboring bin Laden. The Council established a committee of its 15 member states to monitor implementation of the resolution. Because Resolution 1267 was adopted by the Council under Chapter VII of the UN Charter, it created mandatory legal obligations on states to enforce it.[7] Further resolutions were adopted under Chapter VII, before and after September 11, imposing further sanctions against the Taliban and bin Laden and individuals and groups associated with them.[8] Monitoring mechanisms were also established to ensure that these sanction measures were implemented by states.[9]

While many resolutions were designed to respond to a specific incident or to target particular individuals and groups, Resolution 1269 dealt with international terrorism in general by emphasizing the need of member states and the international community as a whole to intensify the fight against terrorism at the national and international levels. It called on all states to take appropriate steps, as set out in the resolution, including becoming parties to and implementing the 12 outstanding international conventions at the time that dealt with terrorism. Because Resolution 1269 was not adopted under Chapter VII of the Charter, it did not have the force of a legally binding obligation on states, and therefore was unenforceable. This action by the Council amounted to nothing more than a political act and was treated as such by most states. It would require the political will of states for its implementation. Such political will was not present at the time.

The Security Council and terrorism After September 11, 2001

As I have written in the past, the events of September 11, 2001, set in motion a new paradigm for the international community to combat international terrorism.[10] The world was largely unprepared; no state had sufficient legal and administrative capacity to deal with the terrorist phenomenon, although many acts had been designated as "terrorist." On September 11 there were 12 international and a number of regional antiterrorism conventions and protocols, none of which had achieved universal implementation.[11] Prior to September 11 only two countries had become parties to all 12 international conventions.[12]

The Security Council's response to the events of September 11 was unprecedented and signaled the emergence of a new dynamic. The level of cooperation among Council members in dealing with terrorism reached new and unprecedented levels,[13] and led to a series of actions. On September 12, 2001, just a day after the attacks, the Security Council unanimously adopted Resolution 1368,[14] which recognized the inherent right of states to act in individual or collective self-defense in accordance with Article 51 of the UN Charter and implicitly acknowledged that the terrorism of September 11 constituted an attack on the United States under the Charter. The resolution also denoted any act of international terrorism as a threat to international peace and security – a required determination in order for the Council to act under Chapter VII of the Charter.[15]

Resolution 1368 provided international legitimacy for potential military action against the perpetrators (and their supporters) of the attacks. In deference to the requirement of Article 51, the United States[16] and the United Kingdom,[17] as well as other coalition partners, provided the necessary notification to the President of the Security Council regarding intended responses to the threats, such that the military response taken by the United States and the supporting international coalition against the Taliban and Al-Qaida in Afghanistan would be authorized under international law by the Security Council.

Having expressed "its readiness to take all necessary steps to respond to the terrorist attacks of 11 September 2001, and to combat all forms of terrorism,"[18] the Security Council, acting under Chapter VII of the Charter, proceeded to adopt Resolution 1373 on September 28, 2001.[19] Unprecedented in the history of the Security Council, Resolution 1373 set out *mandatory* legal obligations for all states to create a legal framework in their national laws and institutions to combat terrorism, and established modalities for cooperation between states, including through mutual legal assistance, intelligence sharing, and tracing and freezing assets related to terrorists and terrorism. States were required to implement border-control measures to prevent the movement of terrorists, to deny them access to weapons, and to deny them safe haven. And very importantly, Resolution 1373 called on all states to become parties to the 12 international antiterrorism conventions and protocols and to implement them fully.

The resolution also established the Counter-Terrorism Committee (CTC)[20] to monitor implementation,[21] and in subsequent resolutions tasked the CTC to facilitate assistance[22] to states to build their counterterrorism capacity pursuant to the requirements of the resolution. States were required to report to the CTC on their actions undertaken to implement the resolution.[23]

The response of states to the requirements of Resolution 1373, like the resolution itself, has been unprecedented. A majority of the member states of the United Nations have now become parties to most of the 12 international antiterrorism conventions and protocols and have implemented the provisions of these legal instruments into their domestic laws, facilitating interstate cooperation in combating terrorism. Through this process, the international community as a whole has significantly strengthened its capacity to suppress and prevent acts of terrorism by nonstate actors, and to prevent state support – active and passive – for terrorists and terrorist groups.

The Council has also undertaken measures to prevent weapons of mass destruction and their precursors from reaching terrorists.[24] As well, other intergovernmental bodies are developing multilateral instruments to contain terrorist threats, such as the UN General Assembly, which on April 15, 2005, adopted the International Convention for the Suppression of Acts of Nuclear Terrorism.[25]

Our only realistic hope to defeat terrorism is through collective efforts – cooperation and collaboration through the framework of an international regime – grounded in multilateralism. The United Nations is leading the way in establishing an international legal framework to facilitate this process. These efforts have been spearheaded by the Security Council through the resolutions discussed above, and by state efforts to comply with them.[26] The Security Council is resolute in its determination to use all available measures to combat terrorism, and despite the widely publicized fallout from the invasion of Iraq by the United States and its coalition states without Security Council authorization, the level of cooperation on terrorism in the Council remains high. Given the patent successes of such multilateral approaches, unilateral policies such as those taken by the US and its allies in Iraq are ill advised.

Unilateral responses to terrorism and realist international relations theory

Despite the advances in responding to terrorism through concerted multilateralism, US unilateralism through actions such as the Iraq invasion threatens not only to undermine international law but also to undermine efforts to control terrorism. Such unauthorized action can be described as the "arrogance of power." Indeed, it has been described by Michael Scheuer, a former Central Intelligence Agency (CIA) officer – writing anonymously while still serving in the CIA – as "imperial hubris."[27] Pierre Schöri, a former ambassador of Sweden to the United Nations, characterized the war on Iraq as "a heavy blow to global governance and the principles of international law."[28] Schöri went on to suggest that such usurpation of power by the United States and its coalition states was "not a defeat for the UN but for the countries that sought Security Council declaration of war, failed, and then proceeded anyway" without being sanctioned by the United Nations.[29] So far the policy response has thus been disappointing, as terrorism shows no signs of abating and Iraq continues to suffer serious political violence and instability. The failure of a policy of unilateralism and preemptive war is in part underpinned by a flawed interpretation of global threats and appropriate responses, underpinned by realism.

An examination of successful and failed responses to terrorism illustrates both the central importance of law in maintaining political order, and the perils that may attend defiance of it. Yet the efficacy of law and multilateral cooperation are both soundly rejected by a realist perspective in international relations scholarship, and policy, as discussed elsewhere in this volume.[30] Such interpretations counsel the powerful to seek security above all else, through armed force where necessary, including through preemptive use of force. They in particular counsel the world's only remaining superpower that it may act unilaterally to protect its interests, and need not concern itself with law. Often these arguments suggest that law is an unnecessary impediment, ill designed to address contemporary threats such as terrorism. Further, law has no binding force: state sovereignty is the preeminent concern. Multilateral cooperation is not only ineffective but also risky – it may prevent a state from taking actions to protect its vital interests. It is now argued in certain quarters that the sole existing superpower has earned the right, through might, to ascribe unto itself the authority to police the world.

I argue the reverse. The absence of rules will inevitably lead to global anarchy. Centuries of practice in the relations of states have evolved into international norms – customary international law – which, particularly during the past hundred years, have seen significant strengthening and in many cases codification. A vast number of multilateral conventions and other international legal instruments covering myriad interstate relations and the behavior of states have evolved, adding to the international legal framework for the conduct of international relations.

Without the constraints of international behavioral norms, there is the possibility that a sole superpower could create its own rules, exempting itself from the constraints of clearly established international law – there is ample evidence to support this premise – and seek to impose its will on the rest of the world without any constraints on the use of its superior might. Such unrestrained exercise of power, no matter how well intentioned, would lead to global chaos and global anarchy, which is neither a desirable nor an acceptable option. The proponents of unipolar hegemony have great difficulty understanding this concept.

No country, no matter its moral authority and no matter the circumstances, can be expected to act unselfishly at all times on behalf of the world community if such action conflicts with its national interest. Action taken under this privileged authority would be unpredictable and have an uncertain result. An acceptance of American exceptionalism, therefore, without significant qualifications, would be to subscribe to the view that there is no need for international order except as determined and applied by the superpower of the day acting in its own national interest.

The responsibility for the maintenance of global order, however, is best left to a global community acting collectively within the framework of international law, in particular the UN Charter, and international conventions and treaties. The United Nations was established with a mandate given by all member states to the Security Council for the maintenance of international peace and security.[31] The authority of the Security Council to act on behalf of all member states of the United Nations is not in doubt.[32] It is enshrined in the UN Charter – a document having its genesis in international law and established practice in international relations. The responses to terrorism at their most successful, as outlined above, have relied upon the authority and legitimacy of the Security Council. Responses that have sidelined the Council, multilateralism, and international law, such as the invasion of Iraq, have had notable failings. The chapters in this volume clearly highlight the failings of policies grounded in "realism," but also more generally the failings of the discipline of international relations given its state-centric nature. A prime failing has been the inability to understand or deal with nonstate actors, of which terrorists are but one example.

Combating violent nonstate actors

Fiona Adamson rightly observes that "the problem of international terrorism presents a conceptual challenge to the discipline of international relations, which has traditionally been concerned with understanding conflict and cooperation among state actors, rather than the role that nonstate actors play in the international security environment."[33] Indeed, nonstate actors challenge the traditional modus operandi of states, in which state sovereignty is supreme and threats are expected to derive from other states, not from substate actors. Terrorism perpetrated by nonstate actors is a threat to international security, and requires thoughtful policy responses informed by the disciplines of both international law and international relations.

Yet much of the failed responses to terrorism have sought to ignore the nonstate-actor dimension of the threat, and tried to refocus attention on states as the source of the security threat. They try to cast nonstate actors as marginal to problems of international peace and security. They thus view violent nonstate actors as agents of states, or selectively ascribe to nonstate actors a "statelike" status. In this way they seek to insist that the fundamental actors in the international system are still states, and that nonstate actors, while they may engage in international or transnational activities, have not altered the fundamental structure of international politics.

The realists' misunderstanding of the nature and roles of nonstate actors such as terrorist groups results in inconsistent statements and actions. It results in the declaration that Iraq, Iran, and North Korea are the "Axis of Evil" and, at the same time, the declaration of war against an abstract phenomenon – terrorism. Furthermore, the attempt to treat nonstate actors as mere proxies for states is not supported empirically. The link between specific states and terrorism perpetrated by nonstate actors often cannot be proven. The relationship between the Taliban in Afghanistan and Osama bin Laden and Al-Qaida is a qualified exception. Focusing on so-called presumed state sponsors of terrorism and not on strengthening global measures against nonstate actors cannot be mutually exclusive, and pursuit of such a course in combating terrorism is tantamount to treading water. Thus it is perhaps not surprising that policy responses premised upon state-centrism have failed to address the real threats from nonstate actors.

And so too it is not surprising, then, that realists have difficulty understanding the new wave of terrorism – not just Al-Qaida-sponsored terrorism, but also terrorism carried out by homegrown movements comprising nonstate actors, generally viewed as domestic terrorism, that have morphed into a coalescing global network of terrorists in the post-September 11 period. Aided by globalization, what was conceived of as domestic terrorism now has widespread implications beyond the borders of the home state. Jamaah Islamiyah, an Indonesian Islamist terrorist group – a nonstate actor – that is often identified as being most closely linked to Al-Qaida, is a case in point.[34] Needless to say, terrorism has benefited from globalization – facilitated by the ease of global communication, travel, banking, and use of the Internet – and can only be dealt with effectively through global measures, including cooperation and collaboration among states within a multilateral legal framework.

Unquestionably, international politics is fundamentally affected by nonstate actors precisely because of the transnational nature and effect of their activities – whether transnational organized crime, drug trafficking, illicit arms trade, trafficking in persons, or terrorism. These problems cannot be resolved by any one state, no matter how powerful and fully resourced. In particular, a potential terrorist attack against any given country cannot be prevented by simply securing its border, if that were at all possible, or by sustained military response, whether in the form of preemptive strikes or otherwise – a militarized approach. The fact that there has not been a successful terrorist attack on US soil since September 11 is by no means an indication that the United States has successfully secured its borders or has successfully "taken the fight to the terrorists," wherever they may be found. Multilateral responses, and responses that take seriously the non-state nature of many contemporary threats, are clearly needed.

Compounded failings: unilateralism and nonstate actors

Because violent nonstate actors may be located almost anywhere, and responses cannot simply be military ones that single out an individual state or a group of states as "the enemy," multilateral responses are needed. Yet the response of the United States, driven by realism, has been unilateralism, which has only compounded the problem. The policy of preemption has resulted in a sustained militarized response to the events of September 11, 2001, extending well beyond the right to self-defense pursuant to Article 51 of the UN Charter.[35] However, after four years of pursuing this course of action, it should now be patently clear that a military response against nonstate actors with a global and fleeting presence has outlived its usefulness and was only viable as a short-term security measure. This course of action – a sustained militarized response – was the basic rationale for the invasion of Iraq and the continued prosecution of war there.

The diversion of attention away from Al-Qaida, a nonstate actor operating partially from Afghanistan, in order to invade Iraq, a state accused of supporting Al-Qaida and other terrorist groups, is a reflection of the prevailing influence of the so-called realists over American foreign and security policies.[36] The mistakes resulting from this course of action are now contributing significantly to America's vulnerability to potential acts of terrorism. According to former US senator Bob Graham, relating information provided by General Tommy Franks,[37] "in the time that America was fully committed to the war on terror, and not devoting resources, energy, or focus to Iraq, al-Qaeda was rendered harmless."[38] Senator Graham concluded that, "At best, the war in Iraq distracted from the war on terror. At worst, it set us back significantly."[39] I would argue that this illustrates the failings of relying upon realist interpretations and prescriptions.

Conclusion: the promise of liberal responses

Analyses and possible policy prescriptions derived from liberal theories in international relations have merit, and are much more in sync with the realities before and after September 11, 2001. In particular, liberal institutionalism's emphasis upon the importance of multilateral cooperation and institutions, and international law, in constraining state behavior, may provide useful guidance.

The emphasis on international organizations to which member states have a legal obligation, in particular the United Nations,[40] makes a lot of sense. Transnational problems require transnational solutions and modalities for cooperation – legal and operational measures that, prior to September 11, were lacking in all states, including the United States. In this regard, the response of the UN Security Council has been exceptional.

Success in defeating terrorism will only be possible if all countries demonstrate the political will to commit to the measures necessary to achieve the objective. It cannot be done without the full and unconditional support of the United States. The multilateral system must be strengthened, not weakened. The United Nations is a starting point; it is not necessarily the only solution in the sphere of global mechanisms. However, the UN must remain at the center of the process. There are already ideas about creating a new mechanism for coordinated action against terrorism. Whether such a supranational organization will operate within, or as a complement to, the United Nations will be the subject of intense debate.

In a world in which national democracy is vigorously promoted, we must also promote democracy at the multilateral level. Where there are weaknesses – and there are many – corrective measures must be taken to strengthen the multilateral organizations and institutions, including making them more representative, more democratic, and more effective in carrying out their assigned tasks. And by all means, the rule of law – international law – must be allowed to prevail.

Notes

1 J. L. Brierly, *The Law of Nations*, 6th edn, edited by Sir Humphrey Waldock (New York: Oxford University Press, 1963), p. 78.

2 Action by the Council under Chapter VII of the UN Charter creates mandatory obligations on states to implement measures taken pursuant to Articles 39, 41, and 42 to address any threat to peace and to maintain international peace and security.

3 ICTY, Resolution 827, UN Doc. S/RES/827 (May 25, 1993).

4 ICTR, Resolution 955, UN Doc. S/RES/955 (November 8, 1994).

5 UN Doc. S/RES/1267 (October 15, 1999). All Security Council resolutions are available online at www.un.org/documents/scres.htm.

6 UN Doc. S/RES/1269 (October 19, 1999).

7 Under Article 25: "The Members of the United Nations agree to accept and carry out the decisions of the Security Council in accordance with the present Charter." And under Article 49: "The Members of the United Nations shall join in affording mutual assistance in carrying out the measures decided upon by the Security Council." Also, Article 48(1) of the UN Charter states: "The action required to carry out the decisions of the Security Council for the maintenance of international peace and security shall be taken by all the Members of the United Nations or by some of them, as the Security Council may determine."

8 UN Security Council, Resolution 1333, UN Doc. S/RES/1333 (December 19, 2000); Resolution 1363, UN Doc. S/RES/1363 (July 30, 2001); Resolution 1390, UN Doc. S/RES/1390 (January 16, 2002); Resolution 1526, UN Doc. S/RES/1526 (January 30, 2004); Resolution 1617, UN Doc. S/RES/1617 (July 29, 2005).

9 Currently the Analytic Support and Sanctions Monitoring Team, established pursuant to Resolution 1526, UN Doc. S/RES/1526 (January 20, 2004) and tasked with reporting at certain intervals on the implementation of the sanctions and making recommendations to the 1267 Sanctions Committee (regarding Al-Qaida and the Taliban) for improving the effectiveness of the measures.

10 Curtis A. Ward, "Building Capacity to Combat International Terrorism: The Role of the United Nations Security Council," *Journal of Conflict & Security Law* vol. 8, no. 2 (October 2003), 289–305.
11 The 1st of the international antiterrorism conventions is the Convention on Offences and Certain Other Acts Committed on Board Aircraft (1963), and the 12th is the International Convention for the Suppression of the Financing of Terrorism (1999). For a full listing of the international and regional antiterrorism conventions, see Ward, "Building Capacity to Combat International Terrorism," nn. 4, 6, pp. 290, 291. Also, for full description of these conventions, see M. Cherif Bassiouni, *International Terrorism: Multilateral Conventions (1937–2001)* (Ardsley, NY: Transnational, 2001).
12 The two countries were Botswana and the United Kingdom.
13 The 15 members of the Council at the time were: Bangladesh, China, Colombia, France, Ireland, Jamaica, Mali, Mauritius, Norway, the Russian Federation, Singapore, Tunisia, Ukraine, the United Kingdom, and the United States.
14 UN Security Council, Resolution, 1368, UN Doc. S/RES/1368 (September 12, 2001).
15 *UN Charter,* Art. 39.
16 United Nations, *Letter from the Permanent Representative of the United States of America to the President of the Security Council*, UN Doc. S/2001/946 (October 7, 2001).
17 United Nations, *Letter from the Charge d'Affaires of the United Kingdom to the President of the Security Council*, UN Doc. S/2001/947 (October 7, 2001).
18 UN Security Council, Resolution 1368, para. 5.
19 UN Security Council, UN Doc. S/RES/1373 (September 28, 2001).
20 For a discussion on the role of the CTC, see Ward, "Building Capacity to Combat International Terrorism," pp. 297–305; Eric Rosand, "Security Council Resolution 1373 and the Counter-Terrorism Committee: The Cornerstone of the United Nations Contribution to the Fight Against Terrorism," in Cyrille Fijnaut, Jan Wouters, and Frederik Naert, eds, *Legal Instruments in the Fight Against International Terrorism: Transatlantic Dialogue* (Leiden: Brill Academic, 2004), pp. 603–31.
21 The CTC is organized pursuant to paragraph 6 of Resolution 1373.
22 UN Doc. S/RES/1377 (November 12, 2001); subsequent resolutions and statements of the President of the Security Council.
23 UN Security Council, Resolution 1373, UN Doc. S/RES/1373 (September 28, 2001), para. 6.
24 UN Security Council, Resolution 1540, UN Doc. S/RES/1540 (April 18, 2004).
25 UN General Assembly, Resolution A/RES/59/290 (April 15, 2005), adopting the International Convention for the Suppression of Acts of Nuclear Terrorism.
26 UN Security Council, Resolution 1390, UN Doc. S/RES/1390 (January 16, 2002); Resolution 1455, UN Doc. S/RES/1455 (January 17, 2003); Resolution 1526, UN Doc. S/RES/2004 (January 30, 2004); Resolution 1617, UN Doc. S/RES/1617 (July 29, 2005). Also, for a discussion of Security Council efforts to monitor implementation of sanctions against Al-Qaida and the Taliban, see Eric Rosand, "Current Developments: The Security Council's Efforts to Monitor the Implementation of Al Qaeda/Taliban Sanctions," *American Journal of International Law* vol. 98, no. 4 (October 2004), pp. 745–63.
27 Anonymous, *Imperial Hubris: Why the West Is Losing the War on Terror* (Dulles, VA: Brassey's, 2004).
28 Pierre Schöri, "Painful Partnership: The United States, the European Union, and Global Governance," *Global Governance* vol. 11, no. 3 (July–September 2005), p. 274.
29 Ibid.

30 Raffo *et al.*, "International Law and International Politics: Old Divides, New Developments," Chapter 1 in this volume.

31 Article 24(1) of the UN Charter reads: "In order to ensure prompt and effective action by the United Nations, its Members confer on the Security Council primary responsibility for the maintenance of international peace and security, and agree that in carrying out its duties under this responsibility the Security Council acts on their behalf."

32 *UN Charter*, Arts 25, 48(1), 49; see nn. 2, 7.

33 Adamson, "International Terrorism, Nonstate Actors, and the Logic of Transnational Mobilization: A Perspective from International Relations," Chapter 5 in this volume.

34 Jessica Stern, *Terror in the Name of God* (New York: HarperCollins, 2003), pp. 77–8, 253, 259, 277–8.

35 Article 51 of the UN Charter accords each member state the right to self-defense if attacked. It provides in part: "Nothing in the present Charter shall impair the inherent right of individual or collective self-defense if an armed attack occurs against a Member State of the United Nations." Preemptive measures are implied where justified by the certain existence of an imminent threat of an attack.

36 Senator Bob Graham with Jeff Nussbaum, *Intelligence Matters* (New York: Random House, 2004) pp. 125–7.

37 General Tommy Franks, at the time of the invasions of Afghanistan and Iraq, was the officer in charge of CENTCOM (US Central Command) headquarters at MacDill Air Base in Tampa, Florida.

38 Graham with Nussbaum, *Intelligence Matters*, p. 218.

39 Ibid.

40 See Article 2(5) of the UN Charter, which reads in part: "All Members shall give the United Nations every assistance in any action it takes in accordance with the present Charter."

Part III

INTERNALLY DISPLACED PEOPLE

9

THE GUIDING PRINCIPLES ON INTERNAL DISPLACEMENT AND THE DEVELOPMENT OF INTERNATIONAL NORMS

Francis M. Deng

Introduction

How do international norms develop? Do they really affect the behavior of states? Do different types or levels of norms affect behavior differently? Are there optimal strategies for growing norms that make a difference? The two disciplines that have examined these questions the most closely – international relations theory and law – have provided a multitude of theories and little unanimity. Yet answers to these questions are pressing human rights activists hoping to find ways to mold state behavior in favor of the victimized and downtrodden.

Just over ten years ago, as the newly appointed Special Representative of the UN Secretary-General on internally displaced persons (IDPs), I and my dedicated team of human rights experts and advocates faced the dilemma of how to respond most effectively to the spiraling global crisis of internal displacement. We recognized that persons forced to flee their homes for such reasons as armed conflict, situations of generalized violence, violations of human rights, or natural or human-made disasters, but who remained within the borders of their own countries – internally displaced persons, or IDPs as they became known – had particular assistance and protection needs that were not being met either by national authorities or by the international community. Our primary mechanism for addressing the problem was an attempt to create or invigorate (depending upon your point of view) a set of international norms in favor of the rights of IDPs based on existing human rights, humanitarian, and analogous refugee law. We deliberately chose to try to do so by means of a "soft law" instrument, derived by experts rather than directly by states. This endeavor eventually led to the formulation of the Guiding Principles on Internal Displacement in 1998. While it seems highly unlikely that the process can be reversed, the long-term success of the Guiding Principles as a normative instrument is not yet ensured.

Although now over five years old, the Guiding Principles are still a work in progress in terms of acceptance by states and visible effect on the ground. Still, we believe that we have seen measurable progress in both areas. At the same time, the standing of the Guiding Principles, the process by which they were developed, and their potential impact have not been without controversy. For these reasons, the Guiding Principles offer an interesting case study for examining the strength of the various theories about norms. At the same time, we as developers and promoters of what we hope will become norms, which, in turn, we hope will improve the lives of those threatened or affected by internal displacement, would still greatly benefit from any strategic pointers that theory can offer. In this chapter I examine both the theory behind, and our experience with, the Guiding Principles with these twin goals in mind.

The chapter tries to illuminate the theoretical debate about norms, norm building, and the impact of norms through the lens of the Guiding Principles. I begin with a discussion of the general conceptual issues and theoretical debates about norms, particularly those pertaining to rights. I next describe the process by which the Guiding Principles were developed, the reasoning behind our recourse to soft law, and the reception of these principles at the international, regional, and national levels. I conclude with some reflections on the current and potential impact of the Guiding Principles as a budding international normative framework, some general conclusions about norms that can be drawn from the development of these principles, and some observations about the accepted and applied progress achieved.

Conceptual issues

Definition and provenance of norms

There is broad consensus across the fields of international relations and legal studies that a "norm" represents a shared standard of behavior for a given set of actors.[1] Along these lines, norms have variously been described as "standard[s] of appropriate behavior,"[2] "collective expectations for the proper behavior of given actors,"[3] "shared (thus social) understandings of standards of behavior,"[4] and "prescriptions for action in situations of choice carrying a sense of obligation, a sense that they *ought* to be followed."[5] Some scholars also refer to the other vernacular understanding of the term "norm" as "average," "typical," or "common,"[6] asserting that norms refer not only to what ought to be done, but also to "actual patterns of behavior" that generate expectations regarding future behavior.[7] However, these two meanings are frequently at odds. As Ramesh Thakur points out, corruption is ubiquitous in many countries, but revulsion against corruption is unquestionably universal; thus, whereas corruption may be the "norm" in the sense that it is common, it is certainly not the "norm" in the sense of a socially approved standard of behavior.[8] Inconsistent behavior does not necessarily negate the existence of a norm.[9]

At the social level, norms spring from numerous sources, including religious, ethical, and cultural beliefs. Thomas Risse and Kathryn Sikkink assert that norms derive fundamentally from "principled ideas," which are "beliefs about right and wrong held by individuals."[10] Finnemore and Sikkink elaborate that an inherent moral element to all norms therefore exists, at least from the vantage point of those who espouse them.[11] In this sense, norms are necessarily distinct from "interests" or the economic concept of "rational choice."[12] At the level of international relations, however, the notion that norms are necessarily "moral" is contested. Regime theorists, for instance, posit that norms are merely collective rules meant to overcome difficulties in achieving cooperation in an anarchical environment.[13]

Norms may be embodied in laws, codes, guidelines, and other similar mechanisms. Conversely, the absence of a formal and legally binding requirement does not necessarily imply the absence of a norm. Finnemore and Sikkink point out the many explanations that the United States felt it needed to give for its use of landmines in South Korea, notwithstanding the fact that it is not a party to the Ottawa Landmine Treaty, indicating its recognition of an emerging norm against the use of such weapons.[14]

The function of norms

While the basic elements of norms are relatively uncontroversial, the question of how they function is at the heart of the battleground between various schools of thought within international relations and international legal theory.[15] Scholarly opinion in this area ranges from the conviction that norms are nothing more than window-dressing, to the assertion that they are as important as self-interest in guiding state behavior. Moreover, the extent to which norms guide the behavior of nonstate actors in the international arena has only recently come under the scrutiny of these fields of inquiry.

Modern international relations theory was born out of disappointment, in light of the devastation of the Holocaust and World War II, with the formerly ascendant Wilsonian worldview, which foresaw progressive perfectability of the social order through increasingly legalized relationships between states.[16] Reacting against this idealism, so-called realists such as Hans Morgenthau and E. H. Carr (as well as their more recent intellectual progeny, the so-called neorealists) argued that interaction between states could only be explained through their clash of interests, with power as the determining factor.[17] Accordingly, norms had no independent force to shape behavior, figuring in international discourse only as a means to cloak expressions of raw interests by the most powerful states.[18]

Other schools of thought have challenged this view. Liberal theorists, for example, such as Andrew Moravcsik and Anne-Marie Slaughter, see domestic politics as the determining factor of the international behavior of states.[19] States are controlled by individuals and private groups who act according to their own interests, but also to their own values. The position of a state on a given norm will be based on the ruling group's determination about the impact of the norm on its own internal political situation.[20] Human rights norms are more likely to be adopted and championed by liberal states, because they accord with domestic values. In particular, new democracies are likely to adopt human rights norms to shore up the legitimacy and power of a new ruling class.[21] By comparison, entrenched democracies will resist infringements on their autonomy, unless political advantage can be gained from supporting unenforceable norms.[22]

Proponents of rationalist or regime theory posit that states will act in compliance with international regimes, made up of collectively agreed rules, norms, and principles, even when it is contrary to their "myopic self-interests," in order to further their long-term interests in certainty, order, and maintaining their reputations with other states as dependable partners, as well as in facilitating collective action.[23] Human rights norms, however, unlike norms or regimes having to do with trade, military intervention, environment, or resource usage, have little inherent benefit for self-interested states.

Alternatively, constructivists such as Friedrich Kratochwil, Martha Finnemore, Kathryn Sikkink, and Hans Schmitz argue that norms have independent weight in international relations, and draw strength from their intrinsic quality of "appropriateness."[24] Most important, the acceptance of norms helps to shape the identity of states (and other actors) and therefore their behavior.[25] Nations want a reputation of principled behavior, which generates a "virtuous circle" that can establish more inclusive notions of identity, and alter state behavior.[26] There is a mutually constitutive relationship between states, international structure, and norms.[27]

There is a similar tension in the debate among international legal scholars and legal institutions about the function of norms. Early figures in international legal thought, such as Hugo Grotius, identified two bases for international law: consent of states, and "natural law" based on biblical prescription.[28] Thus, religious norms directly justified certain rules of law. Since the Renaissance, however, "natural law" had fallen out of favor, although it continued to play a role in international law and legal theory up to the late eighteenth century. Positivism assumed the dominant position in the nineteenth century as the principal basis for international law.[29] For positivists, the primary constitutive force of law is the consent of states to be bound by it.[30] Like the realists, they hold that the international scene is anarchical, at least in its natural state, where states are free to act in their own interests. However, states can and do create islands of order within the chaos through agreements with each other. This may be by way of express agreement (i.e. treaty), or through implied agreement (i.e. customary law). Whether the resulting rules derive from "norms" in the sense of ethically required standards of behavior, or from mere cooperative self-interest, is irrelevant for the legal analysis.[31] This view was widely shared by legal scholars and legal institutions alike.

The rise of human rights since World War II, however, has shaken assumptions concerning the primacy and form of consent. For example, it has been well established that binding custom is created by two elements: general state practice, and *opinio juris et necesitatis* – the belief by states that the practice is legally required.[32]

Traditionally, custom has been determined by an inductive process looking first for a pattern of state action over a substantial period of time and then seeking contemporary statements indicating the required *opinio juris*.[33] The Permanent Court of International Justice, for example, demonstrated this mode of analysis in reaching its judgment in the SS *Lotus* case.[34]

Scholars such as Oscar Schachter have subsequently recognized that "[w]hether human rights obligations have become customary law cannot readily be answered on the basis of the usual process of customary law formation."[35] The order of inquiry has therefore increasingly been reversed to a deductive process that first looks to general statements of rules and then seeks out instances of practice.[36] The International Court of Justice employed this "modern" type of inquiry in the "Paramilitary Activities in and Against Nicaragua" case.[37]

The former "traditional" method of analysis of custom favors description (i.e. what states are already doing) and is therefore more likely to accord to their consent than the latter method, which favors "normativity" (i.e. what states should be doing).[38] A number of scholars have suggested that the degree to which practice or *opinio juris* is favored should be determined according to a sliding scale based on the moral substance of the rule involved.[39]

An even greater blow to the centrality of consent is the phenomenon of *jus cogens* or "peremptory" norms, which has gained increasing acceptance.[40] The Vienna Convention on Treaties defines *jus cogens* as "a norm accepted and recognized by the international community of States as a whole as a norm from which no derogation is permitted and which can be modified only by a subsequent norm of general international law having the same character."[41] Any treaty provision contravening a *jus cogens* norm is void.[42] Thus, in contrast to treaties and general customary law,[43] a *jus cogens* or peremptory norm is deemed to be binding on all states, even those that object. Exactly which norms have attained the status of *jus cogens* is subject to dispute,[44] but the highly regarded treatise, "Restatement of the Foreign Relations Law of the United States," asserts that prohibitions on genocide, slavery, murder, disappearance, torture, arbitrary detention, and systematic racial discrimination all qualify.[45]

Academic legal theory has also accorded increasing importance to norms in its reflection on law. Feminist scholars have sought to demonstrate how supposedly neutral processes and rules are based on norms favoring men.[46] The "New Haven School" views international law as a means to create a "world public order of human dignity."[47] Even natural law has its modern representatives, such as Fernando Tesón, who insist that international law must be girded by principles of justice.[48] Thomas Franck posits that international law's power to compel springs mainly from perceptions of its legitimacy.[49] Although legal positivism retains many academic and practitioner adherents,[50] a more dynamic view of law is gaining momentum. Norms related to human dignity play an important role in world public order and more specifically, in the development of human rights law.[51] The development of customary international law has become a source of "transnational protection of human rights," humanitarianism in laws of war, and the doctrine of humanitarian intervention.[52] Indeed there seems to be a long-term trend toward "humanizing the other," which resonates with basic ideas of human dignity common to most cultures.[53] Finnemore and Sikkink see this as explaining why certain norms succeed at reaching a "tipping point" (a concept described below) and some do not.[54] A norm that has a strong moral backing even if it is not a legal norm can have an important impact on behavior. The absence of strong legal sanction will not hinder the effect of the norm, since it is driven by compelling values.[55] The moral forces of a norm will lead it to be prescriptive and thus affect behavior (norms are a cause rather than an effect).[56]

Assuming that norms do have an effect on the behavior of states and other actors, the next important question concerns how they develop. Realists, liberals, and regime theorists see norms primarily as instruments for the promotion of state interests and generally have little to say about norm creation. As a norms-based theory, however, constructivism provides an important model.

For constructivists, international norms develop through a process of "socialization."[57] Thomas Risse, Stephen Ropp, and Kathryn Sikkink identify three types of socialization: tactical adaptation in the face of pressure (e.g. from human rights activists), persuasion of state actors as to the moral imperative of the norm, and institutionalization and habituation.[58] Similarly, Finnemore and Sikkink describe a three-stage "life cycle" of norms.[59] The first stage, "norm emergence," is facilitated by "norm entrepreneurs" who focus attention on new norms by creatively "framing" them within political discourse.[60] The norm entrepreneurs make use of organizational platforms such as intergovernmental organizations and nongovernmental organizations (NGOs) to promote their new norms. If they are successful, states gradually begin to accept the norm. The second stage comes about when a "tipping point" is reached in the adoption of the norm, after which a "norms cascade" occurs, with numerous states rapidly adopting the norm, even without domestic pressure.[61] This happens through international socialization of target states by others that have accepted the norm. The third stage is internalization, the point at which norms have been accepted so widely as to be taken for granted and such that compliance with them becomes uncontroversial.[62] Harold Koh describes a similar concept, which he calls "transnational legal process."[63] States move from mere "compliance" (norm-conforming behavior imposed by outside pressure) to "obedience" (norm-conforming behavior based on internal value systems) through the work of networks of domestic "transnational actors" (individuals, NGOs, civil society, corporations, and government agents) in interaction with international actors (international NGOs and regional and international organizations).

"Acceptance" of a norm can take several different forms, including political, moral, and legal obligations. For legal scholars, a central question concerns whether a norm has reached the status of "law." With the caveats discussed above, treaties and customary law remain the backbone of international law, and the basics of how they may be formed are well established. However, there has been a rise in the use and status of "soft law." Although much discussed in legal literature,[64] there is no universally accepted definition of soft law.[65] One particularly useful and broad description of soft law holds that it

> range[s] from treaties, but which include only soft obligations . . . , to non-binding or voluntary resolutions and codes of conduct formulated and accepted by international and regional organizations . . . , to statements prepared by individuals in a non-governmental capacity, but which purport to lay down international principles.[66]

Thus soft law is something less than an entirely binding and enforceable rule and something more than mere political statement.[67]

The use of soft law instruments can facilitate and signal the emergence of a norm where states are not yet ready to bind themselves formally.[68] They may be an exploratory step toward the creation of "hard law" instruments[69] and may in some cases evolve into hard law themselves. The classic example of the latter case is the Universal Declaration of Human Rights, originally agreed to as a nonbinding set of principles, but now generally regarded as having passed (at least in part) into customary law.[70]

Even soft law instruments can intrude into hard law as interpretative guides for courts, arbitral tribunals, and other forums at the international and national levels when hard law is unclear.[71] Most important, they serve as tools of political persuasion and consensus building.[72] A potent example of the latter function is the 1975 Helsinki Final Act, which formed the Conference on Security and Cooperation in Europe (now known as the Organization for Security and Cooperation in Europe) and which was instrumental to promoting human rights in Europe and bringing an end to the Cold War.[73]

Of particular interest here is the last type of soft law instrument described above: instruments drafted by experts without state involvement or endorsement. Somewhat surprisingly, a number (although by no means all) of such instruments have achieved wide acceptance. Instruments such as the Johannesburg Principles on National Security, Freedom of Expression and Access to Information,[74] the Siracusa Principles on the Limitation and Derogation of Provisions in the International Covenant on Civil and Political Rights,[75] the Principles Relating to the Status and Functioning of National Institutions for Promotion of Human Rights ("Paris Principles"),[76] as well as the many draft declarations, conventions, and articles produced by the UN's International Law Commission, have been widely utilized by human rights advocates and states alike.

Compliance with norms

Once a norm is "accepted," the final and perhaps most important question concerns the extent to which the relevant actors comply with it. It is generally assumed that legalized norms (i.e. those codified in treaties or having become recognized as binding custom) are more likely to achieve compliance than others. However, this is not always the case, and theorists have therefore sought to identify other factors that may explain compliance or noncompliance with norms.

Compared with domestic legal systems, mechanisms on the international level for effective sanctions against law violators have traditionally been weak or nonexistent. Nevertheless, Louis Henkin has famously declared that "almost all nations observe almost all principles of international law and almost all of their obligations almost all of the time."[77] Abram Chayes and Antonia Chayes point out that it is effectively impossible empirically to prove or disprove Henkin's maxim,[78] although Edith Weiss observes that states neither fully comply with all obligations nor ignore them entirely.[79] With certain challengers, Henkin's assumption is widely shared among legal scholars, less so among political scientists.[80]

There is growing anecdotal evidence that the formal acceptance of a norm does not necessarily guarantee better compliance with it. Daniel Thomas's study of the Helsinki Final Act concludes that "a state's formal acceptance of human rights norms does not necessarily guarantee significant changes in its behavior, much less in its identity and interests."[81] A 1999 study found that there was no significant statistical correlation between the increase in ratifications of the International Covenant on Civil and Political Rights and state behavior on the ground as measured by the "Political Terror Scale."[82] At the same time, a number of studies indicate that compliance with certain soft law instruments is quite high.[83] In this vein, Gunther Handl has noted the growing "discrepancy between formal status and legal significance" of normative instruments. [84]

A number of potential factors other than legal status have been suggested as possible reasons for the success of some norms, and the failure of others, to obtain compliance: the power (realists), identity (liberals), and numbers (constructivists) of existing adherents to a norm; the simplicity of the norm; the "fit" or "concordance" of the norm with a particular state's domestic situation and with other existing norms; the perceived legitimacy of the norm itself and the process by which it was developed; the durability; and the availability of monitoring mechanisms.[85] Moreover, different environments may produce different results. Thus, Ramesh Thakur argues that norms are more effective as social mores than as laws at the local and regional level, that laws are more effective at the national level, and that both are important at the international level.[86] The truth of all these hypotheses has yet to be demonstrated empirically. It is therefore useful to turn to our case study to see to what extent they are descriptive of our experience "on the ground."

Development of the Guiding Principles on Internal Displacement

Genesis of the Guiding Principles

Internally displaced persons, as we have functionally defined them, are

> persons or groups of persons who have been forced or obliged to flee or to leave their homes or places of habitual residence in particular as a result of, or to avoid the effects of, armed conflict, situations of generalized violence, violations of human rights, or natural or human-made disasters and who have not crossed an internationally-recognized State border.[87]

Although everyone living through the sorts of crises described in this definition is profoundly affected, persons uprooted from their homes are especially vulnerable to physical attack, sexual assault, abduction, disease, and deprivation of shelter, food, and health services.[88] Even in war settings, displaced persons suffer significantly higher rates of mortality than does the general population; in Somalia in 1992, for example, the rate was 50 times greater.[89]

For persons who cross state borders, international attention, assistance, and protection are available through the international refugee regime, codified in the 1951 Convention Relating to the Status of Refugees and its 1967 protocol (in addition to important regional instruments), and institutionalized in the United Nations High Commissioner for Refugees, an agency with an annual budget of over $1 billion.[90] As of the end of the twentieth century, however, there was no international legal or institutional regime dedicated to persons in the same circumstances who did not or could not cross state borders, leaving them at the mercy of states that frequently could not or would not provide them with assistance and protection.

The plight of the internally displaced emerged into international consciousness in the late 1980s and early 1990s, for reasons connected to the end of the Cold War. Foremost among these was the steady rise in their number associated with the increase in internal conflict associated with the post-Cold War period. When they were counted for the first time in 1982, it was estimated that there were 1.2 million internally displaced persons.[91] By 1992 the number had increased by a factor of 20, to 24 million.[92] At the same time, as superpower rivalry came to an end, Western governments' geopolitical advantage in accepting refugees was extinguished and their willingness to do so began to wane.[93] This led to a desire to find ways to protect and assist displaced persons in their own countries and discourage them from seeking asylum abroad.[94] The end of the Cold War also marked a shift in the international attitude toward intervention in domestic affairs, particularly where states caused or failed to react to massive humanitarian crises within their own borders.[95]

As a result, the late 1980s saw the stirrings of an international response to internal displacement. The issue of the reintegration of internally displaced persons figured prominently in two major international conferences at the end of the decade: the 1988 Conference on the Plight of Refugees, Returnees, and Displaced Persons in Southern Africa, and the 1989 International Conference on Central American Refugees.[96] Likewise, in 1989, the UN General Assembly called upon the Secretary-General to consider mechanisms for coordination of relief programs for internally displaced persons.[97] In 1990 the UN Economic and Social Council requested the Secretary-General to initiate a systemwide review of UN entities with regard to relief and protection of refugees and internally displaced persons.[98]

Importantly, however, "the major impetus behind international recognition of the problem of internal displacement lay with a group of NGOs, mobilized as a result of problems encountered in gaining access in the field to large numbers of 'internal refugees' who were in need of assistance and protection."[99] Simon Bagshaw describes the "global policy network" that coalesced around the issue of internal displacement in the early 1990s, where a few individuals associated with these NGOs, including Martin MacPherson of the Friends World Committee for Consultation (Quakers), Beth Ferris of the World Council of Churches, and Roberta Cohen of the Refugee Policy Group, set in motion a process that eventually resulted in the United Nations becoming actively seized of the issue of internal displacement.[100]

In 1990 these activists convened a meeting of diplomats and representatives of intergovernmental and nongovernmental organizations in Washington to discuss the issue, but found the response too cautious.[101] After considering and rejecting various avenues within the UN, they decided to approach the Commission on Human Rights, as the forum most accessible to NGOs. MacPherson drafted a statement on the issue on behalf of the Commission of Churches on International Affairs and the Friends World Committee for Consultation (Quakers) for submission to the Commission on Human Rights in 1991.[102] He then raised the issue at a meeting of diplomats and NGOs during the Commission on Human Rights and won the support of the Austrian delegate; Austria subsequently introduced a draft resolution on internally displaced persons based on MacPherson's statement. [103]

The 1991 resolution called upon the Secretary-General to prepare "an analytic report on internally displaced persons."[104] The resulting report of the Secretary-General concluded that there was "no clear statement of the human rights of internally displaced persons, or those at risk of becoming displaced" and recommended the elaboration of guidelines that would clarify "the implications of existing human rights law for persons who are internally displaced and fashioning from existing standards one comprehensive, universally applicable body of principles which addressed the main needs and problems of such persons,"[105] and recommended the creation of a "focal point within the human rights system" to facilitate the coordination of the UN response to internal displacement.[106]

In response to the report (and with the substantial involvement of MacPherson and Cohen), Austria introduced another draft resolution calling for a comprehensive study "identifying existing laws and mechanisms for the protection of internally displaced persons, possible additional measures to strengthen implementation of these laws and mechanisms and alternatives for addressing protection needs not adequately covered by existing instruments."[107] The establishment of a focal point was also an important goal of the resolution. Various parties had recommended mechanisms ranging from a working group to a "world court" on the rights of the internally displaced.[108] However, many states feared such an option would encroach on their sovereignty. The initial draft of the resolution asked for the designation of an "independent expert," but in response to India's preference that the mandate remain with the Secretary-General, the final version of the resolution was changed to call upon the Secretary-General to "designate a representative" to seek the views of governments, United Nations agencies, regional and nongovernmental organizations, and experts to perform the requested task.[109] In July 1992 the Secretary-General designated the author of this chapter as his representative.

Development of a normative framework

The foundation of the Guiding Principles is the norm of sovereignty as responsibility. Soon after my appointment as Special Representative of the UN Secretary-General on IDPs, I circulated a questionnaire and engaged in extensive consultations with states and other interested parties, both within and outside the UN framework, eliciting in particular the assistance of legal scholars at Harvard and Yale to assist in identifying existing legal rights. My so-called comprehensive study was presented to the Commission on Human Rights in 1993.[110] The study concluded that, with the exception of some important gaps, existing international law provided wide coverage for the protection needs of internally displaced persons.[111] The principal problem lay in the lack of implementation.

The study noted that a new legal instrument specifically addressing the needs of internally displaced persons might bridge the gaps in the existing normative framework and encourage greater compliance. However, the urgent need for international guidance required the development in a "transitional phase" of an initial, nonbinding set of principles to "focus international attention, raise the level of awareness and stimulate practical measures for alleviating the crisis." A process involving three steps was envisaged for the transitional phase: a compilation of existing law, the drafting of "guiding principles" as an informal code of conduct, and finally an authoritative legal document, perhaps in the form of a declaration. I suggested, however, that given the pressing demands of time, those steps might be pursued simultaneously.

The Commission on Human Rights adopted a resolution specifically "noting" my recommendations for the compilation of existing legal norms and developing guiding principles, "tak[ing] note with appreciation" of my study generally "and of the useful suggestions and recommendations contained therein" and calling upon the Secretary-General to extend my mandate for two years.[112] I then convened a series of meetings in collaboration with the American Society of International Law and the Human Rights Law Group in Washington, under the auspices of the Brookings Institution and in collaboration with international legal experts, to assist in the compilation of existing law and to develop guiding principles. Professor Robert Goldman of the American University Law School became a critical legal partner. The team was soon joined by Manfred Nowak of the Boltsman Institute in Vienna. Goldman and Nowak oversaw the work of researchers in their respective institutions toward the completed standards in human rights law, humanitarian law, and analogous refugee law pertinent to the needs of the internally displaced. The task of bridging the gaps between the differing approaches of the two teams was accomplished largely through the genius of Walter Kälin of the University of Berlin.

Out of this process emerged two complementary parts, what became known as the "Compilation" and the "Analysis." The first examined international law applicable to persons who had already been displaced and was presented to the Commission on Human Rights in 1996.[113] The second focused on protections against displacement in the first instance and was presented in 1998.[114] Both studies concluded, as with the 1992 report, that existing law theoretically provided wide coverage of the protection needs of the internally displaced, but that gray areas and gaps existed that needed to be remedied. Moreover, the existing standards were dispersed in a number of different instruments without specific focus on the internally displaced.

In response to the first part of the Compilation, the Commission on Human Rights adopted a resolution in 1996 directing me to "continue, on the basis of [the] compilation and analysis of legal norms, to develop an appropriate framework in this regard for the protection of internally displaced persons."[115] There was a subtle resistance to the development of a legally binding instrument. In the informal consultations, the term "normative framework" was suggested, but some states objected that it implied "legal." The formulation of an "appropriate framework" was therefore considered less controversial, although what was meant was a legal framework.

While the second part of the study was under way, we began to work on an "appropriate framework" without regard to its eventual status as a declaration, a convention, a code of conduct, or a set of guidelines. Once again, we engaged in extensive consultations, now consistently chaired by Walter Kälin, with representatives of various UN agencies, NGOs, and other interested actors, in particular through a series of consultative meetings that not only brought in the substantive input of the various parties, but also encouraged their commitment to the success and acceptance of the eventual product.[116] Of particular importance was reaching out to, and addressing the concerns of, the International Committee of the Red Cross (ICRC), which had warned about the possibility that new guidelines might weaken the standing and application of existing humanitarian law. The participation of the ICRC in the process became one of the most significant elements in the development of the Guiding Principles.[117]

As we were finalizing "the appropriate" framework in a final meeting of the expert team, we decided by spontaneous consensus that, although in my 1992 report I had raised the possibility of seeking a declaration or even a legal instrument, we should instead concentrate on presenting the framework as a set of nonbinding principles. In doing so, we were guided in part by the concerns of the ICRC about the negative potential of "reopening the door" on already accepted rights, thereby undermining them, and also by the desire to avoid the delay inherent in state negotiations on such a potentially contentious issue.[118]

The resulting Guiding Principles on Internal Displacement[119] restate, interpret, and apply standards from human rights, humanitarian, and analogous refugee law. They are divided into four sections, addressing protection against displacement, protection and assistance during displacement, access to humanitarian assistance, and return, resettlement, and reintegration. By their terms, the Guiding Principles apply not only to states, but also to "all other authorities, groups and persons in their relations with internally displaced persons,"[120] including nonstate actors, intergovernmental and nongovernmental organizations, and internally displaced persons themselves. Underlying the Guiding Principles is the fundamental notion that the primary responsibility for ensuring the protection and assistance of internally displaced persons resides with states as an aspect of their sovereignty. Should they fail to discharge their responsibility, however, either for lack of capacity or for lack of will, the international community has a role to play.

The draft principles were finalized at an expert consultation hosted by the government of Austria in January 1998 and attended by representatives of the UN agencies, nongovernmental organizations, and regional organizations. Following the consultation, we held a strategic meeting with our core team to discuss how to approach the Commission on Human Rights. Our agreement was that we should not seek formal adoption by the commission, which was bound to be controversial, but should instead have the commission take note of the Guiding Principles. The Austrian draft resolution for the Commission on Human Rights did just that.

Reception and application of the Guiding Principles

Soon after they were finalized and before they were even presented to the Commission on Human Rights, I shared the Guiding Principles with the United Nations Inter-Agency Standing Committee (IASC), a forum created in 1991 to enhance coordination among agencies. The IASC at its March 1998 meeting welcomed the Guiding Principles and encouraged its members to share them with their executive boards and their staff, especially those in the field, and to apply them in their activities on behalf of internally displaced persons.

The momentum of the IASC decision provided important support for the reception of the Guiding Principles at the Commission on Human Rights several weeks later, when, despite years of reports and resolutions encouraging the development of an "appropriate" normative framework, consultations by the Austrians indicated that a number of states were still fearful about the potential impact on their sovereignty. In the end, however, only the representative of Mexico expressed reservations on the manner in which the Guiding Principles had been developed, but even he voted for the resolution, which took note of the principles and my intention to use them in my dialogues with governments and intergovernmental and nongovernmental organizations and the prior decision of the IASC to make use of them.[121]

In the years following the initial presentation of the Guiding Principles, both the Commission on Human Rights and the General Assembly have adopted resolutions encouraging and welcoming their dissemination, promotion, and application, welcoming my use of them in dialogues with the relevant parties, and requesting that I continue my efforts in this regard.[122] In April 2003, the commission recognized the Guiding Principles as "an important tool" and noted their increasing use "as a standard" by states, United Nations agencies, and regional and nongovernmental organizations.[123] Their use has been recognized in other international forums as well, including the Durban Declaration and Programme of Action, adopted in September 2001 by the World Conference Against Racism, Racial Discrimination, Xenophobia, and Related Intolerance, and in presidential statements of the UN Security Council.[124]

My office has also collaborated with regional bodies, cosponsoring seminars, conferences, and studies with the Organization of African Unity (now transformed into the African Union), the Economic Community of West African States, the Organization of American States, the Organization for Security and Cooperation in Europe, and the Council of Europe.[125] Several of these organizations have issued statements and declarations in support of the Guiding Principles and have begun integrating them into their work. More recently, we have been working with the Inter-Governmental Authority on Development, the Commonwealth, and the Southern Africa Development Community to the same end.

Most important, the Guiding Principles are seeing increasing acceptance and use at the national and local levels, where they are most needed. In 2000, Angola became the first state to enact legislation expressly based on the Guiding Principles, in its "Norms on Resettlement." The government of Uganda has drafted similar legislation. In 2001 the government of Burundi signed its "Protocol for the Creation of a Permanent Framework of Cooperation for the Protection of Displaced Persons," to be undertaken with humanitarian organizations operating in the country, and noting in its preamble that the government considered itself to be bound by the principles.[126] In Colombia the Constitutional Court has cited the Guiding Principles in two judgments,[127] which were bolstered by a presidential directive issued in 2001.[128] The government of Afghanistan is currently preparing a decree on the return of the internally displaced using the Guiding Principles as reference.

Of equal importance are the acknowledgment and use of the Guiding Principles by nonstate actors. During my mission to Georgia in 2000, the de facto Abkhaz authorities acknowledged the importance of the Guiding Principles and called for them to be translated into their language. In Sudan, with the prompting of several workshops conducted serially by the Office for the Coordination of Humanitarian Affairs IDP Unit and my office, representatives of the then-insurgent Sudan People's Liberation Movement/Army have drafted a formal policy on internal displacement, although it has not yet been endorsed by the top leadership.

NGOs, civil society institutions, and internally displaced persons themselves are making increasing reference to the Guiding Principles in their advocacy with states and nonstate actors to promote the rights of the internally displaced. For example, in Sri Lanka, the Consortium of Humanitarian Agencies, a group of more than 50 NGOs, has been conducting an outreach program based on the Guiding Principles for government officials, nonstate actors, international organizations, international and national NGOs, and displaced communities. As part of these efforts, the consortium has published a "toolkit" on the Guiding Principles in English, Sinhalese, and Tamil, as well as a variety of other training materials for use in ongoing workshops and roundtables. Similar efforts are under way in other countries around the world – for instance, in Colombia by the Grupo de Apoyo a Organizaciones de Desplazados, in Georgia by the Georgian Young Lawyers Association, and in the Philippines by the Ecumenical Commission for Displaced Families and Communities. Groups such as the Georgian Young Lawyers Association and the Colombian Council of Jurists have also used the Guiding Principles as a means of measuring the compliance of existing national law with international standards.[129]

The Guiding Principles have now been translated into 32 languages and have been widely disseminated by United Nations agencies, my office, NGOs, and governments. A number of secondary materials explaining the Guiding Principles and suggesting means to implement them have also been developed. A number of partners are working to foster understanding and use of the Guiding Principles, most notably the Global IDP Project of the Norwegian Refugee Council and the IDP Unit of the Office for the Coordination of Humanitarian Affairs, both of which structure their efforts for the internally displaced around the Guiding Principles, and have engaged in training representatives of governments, civil society, and humanitarian actors on the Guiding Principles around the world.

The Guiding Principles as international norms

The Guiding Principles and international norm building

Our experience with the Guiding Principles could be seen to support aspects of a number of the theories about norms described in this chapter. Clearly Finnemore and Sikkink's notion that just a few "norms entrepreneurs" can start a process leading to the establishment of an international norm seems to be borne out in our experience. Prior to 1992, discussion of internal displacement was practically taboo at the international level. Through the inspiration and persistence of just a few key players, however, the Commission on Human Rights was induced to take on the issue in 1992, and resolutions discussing the responsibilities of states and the international community with regard to the internally displaced have been passed by consensus ever since. This has led to the passage of laws in several states, and formal policy among humanitarian agencies (led by the IASC) requiring that the assistance and protection needs of the internally displaced be met.

The realist perspective asserts that human rights norms will only be accepted if pressed by powerful states, and only if the norms further those powerful states' interests. A realist would likely argue that the support of Western countries for the cause of the internally displaced is rooted in their desire to prevent the outflow of potential asylum seekers by making conditions for them more tolerable at home. However, if this were the sole explanation, we would expect to find that the states receiving the largest numbers of asylum seekers would be the strongest supporters of the Guiding Principles, and this has not always been the case.

From the legal standpoint, the Guiding Principles have obtained important recognition despite the fact that they were not drafted by states, although it should always be remembered that they were requested and guided by the relevant resolutions of the UN system. As described above, exhaustive efforts were made to include the viewpoints of relevant actors during the drafting process. These principles were however primarily the product of a small team of legal experts. Although the manner by which the Guiding Principles were "taken note of" has perturbed some states, including some with no issue of internal displacement within their borders, this discomfort has never blocked the consensus resolutions in the General Assembly and Commission on Human Rights welcoming the use of the Guiding Principles. [130]

Are the Guiding Principles "law"? In at least one respect, the answer is certainly yes. As noted by Kälin, the Guiding Principles are well grounded in existing international law, frequently reiterating existing treaty language, and otherwise deducing provisions from interpretations of existing law.[131] States parties to the quoted treaties are thus independently bound by the quoted language and, to the extent that the Guiding Principles' interpretations of existing law are correct and accepted, by the deductive provisions as well.

Even if the provisions of the Guiding Principles are not binding, it is possible for them to become customary international law through state reactions to them. As noted above, resolutions of the General Assembly and other international forums are considered to be of increasing importance in the determination of the element of *opinio juris* required for customary law, especially for human rights norms. Consensus resolutions acknowledging the Guiding Principles at the

Commission on Human Rights and General Assembly have grown progressively more affirmative since they were first "noted" in 1998. The most recent language in the Commission on Human Rights recognizing their use "as a standard" by states, UN agencies, and other parties is an important development, although it is still not an explicit statement concerning the binding nature of the Guiding Principles. There is also demonstrable evidence of state practice, from the incorporation of the Guiding Principles into the national law of Angola, Burundi, and Liberia, and the judicial recognition of the Guiding Principles by the courts of Colombia. These states are admittedly still few in number, but signs are positive that they will soon be joined by Afghanistan and Uganda, and more may be expected in the future. Whether there is sufficient evidence of a general or "special" [132] custom, the Guiding Principles may yet "harden" into law.

The Guiding Principles also demonstrate good prospects under most of the nonlegal indicators of potential success for emerging norms mentioned above. With 53 cosponsors for the last Commission on Human Rights resolution from various parts of the globe, and the active promotion by a number of key states, the Guiding Principles have a great deal of state support, if not adherents on the ground. The Guiding Principles were designed to be simple and comprehensible to states and other users. As a compilation and restatement of existing human rights law, they have an easy "fit" with existing norms and have proven adaptable to local conditions. Although the process of their drafting has raised some controversy, their substantive legitimacy has not been questioned. It still remains to be seen whether the Guiding Principles will prove durable and whether (as discussed below) viable monitoring mechanisms for compliance can be devised.

The Guiding Principles and the effectiveness of norms

In many respects, the level of recognition and increasing use of the Guiding Principles has exceeded our expectations and already represents a substantial achievement of the international community. This was also the conclusion at a symposium in Vienna hosted by the governments of Austria and Norway in December 2003 taking stock of the progress of the mandate of the Special Representative of the Secretary-General on IDPs and laying out the challenges ahead.[133] Participants concluded that the "soft law" approach had proven effective. One civil society representative noted that it "was impossible to overestimate the value of the Guiding Principles and how they help the work of local NGOs."[134] In his independent analysis of the mandate prepared for the symposium, Thomas Weiss[135] concluded that there had been a palpable and significant switch in international opinion about the notion that sovereignty entails responsibility and the legitimacy of international intervention on behalf of internally displaced persons.[136]

On the other hand, it must be admitted that while the rhetorical adoption of the Guiding Principles is spreading relatively quickly, actual implementation of their contents has lagged behind. Even in countries that have passed domestic law based on the Guiding Principles, compliance has not been ensured. For instance, only an estimated 30 percent of the returns carried out by the government of Angola in 2002 actually complied with its own law.[137] Both Burundi and Liberia, notwithstanding their new policies, are currently experiencing exploding levels of new displacement. In Colombia, despite the strong language of the Constitutional Court and rhetorical support of executive authorities, displacement is rising precipitously and the conditions of the displaced remain extremely poor. A number of states with significant problems of internal displacement have yet to engage with the Guiding Principles or effectively to address the problem on the ground. Nonnormative theories of international relations would see in these problems evidence that the Guiding Principles simply do not converge closely enough with the interests of dominant states or their leaders, and that these states have failed to employ adequate pressure on states experiencing internal displacement to ensure their implementation. Constructivists, however, might say that the Guiding Principles are still early in their "life cycle," and that rhetorical adoption without substantial compliance on the ground is a necessary and expected first step in the socialization process.

Lawyers usually prefer to seek binding rather than nonbinding rules to facilitate enforcement. The status of "soft law" limits the available enforcement mechanisms to prompt better compliance with the Guiding Principles. On the other hand, by taking the soft law approach, we have arguably moderated concerns about state sovereignty that might otherwise have blocked any international action or consensus on the question of internal displacement.

The Guiding Principles have helped to focus the attention of states, international humanitarian agencies, and other interested parties on the individual rights of internally displaced persons, who have frequently been seen in the past as an undifferentiated mass and a political or humanitarian rather than human rights issue. This shift in attitude is already having an important effect on how states and the international community approach displacement crises. A good example was the prominent place given to responding to the predicted internal displacement crisis in Iraq in the contingency planning and fundraising appeals by the UN humanitarian system, and in responses by donor states.[138] At the state level, I might cite the still-troubled but largely successful peace negotiations in Sri Lanka, in which the needs and rights of those displaced by that country's conflict have played a formal part.[139] Likewise, the interest of certain then-nonstate actors (like the Sudan People's Liberation Movement/Army) in adopting the Guiding Principles even when they were not bound by human rights law, is an important breakthrough for the protection of the rights of internally displaced persons. In these respects, if no other, I am convinced from my experience with the Guiding Principles that the (neo)realist point of view of the ultimate irrelevance of norms cannot be sustained.

What the theory suggests about next steps

What next? Some activists still hope that the Guiding Principles will serve as a stepping-stone for the creation of a "hard law" instrument, such as a multilateral treaty.[140] While this might indeed become desirable in the future, as I mentioned in my first report to the Commission on Human Rights, initial indications of success persuade me that, for the medium-term, further promotion of the Guiding Principles is the better course. In doing so, international relations and legal theory suggest several courses of action, which (at the risk of academic heresy) I will attempt to harmonize for our practical purposes even though the underlying theories conflict.

First, it is important to continue to broaden the consensus about the Guiding Principles and to encourage states to incorporate their norms into domestic law and policy. We should endeavor to demonstrate to powerful states – the primary agents of international change in the realist worldview – that effective, rights-based solutions to displacement issues promote international security and that it is therefore in the interests of powerful states to support such resolutions. We should try to convince affected states that rights-based solutions to internal displacement issues favor their interests, enhancing stability and economic potential. In line with liberal thinking, we should call upon the international community, and democracies in particular, to stress to governments struggling with displacement the legitimizing effect of commitment to the Guiding Principles. To do so, of course, we will have to make the case to all states of the "appropriateness" of the Guiding Principles and their underlying concept that states' sovereignty entails an obligation to recognize the human rights of persons within their borders. By persuading more states to adopt elements of the Guiding Principles into domestic policy, we might soon reach the "tipping point," after which acceptance will spread more quickly.

Second, we must continue to support "norm entrepreneurs," including governmental institutions, NGOs, and civil society representatives, in their attempt to increase compliance with the norms described in the Guiding Principles. Activists in Colombia, Georgia, the Philippines, the Russian Federation, and elsewhere have actively set about the task of applying the Guiding Principles to their local circumstances and in calling for additional assistance from the international community. National human rights institutions represent a powerful potential for bringing international standards such as the Guiding Principles into play at the domestic level.[141]

Finally, we should encourage greater international monitoring of compliance with the norms in the Guiding Principles. I have done so in my capacity as Special Representative of the Secretary-General on IDPs, primarily through country missions, as have other key players such as the UN Office for the Coordination of Humanitarian Affairs IDP Unit, and NGOs such as the Norwegian Refugee Council's Global IDP Project. However, with 25 million internally displaced person worldwide, much more capacity for monitoring is required.

My office has been examining ways to encourage existing human rights monitoring mechanisms, such as the treaty bodies and other special mechanisms of the Commission on Human Rights, to address the rights of the internally displaced, and has encouraged regional organizations to develop their own monitoring capability. Efforts might also be made to involve the Security Council in promoting the Guiding Principles.[142]

Conclusion

Our experience with the Guiding Principles so far indicates that it is possible to invigorate or create new norms at the international level, and to do so relatively quickly. If there is such a thing as a "tipping point" after which a norm finds quick and comprehensive acceptance around the globe, we have not yet reached it, and domestic internalization remains limited. However, I am confident that we are well on our way.

The jury is still out, however, on the question of effectiveness. If states' behavior is driven only by their narrow interests, the rights of the internally displaced are unlikely ever to be ensured. Absent other reasons for rivalry, it is rarely in one state's interest to complain about how another treats its own citizens, and states with large displaced populations are frequently unable or unwilling to deal with the issue in a manner respectful of the dignity and needs of those affected. For their sake, and although I am not above appealing to state interests where it appears useful, I hope that the Guiding Principles will eventually prove that norms, irrespective of interests, can substantially improve the behavior of states and other actors and bring real change into the lives of human beings.

Acknowledgments

I am deeply indebted to David Fisher and Sophie Haspeslagh for their substantive contribution to the preparation of this chapter.

Notes

1 For example, Martha Finnemore and Kathryn Sikkink, "International Norm Dynamics and Political Change," *International Organization* vol. 52, no. 4 (Autumn 1998), pp. 887, 891; Peter J. Katzenstein, *The Culture of National Security: Norms and Identity in World Politics* (New York: Columbia University Press, 1996), p. 5. United Nations, *Guiding Principles on Internal Displacement*, UN Doc. E/CN.4/1998/53/Add.2, Principle 2.

2 Finnemore and Sikkink, "International Norm Dynamics and Political Change," p. 889.

3 Katzenstein, *Culture of National Security*, p. 5.

4 Audie Klotz, *Norms in International Relations: The Struggle Against Apartheid* (Ithaca: Cornell University Press, 1995), p. 4.

5 Abram Chayes and Antonia Handler Chayes, "Regime Architecture: Elements and

Principles," in Janne E. Nolan, ed., *Global Engagement Cooperation and Security in the 21st Century* (Washington, DC: Brookings Institution, 1994), p. 65.
6 In the *Oxford Dictionary* (1995), one definition of the term *norm* is a "standard or pattern, especially of social behavior, that is typical of a group."
7 See, for example, Andrew Hurrell, "Norms and Ethics in International Relations," in Walter Carlsnaes, Thomas Risse, and Beth A. Simmons, eds, *Handbook of International Relations* (London: Sage, 2002), p. 143.
8 Ramesh Thakur, "Global Norms and International Humanitarian Law: An Asian Perspective," *International Review of the Red Cross* no. 841 (March 31, 2001), pp. 19–44.
9 See Daniel C. Thomas, *The Helsinki Effect: International Norms, Human Rights, and the Demise of Communism* (Princeton: Princeton University Press, 2001).
10 Thomas Risse and Kathryn Sikkink, "The Socialization of International Human Rights Norms into Domestic Practices: Introduction," in Thomas Risse, Stephen Ropp, and Kathryn Sikkink, *The Power of Human Rights: International Norms and Domestic Change* (New York: Cambridge University Press, 1999).
11 Finnemore and Sikkink, "International Norm Dynamics and Political Change," p. 892. Compare Peter J. Katzenstein, introduction to Katzenstein, *Culture of National Security*, p. 5 and n. 12.
12 Gary Goertz, *Contexts of International Politics* (New York: Cambridge University Press, 1994).
13 Robert Keohane, *After Hegemony: Cooperation and Discord in the World Political Economy* (Princeton: Princeton University Press, 1984), pp. 25–7.
14 See Finnemore and Sikkink, "International Norm Dynamics and Political Change," p. 892.
15 See Ole Waever, "Figures of International Thought: Introducing Persons Instead of Paradigms," in Iver B. Newmann and Ole Waever, eds, *The Future of International Relations: Masters in the Making?* (New York: Routledge, 1997).
16 See Friedrich V. Kratochwil, "How Do Norms Matter?" in Michael Byers, ed., *The Role of Law in International Politics: Essays in International Relations and International Law* (Oxford: Oxford University Press, 2000).
17 Ibid.; Hans Peter Schmitz and Kathryn Sikkink, "International Human Rights," in Carlsnaes, Risse, and Simmons, eds, *Handbook of International Relations.*
18 See Hurrell, "Norms and Ethics in International Relations," p. 144.
19 See Andrew Moravcsik, "Taking Preferences Seriously: A Liberal Theory of International Politics," *International Organizations* vol. 51 (1997), pp. 513–53.
20 See Thomas, *Helsinki Effect*, p. 10.
21 Ibid., p. 11.
22 Ibid.
23 See Keohane, *After Hegemony*, pp. 103–6; Andreas Hasenclever, Peter Mayer, and Volker Rittberger, *Theories of International Regimes* (New York: Cambridge University Press, 1997), p. 4.
24 See Schmitz and Sikkink, "International Human Rights," p. 522.
25 Ibid., pp. 521–2.
26 See Kratochwil, "How Do Norms Matter?" p. 57.
27 See Thomas, *Helsinki Effect*, p. 15.
28 See John Head, "Supranational Law: How the Move Toward Multilateral Solutions Is Changing the Character of International Law," *Kansas Law Review* vol. 42 (1994), pp. 605, 615.
29 Ibid.
30 See Peter Malanczuk, *Akehurst's Modern Introduction to International Law* (London: Routledge, 1997).

31 See, for example, Philip R. Trimble, "A Revisionist View of Customary International Law," *U.C.L.A. Law Review* vol. 33 (1985), pp. 665, 684.
32 See Malanczuk, *Akehurst's Modern Introduction to International Law*, p. 39.
33 See Anthea Roberts, "Traditional and Modern Approaches to Customary International Law: A Reconciliation," *American Journal of International Law* vol. 95 (2001), pp. 757–58.
34 Ibid. (citing SS *Lotus* case, 1827 P.C.I.J. [ser. A] No. 10, pp. 18, 29).
35 Oscar Schachter, *International Law in Theory and Practice* (Norwell, MA: Martinus Nijhoff, 1991), p. 336.
36 See Roberts, "Traditional and Modern Approaches to Customary International Law," p. 758.
37 Ibid. (citing *Military and Paramilitary Activities In and Against Nicaragua [Nicaragua* v. *U.S.]*, Merits, 1986 I.C.J. Rep. 14 [June 27]).
38 Roberts, "Traditional and Modern Approaches to Customary International Law," p. 762.
39 Ibid., p. 778.
40 See Schachter, *International Law in Theory and Practice*, p. 343.
41 United Nations, *Vienna Convention on the Law of Treaties*, UN Doc. A/CONF 39/28, UKTS 58 (1980), 8 ILM 679, Art. 53.
42 Ibid.
43 Customary law is not binding on a state that openly and persistently objects to the standard. See Malanczuk, *Akehurst's Modern Introduction to International Law*, p. 39.
44 Robert Jennings and Arthur Watts, eds, *Oppenheim's International Law*, 9th edn (Harlow: Longman, 1992), p. 7.
45 See *Restatement (Third) of the Foreign Relations Law of the United States* (1987), sec. 702 and comment n.
46 See Robert J. Beck, "International Law and International Relations: The Prospects for Interdisciplinary Collaboration," in Robert J. Beck *et al.*, eds, *International Rules: Approaches from International Law and International Relations* (New York: Oxford University Press, 1996).
47 See Myres S. McDougal, Harold D. Lasswell, and Lung-chu Chen, *Human Rights and World Public Order: The Basic Policies of an International Law of Human Dignity* (New Haven: Yale University Press, 1980).
48 See Fernando Tesón, "The Kantian Theory of International Law," *Columbia Law Review* vol. 92 (1992), p. 53.
49 Thomas Franck, *Fairness in International Law and Institutions* (Oxford: Oxford University Press, 1995).
50 See, for example, G. M. Danilenko, *Law-Making in the International Community* (Boston: Martinus Nijhoff, 1993); Philip R. Trimble, "A Revisionist View of Customary International Law," *U.C.L.A. Law Review* vol. 33 (1986), p. 665.
51 See McDougal, Lasswell, and Chen, *Human Rights and World Public Order*, Preface.
52 Ibid., p. 181.
53 See Finnemore and Sikkink, "International Norm Dynamics and Political Change," p. 907.
54 Ibid.
55 Ibid., p. 243
56 See Gary Goertz, *Contexts of International Politics* (New York: Cambridge University Press, 1994), pp. 237–8.
57 See Risse, Ropp, and Sikkink, *Power of Human Rights.*
58 Ibid., pp. 11–17.

59 See Finnemore and Sikkink, "International Norm Dynamics and Political Change," p. 895.
60 Ibid., pp. 896–7.
61 Ibid., p. 902.
62 Ibid., p. 904.
63 Harold H. Koh, "Why Do Nations Obey International Law?" *Yale Law Journal* vol. 106 (1997), p. 2599.
64 C. M. Chinkin, "The Challenge of Soft Law: Development and Change in International Law," *International and Comparative Law Quarterly* vol. 38 (1989), p. 850, n. 1.
65 Tadeusz Gruchalla-Wesierski, "A Framework for Understanding 'Soft Law,'" *Revue de Droit de McGill* vol. 30 (1984), pp. 37, 44.
66 Chinkin, "Challenge of Soft Law," p. 851.
67 See Malanczuk, *Akehurst's Modern Introduction to International Law*, p. 54.
68 Ibid.
69 Ibid.
70 Ibid., p. 213; Henry J. Steiner and Phillip Alston, *International Human Rights in Context: Laws, Politics, Morals* (Oxford: Oxford University Press, 2000).
71 See Gruchalla-Wesierski, "Framework for Understanding 'Soft Law,'" p. 65.
72 Ibid., p. 66.
73 See Thomas, *Helsinki Effect*, p. 4.
74 UN Doc. E/CN.4/1996/39 (1996).
75 UN Doc. E/CN.4/1984/4 (1984).
76 UN Doc. E/CN.4/1992/54 (1992), Annex.
77 See Louis Henkin, *How Nations Behave: Law and Foreign Policy* (New York: Columbia University Press for the Council on Foreign Relations, 1979), p. 47.
78 See Abram Chayes and Antonia Handler Chayes, "On Compliance," *International Organization* vol. 47 (1993), pp. 175, 177.
79 See Edith Brown Weiss, "Understanding Compliance with International Environmental Agreements: The Baker's Dozen Myths," *University of Richmond Law Review* vol. 32 (1999), p. 1555.
80 See ibid.
81 See Thomas, *Helsinki Effect*, p. 287.
82 See Schmitz and Sikkink, "International Human Rights," p. 529.
83 See Kal Raustiala and Anne-Marie Slaughter, "International Law, International Relations, and Compliance," in Carlsnaes, Risse, and Simmons, *Handbook of International Relations*.
84 See "A Hard Look at Soft Law," in *Proceedings of the 82nd Meeting of the American Society of International Law* (April 20–23, 1988), p. 372 (remarks by Gunther Handl).
85 See Finnemore and Sikkink, "International Norm Dynamics and Political Change," pp. 905–9; Richard Price, "Compliance with International Norms and the Mines Taboo," in Maxwell Cameron *et al.*, eds, *To Walk Without Fear: The Global Movement to Ban Landmines* (Toronto: Oxford University Press, 1998).
86 See Thakur, "Global Norms and International Humanitarian Law."
87 United Nations, *Guiding Principles on Internal Displacement*, para. 2.
88 See Roberta Cohen and Francis Deng, *Masses in Flight: The Global Crisis of Internal Displacement* (Washington, DC: Brookings Institution, 1998); United Nations High Commissioner for Refugees, *The State of the World's Refugees: A Humanitarian Agenda* (New York, 1998), pp. 112–15.
89 World Health Organization, "Internally Displaced Persons, Health, and WHO," paper presented at the humanitarian affairs segment of the substantive session of the Economic and Social Council for 2000, p. 5.

90 United Nations High Commissioner for Refugees, *UNHCR Global Report 2002* (New York, 2003), p. 20.
91 Cohen and Deng, *Masses in Flight*, p. 3.
92 United Nations, *Report of the Representative of the Secretary-General on Internally Displaced Persons*, Francis M. Deng, submitted pursuant to Commission on Human Rights Resolution 2002/56, E/CN.4/2003/86 (January 21, 2003), para. 4.
93 Cohen and Deng, *Masses in Flight*, pp. 3–4.
94 Ibid.
95 Ibid.
96 Ibid., p. 5.
97 UN General Assembly, Resolution 43/116 (1998).
98 UN Economic and Social Council (ECOSOC) Resolution 1990/78. See UN Doc. E/1991/109/Add.1.
99 Simon Bagshaw, *Developing the Guiding Principles on Internal Displacement: The Role of a Global Public Policy Network*, available online at www.globalpublicpolicy.net.
100 Ibid., p. 7.
101 Ibid.
102 Ibid.
103 Ibid.
104 UN Doc. E/CN.4/1991/25 (1991).
105 UN Doc. E/CN.4/1992/23 (1992).
106 Ibid.
107 UN Doc. E/CN.4/1992/73 (1992).
108 UN Doc. E/CN.4/1992/23 (1992).
109 See Bagshaw, *Developing the Guiding Principles on Internal Displacement*, p. 9; UN Doc. E/CN.4/1992/73 (1992).
110 Comprehensive study prepared by Mr. Francis M. Deng, Representative of the Secretary-General on the human rights issues related to internally displaced persons, pursuant to Commission on Human Rights Resolution 1992/73, E/CN.4/1993/35 (1993).
111 Ibid., para. 281.
112 UN Doc. E/CN.4/1993/95 (1993), paras. 1, 3, 4. The mandate has subsequently been renewed three times for periods of three years each. See UN Doc. E/CN.4/1995/57, UN Doc. E/CN.4/1998/50, UN Doc. E/CN.4/2001/54.
113 United Nations, *Report of the Representative of the Secretary-General*, Mr. Francis M. Deng, submitted pursuant to Commission on Human Rights Resolution 1995/57. Compilation and analysis of legal norms, E/CN.4/1996/52/Add.2 (1996).
114 United Nations, *Report of the Representative of the Secretary-General*, Mr. Francis M. Deng, submitted pursuant to Commission on Human Rights Resolution 1997/39, Addendum. United Nations, *Compilation and Analysis of Legal Norms*, Part 2, *Legal Aspects Relating to the Protection against Arbitrary Displacement*, UN Doc. E/CN.4/1998/53/Add.1 (1998).
115 UN Doc. E/CN.4/1996/52 (1996), para 9.
116 See Bagshaw, *Developing the Guiding Principles on Internal Displacement*, pp. 21–2.
117 See Jean-Philippe Lavoyer, "Guiding Principles on Internal Displacement: A Few Comments on the Contribution of International Humanitarian Law," *International Review of the Red Cross* no. 324 (September 30, 1998), pp. 467–80.
118 See Walter Kälin, "How Hard Is Soft Law? The Guiding Principles on Internal Displacement and the Need for a Normative Framework," in *Recent Commentaries about the Nature and Application of the Guiding Principles on Internal Displacement* (Washington, DC: Brookings Institution, 2002), pp. 3–7.

119 United Nations, *Guiding Principles on Internal Displacement*, UN Doc. E/CN.4/1998/53/Add.2 (1998).
120 Ibid., para. 2.
121 UN Doc. E/CN.4/1998/50 (1998), paras. 1, 6.
122 See *Report of the Representative of the Secretary-General on Internally-Displaced Persons*, Francis M. Deng, submitted pursuant to Commission on Human Rights Resolution 2002/56, E/CN.4/2003/86 (2003) (hereinafter 2003 CHR Report), para. 17.
123 UN Doc. E/CN.4/2003/51 (April 23, 2003), para. 7.
124 See 2003 CHR Report, paras. 18, 20.
125 Ibid., paras. 30–7.
126 See *Protocole Relatif a la Creation d'un Cadre Permanent de Concertation Pour la Protection des Personnes Deplacees* (February 7, 2001).
127 See Colombian Constitutional Court Decisions T-327 and SU-1150 (March 2001 and August 2000).
128 White House, *Presidential Directive No. 6* (2001).
129 See Roberta Cohen, Walter Kälin, and Erin Mooney, eds, "The Guiding Principles on Internal Displacement and the Law of the South Caucasus: Georgia, Armenia, Azerbaijan," *Studies in Transitional Legal Policy* no. 34 (2003).
130 *Report of the Representative of the Secretary-General on Internally Displaced Persons*, Francis M. Deng, submitted pursuant to Commission on Human Rights Resolution 2001/54, E/CN.4/2002/95 (2002), para. 17.
131 See Kälin, "How Hard Is Soft Law?" p. 8.
132 See Anthony D'Amato, "The Concept of Special Custom in International Law," *American Journal of International Law* vol. 63 (1969), p. 211.
133 See *International Symposium on the Mandate of the Representative of the Secretary-General on Internally Displaced Persons: Taking Stock and Charting the Future*, Brookings-SAIS Project on Internal Displacement, December 2003.
134 Ibid., p. 8.
135 See Thomas G. Weiss, "International Efforts for IDPs after a Decade: What Next?" in *International Symposium: Taking Stock and Charting the Future*, p. 43.
136 Ibid., p. 7.
137 See Global IDP Project, "Angola: While Large Numbers of IDPs Are Returning Home, Authorities Have Largely Ignored Minimum Standards" (December 2002), available online at www.idpproject.org.
138 See, for example, United Nations, *United Nations Flash Appeal for the Humanitarian Requirements of the Iraq Crisis: Six Month Response* (March 28, 2003), p. 23.
139 See United Nations High Commissioner for Refugees, "Phase One of the Action Plan for Accelerated Resettlement Programme in Jaffna District Begins: Government, LTTE, and UNHCR Teams Start Work" (January 28, 2003), press release.
140 See *International Symposium: Taking Stock and Charting the Future*, p. 9.
141 See Mario Gomez, "National Human Rights Commissions and Internally Displaced Persons," *Brookings Institution-SAIS Project on Internal Displacement Occasional Paper* (Washington, DC: Brookings Institution, 2002).
142 See *International Symposium: Taking Stock and Charting the Future*, p. 9.

10

COMMENTARY: PRIVATELY GENERATED SOFT LAW IN INTERNATIONAL GOVERNANCE

Kenneth W. Abbott

Introduction

Francis Deng's chapter on the creation and impact of the Guiding Principles on Internal Displacement (GPID) makes a valuable contribution to our understanding of international normative processes.[1] The chapter combines a "practitioner" perspective, based on Deng's decade of service as the Special Representative of the UN Secretary-General on internally displaced persons (IDPs), with an "academic" perspective, informed by constructivist international relations (IR) theory and related approaches that emphasize the role of norms in shaping behavior. The chapter joins the growing and significant genre of "participant-observer" analyses of international governance,[2] and complements recent papers by, or based on interviews with, other participants in the GPID process.[3] Still, Deng's central role makes his analysis unique.

Deng discusses a single case of norm creation and dissemination, so it is difficult to derive general conclusions from it. However, Deng suggests important issues and hypotheses regarding normative processes that should be pursued through comparison with other cases. I focus here on the nature and functions of privately generated soft law. I also consider some issues relating to the creation and dissemination of private soft law norms.

Privately generated soft law

In a recent special issue of *International Organization* devoted to "legalization and world politics," my coauthors and I emphasized the variability of the legal attributes of international norms. Legal *obligation* (the degree to which rules or commitments are accepted as legally binding), the *precision* and elaboration of rules, and the *delegation* to independent bodies of authority to interpret, apply, and elaborate rules are each matters of degree. States – and other participants in normative processes – can vary each element independently to produce a fine-grained continuum of legalization, from hard law through various forms of soft law, to the virtual absence of legal characteristics.[4]

This conceptualization helps characterize the GPID in terms of legalization. Legal obligation is their most complex characteristic; I discuss it further below. To summarize, as "guiding principles" merely "taken note of" by the UN Commission on Human Rights (UNCHR), the GPID as such were clearly intended not to create binding legal obligations. Indeed, the UNCHR earlier balked at authorizing a "normative framework" on internally displaced persons out of concern that the quoted term might imply too great a legal commitment. Yet the text of the GPID suggests that some norms embodied in the principles carry a higher level of obligation. The introductory section states that the GPID "reflect and are consistent with" international human rights and humanitarian law, and "identify rights and guarantees."[5] In short, as with many soft law instruments, the exact legal status of the principles is somewhat ambiguous.

In terms of precision, the GPID state fairly precise and detailed norms for the treatment of IDPs. In terms of delegation, no legal institution is authorized to interpret, apply, or elaborate the principles. It is simply contemplated that the GPID will "provide guidance" to states, international organizations (IOs), non-governmental organizations (NGOs), and "all other authorities" that deal with IDPs.[6] The UNCHR did, however, take note of Deng's intention as UN Special Representative (carried on by his successor, Walter Kälin) to disseminate the GPID through dialogue with governments, IOs, and NGOs, and of their approval by the UN Inter-Agency Standing Committee (IASC), which encouraged its member agencies to apply them.

In sum, while the GPID resemble other soft law instruments characterized by low levels of formal obligation coupled with the incorporation of legally binding norms, low to moderate delegation, and relatively high precision – such as the Helsinki Final Act and the Rio Declaration on Environment and Development – they strike their own unique balance on the scale of legalization.

While the international organization framework helps characterize the GPID, it misses entirely the fact that Helsinki and Rio were adopted by representatives of states, while the GPID were drafted and finalized primarily by private experts. Deng rightly highlights the significance of such privately generated soft law, created "without state involvement or endorsement."[7] He notes that privately drafted instruments ranging from the Johannesburg Principles on National Security, Freedom of Expression and Access to Information, to the draft conventions of the International Law Commission (ILC) have achieved wide acceptance and impact.

The phenomenon of privately generated soft law deserves more systematic study.[8] As a threshold issue, however, it is important to recognize that the "private" character of international norms and normative processes varies widely: most are hybrids, linked in diverse ways to states, IOs, or other "public" actors. Consider the examples just given. The Johannesburg Principles were drafted by private experts convened by an NGO, although representatives of human rights bodies from the UN and other IOs also participated, and the UN Special Rapporteur on freedom of expression presented the Johannesburg Principles to the UNCHR.[9] In contrast, while the members of the ILC serve in their individual capacities, the UN General Assembly created the institution and elects its members.

The International Commission on Intervention and State Sovereignty (ICISS) – which elaborated the state's "responsibility to protect,"[10] a norm that earlier informed the GPID[11] – represents a more complex hybrid process. The ICISS had no formal public status. The Canadian government and a group of foundations created and funded it.[12] Most (though not all) ICISS members were private citizens.[13] Yet the founders cast the ICISS not only as "an independent body intended to support the UN,"[14] but also as a direct response to the Secretary-General's call for a new consensus on humanitarian intervention. The prime minister of Canada announced its creation during the UN Millennium Summit, and its report was released at the next General Assembly session. UN bodies have taken up the ICISS recommendations, giving the commission significant impact.[15]

The GPID process also had strong UN links. As Deng relates, the UNCHR called on the Secretary-General in 1991 to report on the problem of IDPs; he recommended preparing normative guidelines. The UNCHR accordingly called for a study, and later for preparation of an appropriate framework, by a representative of the Secretary-General. The UNCHR was asked to take note of each phase of the study and of the final product. The General Assembly acknowledged the GPID, and the IASC – which coordinates humanitarian assistance in complex emergencies by the UN relief agencies and other international bodies, as well as NGOs[16] – encouraged its members to use the principles. Other UN agencies participated in drafting and consultations, as discussed below. In sum, the GPID process was far from purely "private"; what is notable, though, is the surprisingly limited role played by states.[17] Future research could fruitfully examine the extent to which subtle variations in the "private" character of institutions and processes affect the production, content, and impact of norms.

In all its forms, privately generated soft law appears to serve many of the same political functions as state-generated soft law.[18] In both cases, actors sacrifice some advantages of hard law, which can increase the credibility of commitments, provide new legal strategies, and allow actors to fill out incomplete bargains through delegation. In return, however, actors gain other advantages: soft law typically reduces the costs and delay of reaching agreement, reduces the perceived "sovereignty costs" of norms, and provides new opportunities for compromise. Soft law is not a mere precursor to hard law, then; it can be optimal on its own terms. Private soft law can further reduce costs and delay and mute state opposition. Participants in the GPID process recognized all of these advantages, abandoning their original plan to proceed to a binding legal document.

Yet NGOs and other advocates often expect privately generated soft law like the GPID to develop greater normative authority than sovereignty-conscious states and other objectors anticipate, in part by mobilizing and empowering affected groups. Consider, for example, the "boomerang" process described by Margaret Keck and Kathryn Sikkink. In this scenario, local civil society groups, unable to obtain redress from their governments on human rights or similar issues, reach outside their countries, enlisting transnational NGO coalitions, IOs, and other states to invoke international norms, to "shame" and pressure those governments, and to support and protect the local groups.[19] In many cases, private soft law can serve as the fulcrum of this process as well, or nearly as well, as more traditional soft law or hard law. Advocates hope that the GPID will enmesh governments in a web of norms and pressures from above (other states and IOs) and below (civil society), much as the human rights provisions of the Helsinki Final Act affected the Soviet Union.[20] As Deng notes, soft law can also "intrude" into hard law and harden into customary international law, quite easily in his view.[21]

This analysis raises fundamental questions about the value of international law. If soft law, even privately generated soft law, can have such potent political effects, what if anything does hard law add? Would it be even more effective, although more difficult to attain? While the GPID raise these questions, they do not cleanly pose them, because of their complex legal character. On one hand, as Deng has recognized, the GPID "do not constitute a binding instrument."[22] Yet on the other, the principles are said to "reflect" legal rules and "identify [at least some] rights." This dual character flows directly from the process by which the GPID were created.

Deng's legal team began by preparing a "Compilation and Analysis of Legal Norms" relevant to IDPs.[23] They found that many principles of human rights and humanitarian law applied to IDPs, although few referred to them specifically. Yet a number of these principles were too general to provide practical guidance, and the law was silent on several issues important to IDPs.[24] In drafting the GPID, then, the team tried to "clarify grey areas and fill in the gaps."[25]

The GPID thus include three types of norms: (1) some principles restate legal rules binding as a matter of treaty or custom – although even here the US legal experts on the team favored the broad "deductive" or "normative" approach to identifying customary international law supported by Deng,[26] while the European experts took a more traditional positivist view;[27] (2) other principles are newly drafted applications of general legal rules, which may well add new substantive content;[28] and (3) a few principles are wholly new, created by analogy to existing norms.[29] The GPID themselves do not identify which principles fall into each category.

It is illuminating to compare this approach with the strategies used by the High Commissioner on National Minorities (HCNM) of the Organization for Security and Cooperation in Europe (OSCE), to give effect to analogous norms, as analyzed by Steven Ratner.[30] To be sure, the HCNM was involved in mediation and other operational activities designed to resolve ethnic conflicts, not in drafting norms. Yet the HCNM utilized hard and soft law in much the same way as did Deng's team.

One strategy the HCNM pursued was to "translate" general or abstract norms into more precise terms applicable to ethnic conflict. This enabled him to provide concrete practical guidance during conversations with governments, ethnic factions, and other groups. The HCNM also "developed" norms, freely interpreting them and filling gaps to cover specific situations.[31] Like the drafters of the GPID, in other words, the HCNM freely blended hard law and soft law in pursuit of the desired results.

Remarkably, Ratner finds that most elites in governments and ethnic communities drew little distinction between hard law and soft law norms. A few rejected all international norms, but most viewed political and legal commitments as equally weighty.[32] Both the GPID and HCNM cases, then, reveal a serious need for theoretical and especially empirical research investigating whether, and under what circumstances, we can expect hard law to have any greater effect on the behavior of states and nonstate actors than would soft law or privately generated soft law.[33]

Creating privately generated soft law

Deng observes that most schools of IR theory – specifically realist, liberal, and institutionalist theory – say little about norm creation; his chapter suggests that this is because those schools view norms as instrumental. I doubt this is the reason for the lacuna. It seems more likely that scholars in all three camps focus on comparative statics because of the difficulties of analyzing dynamics; if those could be controlled, all would likely offer valuable insights into norm creation. Constructivist IR scholarship, which Deng heavily relies on, has explored norm dynamics more intensively, although a number of the works cited in his paper focus on later stages, especially norm internalization. The creation of the GPID suggests significant aspects of private soft law processes that scholars in all theoretical schools might fruitfully explore.

Most notable, the story of the GPID suggests that private soft law processes may have unique political advantages beyond those of soft law generally. Duncan Snidal and I argue elsewhere that, all else being equal, particular types of actors will prefer norm creation processes that afford them the greatest access and influence on outcomes.[34] One can hypothesize in this vein that private soft law processes have particular appeal for specific actor groups:

1 NGOs and activists generally prefer soft law processes for their greater openness, even when administered by states. They should in general find private processes even easier to initiate and bring to fruition "under the radar" of potentially objecting states, and even more open to civil society participation, than state-based soft law procedures.
2 IO officials should see private soft law processes, when coordinated with their own work, as facilitating pursuit of their normative agendas while reducing the risk of damaging confrontations with objecting states.

3 Weak states should likewise find that private soft law processes facilitate pursuit of their normative agendas, while eliminating the need to gain the approval of strong states and reducing the likelihood of costly confrontations with powerful objectors.

The GPID process provides support for all three hypotheses. First, human rights NGOs, religious groups, and IDP advocates like the Refugee Policy Group placed the issue of IDPs on the international agenda, sought action by the UNCHR precisely because of its openness to nonstate actors, participated actively in drafting the GPID, and organized consultations with the humanitarian community that garnered support for the principles while keeping "the NGOs . . . firmly in the driving seat."[35] Roberta Cohen of the Refugee Policy Group codirected with Deng a research project on IDPs at the Brookings Institution; she worked closely with him to solicit funds and legal volunteers, helping shape the GPID process.[36] Throughout that process, the activist coalition and Deng's team used a range of political and linguistic strategies to deflect concern over the limited role of states.[37]

Second, the UNCHR, the UN Secretary-General, the IASC, and other UN bodies actively supported the GPID process.[38] Officials of the UN High Commissioner for Refugees (UNHCR), the UN Department of Humanitarian Affairs, the UN Centre for Human Rights, and the UN Children's Fund (UNICEF) also participated in strategy sessions, conferences designed to build political momentum, and expert consultations. Simon Bagshaw argues that a "fundamental and distinctive feature" of the process was "the role played by non-governmental and intergovernmental actors . . . brought together within the framework of a global public policy network."[39] Indeed, at points the process resembled an IO–NGO alliance designed to bypass potentially obstructionist governments.[40]

Third, Austria and Norway took the lead in gaining official UN support. Their representatives introduced authorizing resolutions in the UNCHR and General Assembly – in consultation with Deng, the coalition, and the legal team – and worked to overcome state objections. Austria brought in a major legal research institution and hosted roundtables to resolve legal and political issues. Both states provided financial support, along with the Netherlands and Sweden (and several nonstate actors).

The GPID case also suggests that the process of researching and drafting legal or soft law norms, which may appear technical and politically neutral, grows directly out of the overtly political work of shaping the policy agenda. In the first stage of the "life cycle" of norms developed by Martha Finnemore and Kathryn Sikkink,[41] norm entrepreneurs – often NGOs or other nonstate activists – recognize when the political climate is ripe for action on a particular issue, frame the issue in a politically appealing way, place it on the international policy agenda, and use tactically suitable organizational platforms to persuade states to adopt it. Deng explores how the technical work of legal drafting fits into this process of "strategic social construction."[42]

Human rights activists began by publicizing the plight of IDPs. The end of the Cold War, a dramatic increase in the number of IDPs, and widely publicized problems in providing relief to IDPs in Africa and elsewhere made the issue ripe for action. Advocates worked through a variety of organizations, but settled on the UN, especially the UNCHR and the Secretary-General's office. Advocates framed the situation of IDPs in contrast to that of refugees, who enjoy superior legal protections.[43] This appealing approach led naturally to an expert process that could rectify the legal disparity.

Deng established a working team staffed by human rights and humanitarian law specialists, many of whom were also advocates. Adopting a "needs-based approach," the team developed norms that addressed the perceived problems facing IDPs, including the first articulation of a right not to be arbitrarily displaced. While technical and expert, this work was shaped by the strategic decisions of the advocates. At the same time, Deng and his team consulted and worked closely with the NGOs driving the campaign and other humanitarian groups, providing them an ideal organizational platform.

Finally, Deng's chapter suggests that the leaders of a private soft law process face a dilemma: they must develop and maintain legitimacy and authority without sacrificing the flexibility and nonthreatening character that made a private process desirable. The dilemma was especially challenging in the GPID case due to the "extremely limited involvement of States."[44] Deng and other process leaders used two techniques to walk this fine line.

Organizationally, Deng sought legitimacy by linking the team's work to international institutions, much as the NGOs had done.[45] He acted throughout as Special Representative of the Secretary-General. He began work on the GPID only pursuant to a UNCHR resolution, and submitted each phase of the work to the UNCHR. He also relied on supportive General Assembly resolutions for authority. Deng was careful to cast the team's work as furthering these resolutions. The IASC provided further legitimacy, and the team consulted widely with other IOs. At the same time, the team dealt with these bodies through procedures designed to forestall adverse state reactions: in particular, requesting the UNCHR only to "take note" of the GPID. One can imagine very different legitimizing techniques, such as casting a private soft law process as a response to the failings of IOs, but the opposite approach was chosen here.

Substantively, the team drew authority from international law. Built around legal experts from recognized institutions, it framed its work in neutral, professional terms. In the early stages, the team produced a "compilation" of extant rules and analyzed their applicability to IDPs. Subsequently, Deng and the team presented the GPID as a restatement and interpretation of established legal rules, even though some principles were at best implicit in positive law.[46] The legal approach appears to have been quite successful in building legitimacy for the process – even as the UNCHR refused to authorize preparation of a "legal framework" and as the team decided to stick with private soft law rather than risk unpredictable negotiations on a binding convention.

Disseminating and adopting privately generated soft law

Successful norms pass through a "life cycle" of three relatively distinct stages.[47] In the first stage, advocates frame an issue and place it on the political agenda, identify or formulate an appropriate norm, and persuade some states (or other actors) to subscribe to it. In the second stage, advocates further disseminate the norm and the "early adopter" states persuade others to sign on. Eventually a "tipping point" is reached at which states widely acknowledge the norm, even if many do so insincerely. In the final stage, the norm is invoked and brought to bear against recalcitrant states, until social pressure and domestic adjustments lead them to internalize it, rendering compliance routine.

The GPID remain in the second stage, dissemination and adoption, and they remain a "work in progress."[48] One would predict that some strategies pursued earlier might now lead to problems, especially with adoption by states. After all, states played a limited role in developing the GPID and did not approve their final text. On the other hand, Deng's efforts to link the GPID to international institutions and law should facilitate adoption.

In considering dissemination, it is again instructive to compare the work of the OSCE High Commissioner for National Minorities. Ratner suggests that the HCNM pursued three strategies to encourage observance of international norms in addition to norm "translation" and "development," discussed above.

First, the HCNM disseminated relevant norms through explanatory seminars for public and private leaders, mediation, and other interventions. Deng has followed similar approaches.[49] He has had the GPID translated and widely distributed. He has presented them at international conferences, some cosponsored with regional organizations, and in meetings with international agencies. He has conducted missions in several countries, some with IDP problems, explaining and invoking the GPID in workshops and discussions with governments, IDP leaders, and other nonstate groups. In these conversations he has presumably continued to "translate" and "develop" the GPID for specific contexts.

Second, the HCNM used international norms to mobilize support for his political interventions among nonstate actors. In the present context it is more important to mobilize support for the GPID themselves, but nonstate actors remain important. Human rights and humanitarian NGOs were central to the GPID process from the outset; many have adopted the principles, using them as tools of advocacy and guides for their own operations. Deng refers somewhat tepidly to "stirrings of acknowledgment and use" by civil society,[50] but it appears that NGO adoption has been quite widespread, even within developing countries. IOs, likewise central to the process, have also responded positively. As already noted, the IASC, which brings together the main UN humanitarian agencies, has encouraged its members to apply the GPID;[51] other IOs also use them in their work.

Interestingly, NGOs and IOs apparently felt a strong need for a single clear normative statement by which they could benchmark their own field operations and assess the conduct of states and nonstate actors in diverse contexts.[52] This situation has elements of a coordination game, in which a common standard has value as a focal point, at least partially independent of its precise content and wholly independent of its legal status.[53] Overall, one can interpret the GPID process as a collaboration between IOs and NGOs – acting above and below the state – first to create the GPID, then to apply them in their operations and advocacy, all with little state involvement. Since these organizations conduct so much of the world's humanitarian work, this is a significant success.

Still, adoption and compliance by states remains crucial: states create many internal displacements, have the most effective tools to prevent other groups from creating them, and have the primary duty to care for IDPs under their "responsibility to protect." On this score, the HCNM tried to "elevate" international soft law norms to hard law status by encouraging states to incorporate them into domestic law. Deng has urged the same action. Here, however, the picture is less encouraging. Deng cites only a few examples of "elevation," or proposed elevation. Even some of the states that have acted are not complying with their new laws or policies.[54] Clearly, soft law norms with weak implementation mechanisms, like the GPID, create a moral hazard problem: states can gain reputational advantages by accepting them even without the intention or capability to comply.[55] Many states with IDP problems have not engaged with the GPID at all.[56]

The future of the GPID therefore poses something of a test for normative theories of international relations. Deng notes that rhetorical adoption of norms by states without a sincere commitment or capacity for compliance is a common feature of the dissemination stage in the life cycle of norms.[57] Yet it is far from clear whether other features of the life cycle necessary to overcome that problem are in place. First, as Deng acknowledges, the GPID have not even reached a tipping point in terms of state acceptance, despite supportive General Assembly votes; it is not clear when they might reach that point. Second, in Finnemore and Sikkink's life cycle theory, committed states play the leading role in persuading other states to sign on; it is not clear whether the GPID have a sufficient core of influential state promoters to make this happen. Third, it is not clear whether there exist adequate implementation mechanisms to bring the GPID to bear against weakly committed states, socialize them, and move them toward deeper commitments and internalization. If the IO–NGO coalition and the small core of states backing the GPID can in fact persuade the broad community of states to adopt the principles, invoke them against recalcitrant states, and bring about widespread internalization, it will be a signal achievement, one that will necessitate further revision in our understanding of international normative processes.

Notes

1 Deng, "The Guiding Principles on Internal Displacement and the Development of International Norms," Chapter 9 in this volume.

2 See, e.g. Steven R. Ratner, "Does International Law Matter in Preventing Ethnic Conflict?" *New York University Journal of International Law and Politics* vol. 32 (2000), p. 591; Michael N. Barnett, *Eyewitness to a Genocide: The United Nations and Rwanda* (Ithaca: Cornell University Press, 2002).
3 See, for example, Simon Bagshaw, "Developing the Guiding Principles on Internal Displacement: The Role of a Global Public Policy Network," paper prepared for the UN Vision Project on Global Public Policy Networks, available online at www.globalpublicpolicy.net/index.php?id=165; Roberta Cohen, "The Guiding Principles on Internal Displacement: An Innovation in International Standard Setting," *Global Governance* vol. 10 (2004), pp. 459-80.
4 See Kenneth W. Abbott, Robert O. Keohane, Andrew Moravcsik, Anne-Marie Slaughter, and Duncan Snidal, "The Concept of Legalization," *International Organization* vol. 54 (2000), pp. 401–19; Special Issue, "Legalization and World Politics," *International Organization* vol. 54, no. 3 (2000), reprinted as Judith L. Goldstein, Miles Kahler, Robert O. Keohane, and Anne-Marie Slaughter, eds, *Legalization and World Politics* (Cambridge: MIT Press, 2001).
5 United Nations, *Guiding Principles on Internal Displacement*, UN Doc. E/CN.4/1998/53/Add.2 (1998), "Introduction: Scope and Purpose," paras. 1, 3.
6 Ibid., para. 3.
7 Deng, "Guiding Principles on Internal Displacement," Chapter 9 in this volume.
8 Some definitions of "soft law" encompass a role for privately generated norms, although few analyze the phenomenon in detail. See, for example, Christine M. Chinkin, "The Challenge of Soft Law: Development and Change in International Law," *International and Comparative Law Quarterly* vol. 38 (1989), pp. 850–1.
9 See Frances D'Souza, "Brief Background to the Johannesburg Principles" (1996), available online at www.article23.org.hk/english/research/johan_and_lima_brief.doc.
10 *The Responsibility to Protect: Report of the International Commission on Intervention and State Sovereignty* (2001).
11 Deng, "Guiding Principles on Internal Displacement."
12 The UK and Switzerland also provided financial support.
13 One of the cochairs was a special adviser to the Secretary-General, one member was a serving national official, and several members were former high state officials. An advisory board of current and former foreign ministers gave political guidance to the commissioners.
14 See www.iciss.ca/mandate-en.asp.
15 The "responsibility to protect" has been adopted by the Secretary-General's High-Level Panel on Threats, Challenges, and Change (see United Nations *A More Secure World: Our Shared Responsibility*, Report of the Secretary-General's High-Level Panel on Threats, Challenges, and Change [2004], paras. 199–203); and by Secretary-General Kofi Annan (see United Nations, *In Larger Freedom: Towards Development, Security, and Human Rights for All*, Report of the Secretary-General of the United Nations for Decision by Heads of State and Government [September 2005], para. 136).
16 See www.humanitarianinfo.org/iasc.
17 As discussed below, two states that did play important roles were Austria, which sponsored the relevant resolutions in the UNHCR, and Norway, which did so in the General Assembly.
18 For a discussion of these functions in the context of state-generated soft law, see Kenneth W. Abbott and Duncan Snidal, "Hard and Soft Law in International Governance," *International Organization* vol. 54 (2000), p. 421.
19 Margaret E. Keck and Kathryn Sikkink, *Activists Beyond Borders: Advocacy Networks in International Politics* (Ithaca: Cornell University Press, 1998). Risse and

Sikkink expand this model dynamically. Thomas Risse and Kathryn Sikkink, "The Socialization of International Human Rights Norms into Domestic Practices: Introduction," in Thomas Risse, Stephen C. Ropp, and Kathryn Sikkink, eds, *The Power of Human Rights: International Norms and Domestic Change* (Cambridge: Cambridge University Press, 1999), pp. 17–35.

20 See, for example, Daniel C. Thomas, *The Helsinki Effect: International Norms, Human Rights, and the Demise of Communism* (Princeton: Princeton University Press, 2001).

21 Deng, "Guiding Principles on Internal Displacement."

22 United Nations, "Introductory Note by the Representative of the Secretary-General on Internally Displaced Persons," available online at www.unhchr.ch/html/menu2/7/b/principles_lang.htm.

23 United Nations, *Compilation and Analysis of Legal Norms*, Report of the Representative of the Secretary-General on Internally Displaced Persons, UN Doc. E/CN.4/1996/52/Add.2 (1995); United Nations, *Compilation and Analysis of Legal Norms*, Part 2, *Legal Aspects Relating to Protection Against Arbitrary Displacement*, UN Doc. E/CN.4/1998/53/Add.1 (1998).

24 See Cohen, "Guiding Principles on Internal Displacement," pp. 463–4. The organization of the drafting process around a "needs-based approach" encouraged the team to highlight these gaps. See ibid., p. 463; Bagshaw, "Developing the Guiding Principles on Internal Displacement," pp. 18–19.

25 United Nations, "Introductory Note."

26 See Deng, "Guiding Principles on Internal Displacement."

27 See Bagshaw, "Developing the Guiding Principles on Internal Displacement," pp. 19–21.

28 An example is the principle prohibiting forcible return of IDPs to places of danger, which the drafters consider a specific application of the general rule against cruel and inhuman treatment. See Cohen, "Guiding Principles on Internal Displacement," p. 464.

29 An example is the principle calling for restitution of property lost as a result of displacement, Principle 29:2. Ibid.

30 Ratner, "Does International Law Matter in Preventing Ethnic Conflict?"

31 Ibid., pp. 623–36, 640–6.

32 Those who drew a distinction were mainly foreign office specialists. Ibid., pp. 661–5.

33 For suggestions as to the design of such research, see Martha Finnemore, "Are Legal Norms Distinctive?" *New York University Journal of International Law and Politics* vol. 32 (2000), p. 699. In the *International Organization* special issue, some case studies found little difference in impact. See, for example, Ellen L. Lutz and Kathryn Sikkink, "International Human Rights Law and Practice in Latin America," *International Organization* vol. 54 (2000), p. 249.

34 See Kenneth W. Abbott and Duncan Snidal, "Pathways to International Cooperation," in E. Benvenisti and M. Hirsch, eds, *The Impact of International Law on International Cooperation: Theoretical Perspectives* (Cambridge: Cambridge University Press, 2004), p. 50.

35 Bagshaw, "Developing the Guiding Principles on Internal Displacement," p. 8.

36 Cohen, "Guiding Principles on Internal Displacement," p. 462.

37 Bagshaw, "Developing the Guiding Principles on Internal Displacement," pp. 26–7. Bagshaw observes that these strategies were essential to keep the process moving "in the direction that Deng, Cohen and the legal team saw fit." Ibid., p. 26.

38 Interestingly, some UN agencies argued initially that the issue of IDPs was too complex and politically sensitive for the organization to address. Bagshaw, "Developing the Guiding Principles on Internal Displacement," p. 7.

39 Bagshaw, "Developing the Guiding Principles on Internal Displacement," p. 4.
40 See, for example, ibid., p. 32.
41 Martha Finnemore and Kathryn Sikkink, "International Norm Dynamics and Political Change," *International Organization* vol. 52 (1998), p. 887.
42 Ibid., pp. 910–11.
43 Refugees also enjoy the support of the UNHCR. Thus, a second strand of the GPID process was to provide a parallel focal point for IDPs in the UN system. The Representative of the Secretary-General fills that role.
44 Bagshaw, "Developing the Guiding Principles on Internal Displacement," p. 26.
45 This strategy is somewhat ironic in the case of the UNCHR, which has been strongly criticized for its *lack* of legitimacy. Secretary-General Kofi Annan has criticized its "credibility deficit" and proposed replacing it with a standing Human Rights Council. See United Nations, *In Larger Freedom*, paras 181–3.
46 See Cohen, "Guiding Principles on Internal Displacement," pp. 467–8.
47 Compare, Finnemore and Sikkink, "International Norm Dynamics."
48 Deng, "Guiding Principles on Internal Displacement," Chapter 9 in this volume.
49 Deng's paper, and those of other participants in the GPID process, are part of the dissemination process.
50 Deng, "Guiding Principles on Internal Displacement," Chapter 9 in this volume.
51 The General Assembly and UNCHR have also continued to encourage their use, in increasingly enthusiastic terms.
52 See Cohen, "Guiding Principles on Internal Displacement," pp. 464–5, 467.
53 For a discussion of types of standards as responses to different strategic situations, see Kenneth W. Abbott and Duncan Snidal, "International 'Standards' and International Governance," *Journal of European Public Policy* vol. 8 (2001), p. 345.
54 Compare Cohen, "Guiding Principles on Internal Displacement," pp. 470–1.
55 See Oona A. Hathaway, "Do Human Rights Treaties Make a Difference?" *Yale Law Journal* vol. 111 (2002), p. 1935.
56 Deng, "Guiding Principles on Internal Displacement."
57 Ibid.

Part IV

INTERNATIONAL CRIMINAL ACCOUNTABILITY

11

THE INTERNATIONAL CRIMINAL COURT AND UNIVERSAL INTERNATIONAL JURISDICTION

A return to first principles

Leila Nadya Sadat

Introduction

In the debate that has taken place over the legitimacy of the International Criminal Court (ICC) exercising jurisdiction over the nationals of states not party to the ICC treaty, a controversy largely sparked by US opposition to the treaty, a series of first principles have been ignored. These principles in the arena of international law and policy are the glue that holds the system together – without them, international law is not a "normative system," as Rosalyn Higgins and others have so passionately argued, but is simply bits and pieces of legal text, a set of discrete rules without any particular coherence.[1] Not only are these principles theoretical rules governing the formation and application of international law, but they also were relied upon by the framers of the Rome Statute in elaborating the text of the ICC treaty, find voice in the draft statutes elaborated by the International Law Commission that formed the basis of the statute ultimately adopted, and informed the discussions of delegates during the preparatory meetings prior to the ICC treaty's adoption as well as the conversations and negotiations that took place during the diplomatic conference held in Rome during the summer of 1998, at which the Court's statute was adopted.

This does not mean that the principles upon which the Court's jurisdiction and establishment are based are without controversy, however, for as I have argued elsewhere, the establishment of the International Criminal Court represented a "constitutional moment" for international law, whereby notions about the legality and legitimacy (under international law) of the extraterritorial jurisdiction of states were transformed into principles governing the exercise of criminal jurisdiction by the international community as a whole.[2] On the other hand, to accept, without reflection, the arguments levied against the jurisdiction of the ICC over the nationals of nonparty states,[3] would not appear to be consistent with either current understandings of international law or state practice, particularly given the high acceptance of the Rome Statute's jurisdictional regime by states, as evidenced by the ICC treaty's widespread signature and ratification.[4]

Critics of the ICC, and more particularly its jurisdictional regimes, make several assertions. In its strongest form, their argument transcends the policy choices involved in the decision to establish the ICC, contending that its establishment was not only a bad idea, but also impermissible under international law.[5] It is important not to overstate the relative weight of these arguments: in fact, relatively few scholars have joined their voices to the loud chorus of political opponents in the United States who have critiqued the Court. Yet if the arguments have been few, they have been influential. In this chapter I take up the principal argument raised against the Court's jurisdictional regime: that the adjudicative jurisdiction of the Court, insofar as it might be exercised over the nationals of nonparty states, is a form of "exorbitant jurisdiction,"[6] because the delegation of universal jurisdiction by states is "impermissible."[7] I conclude, however, that although the expression of universal jurisdiction in the Rome Statute is clearly an extension of existing precedent, it is neither impermissible nor improper under international law.

This chapter briefly examines the negotiating history of the ICC's jurisdiction during the preparatory meetings prior to Rome and during the diplomatic conference itself, to try to tease out, to the extent possible, the extent to which jurisdictional principles featured in the minds of international negotiators as they ultimately crafted the statute in the way that they did. Subsequently, it turns to a more theoretical analysis of the Court's jurisdiction under international law, taken in connection with recent international court decisions exploring the notion of universal jurisdiction as it is exercised before international courts.

Negotiation of the ICC's jurisdiction prior to and during the Rome diplomatic conference

Early drafts of the ICC statute following the establishment of the United Nations generally contained provisions significantly limiting the proposed court's jurisdiction, and, in particular, limiting the cases to be brought to those in which the state of the accused's nationality had consented to the case. Yet a careful reading of the records of the UN General Assembly during the period suggest that this limitation was imposed for practical, not juridical reasons. For example, the draft statute adopted in Geneva in 1951 by the Committee on International Criminal Jurisdiction permitted cases to go to the ICC only if the accused's state or states of nationality *and* the state or states in which the crime was alleged to have been committed had conferred jurisdiction upon the Court.[8] Interestingly, unlike today's ICC, which permits the UN Security Council to trigger the Court's jurisdiction, the 1951 draft would have permitted the General Assembly (or a state party) to do so. Although nationality was imposed as a necessary prerequisite to the exercise of the proposed court's jurisdiction, even at this early juncture in the ICC's development, the 1951 committee did not see the link of nationality as *required*. Some committee members argued that jurisdiction was sufficient if a state had delegated its territorial jurisdiction to the Court. Others opined that nationality should not be a bar if the General Assembly believed that the individual had committed "international crimes." At the same time, members were cognizant of the need for widespread acceptance of the Court's statute, and felt that unless a link to the nationality of the accused was provided for by the statute, it would not be widely adhered to by states.[9]

The work of the Geneva committee, which was composed of 17 member states, was received with a great deal of skepticism by the General Assembly. Belgium's representative argued that the proposed court would violate the most basic principles of international law, by according to the General Assembly a criminal competence that it did not have,[10] and Iraq's delegate stated that the proposed court would "infringe the sovereignty of States."[11] The United States, in contrast, took a fairly benign view of the proposed court, stating that it neither "favored nor opposed the establishment of an international criminal court," but wished merely to see the question fully examined. The General Assembly sent the 1951 report to another 17-member committee of states, which issued a report leaving the jurisdictional provisions of the statute essentially unchanged, at least insofar as the question of nationality was concerned.[12]As is well known, ultimately the question of an international criminal court became the victim of Cold War politics, and it was not until 1989 that work was again resumed.[13]

When the International Law Commission resumed consideration of the question of an international criminal court in 1991, it issued two drafts, the first in 1993 and the second in 1994. Article 24 of the 1993 draft linked the jurisdiction of the Court in a particular case to acceptance of the Court's jurisdiction, and if the suspect was present on the territory of *either* the state of his nationality or the state where the alleged offense was committed, acceptance of the jurisdiction of that state as well. Somewhat confusingly drafted, the implication was that states having jurisdiction to try the accused themselves also had the right to turn him over to the court for prosecution, and in fact the draft makes specific reference to Article VI of the Genocide Convention, which says as much.[14] While the articles on jurisdiction changed fairly significantly between the 1993 and 1994 drafts, Article 21 of the 1994 draft statute (titled "preconditions to jurisdiction") provided that the Court would have "inherent" jurisdiction over the crime of genocide, not subject to state consent, and would have jurisdiction over other crimes, assuming that the Court's jurisdiction had been accepted with respect to the crimes in question by the custodial state (having custody of the accused) *and* the territorial state, where the acts occurred.[15] Note that neither draft gives the state of the accused's nationality a veto over the Court's jurisdiction, a proposal that was apparently made to and rejected by the International Law Commission.[16]

During the four years of negotiations leading to the adoption of the final statute for the Court in Rome, although the question of jurisdiction was often debated, and indeed the question of how the Court would exercise authority over particular cases presented a particularly thorny aspect of the ICC's negotiation,[17] there was never a sense among delegates that international law *required* a state's consent over the trial of its nationals in an international court for crimes committed outside that state's jurisdiction. Instead, the clear working assumption of the negotiators was that because states could exercise jurisdiction over international crimes committed upon their territories under the territorial principle, or over certain *jus cogens* crimes committed elsewhere pursuant to the universality principle, states could cede that jurisdiction to an international court to do so in their stead.[18] There does not even appear to be a reference by the US delegation contesting these basic understandings of international jurisdiction until the debates during the Rome diplomatic conference itself, when the US delegation put forth a proposal to limit the Court's jurisdiction either to cases referred by the Security Council, or to instances in which the state of the accused's nationality consented to the jurisdiction of the Court.[19] That proposal met with considerable resistance, and was ultimately rejected, although the state of the accused's nationality was retained as one of two possible links in the event of a referral to the Court by the ICC prosecutor or a state party to the ICC statute.[20]

A theoretical assessment of the Court's jurisdictional principles

The notion of jus cogens *crimes*

The three crimes codified in the Rome Statute – genocide, crimes against humanity, and war crimes – are essentially the crimes elaborated in Article 6 of the Charter of the International Military Tribunal at Nuremberg (sans crimes against peace, for the time being), as well as the statutes of the Yugoslavia and Rwanda tribunals, and now statute for the Special Court for Sierra Leone (sans genocide) and the statute for the Iraqi Special Tribunal. These are crimes that have been so uniformly accepted by the international community that both the exercise of universal jurisdiction by states, as well as the exercise of universal jurisdiction by the international community as a whole, are generally accepted. In the views of most commentators, they have thus, over time, risen to the status of *jus cogens* crimes embodied in nonderogable peremptory norms of international law.

It is true that the theory of *jus cogens* has been the subject of much dispute and scholarly commentary.[21] Yet the near-universal acceptance of the notion of peremptory or *jus cogens* norms[22] as set out in the Vienna Convention on the Law of Treaties[23] suggests that modern international criminal law both explicitly and implicitly embodies within its prescriptions certain nonderogable norms of peremptory application.[24] Indeed, fundamental to the notion of a duty to prosecute international crimes, a duty incumbent upon all states, is the nonderogability of the norms at issue.[25] As the International Criminal Tribunal for the Former Yugoslavia opined in *Prosecutor* v. *Furundzija*, regarding the crime of torture:

> While the *erga omnes* nature [of the crime] appertains to the area of international enforcement (*lato sensu*), the other major feature of the principle proscribing torture relates to the hierarchy of rules in the international normative order. Because of the importance of the values it protects, this principle has evolved into a peremptory norm of *jus cogens*, that is, a norm that enjoys a higher rank in the international hierarchy than treaty law and even "ordinary" customary rules.[26]

The report issued by the UN Secretary-General establishing the International Criminal Tribunal for the Former Yugoslavia expresses the view that the most serious crimes against the international community as a whole included war crimes, genocide, and crimes against humanity.[27] The Princeton Principles on Universal Jurisdiction refer to these as "serious" crimes under international law, adding to the list piracy, slavery, crimes against peace, and torture.[28] The International Law Commission included, in its 1996 draft regarding "crimes against the peace and security of mankind," aggression, genocide, crimes against humanity, crimes against UN and associated personnel, and war crimes.[29] The US Restatement on The Law of Foreign Relations takes the position that universal jurisdiction crimes include piracy, slave trade, attacks on or highjackings of aircraft, genocide, war crimes, and perhaps certain acts of terrorism.[30]

Paradoxically, most commentators view *jus cogens* norms as representing a floor, a set of lowest common denominator provisions that are truly fundamental to the international legal order, and yet represent norms of a superior hierarchical status in the international legal system.[31] Certainly, most authorities examining the question have concluded that the list of *jus cogens* crimes under international law includes genocide, war crimes, crimes against humanity, crimes against peace (aggression), torture, piracy, and slavery and slave-related practices.[32] Moreover, there are many indications that the exercise of jurisdiction over these crimes is not only permitted under international law, but also required. Many are codified in treaties imposing a duty to try or extradite individuals credibly accused of genocide, war crimes, torture, and acts of terrorism, and as regards aggression and crimes against humanity, a strong case can be made that the *aut dedere aut judicare* principle has risen to the level of customary international law.[33]

The exercise of universal (international) jurisdiction by the Rome Statute for the International Criminal Court over the jus cogens *crimes embodied in the statute*

As regards the exercise of universal jurisdiction, states exist in a horizontal relationship to one another. Their jurisdiction to prescribe norms of criminal law is bounded by their territories, except insofar as some exception permitting the extraterritorial exercise of a state's prescriptive or adjudicative jurisdiction is present. As the SS *Lotus* case suggests, both in the views of the majority as well as the dissent, under the Westphalian system the prescriptive and adjudicative jurisdiction of sovereign states is a creation of international law. At the same time, the case stands for the proposition that "[r]estrictions upon the independence of States cannot be presumed."[34] States generally have jurisdiction only over their territories, with the caveat that international law has generally recognized four exceptions to territoriality: jurisdiction based on nationality, passive personality, the protective principle, and the principle of universality.[35] Application of the theory of universal jurisdiction in these cases is predicated largely on the notion that some crimes are so heinous that they offend the interest of all humanity and, indeed, imperil civilization itself.[36] States seeking to exercise universal jurisdiction over the perpetrator of a *jus cogens* crime are therefore employing their own legislative authority to prescribe as regards an international law norm. Deciding when and under what conditions states may exercise universal jurisdiction therefore presents what I have referred to in earlier writings as a problem of universal "interstate" jurisdiction.[37]

The situation before an international court or tribunal, however, is quite different. The vertical relationship between international and national legal systems, extant as a function of the basic principles of international law, is quite different than the horizontal perspective apparent in cases of universal interstate jurisdiction. Indeed, one of the fundamental contributions of the Rome Statute for the International Criminal Court was to help clarify and codify the status of international, as opposed to national, jurisdictions exercising adjudicative jurisdiction over *jus cogens* crimes. Although some commentators have argued that international courts, whether created by the UN Security Council, international treaty, or amendment to the UN Charter, only exercise jurisdiction delegated to them by states,[38] either directly or through the intermediary of the Charter, this argument appears overstated. Indeed, to accept such a proposition would stand the nature of the international legal order on its head, given that the jurisdictions of states, wrapped up as they are in the essence and definition of sovereignty, are in fact the creation of international law. At the very least, this claim appears insufficient to explain the establishment of the Yugoslavia and Rwanda tribunals and the ICC, and does not appear truly to explain the jurisdictional bases for those courts. To take the International Criminal Court as an example, the ICC statute permits the Security Council to refer a case to the Court even in a situation where neither the territorial state nor the state of the accused's nationality has consented to jurisdiction. Interestingly, the United States has never complained about this capacity of the Court, no doubt because US nationals will be protected in such a case by the veto the United States holds on the Security Council. Is this a case of delegated universal interstate jurisdiction, or a new form of universal international jurisdiction, based upon the notion that there are some harms that are of such vital importance to the international community that they may not only be proscribed by international law, but adjudicated upon as well? The ICC statute's preamble suggests that the latter idea was an important pillar of the Court's jurisdiction, which rests not only upon the notion that the crimes codified in the statute are crimes over which states may exercise universal jurisdiction, but also upon the idea that these grave crimes "threaten the peace, security and well-being of the world."[39]

To the extent that national and international legal orders, each autonomous in their own right, exist in a mutually reinforcing and symbiotic relationship to each other, it would seem deeply problematic to argue that states alone are the ultimate repositories of the international community's prescriptive and adjudicative jurisdictional capacities. Rather, as European scholars suggested during the postwar period, it is more likely that the international community may assert jurisdiction over a problem if it affects a fundamental interest of the international community, or *l'ordre public international.* At the same time, even if the delegation theory explained the permissibility of the ICC's jurisdictional regime, the US argument would not prevail. As others have noted, the idea that the state of an accused's nationality has exclusive jurisdiction over acts committed abroad has no currency in modern international law, but reflects a colonialist concept no longer acceptable in a post-Charter world.[40]

These conclusions have been reaffirmed in several recent international court decisions that have addressed the status of *jus cogens* crimes either directly or in passing, in particular the Special Court for Sierra Leone (SCSL) and the International Court of Justice (ICJ). The Special Court was established on January 16, 2002, by agreement entered into between the United Nations and the government of Sierra Leone.[41] The jurisdiction *ratione materiae* of the Court includes, inter alia, crimes against humanity and war crimes. In a recent opinion on the question of amnesties for international crimes, the Special Court was asked to consider the appeals of two defendants who argued that an amnesty granted under Article IX of the Lomé Accord precluded their trial before the Special Court. Although the United Nations and outside governments were mentioned as "moral guarantors" of the Lomé peace agreement, only two factions of Sierra Leoneans actually signed it, and it was ratified by the parliament of Sierra Leone on July 15, 1999.[42] When rebel forces reneged on the agreement, the president of Sierra Leone wrote to the UN Security Council requesting the establishment of a "court to administer international justice and humanitarian law," and two defendants before the Special Court created subsequently raised the Lomé agreement as a bar to their prosecution. The accused argued that, notwithstanding the international nature of the crimes, the SCSL was bound to respect the amnesty granted by the Lomé agreement because the agreement was an international treaty.

The SCSL disagreed, holding that "[t]he role of the UN as a mediator of peace, the presence of a peacekeeping force which generally is by consent of the State and the mediation efforts of the Secretary-General cannot add up to a source of obligation to the international community to perform an agreement to which the UN is not a party."[43] Instead, the Court found that the agreement could not be characterized as an international instrument. Conversely, it held that Article 10 of the Special Court's statute, forbidding the Special Court from taking into consideration "an amnesty granted to any person falling within the jurisdiction of the Special Court in respect of [international] crimes [within the Special Court's jurisdiction] shall not be a bar to prosecution," did apply. Therefore, any amnesty granted to the accused had no effect. In the words of the Special Court:

> Where jurisdiction is universal, a State cannot deprive another State of its jurisdiction to prosecute the offender by the grant of amnesty. . . . A State cannot bring into oblivion and forgetfulness a crime, such as a crime against international law, which other States are entitled to keep alive and remember.[44]

The Special Court concluded that the crimes within its jurisdiction – crimes against humanity and war crimes committed in internal armed conflict – were subject to universal jurisdiction under international law. It also intimated that the prosecution of such crimes was required, given that "the obligation to protect human dignity is a peremptory norm and has assumed the nature of obligation *erga omnes*."[45] Implicit in the Special Court's opinion is a rejection of the notion that international courts are simply exercising jurisdiction delegated to them by states, rather than acting directly as instruments of the international community (a position it later embraced, as set out below).

This is also the view that the International Court of Justice appears to have rallied behind in its opinion in *Congo* v. *Belgium*. The separate and dissenting opinions filed in that case offer an interesting perspective on the question of universal jurisdiction and universal jurisdiction crimes under international law. Recall that in this case, the ICJ held that Abdulaye Yerodia Ndombasi was immune from Belgium's criminal jurisdiction by virtue of his status as a sitting foreign minister of the Democratic Republic of Congo. However, perhaps to meet the critique that its decision could promote impunity for international crimes, the Court stated that several forums would nonetheless be available for his prosecution – that is, his immunity before the courts of Belgium was not tantamount to *impunity* for the commission of crimes under international law.[46] In particular, the ICJ held that an accused could be tried before the courts of his own state, in a foreign state either if his state waived its immunity or after his tenure in office ceased, and finally, "an incumbent or former foreign minister for Foreign Affairs may be subject to criminal proceedings before certain international criminal courts, where they have jurisdiction."[47] The ICJ referred specifically in this paragraph to the ICC and the ad hoc tribunals for Rwanda and the former Yugoslavia, but did not foreclose other international courts from relying upon this holding in support of their own jurisdiction.

This holding was supported when on May 31, 2004, the Special Court for Sierra Leone issued an opinion on immunity for a sitting head of state, namely Charles Taylor, Liberia's former president. In a fascinating opinion, the Special Court opined that because it was an international and not a domestic court, the immunity invoked by Taylor could not apply.[48] While admitting that it was not "immediately evident" why national and international courts could differ as to their treatment of immunities under international law, the Special Court suggested that, first, the principle of the sovereignty of states was inapplicable, given the Court's status as an international organ; and second, as a matter of policy, states "have considered the collective judgment of the international community to provide a vital safeguard against the potential destabilizing effect of unilateral judgment in this area."[49] Of course, as alluded to above, there is a third explanation for the difference between the jurisdiction of national and international courts in this area, which is that *they are not exercising the same form of universal jurisdiction in the first place.*

The need for comity, complementarity, and balance in the exercise of international criminal adjudication

To some extent, the jurisdictional critique levied at the International Criminal Court by scholars appears really to be a proxy for political concerns that the Court will in fact be meddling in cases best left to national legal systems, or serving as a check upon political decisions properly left to national governments. Both concerns, however, can and have been addressed through various mechanisms in the ICC's statute, as many commentators, including myself, have pointed out in other writings. These protections include the vetting of most of the ICC prosecutor's decisions by the pretrial chamber, the possibility to remove an errant prosecutor or judge, the guarantees of quality and integrity imposed by the statute with regard to the personnel elected to serve as judges and the Court's prosecutor, the principle of complementarity upon which the Court's jurisdiction is premised, and perhaps most fundamentally, the complete absence of any police force at the Court's disposal or direct power of execution of the Court's orders. That is, all rhetoric aside, the ICC is an extraordinary example of *justice sans police* – a Court completely beholden to the goodwill of states for not only its existence, but also its enforcement power. Thus the specter of a runaway Court is more a phantasm than a real possibility.

Rejecting the US claim that the Court's exercise of jurisdiction over the nationals of nonparty states does not entail accepting the Court's jurisdiction in cases in which the exercise of such jurisdiction would interfere with other important values and principles. If conflicts of jurisdiction arise, the principle of complementarity, enshrined in the preamble to the ICC statute, as well as in Articles 1 and 17, mandates that the case be dismissed. Even if a state is not pursuing prosecutions, it may be that the interests of justice, as outlined in Article 53(c) of the Statute, suggest that the ICC prosecutor should not pursue the case. As the recent dialogue between the ICC prosecutor and a visiting delegation of Acholi leaders from northern Uganda makes clear, the Court will need to be mindful in each instance regarding the need to balance traditional justice and reconciliation processes, the interests of victims, and the need to counter the problem of impunity for the commission of international crimes.[50] This kind of case-by-case balancing will not provide US opponents of the Court the kind of bright-line protection they might desire, but it will permit the Court to exercise its jurisdiction in a manner consistent with the best interests of both the international community as a whole and the independent states that compose its membership.

Finally, although there is certainly some truth to the idea that the ICC statute has embodied within it certain revolutionary features, the notion that the Court may exercise jurisdiction over nonstate party nationals is not one of them. Not only does the statute merely confirm, as ambassador (and now ICC judge) Philippe Kirsch wrote some years ago, that "individuals are subject to the substantive and procedural criminal laws applicable in the territories to which they travel, including laws arising from treaty obligations,"[51] but in fact the United States is a party to and promoted the acceptance of more than one dozen treaties based upon the same principle, particularly several important antiterrorism conventions.[52] Indeed, by ignoring perhaps the most fundamental principles of international law – the notions of reciprocity and the sovereign equality of states – the US attack on the jurisdiction of the International Criminal Court weakens, rather than reinforces, the capacity of international criminal law to respond to acts of terrorism,[53] as well as the atrocities the Court's establishment was designed to suppress and prevent.

Notes

1 See generally Rosalyn Higgins, *Problems and Process: International Law and How We Use It* (Oxford: Oxford University Press, 1995).

2 Leila Nadya Sadat and S. Richard Carden, "The New International Criminal Court: An Uneasy Revolution," *Georgetown Law Journal* vol. 88, no. 3 (March 2000), pp. 381–474.

3 See, for example, Madeline Morris, "High Crimes and Misconceptions: The ICC and Non-Party States," *Law and Contemporary Problems* vol. 64 (2001), pp. 13–66.

4 As of this writing, the Rome Statute has 139 signatories and 99 ratifications.

5 US Congress, "Hearing Before the Subcommittee on International Operations of the Senate Committee on Foreign Relations of the United States Senate," July 23, 1998, 105th Cong., 2nd Sess., S. Rep. No. 105 724, p. 13 (statement of Ambassador David Scheffer).

6 Morris, "High Crimes and Misconceptions," p. 27.

7 Ibid. For responses, see, for example, Hans-Peter Kaul, "Preconditions to the Exercise of Jurisdiction," in Antonio Cassese, Albin Esser, Giorgio Gaja, Philip Kirsch, Alain Pellet, Paola Gaeta, and John R.W.D. Jones, eds, *The Rome Statute of the International Criminal Court: A Commentary* (Oxford: Oxford University Press, 2001), pp. 586–92.

8 United Nations, *Report of the Committee on International Criminal Jurisdiction*, UN GAOR, 7th Sess., Supp. No. 11, UN Doc. A/2136 (1952), Art. 27.

9 Ibid., p. 9.

10 UN General Assembly, 7th Sess., Monday, November 17, 1952 (6th Committee, 328th), p. 419.

11 Ibid., p. 430.

12 United Nations, *Report of the 1953 Committee on International Criminal Jurisdiction*, UN GAOR, 9th Sess., Supp. No. 12, UN Doc. A/2638 (1954), Art. 27.

13 Leila Sadat, "The Proposed Permanent International Criminal Court: An Appraisal," *Cornell International Law Journal* vol. 29, no. 3 (1996), pp. 665–726.

14 Report of the Working Group on a Draft Statute for an International Criminal Court, *Report of the International Law Commission on the Work of Its Forty-fifth Session* (1993), pp. 107–9.

15 United Nations, *Report of the International Law Commission*, UN GAOR, 49th Sess., Supp. No. 10, UN Doc. A/49/10 (1994), pp. 79–81.

16 Ibid., Art. 21, Comment (6).

17 Leila Nadya Sadat, *The International Criminal Court and the Transformation of International Law: Justice for the New Millennium* (Ardsley, NY: Transnational, 2002), pp. 103–27.

18 On which state's consent is needed, the debate was lively. See United Nations, *1995 Ad Hoc Committee Report*, GA Supp. No. 22, A/50/22, para. 105.

19 See *Terra Viva* no. 7 (June 23), p. 5; as well as a statement on the bureau's discussion paper of July 9, 1998. Kaul, "Preconditions to the Exercise of Jurisdiction," p. 599, n. 54.

20 *Rome Statute for the International Criminal Court*, Art. 12.

21 See, for example, Anthony D'Amato, "It's a Bird, It's a Plane, It's Jus Cogens," *Connecticut Journal of International Law* vol. 6, no. 1 (Fall 1990), pp. 1–6; Gennady M. Danilenko, "International Jus Cogens: Issues of Law-Making," *European Journal of International Law* vol. 2, no. 1 (1991), pp. 42–65.

22 See, for example, Alain Pellet, "Internationalized Courts: Better Than Nothing . . . ," in Cesare P. R. Romano, André Nollkaemper, and Jann K. Kleffner, eds, *Internationalized Criminal Courts* (Oxford: Oxford University Press, 2004).

23 United Nations, *Vienna Convention on the Law of Treaties*, UN Doc. A/CONF 39/28, UKTS 58 (1980), 8 ILM 679, Art. 53.

24 On treaties that would violate a peremptory norm, see *Yearbook of the International Law Commission* vol. 2 (1966), p. 248.

25 Accord M. Cherif Bassiouni, "Universal Jurisdiction for International Crimes: Historical Perspectives and Contemporary Practice," *Virginia Journal of International Law* vol. 42, no. 1 (Fall 2001), pp. 81–162; Natalino Ronzitti, "Use of Force, *Jus Cogens*, and State Consent," in Antonio Cassese, ed., *The Current Legal Regulation of the Use of Force* (Dordrecht: Martinus Nijhoff, 1986). Compare Claudia Annacker, "The Legal Régime of Erga Omnes Obligations in International Law," *Austrian Journal of Public International Law* vol. 46 (1993), p. 131.

26 *Prosecutor* v. *Furundzija,* Case No. IT-95-17/1-T, Judgement (December 10, 1998), para. 153. It is true that this holding is arguably dicta, being nonessential to the resolution of the case. William Schabas, "Commentary on *Prosecutor* v. *Furundzija*," in André Klip and Göran Suiter, eds, *III Annotated Leading Cases of International Criminal Tribunals* (Antwerp: Intersentia, 1999).

27 The Secretary-General's report does not use the terminology "*jus cogens*," but instead refers to "rules of international humanitarian law which are beyond any doubt part of customary law so that the problem of adherence of some but not all States to specific conventions does not arise." United Nations, *Report of the Secretary General Pursuant to Paragraph 2 of Security Council Resolution 808*, UN Doc. S/25704 (1993), para. 34. The Secretary-General concluded that these rules included the Geneva Conventions for the Protection of War Victims (August 12, 1949); Hague Convention (IV) Respecting the Law and Customs of War on Land and the Regulations Annexed Thereto (October 18, 1907); the Convention on the Prevention and Punishment of the Crime of Genocide (December 9, 1948); and the Charter of

the International Military Tribunal (Nuremberg Charter) (August 8, 1945). Ibid., para. 35.

28 "Princeton Principles on Universal Jurisdiction," in Stephen Macedo, ed., *Universal Jurisdiction: National Courts and the Prosecution of Serious Crimes under International Law* (Philadelphia: University of Pennsylvania Press, 2004). See also *Draft Chicago Principles of Post-Conflict Justice*, Principle 10: Obligation to Prosecute and Extradite.

29 *International Law Commission Articles on the Draft Code of Crimes against the Peace and Security of Mankind* (1996).

30 *Restatement of the Law of Foreign Relations (Third)* (1987), sec. 404. See also M. Cherif Bassiouni, *Introduction to International Criminal Law* (Ardsley, NY: Transnational, 2003), pp. 174–5.

31 For the view that the list of norms achieving *jus cogens* status is too restrictive, see Hilary Charlesworth and Christine Chinkin, "The Gender of Jus Cogens," *Human Rights Quarterly* vol. 15 (1992), pp. 63, 75.

32 *Princeton Principles on Universal Jurisdiction*, Principle 2(1); Bassiouni, *International Criminal Law*, p. 172.

33 M. Cherif Bassiouni and Edward M. Wise, *Aut Dedere, Aut Judicare: The Duty to Extradite or Prosecute in International Law* (Dordrecht: Martinus Nijhoff, 1995), pp. 20–5.

34 *S.S. Lotus (Fr. V. Turk)* (1927), *P.C.I.J.* (Ser. A), No. 10, p. 18. See also Michael P. Scharf, "The ICC's Jurisdiction over the Nationals of Non-Party States: A Critique of the U.S. Position," *Law and Contemporary Problems* vol. 64, no. 1 (Winter 2001), pp. 71–5.

35 Obviously, there are contrary views that have been expressed about the set of "universal jurisdiction crimes." See, for example, the separate opinion of Judge Guillaume in the *Yerodia* case, *Case Concerning the Arrest Warrant of 11 April 2000 (Democratic Republic of the Congo* v. *Belgium),* Separate Opinion of Judge Guillaume (I.C.J., February 14, 2002), para. 12.

36 See Kenneth C. Randall, "Universal Jurisdiction Under International Law," *Texas Law Review* vol. 66, no. 4 (March 1988), pp. 785–841.

37 Sadat and Carden, *Uneasy Revolution*, p. 406; Leila Nadya Sadat, "Redefining Universal Jurisdiction," *New England Law Review* vol. 35, no. 2 (Winter 2001), pp. 241–63.

38 Morris, "High Crimes and Misconceptions."

39 *Rome Statute for the International Criminal Court*, Preamble, clause 3.

40 Scharf, "ICC's Jurisdiction over the Nationals of Non-Party States," p. 75; Bartram S. Brown, "U.S. Objections to the Statute of the International Criminal Court: A Brief Response," *New York University Journal of International Law and Policy* vol. 3 (1999), pp. 855, 871.

41 *Agreement Between the United Nations and the Government of Sierra Leone on the Establishment of a Special Court for Sierra Leone* (January 16, 2002). The negotiations were undertaken pursuant to Security Council Resolution 1315 (2000).

42 *Prosecutor* v. *Kallon & Kamara, Decision on Challenge to Jurisdiction: Lomé Accord Amnesty*, Case Nos. SCSL-2004-15-AR72(E), SCSL-2004-16-AR72(E), para. 25 (SCSL App. Ch., March 13, 2004).

43 Ibid., para. 39.

44 Ibid., para. 67.

45 Ibid., para. 71.

46 *Congo* v. *Belgium*, para. 60.

47 The court created some confusion as to which acts may be chargeable after an official leaves office. Ibid., para. 61.

48 *Prosecutor* v. *Charles Ghankay Taylor*, Case No. SCSL-2003-01-1, *Decision on Immunity from Jurisdiction* (May 1, 2004).
49 Ibid. (citing amicus brief of Diane Orentlicher, p. 15).
50 Statements by ICC chief prosecutor and the visiting delegation of Acholi leaders from northern Uganda (March 18, 2005), available online at www.icc-cpi.int/press/pressreleases/96.html.
51 Philippe Kirsch, "The Rome Conference on the International Criminal Court: A Comment," *American Society of International Law Newsletter* (November–December 1998), p. 1.
52 For a list, see Scharf, "ICC's Jurisdiction over the Nationals of Non-Party States," p. 99.
53 See Leila Nadya Sadat, "Terrorism and the Rule of Law," *Washington University Global Studies Law Review* vol. 3 (2004), p. 135.

12

INTERNATIONAL HUMANITARIAN LAW

State collusion and the conundrum of jurisdiction

Madeline Morris

Introduction

A fundamental dilemma underlies the enforcement of humanitarian law (which term I use broadly to include the law of genocide, war crimes, and crimes against humanity). The problem, at bottom, is the classic conundrum of international law: how to enforce supranational norms in an international system in which states are formally equal and independent. In this sense, the problem is a familiar one. In the context of international *humanitarian* law, however, this problem takes on certain unique features.

In other fields of international law, compliance that might otherwise not be forthcoming is often accomplished largely through reliance on reciprocity: parties tend to comply with their legal obligations lest they lose reciprocal benefits. To some extent, reciprocity induces compliance with international humanitarian law as well: particularly concerning some aspects of the laws of war, states may comply in order to gain reciprocal benefits. For the other aspects of international humanitarian law, however, reciprocity is not effective. States do not gain reciprocal benefits from refraining from genocide or crimes against humanity committed against their own populations. The threat cannot be: "If you murder your citizens, I'll murder mine." And so, for the enforcement of much of international humanitarian law, a different enforcement system is required.

Criminal prosecution has become prominent among the enforcement mechanisms in this field over the past 60 years, most particularly during the past decade. This chapter will consider tensions arising from the use of criminal prosecution in this field within an international system premised on the sovereign equality of states. In particular, this tension will be examined through the lens of the international law of immunities.

On the problem of perpetrator regimes

The most serious violations of international humanitarian law rarely are purely private acts. Governments, all too often, commit or collude in the most serious violations of international humanitarian law. The crimes of the Nazis, the Khmer Rouge, the 1994 government of Rwanda, factions in the former Yugoslavia, and countless others were committed pursuant to official state policy and authority. The problem therefore emerges of how to enforce the norms of international humanitarian law where states themselves are typically the transgressors and where there is no supranational enforcement authority. Because states typically are implicated in the crimes in question, sole reliance on the usual municipal mechanisms of criminal law enforcement would be foolish. It is unlikely that a government that is responsible for the crimes would be efficacious in prosecuting the offenders.

The central problem concerning criminal law enforcement in this field, then, is the need to place prosecutorial authority in the hands of some body other than the very entity responsible for the crimes. Naturally enough, the solutions devised have been largely jurisdictional. Each jurisdictional solution places the power to prosecute in some entity outside of the responsible state – outside of the perpetrator regime – either by placing jurisdiction in the courts of other states, through universal jurisdiction, or by placing jurisdiction in an international court.

These jurisdictional solutions have been controversial. Since the acts that would form the basis for prosecutions typically do involve official state policy and official state actors, the states whose nationals are accused tend to resist the assertion of jurisdiction by third-party states. We see this resistance to jurisdiction both when those third-party states are acting individually (under universal jurisdiction)[1] and when they are acting collectively (through an international court).[2]

Immunities

Increasingly, we see this resistance to jurisdiction manifested in defendants' states of nationality posing claims of immunity against the prosecution of their officials for humanitarian law violations in courts outside of their own states.[3] The international law of immunities includes diplomatic immunity and sovereign immunity.

Some commentators in this field take the view that immunities are not applicable to grave crimes under international law. The argument here is that there is simply an exception to the international law of immunities for the gravest international crimes. This line of thinking is reflected in certain separate and dissenting opinions of judges on the International Court of Justice (ICJ) in the *Yerodia* case (*Congo* v. *Belgium*),[4] in *obiter dictum* in certain decisions of the International Criminal Tribunal for the Former Yugoslavia,[5] as well as in some academic writing on this subject. These arguments rely on the rather compelling point that the crimes in question are so horrific and destructive that the need for their suppression is sufficient to outweigh the costs of abrogating immunities.

We could envision an even stronger version of the claim that immunities do not cover the most serious international crimes. Here, the argument would be that the question is not one of *abrogating* immunities, but rather of identifying the *limits* of immunities. The argument would be, in other words, that immunities were never meant to be absolute, and are not inherently absolute; in other words, that immunities simply do not cover certain acts that are entirely *ultra vires* of any conceivably legitimate state function.[6]

There are two problems with this stronger claim, however. The first is that there is a lack of historical evidence supporting such a view. The second problem is that there is no theory available to reconcile this limit on immunities fully with the overall framework of the international political and legal system. To be sure, the absence of a theory that would fit the exception neatly into the international structure does not mean that there should be no such exception. But it does point up formidable difficulties: not only would the virtue of theoretically coherent and consistent law be compromised, but there would also be a very basic problem concerning the allocation of authority. When allegations of crime were disputed (as they always would be), who would hold the power to determine, as a matter of fact or of law, whether conduct not covered by immunities had occurred? Another state? A supranational authority of some sort? Would presentation of a plausible accusation extinguish immunity such that a foreign court could exercise jurisdiction – jurisdiction to determine guilt or innocence – when guilt of the crime would itself be precisely the basis for that court's jurisdiction? The more traditional view (and that taken by the ICJ in the *Yerodia* case) is that even the international law of immunities applies in relation to grave international crimes.

Under the law of immunities, officials enjoy diplomatic and/or sovereign immunity from the jurisdiction of other states while they are in office. That immunity remains after the official leaves office in relation to the official acts taken while in office. For private conduct undertaken during the period in office, the immunity expires when the official leaves office.[7]

The attempt to handle international humanitarian law violations by conducting criminal prosecution after the individuals leave office, then, is an attempt to treat the offending conduct as private acts. By the same token, the immunity claims lodged by an official's state constitute an attempt to assert or reassert that the former official acted as an agent of that state, even relative to the allegedly offending conduct.

The underlying rationale for treating the acts in question as private acts appears to be that crimes of this type could never be legitimate state functions, and so the acts must, by definition, be private acts. This rationale, however, belies reality. The fact is, the acts often are indeed state policy. If the acts do constitute genocide, war crimes, or crimes against humanity, then they are unlawful state policy. It is also possible that official conduct alleged to constitute genocide, war crimes, or crimes against humanity does *not* constitute those crimes, if the allegations are incorrect as to fact or law. In either case, what is being brought to judgment in these cases is often precisely the official acts of states – lawful or unlawful.

What motivates the attempt to treat these crimes always as private acts, I believe, is the conviction that the crimes in question are so unacceptable, and their suppression so crucial, that the law of immunities and underlying principles of state sovereignty cannot be permitted to stand in the way. Essentially, what is sought is an exception to the limitations otherwise posed by states' sovereignty for the one, compelling purpose of suppressing the most horrific violations of international humanitarian law. But rather than calling the exception an exception, the "private acts" argument is made – in order to avert the difficulties (line-drawing, slippery slopes, and the rest) that are inherent in making exceptions.

In the enforcement of international humanitarian law through criminal prosecutions, the tension between supranational norms and states' sovereign equality – and the relationship of that tension to immunities – is manifested in somewhat different ways depending upon the type of forum asserting jurisdiction. What follows is an examination of these issues as they arise in the distinct contexts of domestic courts exercising universal jurisdiction and in international courts.

Universal jurisdiction

Under the international legal doctrine of universal jurisdiction, the courts of any state may exercise jurisdiction without regard to the territory where the crime occurred or the nationality of perpetrators or victims.[8] The problems of governmental collusion in the crimes, and the resultant unwillingness of those perpetrator governments to prosecute, are ameliorated by vesting jurisdiction in all states.[9] Universal jurisdiction has been exercised on several occasions in recent years as a mechanism for the prosecution of alleged genocide, war crimes, or crimes against humanity committed in third states. Belgium, during the period in which it was the state with the broadest interpretation and application of the doctrine of universal jurisdiction, instituted criminal investigations of potential defendants including Augusto Pinochet, Ariel Sharon, Yasser Arafat, Saddam Hussein, Fidel Castro, George H. W. Bush, Colin Powell, Norman Schwartzkopf, and Yerodia Ndombasi, among others.[10] Other states (mostly in Western Europe) have brought prosecutions under universal jurisdiction as well. In a number of these cases, the defendants' or potential defendants' states of nationality have objected to the criminal proceedings and brought suit in the International Court of Justice, on the ground that the individuals in question enjoyed official immunity from the criminal jurisdiction of foreign states.[11] A brief examination of the historical development of the doctrine of universal jurisdiction reveals that the current controversy and litigation were virtually inevitable.

After World War II the doctrine of universal jurisdiction was extended from its previous coverage of piracy to apply also to the humanitarian law offenses of genocide, war crimes, and crimes against humanity.[12] In both contexts, the doctrine was used to address problems of enforcement, but the particular enforcement problems addressed were distinctly different. In the piracy context, pirates, often lacking identifiable nationality, committed crimes largely on the high seas outside the territory of any state. In many cases, therefore, no state would have jurisdiction over a given act of piracy if establishing jurisdiction required the prosecuting state first to establish its particular nexus with the crime. Universal jurisdiction solved this problem by allowing any state to prosecute without regard to nexus.

In the context of genocide, war crimes, and crimes against humanity, the enforcement problem is not that there is no state that would have jurisdiction, as in the case of piracy. Rather, the problem is that the crimes in question typically involve the collusion of governments. In such a circumstance, the state with the nexus-based jurisdiction is unlikely to prosecute. The problem of governments colluding in the crimes and then shielding perpetrators from justice is ameliorated by vesting jurisdiction in all states under universal jurisdiction.

But solving the problem of state collusion through the mechanism of universal jurisdiction poses a new set of difficulties not encountered in applying universal jurisdiction to piracy. The crucial difference that distinguishes the ramifications of universal jurisdiction as applied to piracy, from the ramifications of universal jurisdiction as applied to genocide, war crimes, and crimes against humanity, is that piracy comprises, by definition, private acts, while crimes under international humanitarian law tend to involve official state practices and official state actors. From its inception, the law of piracy distinguished "pirates," who operated privately and for private gain, from "privateers" or others commissioned or authorized by states.[13] By excluding state acts from the definition of piracy, the law of piracy was designed to prevent universal jurisdiction over piracy from becoming a source or a tool of interstate conflict.[14]

In the aftermath of World War II, a number of tribunals applied a form of universal jurisdiction to prosecute war crimes and crimes against humanity. When universal jurisdiction was applied in the postwar context, it was conceptualized, sometimes explicitly, as analogous to universal jurisdiction over piracy. There was, however, an important flaw in that analogy. While the law of piracy concerned private acts, war crimes and crimes against humanity frequently concern state action. Universal jurisdiction over war crimes and crimes against humanity therefore raises the prospect of one state's courts standing in judgment of the official acts of other states – in precisely the way that universal jurisdiction over piracy was designed to avoid.

Because the scope of universal jurisdiction thus expanded from piracy to more public acts, we now, predictably, see a new set of political and legal difficulties arising from the exercise of universal jurisdiction. These problems have been manifested in diplomatic exchanges and in the legal cases challenging the exercise of universal jurisdiction based on the international law of immunities.

Two such cases have been filed with the ICJ in recent years. Only one – the *Yerodia* case (*Congo* v. *Belgium*) – has yet been decided.[15] In *Yerodia*, decided in 2001, the ICJ ruled that Belgium had violated international law by issuing an international warrant for the arrest of the then foreign minister of the Democratic Republic of Congo, whom Belgium suspected of crimes against humanity. The ICJ majority stated that, under customary international law, sitting foreign ministers enjoy full immunity from the criminal jurisdiction of other states.[16] The Court stated that it found no exception to this rule even when the defendant is accused of grave international crimes.[17] In this respect, the ICJ might appear to have placed principles underlying the legal equality of states above whatever enforcement value might be gained from the application of universal jurisdiction to violations of international humanitarian law.

International tribunals

While holding that absolute immunity from the criminal jurisdiction of foreign states is to be afforded to incumbent foreign ministers, the *Yerodia* court suggested as well, however, that, as an alternative to the prosecution of the official in question in the courts of a foreign state, the official could lawfully be prosecuted before "an international court with jurisdiction." The ICJ cited the International Criminal Court (ICC) as an example of such an international tribunal.[18] The ICJ thus stated that, while covered officials enjoy absolute immunity from criminal prosecution in the courts of foreign states, immunity does not apply before international tribunals. For this proposition, the ICJ offered no support and, indeed, no discussion.

Was the ICJ correct in its *obiter dictum* on this point? Is an international criminal tribunal not encumbered by the immunities that would apply before national courts?

Rather clearly, if the international court in question is created by the UN Security Council under its Chapter VII powers, immunities might be abrogated as part of the Security Council's exercise of those powers. Certainly, the Security Council indicated in its resolutions creating the international criminal tribunals for the former Yugoslavia and Rwanda that those tribunals have competence to exercise jurisdiction regardless of the official capacities of defendants.[19]

But what of a multilateral treaty-based court? The ICC was established on the basis of a multilaterial treaty and not by the Security Council. When the ICJ stated in *Yerodia* that immunities applicable in national courts would not apply before international courts such as the ICC,[20] the ICJ may have spoken too broadly. Contrary to the *Yerodia* court's statement concerning the ICC, and based precisely on the *Yerodia* holding on immunities, we might reason that the ICC would have the power to prosecute an incumbent foreign minister (or other covered official) of a state that is a party to the ICC treaty but not a covered official of a state that is not a party to the treaty. This point becomes clear when we consider the basis for the ICC's purported jurisdiction over nationals of states that are not parties to the ICC treaty.

The ICC treaty provides that, under certain circumstances, the Court may exercise jurisdiction even over nationals of states that are not parties to the treaty and have not otherwise consented to the Court's jurisdiction. Article 12 provides that the ICC will have jurisdiction to prosecute the national of any state when crimes within the Court's subject-matter jurisdiction are committed on the territory of a state that is a party to the treaty or that consents ad hoc to ICC jurisdiction for that case.[21] That territorial basis would empower the Court to exercise jurisdiction even in cases where the defendant's state of nationality is not a party to the treaty and does not consent to the exercise of jurisdiction.

The rationale for this jurisdiction over nonparty nationals is that, when the crime is committed on the territory of a state party or a state consenting ad hoc, that state has *delegated* its territorial jurisdiction to be exercised by the ICC. The reasoning is that, since the territorial state would have the right to prosecute for offenses committed on its territory, the territorial state also has the right to delegate that jurisdiction to be exercised by an international court.[22] Under this theory, the ICC's jurisdiction over nationals of nonparty states rests on the delegated jurisdiction of a party state.

The overbreadth in the ICJ's reasoning concerning immunity before the ICC now becomes clear: states can delegate to the ICC only such jurisdiction as those states have. If states are obliged to recognize a certain immunity from jurisdiction, as the *Yerodia* decision requires, it would seem that those states' delegated jurisdiction logically must carry that immunity with it. The consequence is that, if states would be legally required to afford immunity from prosecution to certain officials, then the ICC would be similarly constrained.[23]

This immunity before the ICC would not apply to officials of states parties to the ICC treaty. States parties waive the immunity of their officials under Article 27 of the treaty, which states that "immunities . . . which may attach to the official capacity of a person . . . shall not bar the court from exercising its jurisdiction over such a person."[24] This treaty provision constitutes a waiver of immunity only by states parties. For nonparty states, there is no such waiver. The official of a nonparty state would therefore appear to maintain immunity.[25]

To reach a conclusion other than the one just delineated – that the ICC must recognize official immunities of nonparty nationals – would require either that, contrary to the statement of the ICJ, immunities do not apply to grave international crimes, or alternatively, that there is a legal or at least logical basis for distinguishing between national and international tribunals for purposes of immunities. The ICJ offered no such rationale (and I am told by one of the judges who sat on the *Yerodia* case that the question of whether a state's delegation jurisdiction carries with it the relevant immunities was not addressed in the Court's deliberations).

As to the first possibility (demonstrating that immunities do not apply to grave international crimes), the problem is that there is no clear legal basis for the exception and there are serious theoretical, political, and practical difficulties that remain unaddressed in the arguments for such an exception. As to the second possibility – that immunities do not apply to prosecutions before international tribunals – no legal or logical basis has been articulated in the *Yerodia* opinion or elsewhere. Although the *Yerodia* decision provided no argumentation or support for its statement that the law of immunities would not apply to prosecutions before an international court, one might surmise that two rationales might have underlain the Court's reasoning.

The first rationale would be that, while criminal prosecution of one state's official in the courts of another state would offend notions of the sovereign equality of states, prosecution in an international tribunal would not offend that principle. (We could easily dispute this point, but it is at least comprehensible as a claim.) The second possible rationale for the ICJ's assertion that immunities would not apply in international courts would be that, while prosecution of one state's officials in the courts of another state might lend itself to politicization, an international tribunal would not be the captive of any one state's interests or biases and thus would be a more neutral forum better suited to the prosecution of states officials. (Once again, while this point is disputable, it is at least arguable as a claim.)

Oddly, while the proposition that immunities would not apply in an international tribunal such as the ICC would seem logically to need to rest on one or both of the two rationales just offered, those rationales were not in fact the ones offered in the *Yerodia* decision. Rather, the ICJ in *Yerodia* based its holding on a functionalist rationale: that foreign ministers must be free to conduct their governmental and international business unimpeded by the coercive authority of foreign states.[26] This functionalist rationale does not sit easily with the ICJ's distinction between national and international courts. An official is equally impeded in his functioning whether he is detained in the custody of a national or an international jurisdiction. In this respect, the *Yerodia* decision is internally incoherent.

In sum, the status of immunities before international criminal tribunals remains quite unresolved. It may be that a somewhat stronger case can be made for abrogating immunities in international courts than in national courts acting under universal jurisdiction. But when we confront forthrightly the underlying tension between criminal enforcement and sovereign equality, even the international nature of the tribunal does not satisfactorily resolve the dilemma.

Conclusion

The fact that the fundamental legal question of the applicability of immunities before international courts remains an open question is emblematic of the fact that the ultimate conundrum of this field remains unresolved. No satisfactory approach has been found to reconcile the demands of effective enforcement of international humanitarian law with the constraints of a state-based international system. This brings us back to the starting point of this chapter: the core problem of the law of genocide, war crimes, and crimes against humanity is the involvement of states in the perpetration of the crimes. The dilemma posed by the available solutions is that they inevitably place a state – or a collectivity of states – in the position of judging the official acts of another state. The issues currently arising in litigation on immunities are a manifestation of this underlying quandary.

The ultimate question concerns whether, when, and how third-party states may regulate other states' conduct in ways that are of great significance both for human security and for the national security and equal independence of individual states. This basic dilemma of enforcing supranational norms in a state-based international system underlies the grand compromise that is the UN Charter. This utterly fundamental tension is reiterated in only somewhat different terms in the current conflict over immunities, jurisdiction, and the law governing the most horrific acts of genocide, war crimes, and crimes against humanity.

Notes

1 See, for example, *Case Concerning Certain Criminal Proceedings in France (Republic of the Congo* v. *France)* (2003), available online at www.icj-cij.org/icjwww/idocket/icof/icofframe.htm.

2 See, for example, *Prosecutor* v. *Slodoban Milosevic, Decision on Preliminary Motions*, Case No. IT-02-54 (November 8, 2001), available online at www.un.org/icty/ind-e.htm.

3 See, for example, *Case Concerning the Arrest Warrant of 11 April 2000 (Democratic Republic of Congo* v. *Belgium)* (February 14, 2002), available online at www.icj-cij.org/icjwww/idocket/icobe/icobeframe.htm.

4 *Yerodia*, dissenting opinions of Judges Al-Khasawneh and Van den Wyngaert.

5 See, for example, *Prosecutor* v. *Slodoban Milosevic, Decision on Preliminary Motions*, para. 28.

6 I am indebted for conversation on this point to Professor Ralf Michaels of the Duke Law School.

7 *Yerodia*, paras 47–62.

8 See *Restatement (Third) of Foreign Relations* (1987), pp. 404, 423.

9 Madeline Morris, "Universal Jurisdiction in a Divided World: Conference Remarks," *New England Law Review* vol. 35 (Winter 2001), p. 337.

10 See Glenn Frankel, "Belgian War Crimes Law Undone by Its Global Reach: Cases Against Political Figures Sparked Crises," *Washington Post Foreign Service* (September 30, 2003), p. A1 (reporting that the broad scope of universal jurisdiction provided under Belgium's 1993 law was cut back substantially by legislation enacted by Belgium in 2003).

11 See notes 1–3.

12 Morris, "Universal Jurisdiction in a Divided World," pp. 341–7.

13 See *Convention on the High Seas* (April 29, 1958), Arts 15, 16, 13 U.S.T. 2312, 450 U.N.T.S. 82. See also United Nations, *Convention on the Laws of the Sea* (December 10, 1982), Arts 101, 102, UN Doc. A/CONF. 62/122, 21 I.L.M. 1261 (1982).

14 Clyde Crockett, "Toward a Revision of the International Law of Piracy," *DePaul Law Review* vol. 26 (1976), pp. 78, 88. See also Morris, "Universal Jurisdiction in a Divided World," p. 340.

15 See *Yerodia*.
16 Ibid., paras 53–5.
17 Ibid., paras 56–8.
18 Ibid.
19 "The official position of any accused person, whether as Head of State or Government or as a responsible Government official, shall not relieve such person of criminal responsibility nor mitigate punishment." See United Nations, *Statute of the International Criminal Tribunal for the Former Yugoslavia*, Art. 7. para 2, UN Doc. S/25704 (as amended May 17, 2002), available online at www.un.org/icty/basic/statut/stat2000.htm; United Nations, *Statute of the International Tribunal for Rwanda* (November 8, 1994), Art. 6, para. 2, UN Doc. S/RES/955, 33 I.L.M. 1598 (1994), available online at www.un.org/ictr/statute.html.
20 *Yerodia*, para. 61.
21 United Nations, *Rome Statute of the International Criminal Court* (July 17, 1998), UN Doc. A/CONF. 183/9, Art. 12.
22 See, for example, Michael P. Scharf, "The ICC's Jurisdiction over the Nationals of Non-Party States: A Critique of the U.S. Position," *Law and Contemporary Problems* vol. 64 (2001), p. 67.
23 Madeline Morris, "Terrorism: The Politics of Prosecution," *Chicago Journal of International Law* vol. 5 (Winter 2005), pp. 405, 417.
24 United Nations, *Rome Statute of the International Criminal Court*, Art. 27.
25 This conclusion appears to be consistent with the thrust of Article 98(1) of the ICC treaty, which provides "that the Court may not proceed with a request for surrender or assistance which would require the requested State to act inconsistently with its obligations under international law with respect to the State or diplomatic immunity of a person or property of a third State, unless the Court can first obtain the cooperation of that third State for waiver of the immunity.'
26 *Yerodia*, para. 53.

13

WHOSE JUSTICE? RECONCILING UNIVERSAL JURISDICTION WITH DEMOCRATIC PRINCIPLES

Diane F. Orentlicher

Introduction

It took only an instant to reverse centuries of diplomatic practice and unsettle the deepest foundations of international law. With the arrest of former Chilean president Augusto Pinochet in London's exclusive Marylebone district in October 1998, the law seemed to lunge forward rather than advance at its more usual plodding pace.[1] For centuries, international law and the practice of states had affirmed a bedrock principle of mutual restraint among nations: courts of one state would not judge the sovereign acts of another. Now, a former Chilean head of state had been arrested by British authorities at the request of a Spanish magistrate on charges that were at heart about how the accused had governed Chile a quarter of a century before. Defying the predictions of seasoned experts, Pinochet's arrest was upheld by England's highest court.

In this way an obscure concept with an ungainly name – "universal jurisdiction" – ended its long exile in the precincts of legal arcana, where it had languished largely unnoticed since Israel's prosecution of Adolf Eichmann in 1961. Inspired by the *Pinochet* precedent, victims of human rights violations in Chad instituted criminal proceedings against former Chadian leader Hissène Habré in Senegal and Belgium in 2000.[2] In June 2001 a Belgian jury broke new ground when it convicted four Rwandans for their roles in the 1994 genocide in Rwanda in a case that relied on universal jurisdiction.[3] Before long – and controversially – Belgium became the world capital of universal jurisdiction. Criminal cases were instituted in Belgian courts against current or former leaders of Chad, Cuba, the Democratic Republic of Congo, Iran, Iraq, Israel, Côte d'Ivoire, the Palestinian Authority, the United States, and other countries.[4]

For some, these developments heralded a long-overdue era of enforcement of the law derived from Nuremberg. In the view of others, Belgium's expansive approach to universal jurisdiction was cause for concern. Several countries pushed back, and Belgium was forced to retreat.

When a Belgian court ruled that a criminal investigation of Israeli prime minister Ariel Sharon could proceed once he left office, Israeli authorities denounced the decision as a "blood libel" and recalled the new Israeli ambassador to Belgium.[5] The American response to a complaint filed in Belgium against senior US officials was even more forceful. Then secretary of state Colin Powell, one of the officials named in the complaint, warned that Belgium risked losing its status as the headquarters of the North Atlantic Treaty Organization (NATO).[6] The Belgian response was swift. The government rushed through parliament legislation that radically reduced the reach of Belgium's law on universal jurisdiction.[7] In the view of the incumbent US administration, the amendments did not go far enough. In June 2003, Secretary of Defense Donald H. Rumsfeld warned that the United States would withhold further funding for a new NATO headquarters building in Brussels and that senior US officials might stop visiting Belgium unless it repealed its already diminished law on universal jurisdiction.[8] Bowing to US pressure, the Belgian parliament amended its law once again,[9] this time leaving scant scope for universal jurisdiction.[10]

It is not hard to fathom why many government officials opposed Belgium's previously expansive law.[11] After all, victims with ready access to Belgian courts had set their sights on national leaders the world over. Yet it is not only senior officials who have misgivings about the exercise of universal jurisdiction.

The most trenchant challenge to universal jurisdiction has been framed in terms of democratic principles. Leading proponents of this challenge make two overlapping claims. First, their core claim is that courts and prosecutors exercising universal jurisdiction "are completely unaccountable to the citizens of the nation whose fate they are ruling upon"[12] and, in consequence, "will invariably be less disciplined and prudent than would otherwise be the case."[13]

In this view, two features of the body of international law supporting universal jurisdiction compound the problems associated with its exercise. First, while classic international law regulated relations between states, contemporary international law intrudes deeply into matters of internal governance.[14] This transformation has special significance for the law establishing universal jurisdiction. In an earlier age, the principle of universality was confined to piracy and the slave trade – conduct that by its nature transpires beyond any nation's exclusive province. Since World War II, however, the writ of universal jurisdiction has expanded to include crimes, like genocide, that usually occur within the boundaries of sovereign states.[15] When a court exercises universal jurisdiction over these crimes, it judges conduct that occurred within another country in light of law that was developed through processes that transcend both states' lawmaking institutions. Second, skeptics note that since there is no consensus about what crimes are subject to universal jurisdiction[16] and how they are defined, courts exercising universal jurisdiction are not even constrained by widely accepted legal interpretations.[17]

The second major objection to universal jurisdiction is the claim that its exercise may "provoke domestic unrest or international conflict."[18] Critics warn that universal jurisdiction may destabilize fragile democracies that have accepted amnesties in exchange for an end to brutal governance. More generally, opponents charge that universal jurisdiction effectively displaces local processes of reckoning with the past – deliberations that belong exclusively to those who have endured unspeakable crimes.

For the most part these challenges have been advanced by writers who are generally skeptical of international law and multilateral institutions that constrain unilateral action. Leading critics of universal jurisdiction have also challenged direct enforcement of customary international law by federal courts in the United States[19] and opposed the International Criminal Court.[20] Their views on universal jurisdiction thus have been seen as one facet of a broader conservative critique of international legal regimes. Perhaps in consequence, their views – which I will call the "conservative critique" of universal jurisdiction – for the most part have not been seriously engaged by other prominent voices in the public debate over bystander justice.

Yet human rights professionals above all should take these claims seriously. The conservative critique lays bare but does not resolve a paradox at the heart of human rights law itself. On the one hand, postwar law affirms that some acts cannot be shielded from global scrutiny – or indeed enforcement – by claims of sovereign prerogative.[21] Yet international human rights law upholds the right of all societies to govern themselves, and questions of self-government are deeply engaged by the question, "What should be done about past atrocities?" Thus while the conservative critique of universal jurisdiction has not been framed in terms of international human rights, its core concern finds significant support in that body of law.

The central aim of this chapter is to develop a framework for resolving the justice/democracy paradox presented by states' recent recourse to universal jurisdiction. As a foundation, I first develop the conservative critique of universal jurisdiction. While I identify legitimate concerns underlying the conservative critique, I reject the stark conclusions reached by its leading proponents – that the exercise of universal jurisdiction is inherently incompatible with democratic principles and is generally likely to derail fragile democratic transitions.

The first claim obscures a crucial fact: many states have *consented* to universal jurisdiction under defined circumstances. The second plank of the conservative critique – the charge that foreign prosecutions may upend national processes of reckoning with past atrocities – rests upon several unsound premises. Most important, it falsely assumes that societies that have endured atrocious crimes are invariably passive objects of foreign hubris when courts exercise a universal jurisdiction. The *Pinochet* case points up the flaws in this premise. Chilean victims initiated the criminal case against Pinochet in Spain, and Chile ratified the treaty that authorized Pinochet's prosecution abroad when Pinochet was president.

In larger perspectives, I argue that the exercise of universal jurisdiction may encourage or deepen normative shifts, with salutary effects in the countries most affected by the crimes in question. Indeed recent experience suggests that, far from destabilizing fragile democracies, the realistic possibility of foreign prosecution for atrocious crimes has enhanced national processes of reckoning and repair and thereby fortified democratic transitions.

The task today is to identify principled guidelines to ensure that universal jurisdiction is in fact exercised in a democratically legitimate – and democracy-enhancing – fashion. Drawing upon insights derived from two very distinct streams of scholarship – US constitutional law and international relations theory – this chapter identifies benchmarks for determining when the exercise of universal jurisdiction is consistent with democratic values.

Transnational lawmaking processes

First, it will be helpful to identify key characteristics of the law underlying universal jurisdiction, as well as the processes involved in making that law. A fundamental feature of universal jurisdiction is its transnational nature. As the term is used in this chapter, "transnational law" is law that is made by more than one state, typically with the participation of nonstate actors, and that is constituted at least in part by national law. As this working definition implies, transnational law typically comprises elements of both national and international law, dissolving traditional dichotomies between the two.[22]

The Convention against Torture and Other Cruel, Inhuman, or Degrading Treatment or Punishment,[23] which proved crucial to the proceedings against General Pinochet in Spain and England, exemplifies this phenomenon. As a multilateral treaty, the Convention against Torture is an instrument of international law: its text was developed and adopted at the international level and it is binding under international law. But the law associated with this treaty also comprises domestic law, both legislative and judicial. States parties are required to "take effective legislative, administrative, judicial or other measures"[24] to prevent torture. Inevitably, then, crucial terms of the convention are left to be clarified by national courts, which embroider onto the treaty text their own interpretive meanings. Thus the law of the convention is "made" at both the international and the national level.

The convention also establishes a transnational architecture of enforcement. Articles 5(2) and 7(1) require states parties either to institute criminal proceedings against persons suspected of having committed torture who are present in their territory or to extradite the alleged torturers for trial in another country. The transnational nature of the Convention against Torture is even wider and deeper than this account suggests. Judicial interpretations of the treaty have drawn upon case law from an eclectic range of international, regional, and national courts. For example, the key British decision judging Pinochet extraditable to Spain to face certain torture-related charges cited decisions of the International Criminal Tribunal for the former Yugoslavia,[25] the European Commission of Human Rights,[26] and courts of countries ranging from the United States[27] to Germany[28] and Israel.[29] Thus states that adhere to the Convention against Torture sign on to a diffuse and decentralized system of lawmaking.

Should transnational lawmaking processes be democratic?

It is not hard to see that this brand of lawmaking challenges traditional notions of self-government, for we have long understood democracy to be inseparable from a bounded political community.[30]

Mindful of this pervasive conception of democratic governance, this chapter examines the challenge to democratic principles presented by emerging patterns of transnational lawmaking, focusing on the lawmaking processes associated with universal jurisdiction. And so a preliminary question merits brief consideration: *Should* transnational lawmaking processes be democratic? The first point to be made here is that international law itself is now deeply committed to democratic principles. Thus the question whether transnational lawmaking processes are democratically legitimate is in part an inquiry into the internal coherence of international law.

Postwar international human rights instruments affirm a universal right to self-government[31] and various regional treaties affirm similar rights.[32] Although states' commitment to promote and enforce these guarantees was shallow until recently, efforts in support of democracy gained powerful momentum in the final decade of the twentieth century.[33] Noting this trend, writers have emphasized its most obvious implication: international law can now concern itself with broad questions of governance within states, matters long deemed off limits to global scrutiny despite states' formal pledges to respect principles of self-government.[34] Only lately has it become clear that democratic principles also have a significant bearing on transnational lawmaking processes. More than ever before, matters touching on how we conduct our daily affairs are regulated through law that transcends the province of state governance.

While transnational lawmaking processes challenge traditional notions of democracy, they are not inherently undemocratic. At a time when states' economies, cultures, ecosystems, and interests are extensively integrated, self-governance would in fact be diminished if national communities were unable to participate in transnational lawmaking processes. The question, then, is how democratic societies can meaningfully choose the terms of their participation – and then ensure the ongoing accountability of lawmaking processes that unfold in significant part beyond their national borders.

Pinochet as paradigm: judge-made law across borders

This is not the place for an exhaustive account of the legal proceedings against the former Chilean leader.[35] For present purposes it suffices to note two aspects of the crucial British ruling that Pinochet could not avoid extradition on certain torture-related charges based on his immunity as a former head of state. On March 24, 1999, the United Kingdom's highest court held that Pinochet was not immune from criminal process for allegations of torture committed after December 8, 1988.[36] Although the reasoning of the six judges constituting the majority varied, the Convention against Torture played a key role in each of their decisions. Yet the Convention is textually silent about head-of-state immunity.[37] Nevertheless, a majority of law lords concluded that substantive head-of-state immunity[38] for the crime of torture would be incompatible with the treaty.

At the proverbial first blush, the *Pinochet* case would thus seem to bolster the charge that the role of judicial interpretation looms especially large when courts exercise universal jurisdiction – a charge that, in the view of critics of universal jurisdiction, exacerbates problems relating to judicial accountability. Yet there is no reason to suppose that treaties are generally vaguer – and thus leave larger scope for judicial interpretation – than domestic legislation. In fact, the more ambiguous law at issue in the British proceedings was a domestic law, the United Kingdom's State Immunity Act of 1978.[39]

Crucially, however, ambiguous domestic laws are normally enforced by judges who are fellow citizens of those whom they judge. As I argue below, this provides a vital resource for ensuring the democratic legitimacy of "judge-made law." The more important question, then, is whether analogous legitimating resources are available in a transnational setting – a question I take up later.

Judicial lawmaking in national proceedings

Concerns about judicial lawmaking are hardly confined to a transnational setting. In a domestic context, they center on the claim that judge-made law is fundamentally undemocratic. For some writers, this claim (which I will call the "democracy critique") proceeds from the belief that the legislature is the preeminent arena for self-government, at least after a country's constitution has been adopted.[40] The critique is thus: judges who effectively modify or invalidate legislation undermine democratic principles by substituting their own preferences for statutes enacted by the elected representatives of "the people."[41]

Scholars and jurists have long questioned key assumptions behind the democracy critique.[42] Understanding its flaws helps us see when and why the peculiar brand of judicial lawmaking at play in the exercise of universal jurisdiction may challenge democratic values – and just as important, when such concerns are misplaced. Many scholars have challenged a key premise of the critique: that the political branches of government are more representative of majority will, and thus more democratic, than the judiciary.[43] This assumption idealizes the legislative process,[44] underestimates the degree to which courts reflect and respond to public opinion,[45] and overlooks the democracy-enhancing role that courts play. Diverse scholars make a common claim: democracies, courts, legislatures, and other actors participate in an ongoing, interactive process of lawmaking – and this anchors the democratic legitimacy of judicial review.[46]

Through myriad forms of interaction, judges remain publicly accountable in ways that secure and sustain democratic government. Most obviously (though in practice rarely), judicial rulings that stray too far from public consensus can be nullified by legislation. In jurisdictions that elect judges, candidates whose views range far afield of public sentiment are unlikely to be reelected. Appointed judges whose views are politically unpopular may imperil their prospects for elevation to a higher court.[47]

But the interaction between judges and society is wider and deeper than the interplay structured by such formal processes as confirmation hearings and elections. As Alexander Bickel wrote, judges engage in "a continuing colloquy with the political institutions and with society at large."[48] The colloquy does not end when judgment is reached. Meanwhile, the ground for further debate has been seeded by dissenting opinions that may some day become the majority view, the arguments marshaled in majority opinions, editorials, speeches, and scholarly critiques. The dialogue includes disagreement, both within the judiciary and among the judiciary, the legislature, the executive, and society. Thus an essential element of the judge's craft is an ability to persuade those who resist his or her interpretations as well as to manage outright opposition to rulings.

The persuasive power of judicial rulings turns in large measure on judges' ability to craft opinions that resonate with widely shared public values. [49] That judges believe they should try to persuade the public that their rulings are correct signifies that the judiciary is a democratically accountable institution, albeit of a different stripe than the legislature. When courts are unable to persuade large segments of the public that their decisions are correct (or even well reasoned), they must draw upon a reservoir of institutional authority to secure acceptance of their rulings as binding.[50] That acceptance derives in large part from two sources, both of which presuppose a court's embeddedness in a political community.

The first is citizens' general commitment to the authority of the government structure to which courts belong. In a democracy, we accept the authority of our courts to interpret our laws because they are *our* courts. In a constitutional democracy, judicial review derives its democratic legitimacy in part from the public's consent, tacit if not explicit, to judicial review itself.[51]

A second basis for accepting decisions we think flawed derives from the respect that courts earn over time through their performance. A precious resource in establishing this brand of legitimacy is the political relationship of the judge to the law he or she interprets – the relationship of a judge who is also a citizen. When judges interpret legislation in a purely national setting, their decisions are shaped in myriad and imperceptible ways by community values, expressed through the daily rituals of self-government as well as at formal moments of legislative enactment. Thus what may on the surface seem to be judge-made law derives from a rich, robust, and continuous process of self-government. When judges make law, they are not so much writing it *for* us as *with* us. In their decisions we recognize public values we have constructed together, much of the time through passionate disagreement,[52] across our common history. As my allusion to disagreement implies, none of this is to suggest that decisions rendered by judges in democratic societies are accepted because they embody values *uniformly* embraced by all or most citizens. Still, the democratic legitimacy of courts turns, in part, on whether citizens recognize that they share a common political project embodied in legal commitments.

In sum, some measure of judicial lawmaking is understood, across a wide spectrum of views, to be integral to self-government. Crucially, however, the embeddedness of courts in a broader framework of self-government and in the social fabric of their communities anchors the perceived legitimacy of judicial review.

Judicial lawmaking in a transnational setting

We can now better grasp what is at stake when judges interpret law in a case, like the attempted prosecution of General Pinochet in Europe, which affects citizens of another country far more than the judge's own compatriots. In a deeply important sense, British and Spanish judges were not making law for Chile by enforcing the torture convention against General Pinochet. By ratifying the convention, Chile had already made the treaty *its* law. Through adjudication, however, British and Spanish judges became coauthors of this law in a case that would have a more profound effect upon Chileans than on British or Spanish citizens. If we believe that citizens should be at least indirect authors of the law that governs them,[53] we instinctively shrink from the thought of Chilean citizens being governed by the law of judges deliberating an ocean away.

Yet despite the differences I have highlighted, cross-boundary lawmaking processes share important qualities with domestic lawmaking. Lawmaking at both levels entails the continuous interplay of multiple law-generating communities. As Harold Koh has noted, "[e]very court in the United States . . . applies law that was not made by its own polity whenever the court's own choice-of-law principles so direct."[54] This perspective helps us see that the fact that lawmaking-across-borders involves multiple communities does not hopelessly undermine its democratic legitimacy.

To grasp the significance of this point it is useful to deepen the discussion of judicial interpretation elaborated so far. Much of my analysis has drawn upon a core insight of communitarian streams in legal scholarship: legal meaning is derived from particular sociocultural matrices.[55] So, too, are the standards we use to assess both the general authority of lawmaking institutions and their performance in specific cases.[56] Even in a purely national setting, however, the legitimating community is always and inevitably plural. The plural nature of discrete political communities is easiest to see when we think of spatially defined substate units, such as federal states, communes, and municipalities. But these are not the only communities that matter when it comes to lawmaking processes. Centrally important here is the kind of community captured in Robert Cover's notion of a *nomos* – a normative universe. *Nomoi* – religious sects, professional communities, and so forth – generate multiple, interdependent meanings for every law.[57] And so while national law, including law established through judicial interpretation, is authoritative and official, its meaning is not unitary but has multiple meanings.

What this tells us is modest but important. The fact that multiple states and an eclectic assortment of actors participate in transnational lawmaking does not irremediably doom the democratic legitimacy of these lawmaking processes. Nor, however, does the multiplicity of actors who participate in transnational lawmaking *demonstrate* the legitimacy of these processes. To the contrary, the multistate nature of judicial enforcement of transnational law presents qualitatively different challenges to democratic values than does judge-made law in a purely national setting. How, then, should we evaluate the democratic legitimacy of the kind of lawmaking processes at play in the *Pinochet* case?

Assessing the democratic legitimacy of transnational adjudication

As a first cut at this question, three benchmarks for appraising the legitimacy of transnational lawmaking phenomena emerge from the preceding discussion. The first is general acknowledgment of the authority of relevant lawmaking institutions, including courts, by those who are subject to the law these bodies generate. Deriving from the democratic principle of consent, this criterion is essentially normative.

At least in well-functioning democracies, the institutional authority of courts is generally accepted by citizens. Their tacit acceptance of the authority of their nation's courts underpins citizens' willingness to accept judicial rulings they consider wrongly decided. In contrast, the notion of tacit acceptance has scant meaning when it comes to the exercise of jurisdiction by a foreign or international court. Reflecting this, international law requires specific acceptance of such a court's exercise of authority, whether expressed through adherence to a relevant treaty, such as the Convention against Torture; case-specific consent;[58] adoption of a national law or decree; or the more diffuse process of establishing customary international law.[59]

In fact, many states have consented to the exercise of universal jurisdiction, and for perfectly valid reasons. Notably, societies recovering from the ravages of mass atrocity have been the first to sign up for transnational enforcement regimes that can provide a backstop in the event their nations once again descend into the abyss of lawless violence.[60] In doing so, they are exercising the prerogatives of democracy – and seeking to safeguard its future.

A second quality associated with adjudicative lawmaking widely accepted as democratically legitimate is the respect that lawmaking institutions earn over time by virtue of their performance. In contrast to the first criterion, this benchmark of legitimacy is more descriptive than normative; that is, it reflects conditions in which citizens tend to accept the legitimacy of judge-made law. Ordinarily, this type of respect derives in large measure from judges' ability to craft decisions that resonate with the deepest commitments of their *own* political communities (though a judge's "own" political community is always plural). A third benchmark of legitimacy is the belief by those who may be subject to judge-made law that adjudicators are accountable to them.

The last two resources for legitimation are manifestly more elusive in a transnational setting than in a purely domestic context. The question, then, is whether appropriate analogues are available in the former. Elsewhere I have developed a response to this question in greater depth than is possible here.[61] A few general observations may, however, be sufficient to demonstrate that transnational lawmaking processes have already generated context-appropriate resources for legitimation, and these can be further enhanced.

Notably, an interpretive community of jurists now plays a disciplining role in transnational adjudication. One need look no further than the *Pinochet* case for evidence. As noted earlier, key decisions by British judges cited judgments by other national courts, regional courts, and international tribunals. This phenomenon is emblematic of contemporary transnational lawmaking: courts enforcing international humanitarian law are talking to each other, shaping each other's understanding of the law, critiquing each other, and, together, constructing a common code of humanity.[62] By providing public and reasoned explanations for their rulings, courts exercising universal jurisdiction can also bridge the distance between themselves and societies particularly affected by their rulings. Moreover, the discipline of providing publicly reasoned decisions operates as a significant restraint on the misuse of judicial power.[63]

There is mounting evidence that the discipline imposed by transjudicial communication can serve to legitimize as well as constrain courts. For example a key source of the "compliance pull" of decisions of the European Court of justice is "the legal language itself: the language of reasoned interpretation, logical deduction, systemic and temporal coherence – the artifacts that national courts would partly rely on to enlist obedience within their own national orders."[64]

Universal jurisdiction and emergent democracies

The final plank of the conservative critique is the charge that the exercise of universal jurisdiction undermines democracies newly emerging from repressive governance. This claim has two principal strands. First, some argue that foreign prosecutions could have a destabilizing effect in the country that endured atrocious crimes, potentially reversing tenuous progress in its transition to democracy.[65] Following the arrest of General Pinochet in London, not a few observers warned that his detention might revive the Chilean military's penchant for political intervention and deepen divisions within Chilean society.[66]

Second, some argue that prosecutions by bystander states upend processes of democratic deliberation that properly belong to the political community directly affected by the crimes in question. John Bolton seemed to have something like this in mind when he denounced the European proceedings against General Pinochet on the asserted ground that, "Morally and politically, what Pinochet's regime did or did not do is primarily a question for Chile to resolve."[67] This critique presumes that questions of punishment belong not to humanity writ large, but to particular communities – above all, to the society most affected by the crimes in question.

This view directly challenges two core justifications of universal jurisdiction: (1) because certain crimes offend humanity writ large, there is a global entitlement to bring perpetrators to account; and (2) unless every state assumes responsibility to prosecute the perpetrators of such crimes, many will likely elude the net of justice. Against these claims, critics say that universal jurisdiction has gone too far. If Nuremberg was justified, they argue, contemporary prosecutions push a noble effort "to extremes that risk substituting the tyranny of judges for that of governments."[68] Before I challenge this statement, however, I will show why it merits close consideration.

Upending democratic deliberations?

Such questions as what behavior should be criminalized and when and how individuals should be punished matter deeply to the community in whose midst the conduct in question occurs. The claim that questions of punishment belong to particular communities has special significance when the crimes in question arise from a pattern of severe repression. Whether a country tries to bury past depredations in a grave of silence, examines and condemns them through the work of an officially sanctioned truth commission,[69] purges from public office those determined to have been responsible for systemic repression, provides reparations to victims, and/or punishes the perpetrators, the path it chooses is constitutive of its political community.

Tellingly, the phrase "transitional justice" has become a term of art for policies of justice devised by societies emerging from repressive governance.[70] Governments that succeed brutal regimes may see criminal trials and other programs of transitional justice as vehicles for the "construction of a permanent, unmistakable wall between the new beginnings and the old tyranny."[71] The deliberations surrounding a program of transitional justice are not the sort that should be displaced by the paternalistic judgment of international law (though I want to reserve for now the question whether universal jurisdiction has any such effect). It is not simply the case that reckoning with past crimes is a matter of unique interest to the community that endured abominations. Societies that have been governed though wholesale repression bear a special burden of reckoning, deriving from both moral and practical imperatives.

Morally, their burden stems from what Karl Jaspers called "political guilt." In Jaspers's lexicon, political guilt, "involving the deeds of statesmen and of the citizenry of a state, results in my having to bear the consequences of the state whose power governs me and under whose order I live."[72] Homegrown justice represents at least partial payment of a country's debt to citizens previously denied protection of the law.

Functionally, transitional justice serves as a vehicle of social and political transformation. By instituting criminal trials or pursuing other policies of transitional justice, a government condemns brutal policies of its predecessor and signals the dawning of a new era. Transitional justice also aims at repairing societies that have endured unspeakable crimes. A key aim of such programs is to restore citizens' capacity to *be* citizens, in part by establishing or restoring public trust in government. Finally, we may be most confident that a country will not once again descend into the abyss of wholesale repression if it addresses past abuses through its own policies of reckoning and repair.[73]

Do transnational processes undermine democratic deliberations? A challenge

If the conservative critique finds support in these considerations, it nonetheless suffers from flawed assumptions and faulty reasoning. We should not uncritically accept the claim that Pinochet's self-amnesty was freely endorsed by a full-fledged democracy. After all, while preparing to relinquish power, Pinochet credibly threatened military force in the event his self-amnesty was challenged.[74] To deliberate under the threat of destabilizing force is hardly an ideal exercise in self-government. More fundamentally, the claim that universal jurisdiction improperly disturbs policy choices resulting from democratic deliberations falsely assumes that political communities decide how to confront past atrocities in a hermetically sealed universe. This assumption is problematic at several levels. To begin, as legal and international relations scholars have recognized, transnational political and social processes are constitutive of the values that shape both domestic and international law and policy.[75] It is not simply the case that domestic politics define state preferences, which are then advanced by a state's diplomatic representatives in their negotiations with representatives of other countries.[76] Rather, interactions across borders often shape participants' values in ways that define their international negotiating positions. In turn, the international norms constructed through these processes, such as the notion that torturers should be punished, loop back into domestic political and lawmaking processes.

The charge that European proceedings against Augusto Pinochet supplanted Chileans' national process of reckoning with his crimes obscures the active participation of Chileans in the transnational legal processes underlying the *Pinochet* case. Notably, the Spanish investigation that led to Pinochet's arrest was triggered by Chilean victims of Pinochet-era crimes (some possessing dual Spanish–Chilean citizenship).

Further, dire warnings about the destabilizing effects of the European proceedings were belied by their salutary impact. The decisions of judges in Madrid and London had a transformative impact on judges and prosecutors elsewhere, exemplifying what Harold Koh calls the "normativity" of transnational lawmaking processes.[77] The unexpected success of the pursuit of Pinochet in turn inspired judges throughout Latin America,[78] as well as Europe and Africa, to pursue dictators previously thought to be legally untouchable.

The most profound reverberations of the European proceedings were in Chile. On December 1, 2000, Chilean judge Juan Guzmán formally charged Pinochet with the kidnapping of political opponents in the aftermath of the 1973 coup that brought Pinochet to power and placed the former president under house arrest.[79] To be sure, even before Pinochet was arrested in England, Chilean society had made significant progress in its national process of reckoning with his crimes, but proceedings abroad had a catalytic effect in Chile.[80] The *New York Times* reported that the case that led to Pinochet's house arrest in Chile "began to gain currency in Chile only after General Pinochet [had been] arrested two years [earlier] in London on a Spanish warrant."[81] Far from displacing Chile's internal project of addressing its past, then, the arrest abroad of General Pinochet reenergized Chile's process of recovering from dictatorship, fortifying its democratic transition. The possibility that Pinochet could be prosecuted outside Chile did not diminish or circumvent that country's democratic deliberations, but rather enlarged the space within which Chilean society could address its past.

Nor is Chile an isolated example. In August 2003, for example, both houses of Argentina's congress voted to annul two 1980s-era amnesty laws. This action has been attributed in part to Spanish magistrate Baltasar Garzón's issuance of warrants seeking the extradition of 45 Argentine military officers and one civilian.[82]

Against these developments, the conservative critique of the *Pinochet* case seems not so much implausible as impoverished. In larger perspective, it would be a mistake to suppose that Chilean society exists, deliberates, and determines its democratic destiny in isolation from transnational processes. Thus to suggest that Chile should determine Pinochet's fate without hindrance from outsiders misses a crucial point: how Chileans exercise their moral autonomy is partly a function of their participation in transnational normative processes.

Acknowledgments

This chapter is adapted from Diane F. Orentlicher, "Whose Justice? Reconciling Universal Jurisdiction with Democratic Principles," *Georgetown Law Journal* vol. 92 (2004), pp. 1057–134. I am grateful to Gregg Bloche, Reed Brody, Richard Falk, Tom Farer, Mark Feldstein, Claudio Grossman, Darren Hutchinson, Steve Macedo, Andy Moravcsik, Jonathan Sarnoff, Anne-Marie Slaughter, and Rick Wilson for providing comments on earlier drafts, sharing their insights, and making other contributions to the article from which this chapter is adapted, and to Christian De Vos, Richard Hamilton, Helen Harnett, Jamal Jafari, Rosy Lor, Jason Maddux, William Martin, and Danica Szarvas-Kidd for first-rate research assistance. I am also grateful to Princeton University's Program in Law and Public Affairs, which awarded me a fellowship during the academic year 2000–1, the US Institute of Peace, which provided a research grant during the same period, both enabling me to begin work on the larger research project of which this chapter forms a part, and to the Washington College of Law of American University for supporting my scholarship in myriad and indispensable ways.

Notes

1 See "Britain Arrests Pinochet to Face Charges by Spain," *New York Times*, October 18, 1998.

2 See Stephen P. Marks, "The *Hissène Habré* Case: The Law and Politics of Universal Jurisdiction," in Stephen Macedo, ed., *Universal Jurisdiction: National Courts and the Prosecution of Serious Crimes Under International Law* (Philadelphia: University of Pennsylvania Press, 2003), pp. 131–67; Human Rights Watch, "The Case Against Hissène Habré, an 'African Pinochet,'" available online at www.hrw.org/justice/habre.

3 See "Rwandan Nuns Jailed in Genocide; Belgian Jury Also Sentences Two Others," *Washington Post*, June 9, 2001; "Mother Superior Guilty in Rwanda Killings," *New York Times*, June 9, 2001.

4 See Diane F. Orentlicher, "Whose Justice? Reconciling Universal Jurisdiction with Democratic Principles," *Georgetown Law Journal* vol. 92 (2004), p. 1060.

5 "Israel Rejects Belgian Court Ruling on Sharon," *New York Times*, February 14, 2003; "Israel Seeks to Counter Belgian 'War Crimes' Ruling," *The Forward* (New York), February 20, 2003; "Israel Scorns 'Anti-Semitic Little Belgium'; Furious Backlash After Court Rules Against Sharon," *Guardian* (London), February 14, 2003.

6 See "Belgium Rethinks Its Prosecutorial Zeal," *New York Times*, April 1, 2003.

7 See "Belgian War Crimes Law Undone by Its Global Reach; Cases Against Political Figures Sparked Crises," *Washington Post*, September 30, 2003.

8 See "Rumsfeld Says Belgian Law Could Imperil Funds for NATO," *Washington Post*, June 13, 2003; "NATO Agrees to U.S. Proposals to Revamp Alliance," *New York Times*, June 13, 2003.

9 *Belgium's Amendment to the Law of 15 June 1993 (as amended by the Law of 10 February 1999 and 23 April 2003) Concerning the Punishment of Grave Breaches of Humanitarian Law*, Art. 18, unofficial translation, 42 I.L.M. 1258, 1267–68 (2003).

10 See "Belgian War Crimes Law Undone."

11 "NATO Agrees to U.S. Proposals to Revamp Alliance."

12 Jack Goldsmith and Stephen D. Krasner, "The Limits of Idealism," *Dædalus* (Winter 2003), p. 51.

13 Ibid.

14 See Curtis A. Bradley and Jack L. Goldsmith, "Customary International Law as Federal Common Law: A Critique of the Modern Position," *Harvard Law Review* vol. 110 (1997), pp. 840–1.

15 See Kenneth C. Randall, "Universal Jurisdiction Under International Law," *Texas Law Review* vol. 66 (1988), pp. 800–15.

16 See Michael Kirby, "Universal Jurisdiction and Judicial Reluctance: A New 'Fourteen Points,'" in Macedo, *Universal Jurisdiction*, p. 250.

17 See Goldsmith and Krasner, "Limits of Idealism," pp. 50–1. See also Jeremy Rabkin, "International Law vs. the American Constitution: Something's Got to Give," *The National Interest* (Spring 1999), pp. 33–4.

18 Goldsmith and Krasner, "Limits of Idealism," p. 51.

19 See, for example, Bradley and Goldsmith, "Customary International Law," pp. 857–9.

20 See, for example, Henry A. Kissinger, "The Pitfalls of Universal Jurisdiction," *Foreign Affairs* vol. 80, no. 4 (July–August 2001), pp. 86–96; Rabkin, "International Law vs. the American Constitution," p. 30.

21 See generally, Diane F. Orentlicher, "Settling Accounts: The Duty to Prosecute Human Rights Violations of a Prior Regime," *Yale Law Journal* vol. 100 (1991), pp. 2537–615.

22 See Harold Hongju Koh, "Transnational Public Law Litigation," *Yale Law Journal* vol. 100 (1991), p. 2349, n. 9.

23 S. Treaty Doc. No. 100-20, 1465 U.N.T.S. 113-122 (December 10, 1984).

24 Ibid., Art. 2(1).

25 See *Regina R.* v. *Bow St. Metro. Stipendiary Magistrate, ex parte Pinochet Ugarte* (No. 3) (2000) 1 A.C. 147, 198 (H.L. 1999), reprinted in 38 I.L.M. 581, 589 (1999) (hereinafter *Pinochet III*) (opinion of Lord Browne-Wilkinson).

26 See ibid., p. 220 (opinion of Lord Goff).

27 See, for example, ibid., p. 241 (opinion of Lord Hope).

28 See, for example, ibid., pp. 255–7 (opinion of Lord Hutton).

29 See, for example, ibid., p. 198 (opinion of Lord Browne-Wilkinson).

30 J. H. H. Weiler, "Does Europe Need a Constitution? Demos, Telos, and the German Maastricht Decision," *European Law Journal* vol. 1 (1995), p. 222.

31 See, for example, United Nations, *Universal Declaration of Human Rights*, Art. 21, GA Res. 217A, UN GAOR, 3rd Sess., pt. 1, 183rd plenary meeting, p. 75, UN Doc. A/810 (1948); *International Covenant on Civil and Political Rights*, Art. 25 (December 16, 1966), S. Exec. Doc. 95-2, 999 U.N.T.S. 171.

32 See, for example, *Protocol to the European Convention for the Protection of Human Rights and Fundamental Freedoms* (as amended by Protocol No. 11), Art. 3, signed at Paris March 20, 1952, entered into force May 18, 1954, 213 U.N.T.S. 262, E.T.S. 9; *American Convention on Human Rights*, Art. 23, concluded at San José November 22, 1969, entered into force July 18, 1978, 1144 U.N.T.S. 123, O.A.S.T.S. No. 36; *African Charter on Human and Peoples' Rights*, Art. 13, concluded at Banjul June 26, 1981, entered into force October 21, 1986, OAU Doc. CAB/LEG/67/3 Rev. 5, reprinted in 21 I.L.M. 59 (1982).

33 See generally, Thomas M. Franck, "The Emerging Right to Democratic Governance," *American Journal of International Law* vol. 86 (1992), pp. 46–91; See also Diane F. Orentlicher, "Democratic Principles and Separatist Claims: A Response and Further Inquiry," in Stephen Macedo and Allen Buchanan, eds, *NOMOS: Secession and Self-Determination*, vol. 45 (New York: New York University Press, 2003), pp. 77–86.

34 Compare W. Michael Reisman, "Editorial Comment: Sovereignty and Human Rights in Contemporary International Law," *American Journal of International Law* vol. 84 (1990), p. 867.

35 The legal proceedings are described in greater depth in Orentlicher, "Whose Justice?" pp. 1070–86.

36 *Pinochet III*.

37 See Orentlicher, "Whose Justice?" pp. 1084–6 (summarizing opinions in *Pinochet III*).

38 Known in international law as immunity *ratione materiae*, this type of immunity is

associated with the official nature of particular acts rather than with an incumbent official's status and persists even after an individual ceases to hold his or her official position.

39 See Orentlicher, "Whose Justice?" pp. 1081–2.

40 See Jane S. Schacter, "Metademocracy: The Changing Structure of Legitimation in Statutory Interpretation," *Harvard Law Review* vol. 108 (1995), p. 594; William N. Eskridge Jr, "Dynamic Statutory Interpretation," *University of Pennsylvania Law Review* vol. 135 (1987), pp. 1498–9; Barry Friedman, "Dialogue and Judicial Review," *Michigan Law Review* vol. 91 (1993), p. 588; Steven L. Winter, "An Upside/Down View of the Countermajoritarian Difficulty," *Texas Law Review* vol. 69 (1991), p. 1925.

41 Alexander M. Bickel, *The Least Dangerous Branch: The Supreme Court at the Bar of Politics*, 2nd edn (New Haven: Yale University Press, 1986), p. 16.

42 See Schacter, "Metademocracy," pp. 598–9.

43 See, for example, Jesse H. Choper, "The Supreme Court and the Political Branches: Democratic Theory and Practice," *University of Pennsylvania Law Review* vol. 122 (1974), p. 815; Winter, "An Upside/Down View," p. 1920; Darren Lenard Hutchinson, "The *Majoritarian* Difficulty: Affirmative Action, Sodomy, and Supreme Court Politics," *Law & Inequality* vol. 23 (2005), pp. 13–20.

44 See William N. Eskridge Jr, "Politics Without Romance: Implications of Public Choice Theory for Statutory Interpretation," *Virginia Law Review* vol. 74 (1988), pp. 285–95; Cass R. Sunstein, "Interest Groups in American Public Law," *Stanford Law Review* vol. 38 (1985), pp. 48–9; Erwin Chemerinsky, "Forward: The Vanishing Constitution," *Harvard Law Review* vol. 103 (1989), pp. 77–81; Hutchinson, "Majoritarian Difficulty," pp. 13–15.

45 See, for example, Friedman, "Dialogue and Judicial Review," p. 590; Barry Friedman, "The Birth of an Academic Obsession: The History of the Countermajoritarian Difficulty, Part Five," *Yale Law Journal* vol. 112 (2002), p. 166; Hutchinson, "*Majoritarian* Difficulty," pp. 15–20.

46 See Orentlicher, "Whose Justice?" p. 1094, n. 196.

47 Hutchinson, "*Majoritarian* Difficulty," p. 18.

48 Bickel, *Least Dangerous Branch*, p. 240; Friedman, "Dialogue and Judicial Review," pp. 653, 655.

49 See Hutchinson, "Majoritarian Difficulty," p. 16, and sources cited in n. 95; Friedman, "Dialogue and Judicial Review," p. 672; Winter, "An Upside/Down View," pp. 1920, 1925–26.

50 See Friedman, "Dialogue and Judicial Review," p. 608; Hutchinson, "*Majoritarian* Difficulty," pp. 16–17.

51 See Choper, "Supreme Court and the Political Branches," p. 848. Compare Louis Michael Seidman, "Ambivalence and Accountability," *Southern California Law Review* vol. 61 (1988), p. 1587.

52 Robert M. Cover, "Forward: *Nomos* and Narrative," *Harvard Law Review* vol. 97 (1983), p. 17.

53 See Pablo de Greiff, "Comment: Universal Jurisdiction and Transitions to Democracy," in Macedo, *Universal Jurisdiction*, p. 126.

54 Harold Koh, "Commentary: Is International Law Really State Law?" *Harvard Law Review* vol. 111 (1998), pp. 1852–3.

55 See Cover, "*Nomos* and Narrative," p. 38; Robert M. Cover, "Violence and the Word," *Yale Law Journal* vol. 95 (1986), p. 1602, n. 2.

56 See Owen M. Fiss, "Objectivity and Interpretation," *Stanford Law Journal* vol. 34 (1982), p. 745.

57 Cover, "*Nomos* and Narrative," pp. 4, 33.

58 See, for example, United Nations, *Independent Study on Best Practices, Including Recommendations, to Assist States in Strengthening Their Domestic Capacity to Combat All Aspects of Impunity, by Professor Diane Orentlicher*, UN Doc. E/CN.4/2004/88 (February 27, 2004), p. 17, para. 50.

59 See *Statute of the International Court of Justice* (June 26, 1945), Art. 38(1)(b), 59 Stat. 1031, p. 1060, T.S. No. 993, 3 Bevans, 1153, p. 1179.

60 Orentlicher, "Whose Justice?" p. 1131, and n. 378.

61 See ibid., pp. 1111–15.

62 See Anne-Marie Slaughter, *A New World Order* (Princeton: Princeton University Press, 2004), pp. 65–103; Amnon Reichman, "'When We Sit to Judge We Are Being Judged': The Israeli GSS Case, *Ex Parte Pinochet* and Domestic/Global Deliberation," *Cardozo Journal of International and Comparative Law* vol. 9 (2001), pp. 41–103; Anne-Marie Slaughter, "Judicial Globalization," *Virginia Journal of International Law* vol. 40 (2000), pp. 1103–24. See also "Thinking Outside the U.S.," *Washington Post*, August 4, 2003.

63 Eskridge, "Dynamic Statutory Interpretation," p. 1537. See also Fiss, "Objectivity and Interpretation," pp. 744–7.

64 J. H. H. Weiler, "A Quiet Revolution: The European Court of Justice and Its Interlocutors," *Comparative Political Studies* vol. 26 (1994), p. 521.

65 See Goldsmith and Krasner, "Limits of Idealism," p. 51; Rabkin, "International Law vs. the American Constitution," p. 33.

66 See David L. Bosco, "Dictators in the Dock," *American Prospect* vol. 11, no. 18 (August 14, 2000), p. 29.

67 *American Servicemembers' Protection Act: Hearing on H.R. 4654 Before the House Committee on International Relations*, 107th Cong. (2000) (testimony of John R. Bolton, then senior vice president of the American Enterprise Institute), July 25, 2000; Kissinger, "Pitfalls of Universal Jurisdiction," pp. 86, 90–9.

68 Ibid., p. 86.

69 See Priscilla B. Hayner, *Unspeakable Truths: Confronting State Terror and Atrocity* (New York: Routledge, 2001), p. 14. See also United Nations, *Updated Set of Principles for the Protection and Promotion of Human Rights Through Action to Combat Impunity,* UN Doc. E/CN.4/2005/102/Add.1 (February 18, 2005), p. 6.

70 See, for example, United Nations, *Report of the Secretary-General: The Rule of Law and Transitional Justice in Conflict and Post-Conflict Societies,* UN Doc. S/2004/616; Neil J. Kritz, ed., *Transitional Justice: How Emerging Democracies Reckon with Former Regimes* (Washington, DC: US Institute of Peace, 1995); Ruti G. Teitel, *Transitional Justice* (New York: Oxford University Press, 2000).

71 Otto Kirchheimer, *Political Justice: The Use of Legal Procedures for Political Ends* (Princeton: Princeton University Press, 1961), p. 308

72 Karl Jaspers, *The Question of German Guilt* (1947), translated by E. B. Ashton (New York: Fordham University Press, 2001), p. 25.

73 See Orentlicher, "Whose Justice?" pp. 1120–3.

74 See Cynthia Brown, *Chile in Transition: Human Rights Since the Plebiscite, 1988–89* (New York: Americas Watch, 1989), p. 73.

75 Judith Goldstein and Robert O. Keohane, eds, *Ideas and Foreign Policy* (Ithaca: Cornell University Press, 1993). See also Ernst B. Haas, *When Knowledge Is Power* (Berkeley: University of California Press, 1990), p. 2; Diane F. Orentlicher, "The Power of an Idea: The Impact of United States Human Rights Policy," *Transnational Law and Contemporary Problems* vol. 1 (1991), pp. 43–79; Kathryn Sikkink, "The Power of Principled Ideas: Human Rights Policies in the United States and Western Europe," in Judith Goldstein and Robert Keohane, eds, *Ideas and Foreign Policy* (Ithaca: Cornell University Press, 1993) p. 139.

76 See Martha Finnemore, *National Interests in International Society* (Ithaca: Cornell University Press, 1996), p. 128.

77 Harold Hongju Koh, "Transnational Legal Process," *Nebraska Law Review* vol. 75 (1996), p. 184. See Siegfried Wiessner and Andrew R. Willard, "Policy-Oriented Jurisprudence and Human Rights Abuses in Internal Conflict: Toward a World Public Order of Human Dignity," *American Journal of International Law* vol. 93 (1999), p. 330.

78 See "'Pinochet Effect' Spreading; Case Opens Way to Other Prosecutions," *Washington Post*, August 5, 2000.

79 See "Pinochet's Arrest Ordered by Judge," *New York Times*, December 2, 2000. See Orentlicher, "Whose Justice?" p. 1070, n. 78, p. 1126, n. 362.

80 See Richard A. Falk, "Assessing the Pinochet Litigation: Whither Universal Jurisdiction?" in Macedo, *Universal Jurisdiction*, p. 103.

81 Reed Brody, "Justice: The First Casualty of Truth? The Global Movement to End Impunity for Human Rights Abuses Faces a Daunting Question," *The Nation* (April 30, 2001), pp. 25–6; "High Court Voids Charges for Pinochet; Sets New Date," *New York Times*, December 21, 2000; Tina Rosenberg, "Editorial Observer: In Chile, the Balance Tips Toward the Victims," *New York Times*, August 22, 2000.

82 See United Nations, *Independent Study on Best Practices*, p. 12, para. 30, pp. 17–18, para. 51; Ellen Lutz and Kathryn Sikkink, "The Justice Cascade: The Evolution and Impact of Foreign Human Rights Trials in Latin America," *Chicago Journal of International Law* vol. 2 (2001), pp. 1–33.

14

BRINGING SECURITY BACK IN

International relations theory and moving beyond the "justice versus peace" dilemma in transitional societies

Chandra Lekha Sriram and Youssef Mahmoud

Introduction: peace, justice, and international relations theory

While transitional justice, domestic and international, has been the subject of an expansive literature, particularly since the political transitions of the 1990s, until recently it has not been a topic of direct interest to international relations (IR) scholars or theorists.[1] However, recent books and articles have begun to examine the challenges of transition, and specifically the virtues and vices of prosecutions and other punitive forms of accountability, through the lenses of theories of international relations, such as realism, liberalism, and constructivism.[2] Theorists have attempted to transform theories of systems, structures, and agencies in international politics, then, into ones that can help to describe the workings and needs of polities after significant violence and atrocities. In this chapter, we will briefly discuss the insights of each of these theories, before turning to a specific case, that of the peace process and hybrid tribunal in Sierra Leone. What we find is that key insights from realism, couched as pragmatism, are of great importance in addressing the needs of transitional societies. However, we argue that realism, like the other theories, does not take a nuanced view of security. Specifically, while a core dilemma for transitional societies is that punishment for past gross human rights abuses may generate instability by provoking retaliation, particularly by armed groups or state security forces, none of these theories seriously engage in consideration of how to prevent or control reactions by these groups in the short and long term. That said, the UN and other actors supporting transitions to peace recognize the importance of accountability for past crimes notwithstanding possible destabilizing effects that this might have. What is vital, then, is to fashion peacebuilding strategies that can achieve accountability while simultaneously limiting the likelihood of instability. This requires going beyond any simple "justice versus peace" dichotomies.

This means that even perpetrators of atrocities must often be treated seriously as agents to be engaged, and not simply in the negotiation of war termination. They must be assisted to transform themselves into participants in society again, whether as civilians or as rights-respecting security forces. Such engagement, through programs of disarmament, demobilization, and reintegration (DDR), and through programs of military and police reform, constitute a critical but often overlooked element of transition. The absence of such transformative programs may virtually ensure that trials provoke backlash, and they may often need to take priority over any accountability mechanisms. Their presence may provoke tension in the short term, but eventually promote stabilization and in some instances even enable accountability. In Sierra Leone, there were initial fears that the institution of a hybrid tribunal and overriding of an agreed amnesty could provoke instability. Some therefore argued that the tribunal was premature, and that its institution ought to have been delayed to allow the country to stabilize. However, it also appears that the relatively rapid implementation of the DDR program helped to limit the possible repercussions of trials in Sierra Leone. Nonetheless, as field research illustrates, there remains significant cause for concern that the security situation will not remain stable, particularly after the withdrawal of the United Nations Mission in Sierra Leone (UNAMSIL) and the reduced presence of other international actors.

The problem of postconflict justice

After countries emerge from armed conflict, severe political repression, or serious political violence, internal and external pressure invariably emerges to impose accountability in some way upon the perpetrators of the most serious human rights violations or violations of the laws of war. These may occur through domestic, international, or hybrid mechanisms, and may involve prosecutions, truth commissions, lustration or vetting, amnesties, and on occasion all of the above. Regardless of the tools used, and the presence or absence of the international community in the development of responses, postconflict justice requires grappling with what is often referred to as the "peace–justice dilemma."[3] Simply put, while there are often strong demands, both within a society emerging from conflict and by the international community, for some form of accountability for perpetrators, there is simultaneously a concern that such a pursuit for justice may bring about a backlash. It is feared that such perpetrators, particularly those who are armed, whether government military or police forces, militias, or nonstate armed groups, might renege on agreements and return to the use of violence if their members are threatened with prosecution. Thus there are those who contend that in order to maintain stability, and pave the way for the (re)installation of a functioning democratic state capable of upholding the rule of law, it might be necessary to condone amnesties.[4] Alternatively, there are those who would argue that some form of accountability is necessary in order to support stability and the rule of law. Prosecutions, it is argued, help to prevent vigilante retribution, serve as a deterrent to future abuses, and facilitate the restoration of the rule of law, and according to some help to challenge a culture of impunity. Both of these views – for and against prosecution – are perhaps too stark, the former in particular suggesting an either/or dichotomy that compels choosing justice or peace. In reality, national practice seems to indicate that some elements of amnesty, and some of punishment, may exist simultaneously.[5] Nonetheless, debate continues among policymakers as to the appropriate responses to the dilemma, and IR theorists may offer insights and recommendations.

International relations theory and postconflict justice

IR theorists have only begun to focus upon the issue of postconflict justice relatively recently. However, several works representing leading IR theories – constructivism, liberalism, and realism – have offered explanations for the creation of international tribunals, domestic trials, and human rights regimes generally. Taken together, these works allow one to sketch out the general arguments and prescriptions arising from each theoretical strain.[6]

Constructivism

Constructivists see justice after transition as part of a normative development, one that might be expected to affect behavior patterns over time. Activists or norm entrepreneurs, they argue, have not only formulated norms over time regarding the unacceptability of severe rights violations and the necessity of a punitive response, but also begun to convince others successfully of the correctness of their arguments. A favorite example is the "justice cascade" in Latin America. According to scholars such as Ellen Lutz and Kathryn Sikkink, responses to past abuses became increasingly possible across Latin America following transitions in the 1980s and 1990s because transnational advocacy networks successfully disseminated their claims that abuses required redress, in order to prevent their recurrence.[7] According to this argument, amnesty is increasingly considered to be unacceptable, not just by human rights advocates, but also by broader swathes of societies who experienced violence and abuses, and even governments have begun to internalize this norm and pursue trials. Such an argument about the power of norms to compel domestic responses to crimes can also be transposed to the international sphere, where advocates of international trials and tribunals, or for that matter trials through tools such as universal jurisdiction, point to the heinous nature of certain crimes, and argue that they are therefore crimes of international concern that can call out a response anywhere. Impunity, it is argued, is something to be globally condemned, and responding to it is imperative. The language of tribunal staff suggests that this is a normative belief, though often linked to claims about deterrence simultaneously.[8]

One critique that has been made of this argument is that the evidence does not support it – we do not see and have not seen significant change in the behavior of abusive leaders, or of combatants in armed conflicts, either out of a belief that atrocities are wrong or out of a fear of punishment.[9] It may yet simply be too early to assess this set of claims: the trends of transitional justice and use of international tribunals are, in international political terms, relatively new and normative shifts often require time. While not rejecting the possibility that a normative shift is under way, we recognize that, in any event, it is far from complete, and some tensions between accountability and stability remain and require coherent strategies to address.

Liberalism

Liberalism in international politics points to the relevance of domestic political orders for international politics, with some variants specifically noting the "democratic peace" among liberal nations and suggesting that liberal states comply with international agreements, engage in cooperative bargaining, and the like. They also suggest that human rights norms are consistent with key liberal values. As such, then, we should expect it to be the case that liberal states engage in support to processes that impose justice after atrocities, whether through the creation of tribunals, or through offering financial and technical support to domestic trials. The record, however, is mixed at best, as many scholars have aptly demonstrated.[10] The most notable case in which democratic values have not resulted in an embrace of international justice is that of the United States in its opposition to the creation of, or cooperation with, the International Criminal Court. As Andrew Moravcsik has argued, it is often not the case that established democracies embrace rights courts – he argues that in postwar Europe and perhaps in Latin America, it was not strong democracies that embraced regional rights agreements, with attendant courts, but weak, new democracies concerned to defend against any return to past patterns.[11]

Realism

In a recent article on international justice, Jack Snyder and Leslie Vinjamuri criticize what might be characterized as constructivist approaches, and take what they refer to as a pragmatic one; in essence their approach draws on realism in IR theory.[12] However, and this is an important distinction, while realism predicts anarchy in the international system because of the absence of a superior and centralized authority, and views this state as inevitable, it contrasts this to the appropriate, rule-governed, hierarchical order within domestic society. After internal strife, this normal state has been destroyed, and according to Snyder and Vinjamuri it is imperative to restore this normalcy, to ensure stability and the rule of law. International justice, on this account, is not particularly well designed to help reinstall justice, stability, or the rule of law; the same, they argue, will be true of domestic or hybrid mechanisms as well. Why is this so? The problem, they argue, is that trials after internal strife may at best do little, and at worst provoke retaliation by the very forces responsible for the abuses. Because those responsible for serious abuses are punished so rarely, it is unlikely that trials can act as deterrents; more generally they may not help support the development of the rule of law and stability in transitional societies. Further, they might well undermine stability by provoking a backlash; it is for this reason that postconflict amnesties are so common. Efforts to upset these amnesties, even years later, they argue, are unwise.

Bringing security back in: (re)constructing stability and the rule of law

Advocating amnesty for the sake of security may have its virtues. However, we argue that it may simultaneously overstate the imperatives of stability over accountability and address insufficiently key elements of stability or security. We argue that both justice and stability need to be addressed. Further, it is important not to view the needs of transitional societies in a static fashion, and in particular not to ignore the role of armed groups, whether state, quasi-state, or nonstate, not only in upsetting postconflict stability, but also as necessary actors in this process. Thus many transitional states may create commissions of inquiry and pursue trials even as they seek to limit those trials.[13] For these are not the only elements in their strategies of transition: they will also engage the men and women with guns, in an attempt to pacify them, and transform institutions. This may be done through DDR programs, through reform of the security sector, and through the inclusion of armed groups in governance and economic recovery as legitimate actors.[14] However, for all of the concern about security that the pragmatic approach emphasizes, it does not confront the need to engage those most responsible for both security and insecurity. In fact, this is what countries frequently do when they are in transition – they attempt some measure of accountability even with amnesty, but also will seek to reform military doctrine, effect civilian control over the military, separate the police forces from the military, vet and integrate former opposition combatants into the regular armed forces, demobilize both state and nonstate armed forces, and so forth. As with prosecutions, these processes, if not properly managed, could run the risk of a backlash. However, they are vital for longer-term prevention of abusive activities. Such efforts, ranging from DDR to military reform and inclusion of former combatants in new security forces, have been central elements of transitional and postconflict strategies for numerous regimes, particularly in Latin America and Africa. The ongoing attempts in Sierra Leone to build peace and also pursue accountability through the use of the hybrid tribunal, the Special Court for Sierra Leone (SCSL), illustrate the importance of pursuing not just accountability, or reinstitutionalization of the rule of law, but also a real engagement with armed actors. However, it must be stressed that such engagement can only be sustainable if the enduring distrust between the armed forces and the civilian leadership is properly addressed.

Security and justice: lessons from Sierra Leone

The history of the conflict in Sierra Leone is well known, and will not be discussed here in any detail.[15] Conflict between the government and the Revolutionary United Front (RUF) erupted in 1991, endured for over a decade, resulting in some 50,000 deaths and widespread atrocities, including mutilation and sexual violence, and was notable for the widespread use of child combatants. It appeared that the conflict might finally end when negotiations in 1999 resulted in the Lomé peace agreement, and the mandate by the UN Security Council for a peacekeeping force, UNAMSIL.[16] The accord provoked concern from the international community for its inclusion of an amnesty for crimes committed during the conflict, and the United Nations, which acted as a "moral guarantor" of the agreement, issued a reservation indicating that it did not consider the amnesty provision to cover international crimes. Despite the agreement, fighting and atrocities continued, along with attacks on UNAMSIL. In May 2000 the notorious RUF leader Foday Sankoh was captured, leading to discussions of the possibility of a tribunal to prosecute him and other war criminals. In June 2000 the government asked the UN to set up a court to try such cases. Ultimately, a complex system comprising a commission of inquiry and a mixed tribunal was created to address accountability for past abuses.[17] The efforts of the tribunal simultaneously to serve the needs for justice and stability in Sierra Leone offer an interesting test case.

The United Nations created the Special Court through an agreement with the government of Sierra Leone and pursuant to UN Security Council Resolution 1315 in August 2000.[18] The Court's statute, completed on January 16, 2002, gives it the power to prosecute persons who bear the greatest responsibility for serious violations of national and international humanitarian law since November 30, 1996.[19] The crimes within the Court's mandate include crimes against humanity, violations of Common Article 3 of the Geneva Conventions and Additional Protocol II, other serious violations of international humanitarian law, and crimes under national law.[20] In March 2002 the agreement for the Court was formally ratified.[21]

Dispute over the validity of the Lomé amnesty

The establishment of the Special Court for Sierra Leone has had significant ramifications for the controversial amnesty embedded in the Lomé peace accord.[22] Article 10 of the Court's statute provides that any amnesty for the crimes covered in the statute would not be a bar to prosecution. Were that blanket amnesty still in force, it would significantly limit the court's temporal jurisdiction, to crimes committed only *after* the signing of the accord in 1999. However, several arguments have been advanced against the amnesty's constraining prosecutions by the Court. First, as noted above, the UN issued a reservation at the time of the signing of the accord, indicating that the amnesty could not cover international crimes such as genocide, crimes against humanity, war crimes, or other serious violations of international humanitarian law. The argument was thus made that to the degree that the amnesty was valid, it was valid only in respect of domestic crimes. The UN, further, was not party to the agreement, but rather, along with a number of other institutions and governments, agreed to act as guarantor of the agreement. Thus, it argued, it was not in breach of any agreements in the creation of the Court. However, the government of Sierra Leone was a party to the Lomé Accord, and entered into a contract with the UN for the creation of the Court. The government has argued, as have others, that the amnesty provision was nullified by the continued violation of the peace accord, through fighting and atrocities, on the part of the RUF.[23] In March 2004 the Court itself had occasion to consider the validity of the amnesty and of Article 10. It found that the Lomé Accord could not be considered a treaty, and thus that the amnesty contained in the Lomé Accord would only have domestic effect and would be regulated by domestic law. As a result, it could have no effect upon an international court.[24]

Dispute regarding head-of-state immunity and the legality of the Special Court agreement

The unsealing of the SCSL's indictment of then president of Liberia Charles Taylor while he was attending peace negotiations in Ghana shocked the diplomatic community, according to many offending African diplomats in particular.[25] Rather than arrest Taylor, Ghana allowed him to leave the country; Taylor has since gone into hiding in Nigeria after the latter acceded to international pressure to accept him. Nigeria refused until recently to surrender him to the SCSL, having granted him "asylum," although in June 2004 the Nigerian High Court decided to review that asylum.[26] However, the Nigerian High Court said that it would honor a request for extradition from a permanent (rather than the current interim) Liberian government.[27] Attorneys for Taylor have filed legal challenges to the SCSL's jurisdiction over him at the Special Court itself, as has the Liberian government at the International Court of Justice.[28] The ICJ has yet to hear the case filed, in which it is claimed that proceedings against Taylor violate head-of-state immunity and the immediate cancellation of the arrest warrant is requested. The SCSL will not take any action with respect to this filing, however, unless Sierra Leone consents to the Court's jurisdiction in the case. Lawyers for Taylor have also challenged the Court's jurisdiction in a filing before the Liberian Supreme Court against the SCSL and the Liberian Ministry of Justice, challenging the legality of searches of homes of Taylor and his associates. They have argued that the jurisdiction of the SCSL does not extend beyond the borders of Sierra Leone.[29] Some Liberian officials have rejected that claim, arguing that Liberia was obliged to respect foreign courts and proceedings; however, the former Liberian parliament has expressly rejected the possibility of allowing Taylor to face charges before the SCSL.[30]

The legality of the agreement establishing the court was challenged before the Special Court itself, and before the Supreme Court of Sierra Leone.[31] The Special Court rejected these challenges, finding that the agreement was valid and was neither an excess delegation by the UN Security Council of its own powers, nor an excess transfer of jurisdiction by Sierra Leone itself. In 2004, hearings regarding the legality of the agreement opened in the national Supreme Court.[32] In 2006, Taylor was surrendered to the SCSL, and the proceedings were transferred to The Hague due to local and regional security concerns.

The Special Court and former combatants

One might expect that former combatants would have a uniform, and negative, view of a court designed to punish their commanders, and condemn by implication their own activities. However, given the complex nature of warring factions in Sierra Leone, the situation is somewhat more complicated. It is true that former combatants of all groups were suspicious of the SCSL, fearing that they themselves would be indicted by it. This suspicion arguably extended beyond the Court, leading many to fear testifying before the Truth and Reconciliation Commission (TRC), despite explicit assurances by the prosecutor that he would not use testimony to the TRC as evidence for indictments or prosecutions.[33] However, this suspicion may or may not have had a lasting impact on the work of the TRC: after a few months this concern abated and they began to testify.[34] Similarly, there have been concerns that fear of indictment might have deterred some fighters from engaging in the DDR process. However, given the extensive nature of DDR in Sierra Leone, and the apparently broad-based buy-in to the process, the ultimate effect appears to have been negligible.[35] However, the primary objection among some former combatants has been the decision to pursue cases against the Civil Defense Forces (CDF), and in particular the case against CDF head Chief Sam Hinga Norman. Former CDF fighters view themselves and Hinga Norman as heroes who defended the democratically elected government, and resent being called to account. This resentment has led to rumors and fears that supporters of Hinga Norman will seek to destabilize the country.[36] One editorial in a Freetown paper expressed its concerns thus: "We only hope this court will not leave behind an ugly legacy that will spark another war in this country. You see, Chief Norman has a very large following that is angry with the treatment currently meted out to him."[37]

Systematic surveys of former combatants conducted by a local NGO with international support suggest that attitudes among former combatants are mixed. The analyses find moderate levels of support for the Special Court and the TRC, which may be attributed to an intense sensitization and information campaign by the SCSL. It is worth noting that support of former RUF combatants, many of whom see themselves as victims of forcible recruitment as well as betrayal by their former commanders, express relatively strong support for the court as well as willingness to testify. Conversely, former CDF combatants, the vast majority of whom joined willingly, and who believe that they helped to defend the nation and the democratically elected government, express greater resistance to the Special Court.[38]

Timing and security: did the Special Court begin work too early?

The UN peacekeeping operation, UNAMSIL, and the DDR process, have been widely viewed as successful.[39] Nonetheless, there were concerns from the outset that the operation of the Special Court for Sierra Leone would begin too early, perhaps undermining DDR if fighters feared indictment. Happily, these fears do not appear to have been borne out.[40] Nonetheless, many skeptical NGO observers suggest that the SCSL did begin operation too early, examining crimes and societal rifts best left to heal; many have even suggested that a delay of five years or so would have been appropriate.[41] Conversely, the SCSL prosecutor points out that any delay might have undermined justice, making it more difficult to obtain perpetrators, witnesses, and evidence; as it stands, one key perpetrator, Foday Sankoh, died while in custody of the Court.[42] As discussed above, the issue of timing has been fraught in other ways, with substantial disagreement as to the viability of operating a commission of inquiry and a court simultaneously.

Relation to other accountability efforts

The brief nature of this chapter does not permit a full examination of the broader scope of the efforts at addressing recent abuses, either the work of the TRC, cases that may proceed in domestic courts, or traditional justice. It is worth noting, however, that many in Sierra Leone, and many international actors seeking to support peacebuilding there, believe that the use of traditional justice, such as cleansing ceremonies, through the country's vast array of secret societies, may be an important tool for justice and reconciliation. They note that while formal justice does not reach many people in the country, particularly those that live upcountry, over 80 percent of Sierra Leoneans belong to some form of secret society.[43]

Such traditional justice mechanisms ought not be a substitute for trials, but may need to act as supplements where trials are not possible. It is worth emphasizing that from the perspective of security, DDR and other processes are critical, but that longer-term security requires justice and reconciliation, and a real account of the needs of the victims as well. Many victims in Sierra Leone object to the narrow scope of the Special Court's jurisdiction, and are more interested in the punishment of those who directly harmed them; they also view DDR processes with suspicion, asking why it is that the very people who harmed them are now being rewarded with DDR payments. A further challenge is that the

DDR process has not always served women, either as combatants or as "bush wives," particularly well; not only have they been victims of the conflict, but they also often have dual status as both victim and combatant. In addition to being underrepresented in DDR processes, the specific gender dimension of crimes during the conflict has not been adequately addressed.[44] A real strategy of peace-building and reconciliation must address women's needs and concerns as well.

After UNAMSIL: prospects for peace, security, and justice

Individuals interviewed for this research from a variety of sectors in Sierra Leone expressed pessimism regarding the future of their country after the withdrawal of UNAMSIL. This was often articulated as an expectation that, simply, after withdrawal, fighting would resume. In some instances this was couched as being likely to come in the form of an attack from outside, in others as a remobilization of combatants. In general, there was skepticism that the government could or would provide basic services or address corruption, which were seen as key "root" causes of the conflict, and far greater faith in international than national actors to provide for services and security.[45] This widespread expectation that conflict will resume may also have a dampening effect upon either the functioning or the impact of the Special Court – the more that people fear retribution for testifying or otherwise cooperating with the SCSL, the less likely they are to do so.

Policy implications

A number of key policy problems for the Special Court for Sierra Leone have emerged throughout this discussion, which for reasons of space could not be discussed in great detail but ought to be acknowledged here. Of particular relevance are those related to mandate and funding. Clearly, for any process of international justice to function properly, it must have proper resources and a real capacity to obtain custody of indictees, which, in the case of Charles Taylor and others, the SCSL does not. Transitional processes, be they juridical or security-related such as DDR, must also deal with the specific challenges faced by women during and after conflict. The Special Court must also seek to complement the functioning of domestic legal structures, both formal and traditional. The work of the Court did seek to complement that of the TRC, but as noted in the case of evidence sharing, may occasionally have undermined these processes. In a more hopeful vein, the Court has explicitly sought to leave behind a "legacy" and is seeking to engage with the process of rebuilding the shattered judicial structures in the country.[46] These observations are more than policy concerns; they may affect the way we think about the so-called peace versus justice dilemma. For to the degree that the practice of accountability can be refined, it may contribute to the restoration of the rule of law, but also ensure greater stability, particularly if strategies of transition seek to integrate both justice and security. We recognize, however, that the pursuit of justice and stability in a transitional society will yield durable results only if integrated within an overall peacebuilding strategy in which the political and socio-economic incentives for peace are fostered from the start and implemented simultaneously.

Conclusion

This chapter has examined the arguments offered by several strands of IR theory about why postconflict justice is on the rise, and whether this is always a positive development. While it has largely concurred with a "realist" assessment – that postconflict justice must be carefully weighed against other security-specific concerns – it has sought to elaborate further upon the positive steps required to address security needs. Specifically, we have advocated for greater recognition that the pursuit of transitional justice must be complemented by strategies of justice that positively engage fighters, whether through processes of reform, inclusion where possible in governance, and DDR. Such inclusion, and positive engagement, of course, must be undertaken cautiously, which was arguably not the case with the inclusion in the Lomé agreement of not only amnesty for combatants but also the provision for control over mining by Sankoh and the RUF. Nonetheless, there will be many instances where former fighters can be included in the armed forces, or police force, or where armed groups may transform themselves into political parties. These efforts alone clearly cannot ensure peace, nor do they address the need for justice and reconciliation at all. However, they may be important supplements to prosecution, commissions of inquiry, and traditional justice, as strategies of transition, which may be part of strategies of justice.

Acknowledgments

The views expressed herein are personal, and do not represent the position of the United Nations. Youssef Mahmoud would like to thank Charles Anyidoho, a Sierra Leone specialist in the Africa II division, for his insights. Chandra Lekha Sriram would like to express gratitude to the British Academy, whose grant no. SG-3725 provided funding for research conducted in Freetown, Sierra Leone, in July and August 2004, and to the Bellagio Study and Conference Center of the Rockefeller Foundation, which provided a conducive environment for writing in August and September 2004.

Notes

1 Some key works include Neil J. Kritz, ed., *Transitional Justice: How Emerging Democracies Reckon with Former Regimes*, 3 vols (Washington, DC: US Institute of Peace, 1995); Priscilla Hayner, *Unspeakable Truths: Confronting State Terror and Atrocity* (London: Routledge, 2001); Aryeh Neier, *War Crimes: Brutality, Genocide,*

Terror, and the Struggle for Justice (New York: Times Books, 1998); Mark Osiel, *Mass Atrocity, Collective Memory, and the Law* (New Brunswick, NJ: Transaction Books, 1997); Martha Minow, *Between Vengeance and Forgiveness: Facing History after Genocide and Mass Violence* (Boston: Beacon Press, 1998); Naomi Roht-Arriaza, ed., *Accountability for Human Rights Violations in International Law and Practice* (New York: Oxford University Press, 1995); see also Chandra Lekha Sriram, *Confronting Past Human Rights Violations: Justice vs. Peace in Times of Transition* (London: Frank Cass, 2004); Sriram, *Globalizing Justice for Mass Atrocities: A Revolution in Accountability* (London: Routledge 2005), chap. 6.

2 Gary Jonathan Bass, *Stay the Hand of Vengeance: The Politics of War Crimes Tribunals* (Princeton: Princeton University Press, 2000); Jack Snyder and Leslie Vinjamuri, "Trials and Errors: Principle and Pragmatism in Strategies of International Justice," *International Security* vol. 28, no. 3 (Winter 2003–4), pp. 5–44; Andrew Moravcsik, "The Origin of Human Rights Regimes: Democratic Delegation in Postwar Europe," *International Organization* vol. 54, no. 2 (Spring 2000), pp. 217–52; Christopher Rudolph, "Constructing an Atrocities Regime: The Politics of War Crimes Tribunals," *International Organization* vol. 55, no. 3 (Summer 2001), pp. 655–91; Martha Finnemore and Kathryn Sikkink, "International Norm Dynamics and Political Change," *International Organization* vol. 52, no. 4 (Autumn 1998), pp. 887–917; Ellen Lutz and Kathryn Sikkink, "The Justice Cascade: The Evolution and Impact of Human Rights Trials in Latin America," *Chicago Journal of International Law* vol. 2, no. 1 (Spring 2001), pp. 1–34; Kenneth W. Abbott, "International Relations Theory, International Law, and the Regime Governing Atrocities in Internal Conflicts," *American Journal of International Law* vol. 93 (April 1999), pp. 361–79.

3 See United Nations, *The Rule of Law and Transitional Justice in Conflict and Post-Conflict Societies: Report of the Secretary-General*, UN Doc. S/2004/616 (August 23, 2004). See "Security Council Says 'Climate of Impunity' Must End in Post-Conflict Nations," *UN Daily News*, Issue DH/4243 (October 6, 2004); "Security Council Stresses Importance, Urgency of Restoring Rule of Law in Post-Conflict Societies," press release, UN Doc. SC/8209 (October 6, 2004), presidential statement released as UN Doc. S/PRST/2004/34.

4 See, for example, Laila Nadya Sadat, "Universal Jurisdiction, National Amnesties, and Truth Commissions: Reconciling the Irreconcilable," in Stephen Macedo, ed., *Universal Jurisdiction: National Courts and the Prosecution of Serious Crimes Under International Law* (Philadelphia: University of Pennsylvania Press, 2003).

5 Sriram, *Confronting Past Human Rights Violations*, pp. 38–77, examines 26 cases.

6 These three approaches are hardly exhaustive but are most relevant for our purposes.

7 Lutz and Sikkink, "Justice Cascade"; see also Thomas Risse and Kathryn Sikkink, "The Socialization of International Human Rights Norms into Domestic Practice," in Thomas Risse, Stephen C. Ropp, and Kathryn Sikkink, eds, *The Power of Human Rights: International Norms and Domestic Change* (Cambridge: Cambridge University Press, 1999).

8 Payam Akhavam, "Justice in the Hague, Peace in the Former Yugoslavia?" *Human Rights Quarterly* vol. 20, no. 4 (1998), pp. 737–816. In an interview with Chandra Lekha Sriram, David Crane, the prosecutor for the Special Court for Sierra Leone, repeatedly emphasized the importance of the tribunal's symbolic effect (Freetown, July 6, 2004).

9 Snyder and Vinjamuri, "Trials and Errors," pp. 11–12.

10 Moravcsik, "Origin of Human Rights Regimes"; Bass, *Stay the Hand of Vengeance.*

11 Ibid.

12 Snyder and Vinjamuri, "Trials and Errors," esp. pp. 12–25.

13 It is important to note that while amnesties are common, it is increasingly rare that

one will see blanket amnesties imposed or respected; these are increasingly challenged by international law and by peacebuilding practice.

14 See Sriram, *Confronting Past Human Rights Violations*, chap. 1.

15 See generally, John Hirsch, *Sierra Leone: Diamonds and the Struggle for Democracy* (Boulder: Lynne Rienner, 2001); Michael Pugh and Neil Cooper, with Jonathan Goodhand, "Sierra Leone in West Africa," in *War Economies in Regional Context* (Boulder: Lynne Rienner, 2004); Comfort Ero and Jonathan Temin, "Sources of Conflict in West Africa," in Chandra Lekha Sriram and Zoe Nielsen, eds, *Exploring Subregional Conflict: Opportunities for Conflict Prevention* (Boulder: Lynne Rienner, 2004). See also Adekeye Adebajo and Ismail Rashid, eds, *West Africa's Security Challenges: Building Peace in a Troubled Region* (Boulder: Lynne Rienner, 2004).

16 United Nations, *Peace Agreement Between the Government of Sierra Leone and the Revolutionary United Front of Sierra Leone*, UN SCOR, annex, UN Doc. S/1999/777. For the mandate of the United Nations Mission in Sierra Leone (UNAMSIL), see UN Security Council, Resolution 1270, UN Doc. S/Res/1270 (1999).

17 See *Special Court Agreement 2002, Ratification Act 2002*, supplement to *Sierra Leone Gazette*, vol. 130, no. 2 (March 7, 2002). See generally, Abdul Tejan-Cole, "The Special Court for Sierra Leone: Conceptual Concerns and Alternatives," *African Human Rights Law Journal* vol. 1 (2001), pp. 107–26.

18 See UN Security Council, Resolution 1315, UN SCOR, 55th Sess., 4,186th meeting, UN Doc. S/Res/1315 (2000).

19 See *Statute for the Special Court, Office of the Attorney General and Ministry of Justice, Special Court Task Force*, Art. 1 (January 16, 2002).

20 See ibid., Art. 2.

21 See *Ratification Act 2002.*

22 See generally, Daniel Macaluso, "Absolute and Free Pardon: The Effect of the Amnesty Provision in the Lomé Peace Agreement on the Jurisdiction of the Special Court for Sierra Leone." *Brooklyn Journal of International Law* vol. 27 (2001).

23 For criticism, see ibid.

24 See *Decision on Challenge to Jurisdiction: Lomé Accord Amnesty*, Appeals Chamber of the Special Court of Sierra Leone, Case Nos. SCSL-2004-15-AR72(E) and SCSL-2004-16-AR72(E) (March 13, 2004).

25 *The Prosecutor* v. *Charles Ghankay Taylor, Indictment*, Case No. SCSL-03-I (March 3, 2003), available online at www.sc-sl.org/taylorindictment.html.

26 "Nigerian High Court Agrees to Review Charles Taylor Asylum" (June 3, 2004), available online at www.globalpolicy.org/intljustice/wanted/2004/0603agree.htm.

27 "Sierra Leone: Taylor Could Be Tried upon Request by Liberian Government," *UN Integrated Regional Information Network* (August 13, 2004), available online at www.irinnews.org.

28 International Court of Justice, "Liberia Applies to the International Court of Justice in a Dispute with Sierra Leone Concerning an International Arrest Warrant Issued by the Special Court for Sierra Leone Against the Liberia President," ICJ press release 2003/26 (August 5, 2003), available online at www.icj-cij.org.

29 "Taylor's Lawyers File Petition against Special Court," *UN Integrated Regional Information Network* (March 16, 2004), available online at www.globalpolicy.org/intljustice/wanted/2004/0313pet.htm.

30 "Liberia: Parliament Rejects Petition for Taylor to Be Tried in Sierra Leone," *UN Integrated Regional Information Network* (August 12, 2004), available online at www.irinnews.org.

31 *Prosecutor* v. *Augustine Gbao*, Case No. SCSL-2004-15-AR72(E) (May 25, 2004);

Prosecutor v. *Allieu Kondewa*, Case No. SCSL-2004-14-AR72(E) (May 25, 2004); Sriram's interviews with human rights NGOs (Freetown, July 2004).

32 Sriram's discussions with Alpha Sesay of the SCSL defense team (Freetown, July 2004). Further information was not available as this volume went to press.

33 Sriram's interview with Lawrence Sesay, and other staff of PRIDE (July 15, 2004).

34 Sriram's interview with David Crane, SCSL prosecutor (July 6, 2004); Sriram's interview with Desmond Molloy, UNAMSIL DDR expert (July 9, 2004). See "Overview of the Sierra Leone Truth and Reconciliation Report" (October 5, 2004) and full report available at www.trcsierraleone/org.

35 Sriram's interview with Desmond Molloy. However, this fear remains a valid one for the future. Sriram's interview with Allison Cooper, SCSL Press and Public Affairs (Freetown, July 16, 2004).

36 "Special Court Lied Against Me ... Norman ... Defence Lawyers Drag Special Court to Court," *Concord Times* (Freetown), January 27, 2004, front page; "As Courthouse Opens Police Clamp Down on Free Norman Supporters," *Concord Times* (Freetown), March 11, 2004; "Kamajor Administrator Arrested for Talking to Norman," *Concord Times* (Freetown), January 28, 2004; "More Headache for Special Court: Hinga Norman Planning a Coup?" *Standard Times* (Freetown), January 22, 2004.

37 "Watch Out, Sierra Leoneans!! The Special Court Could Leave an Ugly Legacy Behind," *The Democrat* (Freetown), April ?, 2004, p. 3 [note: the day was obscured on all pages of this edition of the paper].

38 PRIDE, *Ex-Combatant Views of the Truth and Reconciliation Commission and the Special Court in Sierra Leone* (Freetown, September 12, 2002), available online at www.ictj.org.

39 See Refugees International, *UNAMSIL: A Peacekeeping Success, Lessons Learned* (October 2002, copy on file with current authors). See also Desmond Molloy, "The DDR Process in Sierra Leone" (Freetown: UNAMSIL, June 2004).

40 Sriram's interview with Desmond Molloy (Freetown, July 9, 2004).

41 Sriram's interviews with NGOs (Freetown, July 2004).

42 Sriram's interview with David Crane (Freetown, July 6, 2004).

43 Sriram's interviews with Valnora Edwin, Campaign for Good Governance (Freetown, July 2004) and Alfred Carew, National Forum for Human Rights (Freetown, July 2004).

44 Molloy, "DDR Process in Sierra Leone"; Yasmin Sooka, "Building Peace Through Accountability: A Comparative Experience Between South Africa and Sierra Leone," paper presented at *Conference on Gender Justice in Post-Conflict Situations* (New York, September 15–17, 2004).

45 Sriram's interviews with NGOs and UN officials, not for attribution (Freetown, July 2004). See also Pyt Duoma and Jeroen de Zeeuw, "From Transitional to Sustainable Justice: Human Rights Assistance to Sierra Leone," *CRU Policy Brief* 1 (August 2004), available online at www.clingendael.nl/cru/pdf/2004_policy_brief/20040800_cru_pol1.pdf.

46 *First Annual Report of the President of the Special Court for Sierra Leone* (December 2, 2002–December 1, 2003), on file with current authors.

15

COMMENTARY: INTERNATIONAL CRIMINAL ACCOUNTABILITY AT THE INTERSECTION OF LAW AND POLITICS

Ellen L. Lutz

We live in an era of anniversaries: 60 years since the liberation of Auschwitz, a quarter of a century since the genocide in Cambodia, a decade since a comparable nightmare in Rwanda. I write this commentary on the eve of another anniversary: a decade after the massacre in Srebrenica.

Anniversaries are moments for reflection. They challenge our faith in God, in human nature, in ourselves. How can it be that with all of humanity's technical prowess, scientific knowledge, and globalized sensibility, we have yet to learn how to prevent the repetition of a scenario in which a handful of people, greedy for power and wealth, develop and exploit the insecurity of a large number of people, causing them to commit unspeakable atrocities that under saner conditions they ardently would condemn? As a species we have failed in our most fundamental and obvious collective responsibility: preventing crimes against humanity.

Confronting that failure is a small network of creative legal people who are applying their talents and training to the search for a solution. Marrying their idealism with their expertise in human rights and domestic criminal law, they are taking theories that apply – often only marginally – to small-scale crime, and adapting them to address massive politically based crimes.

The core reasoning is simple: if we cannot prevent genocide and other crimes against humanity, we can at least prosecute and punish those most responsible. Doing so, it is argued, will put the brakes on current power-holders and deter future power-holders from abusing their power lest they wind up in jail. While not the only rationale, deterrence is central to the constellation of reasons offered for all of the accountability mechanisms discussed in this section of the volume. But it is most central in the rationale for universal jurisdiction, which most legal theorists agree is a third-best alternative.[1]

Universal jurisdiction is the legal theory that asserts that if a state will not or cannot fulfill its responsibility to prosecute nationals who are engaged in egregious abuses of power, and the international community will not step in to ensure that justice is done, perpetrators still will not get a free pass. Instead they must live the rest of their days on the lam, hounded by the clamor for their prosecution, as virtual prisoners in the place where they did the most harm. For, as Augusto Pinochet found out when he sought the benefits of medical care available in the United Kingdom, the law does not have so much a long arm, as tentacles everywhere, ready to grasp wrongdoers and reverse their fortunes.

The four foregoing chapters in this section of the volume address international criminal accountability from multiple perspectives. Three are authored by law professors who have been at the forefront of the movement for international justice. The fourth looks at legal developments and trends through an international relations (IR) lens and more comfortably acknowledges the political constraints on both advances in accountability law and states' willingness to enforce it. But regardless of the authors' disciplinary perspective, all of the chapters reflect the growing awareness of international law and international relations scholars that, when it comes to transitional justice and international accountability, explanations of state behavior necessarily require a sophisticated analysis that draws from both disciplines.

Diane Orentlicher solidly refutes the political challenges raised by conservative opponents of universal jurisdiction: that it is antidemocratic and that foreign judicial action could provoke an internal scenario far worse than inaction. Orentlicher brings her broad knowledge of legal process to her analysis of democratic accountability. Courts understand their role in a democratic system and are the foremost proponents of the innate conservatism of law. Because of their caution, they maintain regular dialogue – both formally and informally – with other courts, including the courts of other states.[2] They go to great lengths to avoid making law, and when lack of clarity or a void in the law forces them to explore new legal territory, they almost always craft opinions that are deferential to the lawmaking branches of government. Indeed, courts are at their most conservative where the subject matter of a legal case touches on foreign policy, which states regard as the domain of the executive branch of government.

Judges recognize that maintaining democratic legitimacy requires them to engage in a high-wire act. While they must appear modest and deferential, they must also help manage and contextualize normative uncertainty. At the same time, as the branch of a democratic society that people expect to protect the rights of minorities from overreaching by the majority, courts often must take decisions that are politically contentious.

Similarly, transitional states are not hermetically sealed juridical universes. Today, all states are aware of the purpose and effect of the exercise of universal jurisdiction. Many states have embraced its use for at least some crimes, by not only ratifying international treaties that require them to prosecute or extradite persons alleged to have committed treaty-defined crimes, but also passing domestic implementing legislation, including statutes enshrining universal competence. Yet there is a tension between this expansion of extraterritorial competence and key features of the international legal and political order. The interstate system is founded and largely kept in check through reciprocity, which makes states reluctant to upset their relations with other states lest they lose the benefits of friendly relations, or risk the retaliatory consequences of having set a dangerous precedent. For this reason states may be cautious about extending juridical activities extraterritorially, and conservatives will argue further that such extension is in fact dangerous.

Orentlicher demolishes conservative arguments that universal jurisdiction involves engaging in external action contrary to the internal choices of another state when universal jurisdiction is based on an international treaty that both states have ratified. Such treaties impose identical international legal obligations on both states, and provide a guide for judicial action where the prosecution or extradition of an individual accused of committing a treaty-defined crime is concerned.

She also accurately describes a phenomenon already solidified in Europe and increasingly becoming normative reality in Latin America that Kathryn Sikkink and I have described elsewhere as the "justice cascade."[3] As democracy becomes more embedded, so too does societal acceptance of norms requiring states to prosecute or punish perpetrators of crimes against humanity. But as we have seen in all the successful examples of the exercise of universal jurisdiction to date, courts are only willing to follow nongovernmental activists and political actors down this path where the positive law provides a legitimizing foundation.

What about the case in which the offending state never ratified an enabling treaty allowing for the prosecution or punishment of its public officials? In such circumstances, the only basis for doing so is that the alleged crime is a violation of *jus cogens* norms in international law. *Jus cogens* norms are those rare peremptory norms of international law from which no derogation is permitted, including obligations to refrain from the commission of genocide, slavery, and torture. Unlike ordinary customary international law, however, for which some violations may be permissible in specific circumstances, it is *never* permissible to violate these norms. *Jus cogens* norms, as the International Criminal Tribunal for the Former Yugoslavia opined in *Prosecutor* v. *Furundzija,* "[enjoy] a rank in the international hierarchy [higher] than treaty law and even 'ordinary' customary rules."[4]

But domestic court judges, who tend to be better schooled in national law than international law, are often reluctant to apply customary international law where powerful political counterweights are present. Hence, when the Democratic Republic of Congo sought an International Court of Justice (ICJ) opinion as to whether its foreign minister, Abdulaye Yerodia Ndombasi, had diplomatic immunity from prosecution in Belgium, the Belgian courts likely were relieved to have that question clarified by a higher authority.

As noted above, lawmaking bodies share judges' apprehensions. Again in

Belgium, when victims' representatives filed criminal prosecutions against George H. W. Bush and his foreign policy team for alleged crimes against humanity committed in Iraq in the context of the first Gulf War, Belgium's legislature (albeit under extreme pressure from the United States) reexamined and significantly narrowed its universal jurisdiction legislation.[5]

But the fact that a norm prohibiting crimes as serious as genocide or other crimes against humanity has achieved the status of a *jus cogens* norm of customary international law does not automatically mean that the duty to prosecute persons accused of genocide or crimes against humanity falls on any state in whose territorial jurisdiction the alleged offender is to be found. As Leila Nadya Sadat explains in her chapter, which focuses primarily on the source of jurisdiction of the International Criminal Court (ICC), while under international law universal jurisdiction is recognized as one of the five bases of criminal jurisdiction that states may exercise, emphasis must be placed on the word "may." In other words, it falls to sovereign states to decide, as a matter of their own domestic criminal law, whether to give their courts jurisdiction to try criminal cases on the basis of the universal jurisdiction. Some treaties require that ratifying states either try perpetrators of the prohibited acts who are found on their territories, or extradite them to another state that will do so. However, no international judicial body has ever recognized a comparable basis for compelling the exercise of universal jurisdiction where violations of *jus cogens* norms are concerned.

Sadat is right that the tide seems to be turning in that direction. Distinguished international law commentators, including Sadat herself, are persuasively leading the charge. But it is one thing to argue that a direction is the one in which the law both ought to and is moving, and another to assert that an international national legal norm has been solidly established.

It is troubling to admit that while some terrible human rights crimes are *jus cogens* violations, there is not yet a universal duty for states to prosecute individuals for acts committed anywhere, rather than simply to prosecute or extradite those found upon their own territory. On the other hand, there is comfort in the fact that universal jurisdiction may provide an auxiliary system of justice. When the state where the crimes occurred cannot or will not prosecute, the next line of defense is prosecution by the international community – either through a process established by the UN Security Council exercising its Chapter VII powers, such as the ad hoc tribunals for Rwanda and the former Yugoslavia, or through the International Criminal Court. And, for *jus cogens* crimes committed by power-mongers and their inner circle of cadres in states that have attracted international intervention, Sadat correctly observes that the international community, more and more, is acknowledging its legal obligation to do so. Through the ICC, whose treaty over half of the world's nations have now ratified, the international community will increasingly do so in the future.[6] Thus normative ambiguity and likely domestic judicial reticence to act in the absence of treaty guidance is far less problematic than it otherwise might be.

Madeline Morris examines a different legal impediment that arises when international or third-party state courts assume jurisdiction over defendants charged with crimes against humanity and related crimes: sovereign and diplomatic immunity. Morris correctly narrows the problem where international courts are concerned: in many instances such immunities will not provide successful defenses before international courts. Where a court is established by the Security Council, it is in the Security Council's power to abrogate any immunity defense. Where the ICC prosecutes a defendant from a country that has ratified the ICC statute – which in Article 27 explicitly disallows defenses based on official capacity immunities – there also is no problem. But as Morris explains, the ICJ's decision in *Congo* v. *Belgium* (the *Yerodia* case),[7] does not address whether the ICC or indeed any other international court would have jurisdiction over a sitting head of state or diplomat of a nonmember state alleged to have committed crimes on the territory of a member state. What the *Yerodia* case does do is make clear that individual states, exercising universal jurisdiction, are limited with respect to certain foreign officials: heads of state and diplomats from other states, while in office, are immune from prosecution.

This might appear to be at odds with our intuition that certain acts, even if committed by public officials, cannot be viewed as "official" acts. The legal fiction that atrocities committed by public officials in their official capacities are *ultra vires* and therefore an abuse of state power rather than "acts of state" is one with which courts in countries that permit universal jurisdiction seem to be comfortable.[8] Similarly, US courts before which civil lawsuits for torture, disappearance, crimes against humanity, and genocide have been brought have displayed an equal level of comfort with the "private acts" legal fiction. This was not an issue considered by the ICJ majority. It is worth noting, however, that the dissent in *Yerodia* made a more radical argument: that there are exceptions to the international law of immunities. As Orentlicher aptly notes, judicial dissents prepare the ground "for further debate . . . by seed[ing] it [with] opinions that may someday become the majority view." Through dissenting opinions, "the colloquy continues and . . . the law advances."[9]

Chandra Lekha Sriram and Youssef Mahmoud remove themselves from the debate about where or under what legal theory to try perpetrators of *jus cogens* crimes against humanity, and focus instead on the deeper political questions of whether and, if so, when to do so. They maintain that fashioning peacebuilding strategies that achieve accountability while simultaneously limiting the likelihood of instability requires an analysis that involves going beyond simple "justice versus peace" dichotomies. This, as I have written about elsewhere, is a view with which I agree.[10]

Sriram and Mahmoud recognize that postconflict transitions are messy affairs. From the vantage point of the officials in charge, whether an interim government, a new democratically elected government, or an interim international governing body, transitional justice encompasses multiple, interdependent accountability goals. The failure to ignore any of these goals can increase the risk of instability. At the same time, those governments must balance transitional justice goals with a host of nontransitional justice matters, including ensuring security, consolidating democratic practices and institutions, rebuilding neglected or damaged infrastructure, invigorating the economy, reinserting former soldiers into civilian life, and the return or resettlement of refugees or internally displaced persons. In many cases transitional leaders will face challenges from political opponents, including "spoilers," who oppose the transition or felt excluded from negotiations that led to it. Thus, in any transition, those holding power, even those who genuinely want to redress past violations, will feel pressure to balance transitional justice goals with the other urgent societal and political concerns.

The methods governments or other decisionmakers adopt to achieve their accountability goals *are* nearly always the result of a compromise between these goals and other societal needs that arise in the transitional context. The degree to which those governments take measures that can be interpreted through "constructivist," "liberal," or "realist" paradigms depends upon political calculations rather than IR-theoretical considerations. Some transitions provide greater latitude for immediate action than others, and one of the great lessons of the transitional justice literature has been that no matter how many years or decades pass, the demand for justice for crimes against humanity does not go away until it is addressed through meaningful accountability processes.

Proamnesty arguments by realists like Jack Snyder and Leslie Vinjamuri, which Sriram and Mahmoud cautiously support, maintain that "norm-governed political order must be based on a political bargain among contending groups and on the creation of robust administrative institutions that can predictably enforce the law."[11] In the midst of political chaos or violent conflict, where restoring peace, security, and order is of paramount concern, granting amnesties can help accomplish that goal. Once granted, those amnesties must be respected to shore up fragile political and judicial institutions, which in turn are the best insurance policy against violence breaking out anew. These arguments, I suggest, are unsupported by much of the new transitional justice literature.[12]

For example, in Afghanistan, instead of being disarmed and tried, former warlords were selectively welcomed at both the negotiation table and into the transitional government to reduce the likelihood that violence would continue. The result is a government that is dominated by heavily armed faction leaders whose power comes from the implied threat of renewed violence rather than true leadership or democratic legitimacy. In Sierra Leone, where, as Sriram and Mahmoud point out, a multifaceted accountability process was created despite grave worries that it would produce more political instability, so far the peace has held. Moreover, many of the most feared Revolutionary United Front combatants, who themselves feel victimized or betrayed, have surprised the skeptics with their support for the Sierra Leone court and truth and reconciliation processes.

Sriram and Mahmoud allude to one feature of transitional justice processes that has not received much attention: that the greatest danger to political stability may arise not from those who know where they stand in the transitional scheme of things, but from those whose future is uncertain. Thus, in Argentina, it was not the original nine junta members who were tried for hundreds of acts of disappearance, murder, and torture during that country's dirty war who threatened to destabilize democracy. It was the mid-level military and police officers who had to endure several years of uncertainty about whether they would be tried. Similarly, as Sriram and Mahmoud point out, in Liberia, destabilization is most likely to come from demobilized Liberian fighters who fear that the reach of the Sierra Leonean tribunal will be expanded to include them as well.

One of the things we now know is that a credible public indictment for crimes against humanity or related crimes, by a government or international authority with the police power to back it up, will deter the individual named. Whether the indictee goes underground or seeks refuge abroad, his or her power to do further harm is undermined. In cases in which the indictee was a singular, strong, charismatic force with no obvious successor, such an indictment might be enough to shut down a warring movement, or at least persuade the followers to sit down at the negotiating table.

On the other hand, promises of amnesties now mean little. Whereas a generation ago, a domestic amnesty largely ensured any high-level official responsible for massive human rights violations a comfortable retirement anywhere in the world, in the world after the Pinochet case this no longer applies. The possibility that a state's citizens might be tried in another country, under either a treaty-based or a *jus cogens*-based theory of universal jurisdiction, coupled with establishment of the International Criminal Court, has altered the juridical landscape. Like it or not, states no longer have the capacity to guarantee to those most responsible for genocide or other terrible crimes against humanity that they can escape liability for their crimes. The continuing forward march of both international law and the laws of other states has undercut such promises.

Notes

1 Anne-Marie Slaughter and William Burke-White, "An International Constitutional Moment," *Harvard Journal of International Law* vol. 43, no. 1 (Winter 2002), p. 15.
2 See also Anne-Marie Slaughter, "Judicial Globalization," *Virginia Journal of International Law* vol. 40, no. 4 (2000) pp. 1103–24, noting that this dialogue can also help to promote the adoption of new norms by judges.
3 Ellen Lutz and Kathryn Sikkink, "The Justice Cascade: The Evolution and Impact of Foreign Human Rights Trials in Latin America," *Chicago Journal of International Law* vol. 2 (Spring 2001), pp. 1–33.
4 See Sadat, "The International Criminal Court and Universal International Jurisdiction: A Return to First Principles," Chapter 11 in this volume, quoting *Prosecutor* v. *Furundzija,* Case No. IT-95-17/1-T, Judgment (December 10, 1998), para. 153.
5 Stefaan Smis and Kim van der Borght, "Belgian Law Concerning the Punishment of Grave Breaches of International Humanitarian Law: A Contested Law with Uncontested Objectives," *ASIL Insights* (July 2003), available online at www.asil.org/insights.htm#2003.

6 See list of country ratifications at www.iccnow.org/countryinfo/worldsigsandratifications.html. Ninety-nine countries had ratified as of September 5, 2005.

7 *Case Concerning the Arrest Warrant of 11 April 2000 (Democratic Republic of the Congo* v. *Belgium)* (February 14, 2002), available online at www.icj-cij.org/icjwww/idoctet/icobeframe.htm.

8 Orentlicher makes this point with respect to the British law lords' decision in the Pinochet case.

9 Orentlicher, "Whose Justice? Reconciling Universal Jurisdiction with Democratic Principles," Chapter 13 in this volume.

10 Ellen L. Lutz, "Transitional Justice: The Latest Lessons Learned and the Road Ahead," in Naomi Roht-Arriaza and Javier Mariezcurrena, eds, *Transitional Justice in the Twenty-first Century: Beyond Truth Versus Justice* (Cambridge: Cambridge University Press, forthcoming 2006).

11 Jack Snyder and Leslie Vinjamuri, "Trials and Errors: Principle and Pragmatism in Strategies of International Justice," *International Security* vol. 28, no. 3 (Winter 2004), p. 6.

12 See contributions in Roht-Arriaza and Mariezcurrena, *Transitional Justice in the Twenty-first Century.*

Part V

CONCLUSIONS

16

DISAGGREGATING US INTERESTS IN INTERNATIONAL LAW

Sketching a theory of liberal transnationalism

Peter J. Spiro

Introduction

As events surrounding September 11, 2001, and the invasion of Iraq have brought into yet sharper relief, the United States has been famously resistant to the imposition of international law norms. This resistance runs deep in American constitutional culture, which has rejected the possibility of being made to bow before international law where it does not otherwise serve its national interest. In the American imagination, sovereignty still represents a bulwark against alien encroachment. And given America's unchallenged position as the world's sole superpower, many – including many academics – have assumed a US capacity to persist in this sort of splendid legal isolation, even as its sovereigntist premises are normatively deplored.

But autonomy may no longer present a sustainable strategy, even from a materialist perspective, as the disaggregating tendencies of globalization work to break down the possibilities for exceptionalism. This chapter first adapts the tools of international relations (IR) theory to the question of how international law might be incorporated into US law, the putative global dominance of the United States notwithstanding. IR theory has informed an important strain of recent international law scholarship.[1] It provides a useful frame for situating international law as a matter of institutional interactions rather than a matter of doctrine. IR theory is not, however, typically deployed to explain internal state dynamics salient to the initial incorporation of international law, focusing more on domestic politics as an independent variable.[2] Nor has IR theory been prominently deployed to explain or to project the relationship of the United States to international law. This chapter describes how discrete elements of the United States, including private actors and disaggregated governmental components beyond the traditional foreign policy apparatus, may be developing an institutional interest in the acceptance of international regimes. It thus suggests a future in which international law is absorbed into US law not because it is good

– although it may well be that, too – but because rational institutional action will pull in that direction.

Bringing international relations theory home

International relations theory has until recently been about states, their interests, and their power. Departures from the once dominant realist school have recognized the salience of nonstate actors, but only to the extent that they either exercise political power within domestic structures (liberal IR theory) or seek to persuade states to adhere to particular norms (constructivist IR theory). State action remains the ultimate unit of analysis in all three approaches, which misses the independent consequentiality of nonstate action.[3] While constructivist approaches recognize that nonstate actors operate on a transnational basis, they attribute nonstate influence to the force of ideas rather than power. This chapter attempts to marry constructivist foregrounding of transnational actors with liberal premises of institutional self-interest and domestic power politics.

International law has long suffered a sort of ontological challenge among political scientists as to whether it really qualifies as "law" at all. This difficulty dates to Austinian notions of law and power, under which rules qualify as law only where enforced by superior institutions, able to back commands with the legitimatized use of violence. The system of rules among nation-states did not fit with this pyramidal conception of law. States were not subject to command from above. The enforcement model of the law of nations, as it was known, was a horizontal one among formal equals. Of course, formal equality did not translate into equality on the ground. To the political scientists of the mid-twentieth century, international law thinly masked power relationships and state interests. The realist school of IR theory was particularly devastating in its critique of international law as lacking consequence. Posing an anarchic system of interstate relations, definitionally counterposed to one governed by the rule of law, the realists framed a world in which rational self-interest and geopolitical capacities, not law, explained the global dynamic.

In fact, realism did a good job of explaining the Cold War world. The Cold War marked the zenith of state-centered power. It was a context in which studying the state, to the exclusion of all other actors, comported with power realities. The domination and antagonism of the two superpowers, moreover, made it almost impossible to establish a broadly effective regime of international norms, at least not one that significantly constrained state discretion. The superpowers rejected norms inconsistent with their interests, and nobody else could do anything about it. This created a glaring gap between the formal instruments of what purported to be the new, post-World War II dawn of international law – the UN Charter and the UN Declaration on Human Rights, for instance – and the actual practices of states. International law appeared to be a system of merely paper guarantees, an epiphenomenon of interstate relations. States pursued perceived self-interest, whether or not it complied with international law. States did what they could get away with.

Hence the traction of realist approaches in the latter half of the twentieth century and the corresponding poverty of norm-driven or positivist models. On such issues as the use of force and human rights law, it was power that determined state action. Realism also enjoyed intuitive analytical appeal to the extent that it worked from notions of self-interest rather than obligation. In the absence of systematic enforcement and high stakes, it was not easy to explain why states would or should observe rules that competitors were flouting, at least not where the observance of such rules would diminish relative strength.

Realism faces a more difficult challenge processing the contemporary realities of late-modern world politics. It is hard now to deny the consequentiality of international norms. The number and scope of international instruments, the attention that states and others direct to their negotiation, refinement, and application, and the prominence of international regimes and institutions in important policy debates all point to an enhanced position for international law. Realism might be able to explain some of this activity. In the security context, for instance, state power and self-interest would explain nonproliferation regimes, especially those that privilege more powerful states. In such cases, law may still be more of an indicator rather than a driver.

But there are other new global issues in which realism comes up short, human rights presenting the most obvious case. Human rights regimes have nothing to do with material reciprocal benefits. One country's refraining from torturing its own citizens does not pose a direct benefit to other countries. It is not clear why, from a realist perspective, states would undertake human rights commitments and then live up to them, especially if other states were unwilling to marshal significant resources in their universal enforcement. It is for this reason that realists may be cheap in conceding that human rights regimes have in fact deepened. To the extent that human rights regimes now govern state behavior with no correlation to power relationships, traditional realist conceptions of international relations are undermined.

Hence the emergence of strong competing schools of international relations theory. Liberal international relations theorists break open the "black box" of the state to allow the salience of domestic political actors. In this scheme, international relations becomes a two-stage process in which foreign policy outcomes are explained by the pursuit of state preferences, as determined through domestic politics and as constrained by strategic interactions with other states.[4] In a more radical break from the realists, constructivist IR theorists assert the consequentiality of ideas, as pressed by norm entrepreneurs in transnational political spaces.[5] In this view, international relations adds up to more than the summing out of rational interests.

It is not my purpose here to undertake anything more than a crude primer of international relations theories, nor to offer a freestanding alternative. It does seem possible, however, to extract some utility from all three of these major strands of IR theory. Realism offers the logic of self-interested behavior and the inevitability of relationships defined by power. But realism fails to recognize power outside of the state. Indeed, it refuses to acknowledge power outside of the traditional foreign policy apparatus of states. Constructivist IR theorists highlight the salience of other actors, especially transnational social movements,[6] but only insofar as they are propagators of new ideas. Liberal theorists, meanwhile, understand that "individuals and private groups"[7] are consequential as political actors to the development and effectiveness of international regimes, but only as they are enclosed within the confines of "domestic society" and working at the international level only through their allocated state agents; the possibility of their transnationality goes unacknowledged. As much as the realists, liberal IR reifies the territorial state and hews to the primacy of states on the international scene. Even where states act in a disaggregated manner – that is, through component units – they are characterized as maintaining unitary preferences.

As yet unrepresented among major IR strains is a model that centers the powers and interests, as opposed to the principles, of transnational nonstate actors. Such a model would take the rational-actor, materialist premises of liberal IR theory, and broaden them to include the constructivist focus on transnational social movements as well as corporations and subnational authorities. The model abandons liberalism's state-delimited conception of "society" and constructivism's elevation of norms over material interests. It rejects the essentialization of the state in which all IR theory continues to be grounded, arguing that transnational nonstate activity can be of independent consequence, whether or not it impacts state behavior. The resulting dynamic, which might run under the label "liberal transnationalism," would highlight the rational interests and capacities of various institutions in charting global developments. The approach may not lend itself to the refined modeling of state interaction. Alone, states present a small universe of isomorphic entities, mostly working along the same metrics of interest and power (both ultimately relating to military and economic might and the control of persons and territory). The new actors of international relations, by contrast, project different capacities with differing objectives, and their interactions are complex, especially insofar as states no longer serve a dominant channeling function. Explaining incentive structures beyond state-to-state interactions, a model recognizing the interests and power of nonstate actors – both independently and as determinants of state power – might complement normative justifications for participation in international legal regimes. The model, in other words, supplies a polycentric, interest-based explanation of how international law comes home, to stand alongside those who assert or assume that international law should triumph as an inherent good.

The exceptional case of the United States

Incorporating institutional power and self-interest at levels other than the state, this model could predict the more complete assimilation of the United States into the system of international norms. Unlike most other developed countries, the United States has assumed a skeptical, sometimes openly hostile, posture to international law and institutions. The United States assumes an à la carte model of international law, asserting its prerogative to elect those regimes in which it will participate. In some cases this approach drives nonparticipation in important but discretionary international regimes, as with the Kyoto accords on climate change and the establishment of the International Criminal Court. In other cases, it drives noncompliance with mandatory norms (that is, one from which a state may not opt out), as with the continuing use of capital punishment against juvenile offenders and other practices implicating human rights norms. In that the United States is the sole superpower, realists would expect this nonparticipation and noncompliance where regimes do not further US self-interest. Some elements of the George W. Bush administration clearly work from these sorts of "might makes right" assumptions. The United States, the argument runs, can and should eschew international norms contrary to its national interest.

It is possible that absorption will not occur, and that the United States will successfully resist the imposition of international norms not consistent with its interests and continue to act unilaterally. Empire stands as an alternate basis of global governance going forward, with a hegemonic United States dictating international standards rather than submitting to them. However, to the extent that the United States consents to regimes not of its devising and inconsistent with its interests and preferences, some other explanation would be required.

Players in this debate mostly assume that US acceptance of international law is a matter of choice. My purpose here is to suggest that the choice may become increasingly constrained as the costs of nonparticipation and nonconformity increase for and are increased by various actors within and outside the state. Pressures from multiple quarters will build on disaggregated components of the United States to submit to various international regimes. These pressures will progressively limit opt-out possibilities. This will be true in the constitutional realm as in others. There will likely come a point at which domestic constitutional law is effectively, if not formally, subordinated to international law.

The proposition might be advanced under a constructivist or liberal IR analysis. Constructivism would highlight the influence of transnational activism on US practices, making the shift from what were once characterized as "public interest groups" acting within national parameters to nongovernmental organizations (NGOs) acting across national borders. Transnational NGOs may act on any state, including the United States. Constructivists would highlight the role of ideas in persuading states to accede to international regimes and press them on others. The solidification of these regimes would in turn define the parameters of legitimacy for states. In this sense, international regimes construct (hence the tag for this brand of IR) what it takes to be a state, and that states are socialized by those regimes.[8] Insofar as those parameters are defined in legal terms, states will be drawn into compliance with international law. In the US case, the analysis would assert the possibility that participation with various international regimes will be pressed by transnational NGOs, directly and through other states, and that US interaction with other states and international organizations will draw it to participation in an iterative normative dynamic.[9] As a state, the United States will have to present itself in terms defined by other states.

Constructivism breaks down the wall between domestic and international politics. Unlike other IR theories, constructivism accounts for the fact of globalization. But constructivism does not seem well equipped to explain exactly what it will take to bring a behemoth such as the United States to heel. To the extent that constructivism recognizes power, it is in the form of state power. As for socialization, constructivism does not demonstrate how the bully is socialized where he can afford not to be. It is not clear how the United States will perceive its legitimacy to be defined or diminished by the standards of other states, international institutions, or international norms. Many in the United States seem quite content to establish legitimacy by contrast to rather than consistency with external phenomena. The United States is not among those states that "are keenly aware of the approval of other states,"[10] nor would the label "rogue state" give many Americans much pause. The well-established tradition of American exceptionalism makes it a hard case for the constructivists.

From a liberal IR perspective, two possible pathways might point to greater US submission to international regimes. The first would depend on the willingness of other states to press compliance with international law as a matter of state-to-state relations. Unlike realism, which has difficulty processing the assertion of something like a human rights agenda, liberal IR theorists can explain this willingness in terms of the domestic politics of those states. A new European agenda centering international law may be driven by domestic European political interests. Once adopted as a matter of state policy, it is not conceptually difficult to play out the mechanisms by which international norms might be imposed on the United States. To the extent that other states have something of interest to the United States, international law will be injected into the bargaining mix. Depending on the intensity with which international law compliance was pressed by another state and the bargaining power of that state, the United States would incur costs from continued noncompliance. But other states would need to marshal substantial leverage over the United States and be willing to incur costs in pressing the United States to change its posture. In some contexts this might work, where the leverage is high and costs low. An example would be with respect to the application of the death penalty to persons whose extradition is sought by the United States; other states can extract US undertakings at little cost, and their leverage is complete. But these contexts present the exception. The European response to the Iraq invasion supplies a counter-example. Even though some powerful European states considered the US invasion to constitute a serious breach of international law, their leverage was insufficient to enforce that position against the United States.

New causal pathways for international law

More promisingly, liberal IR would also consider the interests of domestic US groups in particular international regimes as drivers of participation in those regimes. Liberal theorists can readily explain US adherence to free trade regimes, given strong US corporate support for them. But liberal IR would consider this support on something approaching a mercantilist basis. In this approach, US corporations (and other groups supporting free trade) determine the "preference" of the United States. The source of that preference is assumed to be indigenous, that is, not impacted by politics beyond the water's edge. As Andrew Moravcsik writes, preferences are "causally independent of the strategies of other actors and, therefore, prior to specific interstate political actions."[11] Liberal IR also gives rise to an aggregated national position in relation to other nations. The state remains the basic unit of international relations, this notwithstanding the liberal recognition of disaggregated central government actors. In liberal IR theory, the state continues to be a box, albeit one that has become transparent.

Liberal IR theory could be deployed to chart the more complete assimilation of the United States into international institutions. Almost all international regimes can now be paired with some domestic US constituency. In the liberal view, US accession would be expected where that constituency had an interest sufficiently intense to warrant pursuing participation in an international regime and domestic political power sufficient to secure that objective. Adoption of the Kyoto Protocol, on climate change, for example, would be expected at the point when environmentalists were in a position, through the domestic political process, to garner the votes and contributions necessary to secure legislative and executive action. Likewise for human rights agreements, especially those (such as the conventions on race and gender discrimination) that have self-interested constituencies who might at some point have sufficient material incentive and wield sufficient power to secure accession.

But liberal IR theory would seem to miss important additional causal pathways that may point to the more complete participation of the United States in international regimes.[12] The incompleteness of the liberal IR account can be pinned to two core assumptions: (1) that state preferences are generated by domestic politics insulated from outside forces, and (2) that international relations solely comprises government-to-government interactions, rather than being a more polycentric process in which nonstate actors may engage in consequential norms activity even where states are not engaged.

On both counts, the more theoretically challenging "disaggregation" is taking place outside of the realm of central governments. No doubt the state is disaggregating, in the sense that components of the federal government are now directly involved in international relations activity. But society is disaggregating as well, so that it is more difficult to identify groups or corporations (or even individuals) as discretely "American." Where corporations and the organs of civil society once functioned for the most part within the parameters of particular states, they now represent partially distinct transnational identities and enjoy autonomous power. As they dissagregate from the state, these actors can mobilize transnationally to advance international regimes, both by pressuring state actors and by adopting those regimes into their own practices. In the case of the United States, disaggregation creates more effective alternatives to targeting a superpower. Where action against the United States as a whole would in most cases implicate formidable costs, discrete components may be vulnerable to transnational mobilization.

Transnational pressure points

The transnationality of social movements and corporations, first of all, changes the nature of their power and what they represent. Nonstate actors apply leverage against governmental decisionmakers. This leverage can be applied directly, under a standard pressure group model. Political actors respond to organizational power that can command votes, favorable media play, and money. But transnational dynamics open up indirect channels of influence that enhance domestic political power, and extend domestic political power to nondomestic groups. To the extent that Amnesty International or Greenpeace has power within US political structures, for example, it is not fully measured by the length of their US membership rosters. Likewise, the influence of the foreign-based multinationals is not dependent on the size or existence of US subsidiaries.

Because they operate transnationally, these groups can pursue avenues of influence outside of domestic political structures that will enlarge their powers within those structures. They will be in a position to enlist other states to advance their agendas. Constructivists describe a "boomerang" effect in which domestic social movements work with transnational partners to enlist other states and international organizations to pressure their own governments (human rights activity in Latin American providing a paradigmatic example).[13] The US elements of these transnational networks can themselves undertake parallel efforts in foreign and international institutional settings to bolster their domestic political undertakings. A US-based group such as Human Rights Watch will work to enlist other states as part of efforts to influence US human rights practices.

In pressuring the United States, that strategy will make a difference, at least at the margins. Where US action depends on some level or form of multilateral support, and that support is politically controversial in other states, transnational NGO activity can tip the balance. One might suppose, for instance, that the United Kingdom would not support application beyond Iraq of the Bush administration's preemption doctrine, that British nonsupport was generated in part by transnational activists (including American ones), and that the United States would not proceed with additional military incursions without British participation. Insofar as US elements in the transnational political coalition contributed to

British decisionmaking, those elements secured through transnational channels what they could not secure through ordinary domestic ones.

More subversive of both constructivist and liberal IR models are efforts by transnational social movements to advance international law-related agendas by pressuring corporate actors, on the expectation that they will in turn work to secure appropriate governmental action. In this diagram, NGOs mobilize (or threaten to mobilize) the buying power of sympathetic consumers. Target companies may sometimes be singled out because of their identification with a particular country whose conduct the NGO seeks to change, entangling them, in effect, as innocent bystanders. The boycott of Beaujolais wine in the face of French nuclear tests during the 1990s presents an example.[14] Another example – action directed at US companies having no direct connection to global warming because of the US refusal to accept Kyoto.[15] In other cases, the target is implicated in the policy whose modification is sought. The continuing boycott campaign against ExxonMobil relating to climate change fits into this category. ExxonMobil has been singled out both because of the impact of its own corporate policies on climate change (it, unlike Beaujolais wine, is part of the problem) and because of its leverage in Washington. If ExxonMobil faces significant lost profits as a result of US nonparticipation in Kyoto,[16] it could be expected to desist from its support of the Bush administration's refusal to pursue ratification of Kyoto. The campaign against ExxonMobil may have spurred other major oil companies to come out in favor of the protocol.

In the face of economic globalization, this channel for securing governmental action should become more effective. Where transnational corporations are the target, this mechanism politically empowers nonstate actors (individuals and organizations) outside of the United States, typically in partnership with US cohorts. A consumer exercising choice at European pumps will be casting a sort of virtual vote in Washington. In the wake of successful consumer campaigns, moreover, transnational activist groups wield power without resort to boycotts, actual or threatened; they have secured what appear to be permanent seats at the table. Coupled with direct use of domestic political channels, these entry points open up new opportunities for actors seeking to advance US participation in international institutions and compliance with international norms. If US companies face lost business as a result of the Bush administration's unilateralist orientation, as they fear they will, they will work to change it. This offers a more viable channel for applying pressure than has prevailed at the state-to-state level, where the costs of discipline will be high. Nongeopolitical channels will present lower thresholds. The strategy is divide and conquer, both enabled and generated by the disaggregating tendencies of globalization.

Nonstate norm regimes

Equally significant is activism, whose objective is to change the behavior of corporate or other nonstate entities without securing the modification of governmental policy. This strategy is increasingly being deployed in the many contexts in which corporate or other nongovernmental conduct is the source of a perceived harm. The emergence of social responsibility and refined "voluntary" codes of conduct evidence this trend toward advancing agendas outside of public institutions.[17] Much of this activity has been occurring in the context of transnational corporate conduct, and much of it has clear salience to international norms. Prominent examples are found with respect to worker rights and carbon emissions. With respect to worker rights, competing codes of conduct have emerged to set and monitor standards on such issues as child labor, minimum wages, and other working conditions.[18] These codes have significant coverage among major manufacturers as well as important licensers, especially among universities. On emissions standards, environmental groups are securing commitments from some major energy corporations, including giants Shell and British Petroleum, to reduce their emissions of greenhouse gases.[19]

Insofar as these initiatives succeed in changing target entity behavior, they diminish the importance of multilateral governmental action. Success is contingent on coverage and effective monitoring (neither of which are seamless in any regulatory scheme, public or private). Coverage is facilitated by competitive incentives within industries and the risk of being stung by NGO "naming and shaming" boycott campaigns, launched on a transnational basis.[20] Though initial subscriptions to conduct codes may be hard won for so long as a particular industry shows a united front, one finds, as more entities within the targeted community sign on, the nonstate equivalent of a "norm cascade" or "tipping point" after which participation is voluntary in name only.[21] The establishment of conduct regimes advances international regimes even in the absence of state participation. Every additional manufacturer signed on to a worker rights code of conduct represents an incremental gain for international worker rights. If all major energy producers were to reduce their greenhouse gas emissions, that might represent a significant step toward accomplishment of the reduction set by Kyoto, whether or not the protocol were to come into force. In other contexts, direct action against other private actors could obviate altogether the need for US governmental participation. International relations theorists could not process this result insofar as they all aggregate the state for purposes of compliance. An aggregated approach may produce the conclusion that the "United States" is not participating in an international regime when in fact much (or even all) of what constitutes the United States has signed on.[22]

Once major corporations are implicated in codes of conduct and similar regimes, however, they have an incentive to press for their adoption as law. Corporate actors seek certainty, even if certainty means entrenching norms that are costly over the short term, and public law regimes promise greater certainty than do private ones. To the extent that codes of conduct are pressed more effectively on large, multinational manufacturers than on others, the lack of universality gives rise to competitive disadvantages. Those disadvantages can be corrected by universalizing norms generated in the private scheme. The result will be corporate pressure for legalization. In the US context, this may mean pressing the US government to accede to relevant international regimes. This was an important element in US acceptance of international accords limiting the use of chlorofluorocarbons (CFCs).[23] DeBeers was a crucial advocate of the Kimberley Process and related US legislation to address the problem of African blood diamonds. The CFC model could be repeated with respect to the Kyoto accords in the context of greenhouse gases. To the extent that major energy concerns are being held to Kyoto-like requirements as a result of activist pressure at the same time their smaller counterparts slip under the radar screen, they can be expected to advocate US support for the multilateral regime. In the meantime, the success of social responsibility campaigns dilutes the significance of current US intransigence.

Unlike constructivist models and their equivalents in the legal scholarship, this descriptive analysis works from rational actor premises. Unlike liberal IR theory, it allows for the transnational determination of "domestic" interests. The analysis is not meant to dismiss the consequentiality of ideas, which at some level (not always primary) invariably figure in the success of efforts to secure adoption of an international regime. But in confronting the massive power of the United States, it is important to pose an interest-based scenario for the more complete integration of the United States into international legal institutions. The plausibility of such integration is enhanced by the recognition of transnational in addition to intergovernmental and domestic politic determinants.

Disaggregate and conquer

The importance of causal pathways involving private actors is coupled with the emergence of newly paved or widened pathways among governmental ones. These include state and local governments, the courts, Congress, and executive agencies outside of the traditional foreign policy apparatus. These governmental entry points can be visited through both domestic and international channels. This disaggregation of governmental entities facilitates the incorporation of international law into US practice, by lowering the pressure thresholds for institutional action and exploiting the institutional self-interest of disaggregated entities to participate in or conform with international regimes.

Liberal IR acknowledges – indeed it has foregrounded – the role of disaggregated components of central governments.[24] This work has been of breakthrough magnitude in describing the actual conduct of international relations and posing a rich set of normative questions. On the theoretical side, it further undermines realist conceptions of unitary state actors. It is less clear how disaggregation fits into liberal conceptions of international relations. Liberal IR theorists stress the representative nature of disaggregated governmental entities, working from the premise that political preferences within putative domestic society are prior. In effect, if liberal theory generally poses "the state as agent," it appears to process disaggregated activity as "the agent of the state as agent."[25] The liberal transnationalist analysis that follows, by contrast, highlights the transnational determination of disaggregated governmental interests, that is, how they are affected by forces that do not come under the umbrella of "domestic society." The explanatory distinction may promise the facilitation of US submission to international regimes on a more accelerated basis than other theories would predict.

Subnational actors

First of all, IR theorists appear almost completely to ignore the salience of substate actors to international relations and the incorporation of international law, perhaps because their role is subversive of IR's continued privileging of the state. But subfederal jurisdictions in the United States now face weighty, discrete interests on the global stage, interests that create leverage for international actors. The leverage may be exercised to advance international regimes. As I have written elsewhere, noncompliance with entrenched international law norms may result in lost economic opportunities for subnational units, crucial to economic prosperity in a globalized economy.[26] Local jurisdictions in the United States are relatively substitutable. International actors can target resources away from jurisdictions thought to stand in violation of international norms. The approach increases leverage insofar as it can exploit interstate competition in a dynamic resembling consumer and shareholder action against corporations. (Indeed, it may include action against corporations that are identified with a particular state, by way of securing a change in state practices.) Where it would be difficult to sanction the United States as a whole for noncompliance with an international law standard, it might be possible to single out particular subnational jurisdictions.

As with action against private actors, where subnational governmental conduct is the ultimate object of a standard of conduct, securing action at that level will diminish the significance of nonparticipation at the national level. If, for example, all states of the United States are persuaded to modify death penalty practices (over which they command almost complete responsibility) to comport with international standards, then it makes less difference whether such persuasion succeeds in federal institutions.

Congress

Congress, executive branch agencies, and the courts also present discrete entry points for international regimes. At the federal level, disaggregation creates fewer competitive pressures, at least not on anything less than a national scale. It is more costly to exercise economic leverage against the United States as a whole than against territorial subunits or corporate elements. But transnational forces may nonetheless prove increasingly influential with component parts of the federal government, resulting in more effectively applied pressures toward participation in international regimes.

Congress remains most resistant to these forces. Its default position continues to be one of nonparticipation. Congress has historically stood at the center of American exceptionalism, and it will likely suffer exceptionalist tendencies into the future. But it can be moved from these tendencies through the standard channels of legislative influence (money and votes), as in the international economic law context. Much of this influence will be undertaken on behalf of indentifiably domestic interests, including US citizens and corporations, thus appearing to fit neatly within the liberal IR paradigm. But even these channels are no longer cleanly "American." All publicly traded corporations will now include foreign shareholders, and many will include other significant non-US stakeholders. Many US citizens hold additional citizenships in other states.[27] And these elements, even if dominantly American, can be the agents of transnational influence, as where US corporations face the sort of transnational consumer pressure described above.

More clearly outside the "domestic" box are campaign contributions by resident aliens and the wholly owned US subsidiaries of foreign corporations. Foreign corporations are independently active lobbyists on the Hill, where they can exercise influence by delivering information if not dollars. This activity will tend to support participation in international regimes, insofar as such regimes benefit foreign entities in the US and global context. Progress may lag in contexts lacking corporate advocates. It will be especially difficult to budge Congress on meaningful participation in human rights regimes, on which the most intense contemporary manifestations of modern American exceptionalism have focused, from the Bricker Amendment episode forward. As liberal IR theorists have highlighted, the structure of Congress creates minority veto opportunities, and those opportunities will continue to be exercised in the international human rights context. To the extent that domestic interests mobilize in support of participation, one could expect an evolution in practice towards participation. The change would be accelerated if US corporate interests began to face related transnational activist pressure, along the lines of the "innocent bystander" model sketched above. Action broadly equating US corporate activity with US nonparticipation in human rights regimes remains a long way over the horizon. But one can construct scenarios in which Congress becomes more institutionally amenable to pressure to participate in international human rights and other noneconomic international regimes.

Executive branch agencies

Closer to the core of disaggregation theory, executive branch agencies beyond the traditional foreign policy apparatus now have institutional incentives to incorporate international legal regimes. Though this incorporation is largely out of the public eye, it points to the globalization of regulatory activity. The emerging transnational government networks are at the leading edge of disaggregation. The US nodes of these networks constitute another discrete entry point for international law. Here, too, there are transnational determinants of institutional interests that should point to increased US participation in international regimes over the long run. Although agencies cannot be directly plied with contributions, foreign entities can supply them with information. Especially where coordinated with US-based entities, these deliverables can affect outcomes.[28] Regulatory constituencies are likely to be transnational, even if they are not organized as such. For instance, the US Securities and Exchange Commission (SEC) now protects a significant number of foreign shareholders in US-based corporations. Insofar as SEC regulatory effectiveness is contingent on global harmonization, one could expect that transnational constituency to press both US and foreign regulators to undertake regulatory coordination. That the resulting regime is largely (though not completely) of the SEC's devise does not render it representative only of US interests. The transnational constituencies will press for the adoption of transnational regulatory regimes.

The regulators will have a strong independent interest in coordinated action, insofar as in an increasing number of regulatory spaces, regulation will be ineffective if undertaken on a domestic territorial basis only. Together, these forces should lead component elements of the federal executive branch to buy into transnational regimes. Although a US regulator will often be the most powerful player in a transgovernmental network, even where dominant the process of coordination will involve compromises. As adopted by the United States, then, the harmonized regime – whatever the vehicle, a form of international law – will constitute an incorporation of international law standards. As disaggregated from the central organs of foreign policy, agencies pose another entry point for international law.

The judiciary

Even though they are not directly subject to interest-based politics, federal judges and the courts are also developing institutional interests that point toward greater orientation to international law standards. In the context of life tenure, judges may be more focused on reputational standing. As domestic courts come increasingly to identify themselves as part of a global community of courts,[29] this interest should open up the courts as an additional entry point for international law.

Federal judges may now define their peer group to include foreign and international jurists, as a result of increasingly structured contacts with those counterparts. This identification gives US judges an incentive to act in a way that will enhance their reputation with those groups. The incentive can play out at the level of individual contact; judges will naturally want to garner respect rather than opprobrium when they find themselves, on a repeat basis, interacting with non-US judges. To the extent that judging involves dialogue among courts – with citation frequencies as a measurement of both individual and institutional reputation[30] – federal judges may come increasingly to value the attention of foreign and international tribunals.

On both counts, the interests of federal judges will be served by the deployment of international law norms. Recognition is, first of all, a two-way street, especially among those who are not assigned a formal hierarchical relationship. Foreign and international tribunals are more likely to take notice of US judicial decisions to the extent US judges take notice of them. Second, US jurists have lagged in their comfort with and use of comparative and international law sources relative to their non-US counterparts. In the context of twentieth-century America, that was never a problem; indeed, it may have been a badge. Today, US judges may be more responsive to the harsh critiques launched by global jurists highlighting the failure of US courts to take account of international law.[31]

This amenability to international law sources is being reinforced among domestic audiences. Litigants are coming increasingly to bring international law sources before US courts; gone are the days when resort was made to international legal authority only when none was to be had among domestic sources. Leading US legal academics, including some who would identify themselves as constitutional rather than international law scholars (another group with which many judges will seek to build reputational capital), are asserting the salience of international and foreign law to the task of judging domestically.[32] Federal judges now enjoy significant backup support as they begin to shed their blinders. But that support is itself far from indigenous, as it will have been transnationally generated. Litigants and law professors are themselves increasingly situated in transnational spaces and are being buffeted by transnational forces.

Long emerging, these influences are showing results in US judicial decision-making. Opinions in three important recent Supreme Court decisions have adverted to international norms. The majority in *Atkins* v. *Virginia* noted the near-global consensus against executing the mentally retarded.[33] In *Lawrence* v. *Texas*, the Court highlighted decisions of the European Court of Human Rights and other nations on the way to striking down a state measure criminalizing homosexual sodomy.[34] And perhaps most dramatically, with respect to the execution of juvenile offenders the decision in *Roper* v. *Simmons* dwelled at length on the near universal international prohibition on the practice.[35] One might expect to see a growing number of cases in which majority opinions from the Court cite international law sources as support. Such deployment of international and foreign law may continue to draw ferocious dissents[36] and other opposition.[37] The possibility of provoking anti-internationalist elements in Congress, which would have some capacity to fight the practice, will likely find the Court treading lightly for now. But the trend toward the judicial incorporation of international norms is unlikely to be reversed.

As the state is disaggregated and made permeable to discrete international activity, these actors beyond the foreign policy organs of the central government will render the United States vulnerable to the imposition of international norms. As permeability broadens, actors whose interests will be served through international norms will be afforded multiple strategic opportunities denied them in the era of highly channeled state-to-state relations. The United States is no longer a monolith for purposes of international law and relations; it is now, rather, an arena in which global forces can play at the game of transnational politics and rational institutional action.

That is not to say that traditional, aggregated models of state action all reject the possibility of more complete US participation in international regimes. Long-established models of international relations working from standard statist geopolitical premises, focusing on the White House and traditional foreign policy agencies, including the Departments of State, Defense, and Treasury, still apply on a nonexclusive basis, and there are an increasing number of contexts in which they implicate international law. To the extent that other states press an international law agenda on the United States, the traditional foreign policy apparatus may have cause to accept international legal regimes that it would otherwise reject. Assuming rational decisionmaking, it all depends on what is on the table; if the cost of the action threatened by the other state outweighs the benefit of nonparticipation in the regime, then one would expect a change in the US posture toward the regime.

Such discipline has been difficult to apply, because the United States looms so powerful and because other states have been unwilling to expend significant resources to back international law where it does not promise direct payoffs. But some examples may loom over the horizon. In the post-September 11, 2001, context, for example, European states have been turning up the heat on the indefinite Guantanamo detentions, secret detention facilities elsewhere, and interrogation techniques in such a way as to secure action consistent with their view of applicable human rights standards. Left to its own devices, the United States would likely continue these elements of its antiterrorism strategy, which have generated growing opposition among other states. European states may threaten to withhold important cooperation along other fronts in the war on terrorism if the practices persist. That could tip the balance against the offending policies, and find even this Administration, so rhetorically hostile to international law, relenting to its power on the ground.[38]

Conclusion

Existing models of international law and international relations are ill equipped to project the more complete assimilation of the United States into international norm regimes. On the one hand, norm-driven theories fail to explain how international actors will overcome entrenched US resistance to international lawmaking. The United States does not require the approbation of other states by way of maintaining a sense of national legitimacy. On the other hand, rationalist theories systematically underestimate the incentives that the United States may have for buying into international regimes. By segregating interests and actors along national lines, these models miss transnational accelerants of international norms. The interests of the full spectrum of US actors – disaggregated governmental and private entities – are increasingly determined in transnational political spaces. Transnationality affords nondomestic actors enhanced leverage in pressing US participation in international regimes. The model suggested in this chapter explains how the United States could be more fully drawn into international law as a matter of rational institutional action.

Notes

1 See, for example, Kenneth W. Abbott, "Modern International Relations Theory: A Prospectus for International Lawyers," *Yale Journal of International Law* vol. 14 (1989), p. 335; Anne-Marie Slaughter, "International Law and International Relations Theory: A Dual Agenda," *American Journal of International Law* vol. 87 (1993), p. 205.

2 See Anne-Marie Slaughter *et al.*, "International Law and International Relations Theory: A New Generation of Interdisciplinary Scholarship," *American Journal of International Law* vol. 92 (1998), pp. 367, 369.

3 See Peter J. Spiro, "Globalization, International Law, and the Academy," *New York University Journal of International Law and Politics* vol. 32 (2000), pp. 567, 582–6.

4 See, for example, Andrew Moravcsik, "Taking Preferences Seriously: A Liberal Theory of International Politics," *International Organization* vol. 51 (1997), pp. 513, 544.

5 See, for example, Martha Finnemore and Kathyrn Sikkink, "International Norm Dynamics and Political Change," *International Organization* vol. 52 (1998), p. 887.

6 See Margaret Keck and Kathryn Sikkink, *Activists Beyond Borders: Advocacy Networks in International Politics* (Ithaca: Cornell University Press: 1998), chap. 1.

7 Moravcsik, "Taking Preferences Seriously."

8 See Abram Chayes and Antonia Handler Chayes, *The New Sovereignty: Compliance with International Regulatory Agreements* (Cambridge: Harvard University Press, 1998); Harold Hongju Koh, "Why Do Nations Obey International Law?" *Yale Law Journal* vol. 106 (1997), pp. 2599, 2650–1.

9 See Harold Hongju Koh, "Bringing International Law Home," *Houston Law Review* vol. 35 (1998), pp. 623, 643.

10 Thomas Risse and Kathryn Sikkink, "The Socialization of International Human Rights Norms into Domestic Practices: Introduction," in Thomas Risse *et al.*, eds, *The Power of Human Rights: International Norms and Domestic Changes* (Cambridge: Cambridge University Press, 1999), p. 38.

11 Moravcsik, "Taking Preferences Seriously," p. 519.

12 See Andrew Moravcsik, "Why Is U.S. Human Rights Policy So Unilateralist?" in Stewart Patrick and Shepard Forman, eds, *Multilateralism and U.S. Foreign Policy: Ambivalent Engagement* (Boulder: Lynne Rienner, 2002), p. 345.

13 See Keck and Sikkink, *Activists Beyond Borders*, p. 13.

14 See Peter J. Spiro, "New Global Potentates: Nongovernmental Organizations and the 'Unregulated' Marketplace," *Cardozo Law Review* vol. 18 (1996), pp. 957, 960.

15 See Andrew Marshall, "Boycott Targets Friends of Bush," *Christian Science Monitor*, April 20, 2001, p. 6.

16 See, for example, Activists at the Gates, "Whether They Like It or Not, Companies Cannot Afford to Ignore Campaigning Groups," *Financial Times*, June 5, 2002, p. 12.

17 See, for example, John Gerard Ruggie, "Embedded Liberalism Global: The Corporate Connection," in David Held and Mathias Koenig-Archibugi, eds, *Taming Globalization: Frontiers of Governance* (Cambridge: Polity Press, 2003); Gary Gereffi *et*

al., "The NGO-Industrial Complex," *Foreign Policy* (July–August 2001), p. 125; Spiro, "New Global Potentates," pp. 958–62. See Amy Cortese, "The New Accountability: Tracking the Social Costs," *New York Times*, May 24, 2002, sec. 3, p. 4.

18 See generally, Eliot J. Schrage, *Promoting International Worker Rights Through Private Voluntary Initiatives: Public Relations or Public Policy?* (Iowa City: University of Iowa Center for Human Rights, 2004).

19 See Joseph F. C. DiMento, *The Global Environment and International Law* (Austin: University of Texas Press, 2003), pp. 66, 69; "Pew Center on Global Climate Change, Climate Change Activities in the United States: 2004 Update," pp. 21–50, available online at www.pewclimate.org /what_s_being_done/us_activities_2004.cfm. See generally, Gereffi *et al.*, "The NGO-Industrial Complex." In 2000, UN Secretary-General Kofi Annan launched the UN Global Compact, an undertaking in which more than 1,500 corporations have directly subscribed (that is, in their own capacity and not through home states) to nine principles relating to human rights, labor rights, and environmental protection. See www.unglobalcompact.org. Participating US companies include Amerada-Hess, Dupont, Nike, and Pfizer. Ibid.

20 See Joseph S. Nye Jr, *The Paradox of American Power* (Oxford: Oxford University Press, 2002), p. 99.

21 See Finnemore and Sikkink, "International Norm Dynamics," p. 895.

22 Compare Harold Hongju Koh, "American Exceptionalism," *Stanford Law Review* vol. 55 (2003), pp. 1479, 1484.

23 See Richard Benedick, *Ozone Diplomacy* (Cambridge: Harvard University Press, 1998).

24 See, for example, Anne-Marie Slaughter, "International Law in a World of Liberal States," *European Journal of International Law* vol. 6 (1995), pp. 503, 505; Kal Raustiala, "The Architecture of International Cooperation: Transgovernmental Networks and the Future of International Law," *Virginia Journal of International Law* vol. 43 (2002), pp. 1, 11, 19.

25 See Moravcsik, "Taking Preferences Seriously," p. 519; Slaughter, "International Law in a World of Liberal States," p. 534; Anne-Marie Slaughter, "Breaking Out: The Proliferation of Actors in the International System," in Yves Dezalay and Bryant G. Garth, eds, *Global Prescriptions: The Production, Exportation, and Importation of a New Legal Orthodoxy* (Ann Arbor: University of Michigan Press, 2002), pp. 12, 28.

26 See Peter J. Spiro, "Globalization and the (Foreign Affairs) Constitution," *Ohio State Law Journal* vol. 63 (2002), pp. 649, 672; Peter J. Spiro, "Foreign Relations Federalism," *University of Colorado Law Review* vol. 70 (1999), pp. 1223, 1227.

27 See generally, Peter J. Spiro, "Dual Nationality and the Meaning of Citizenship," *Emory Law Journal* vol. 46 (1997), p. 1411.

28 See, for example, Maria Green Cowles, "The Transatlantic Business Dialogue: Transforming the New Transatlantic Dialogue," in Mark A. Pollack and Gregory C. Shaffer, eds, *Transatlantic Governance in the Global Economy* (Lanham: Rowman and Littlefield, 2001), p. 213.

29 See, for example, Anne-Marie Slaughter, "The Global Community of Courts," *Harvard Journal of International Law* vol. 44 (2003), p. 191.

30 Compare Richard Posner, *Cardozo: A Study in Reputation* (Chicago: University of Chicago Press, 1989), p. 71.

31 See, for example, Claire L'Heureux-Dubé, "The Importance of Dialogue: Globalization and the International Impact of the Rehnquist Court," *Tulsa Law Journal* vol. 34 (1998), pp. 15, 27.

32 It is particularly significant that it is not only international law theorists who are pressing the use of international sources in domestic judging. See, for example, Mark

Tushnet, "The Possibilities of Comparative Constitutional Law," *Yale Law Journal* vol. 108 (1999), p. 1225; Sanford Levinson, "Looking Abroad When Interpreting the Constitution: Some Reflections," *Texas International Law Journal* vol. 39 (2004), p. 353.

33 536 U.S. (2002), 304, 316 n. 21.

34 123 S.Ct. (2003), pp. 2472, 2483.

35 123 S. Ct. (2005), pp. 1183, 1198-200.

36 See *Lawrence*, 123 S.Ct. (2003), p. 2495 (Scalia, J. dissenting); *Atkins*, 536 U.S., p. 325 (Rehnquist, C. J., dissenting); ibid., p. 346 (Scalia, J., dissenting). See also Antonin Scalia, "Commentary," *St. Louis Law Journal* vol. 40 (1996), p. 1119.

37 See, for example, "And the Verdict on Justice Kennedy Is: Guilty," *Washington Post*, April 9, 2005, at A3. See also H. Res. 568 (108th Cong.).

38 For an elaboration, see Peter J. Spiro, "Realizing Constitutional and International Norms in the Wake of September 11," in Mark Tushnet, ed., *The Constitution in Wartime* (Durham, NC: Duke University Press, 2005).

17

NEW DIRECTIONS, NEW COLLABORATIONS FOR INTERNATIONAL LAW AND INTERNATIONAL RELATIONS

Martha Finnemore

Introduction

The time is ripe for new thinking about collaboration between international law (IL) and international relations (IR). Intellectually, both disciplines have opened themselves to new perspectives and new ways of thinking in recent years. State-centric understandings of international order, on which both IR and IL were built, are being questioned now by scholars in both fields. Interest in the role of nonstate actors, in international organizations, substate actors, and transnational advocacy groups, has permeated both fields. Both fields, too, have become interested in "international regimes" and the array of logics by which rules can channel self-seeking behavior into more cooperative paths.[1] In IR this move has been supplemented by a renewed interest in the power of ideas to transform politics. Constructivists in IR have spent the past 15 years demonstrating and analyzing the ways in which shared ideas and social norms, legal and otherwise, construct new actors in the world (like "human rights monitors") and construct new interests or shared tasks (for example, "promoting good governance" or "participatory development"). As IR became more attuned to the power of international norms and rules, collaboration with international law became newly attractive and important.

Real-world political changes have reinforced, perhaps even caused, these intellectual shifts. The end of the Cold War and accelerating globalization have created new types of social, economic, and security challenges. The disappearance of bipolarity and its superpower police who could and would keep some kind of order in far-flung corners of the globe means that places that previously enjoyed (or suffered) superpower attention, like Somalia, Congo, and Cambodia, are now left to local elites who often lack the capacity to govern. Indeed, the erosion of national capacity in many parts of the world has become central to many contemporary security challenges. States that are juridically sovereign – recognized by others and by international law – often are not empirically sovereign in the sense of being able to exercise control on the ground. This lack of local capacity has exacerbated many of the challenges presented by ever-expanding globalization. Small arms trafficking, terrorism, and internally displaced persons (IDPs) are not new security problems, but they were previously overshadowed by Cold War threats of mass annihilation. With the Cold War over, the pace of transnational flows of people and goods increasing, and state capacity to manage these flows declining, these problems are newly important and increasingly worrisome.

As problems like these rise to the top of the security agenda, our old state-centric toolkits provide little intellectual help in understanding them. As the cases discussed in the volume make clear, these are not only, or even primarily, state-to-state problems that can be resolved by decisions of national governments. These are complex problems involving myriad substate, transnational, and supranational actors. Governments often lack technical capacity, political authority, and legal instruments to deal with them. Scholars, lacking intellectual tools, are not providing as much help as they should and probably could.

Participants in this project are united by a belief that successful approaches to many contemporary problems require both political knowledge and legal tools. As we have explored both the theoretical possibilities and the practical issues involved in this marriage, at least three themes have surfaced repeatedly. First, participants share an interest in the *dynamics* of international law and politics; they seek understandings of change, not static legal application or political equilibrium, which are prevalent concerns in the home disciplines of IR and IL scholars. Second, they are also deeply interested in the *social context* of both law and political action, and the effects of context on potential solutions. Norms and rules work differently, sometimes perversely, in different contexts, and conversely, different contexts give rise to different norms. We wanted a better understanding of this variation. Finally, participants are consistently engaged with the role of *nonstate actors* not only in creating policy challenges but also in solving them using legal tools.

In this chapter I examine these three themes and draw from them some lessons suggested by the project. This volume amply demonstrates shared policy interests among practioners and scholars in both IR and IL. Here, I will argue that there are also important theoretical synergies between the two academic disciplines as well – synergies that offer opportunities to scholars in both fields that have not yet been exploited.

Grounds for collaboration: shared interests and where they might lead

Dynamics of law and politics

Addressing the policy challenges examined in this volume requires changes – in law, norms, and political agendas. Practitioners made this abundantly clear in our project meetings and in their papers. All their efforts are directed toward change. Francis Deng has spent more than a decade working to develop new international norms, rules, and practices that will improve the situation of internally displaced people. Activists strategize hard about ways to change norms and rules to limit the flow of small arms, and continue to struggle for improved international criminal accountability. Understanding what these practioners do and how their efforts succeed or fail should be central for IR and IL as academic disciplines, but in fact has not been so.

Much of the dominant intellectual apparatus in IL and IR fails to provide good understandings of when change will occur, how, or why. In IR this is particularly clear. The structural or "neo" theories (neoliberalism, neorealism) that have dominated IR for several decades are built around equilibrium, not change.[2] They draw explicitly and extensively on microeconomics for their intellectual architecture and use formal models (equilibrium models) to analyze political interaction (e.g. Prisoners' Dilemma games). Philosophically, political realism is very much a theory about continuity, not change. It explains why the strong do what they can and the weak suffer what they must across the ages, underscoring similarities between the fifth-century Greek city-state and contemporary politics rather than placing change at the center of analysis.

With the development of constructivist theory and the elaboration of (or sometimes resurrection of) non-"neo" variants of liberalism, IR now has more and better equipment for thinking about processes of change. It is no accident that Peter Spiro finds these strands of IR theory most useful in exploring the dynamic forces pushing the United States toward greater involvement with international law.[3] Spiro is modest, however, in the demands he places on these arguments, and leaves unexplored some of the deeper forces for change embedded in both strands of theorizing. Harnessing some of these strains of theory could lead to a very rich shared research agenda on the dynamics of law and politics among IL and IR scholars.

Constructivist and liberal theories are much broader and deeper than simple recognition of nongovernmental organizations (NGOs) and pluralist dynamics of domestic interest groups emphasized by Spiro. Important strands of constructivist theory talk not just about NGOs and norms, but also about identities – of states, of individuals, of groups. How people come to understand their identities and how identities shift, matter hugely to compliance and the spread of rule-of-law internationally. For example, creating "rule-of-law states" and spreading that identity is a major enterprise of many of the world's most powerful actors, states, and international organizations alike. Much of the effort to help the former Soviet-bloc states make successful transitions to join the West has involved explicit effort to establish rule of law as the West understands it, in the politics and economy of these places. State-building programs in failed states and postconflict states similarly emphasize instilling respect for rule of law as a cornerstone of their new identity. Defining identities – for example, "Europe" and a "European state" and what it means to be "European" – logically precedes that applicability of a great many norms, since the very dense network of European norms would not have claims in places that do not think of themselves as European. Defining identities has also been a major international project outside Europe.[4] More relevant to Spiro, a very strong and distinctive American identity has been argued to be central to US foreign policy decisionmaking, including its relation to law.[5] Identity logically must precede the cost–benefit analysis Spiro emphasizes, since it is only by knowing "who we are" that we can decide what we want, what is good for us, and what policies we should pursue in law or any other domain. Change in identities is thus a crucial theoretical component of political and legal change. Research on how identities change – on how states rethink their own place in the world and how they attempt to persuade others to do the same – would seem to be a clear shared interest for IR and IL scholars.

Other strands of constructivist theory push the ideational argument further. In sociology, scholars calling themselves "institutionalists" focus not on NGOs, activists, or identities, but on a broad and powerful world culture that shapes contemporary politics in all dimensions.[6] Nongovernmental organizations, intergovernmental organizations, and even states, in this argument, are accretions of this world culture as much as constructors of it, and treating these actors as free agents, operating independently of the powerful global culture that generates and enables them, misses much of the causal story in this view.[7] The entire legalized, bureaucratized, marketized character of all contemporary world politics is an artifact of the larger (now global) culture in which it resides – a culture one might call "modern" or perhaps "developed." We do not see this culture precisely because it is *our* culture; it thus seems natural to us and we take it for granted. But states, markets, and bureaucracies (including intergovernmental and nongovernmental organizations) are distinct cultural forms, particular to a specific historical moment – our own.

These arguments predict growing homogenization of law and political organization as Western global culture spreads. They predict the adoption of similar "modern" legal and bureaucratic forms, even in places where such forms are ill suited and may produce perverse outcomes. Thus they predict the dissemination of Western-style markets and democracy even in places that lack the underlying local traditions and cultural norms to support such transplants. Sociologists working in this vein have already extensively researched the spread of various Western "rights" (human, women's, children's), the elaboration of national constitutions, and characteristics of citizenship, marshaling evidence that spreading global culture increases isomorphism in rules, law, and organizational forms.[8] This group of scholars would fully agree with Spiro's prediction that the United States must eventually embrace international law, but would argue this is a cultural phenomenon, not an artifact of rational choice among costs and benefits.[9] Understanding the role of a global world culture in changing the law and politics of the non-Western world would again seem to be a shared topic of interest for both IR and IL.

Liberal arguments are similarly broad and deep as explanations for change.[10] They often emphasize not the cost–benefit calculations of domestic interest groups (as Andrew Moravcsik and Peter Spiro do), but adherence to and promotion of liberal values. The liberal canon, after all, includes much more than simple Benthamite utilitarianism. Individuals may indeed make their choices by weighing costs and benefits, but this hardly exhausts the possibilities for human action. The "habits of the heart" so crucial to Tocqueville's understanding of American democracy rely on mechanisms distinct from cost–benefit analysis and rational choice. They rely on education, not in the sense of transferring information, but in the sense of deep persuasion and shaping of worldviews. They also rely on emotion, something many of our activist practioners understand very well.[11] Instilling devotion to liberal values of human equality and toleration requires manipulation of emotion as much as reason, and activists' use of testimony and their personalizing of human rights abuses or atrocities are designed specifically to appeal to hearts as well as heads.[12]

This line of argument has obvious synergies with constructivist arguments about identity and identity construction. Becoming "democratic" or "European" has an affective component. Certainly many people believe they will be better off materially by joining the European Union and the Western "club" of democracies, but lasting change requires internalization of these values in a deeper sense, one that involves redefinition of who we are and what we value. In more contemporary debates, Fareed Zakaria's well-known arguments about the perils of "illiberal democracy," for example, emphasize that creating liberalism is a matter of instilling liberal values (toleration, love of liberty, respect for human dignity and autonomy), which is not obviously or primarily achieved by leaving people to make cost–benefit calculations.[13]

Beyond formalism and structure: the importance of social context

Another recurrent theme in our project has been the importance of social context to the way law and politics do their work in the world. Scholars in this project share an interest in looking beyond formal legal rules and formal organizations to understand the dynamics they see. Indeed, we chose the cases we did in part because formal rules and norms did not exist, were not commanding compliance, or were not producing effective governance in these areas. In all of these cases, law is being contested or created by people working outside government and formal legal structures. These actors sometimes work by trying to persuade others inside formal structures – government officials, staff of international organizations or tribunals – to change the way they do business, but activists also look for leverage by appealing to publics. Mobilizing social sentiment behind an issue can be a very effective way of creating change.

Social context is a crucial bridge between IL and IR for three reasons. First, it speaks to a shared interest in legitimacy and authority. Sources of legitimacy and authority are crucial to the workings of both politics and law, but are inadequately theorized in both fields, as noted in the introduction to this volume. IR theorists have thought a great deal about power but much less about authority. Authority is different from power. It is a social construction and requires some recognition, if not acquiescence, from those over whom it is exercised. Power may be seized or taken regardless of the opinions of others, but an actor is only authoritative if others recognize her or him as such. In that sense, authority is a particular type of legitimated power.[14] Whether organizations or formal laws are authoritative and command deference thus depends only partly on the formal structure or content of the law or organization in question. It depends equally on the audience, on the group over whom authority is being claimed. Their recognition is essential to authority's existence and influence. Shifting our focus to consider the social context of law as well as its form and content helps us better understand compliance with international law and norms, and the various pressures to change them.

Second, and related, social context strongly shapes senses of obligation and compliance with new and changing norms. A central issue for both IR and IL concerns what generates a sense of obligation to follow new law, rules, and norms. Scholars in both IR and IL have long understood that formal rules or contractual agreements are unreliable at best as generators of a sense of obligation or guarantors of compliance in the international realm. The history of law and politics is littered with optimistic attempts to legislate behavior that have little success. Effective law generates a sense of obligation, not just in a formal sense but also in a felt sense. Thomas Franck has famously discussed the "compliance pull" of law, but the social science underlying this or any other sense of felt obligation has remained poorly theorized.[15] Many of the practioners in our project are precisely in the business of generating this kind of obligation, however. Particularly for new or emergent normative claims where few "hard" law obligations exist, activists seek to generate this kind of felt obligation as a means of promoting "harder" legal obligations in the future. The campaign to ban antipersonnel landmines had very effective and conscious strategies for generating emotional responses to these devices. Campaigners worked hard to frame the issue not as one of arms control, but as a human rights issue, highlighting the human cost to innocent civilians, especially children, of these mines.[16] Similarly, the small arms campaign was very much conscious of these strategies in its work. Emotional appeals have been called into service on behalf of IDPs as well.[17] People make decisions for many reasons besides utilitarian cost–benefit calculations; conversely, many nonutilitarian components make up most people's preference structure of "benefits" and "costs." What constitutes a cost or benefit or appropriate action depends very much on social context. Much of the work of activists and "norm entrepreneurs" aims at changing social context – reframing issues, personalizing policy problems, creating identification with victims – in ways that will generate senses of obligation and compliance with the new norm.

Third, attention to social context helps us better understand much of the variation we see in both the effects of law and its dynamics. The goal of most international law and formal international organizations is to create general rules – to govern small arms, IDPs, human rights violations. General rules play out differently, though, in different social contexts. It is common to find that laws and organizational forms developed for economies and societies in the West do not work the same way when transplanted elsewhere. Western democracy is certainly complicated to transplant, as the extensive literature on democratization makes abundantly clear. However, social context helps explain other kinds of variation as well. For example, it helps us explain why some attempts to generate or change law and norms work when others fail. The success of the landmines ban loomed large over the small arms activists in our case study.[18] Why did the former succeed when the latter are having so much difficulty? One could say that particularities of the issue mattered. Unlike landmines, small arms have a variety of legitimate nonmilitary uses in most countries, ranging from police enforcement in virtually all states, to hunting and personal protection in a more limited number of states. This "dual-use" character, however, is not a physical property of the weapons themselves. It is a function of social context. Different societies understand legitimate uses of small arms differently, and support or oppose efforts to regulate them accordingly.[19]

More careful attention to social context is thus essential to shared concerns of IR and IL. Context is intimately connected with both the authority of laws, rules, and norms as well as their "compliance pull." Variations in context consequently may tell us a great deal about why general or universal laws and norms create such varied effects around the world and over time. A better theorization of the ways in which context shapes authority and obligation would seem another promising shared avenue for research.

Unpacking assumptions: nonstate actors and national capabilities

Underlying much of the inadequacy of IL and IR to grapple with contemporary policy challenges is the widening gulf between actual political practice and the assumptions on which these bodies of knowledge rest. The state has been the cornerstone of intellectual architecture in both IL and IR. Both academic disciplines assume, implicitly or explicitly, that states are the source of international problems, that solutions depend primarily on state action, or both. The cases examined in this volume call these assumptions into question. States are not the source of many of the problems investigated here, nor can they provide effective solutions.

Two issues, in particular, have been highlighted here. First, many contemporary problems involve actors besides states in pivotal roles. As the introduction to this volume points out, other actors are increasingly prominent in determining political and legal outcomes. NGOs, substate groups, and international organizations have all become increasingly influential in determining policy and outcomes in many issue areas. Practioners have become increasingly creative in mobilizing nonstate, substate, transnational actors to pursue their goals in ways not easily accounted for by state-centric notions of law or politics. Understanding why states, themselves, define their interests and act as they do has become increasingly difficult without attention to these other types of actors. NGOs, activists, and other nonstate entities often penetrate states, shaping the kinds of policies that are crafted at the substate level. While states remain crucial, we need better theoretical tools for understanding and prescribing action for these other types of actors. Second, the capacity of states, particularly weak states, to exert the practical control assumed by dominant approaches to IR and IL, is limited in a great many parts of the world. Even assuming that states agree on some policy, successful application of international law and political instruments is often frustrated by the inability of states to deliver on their commitments and meet their responsibilities. Capacity is not simply a developing-world problem, however. Difficulties in thwarting transnational terrorism have challenged the most powerful states, as have narcotrafficking and other transnational issues not examined here.

Reimagining law and politics in ways that accommodate diverse actors and processes has been a central concern throughout this project. Some theorizing of this type already exists, and appears in a variety of the chapters here. For example, the constructivist work on the mechanisms or processes by which NGOs and activists achieve their goals has been widely influential in both IR and IL, and is cited by several contributors.[20] In this volume, Francis Deng, Fiona Adamson, Peter Spiro, and Harold Koh's contributions draw on this line of theory. Anne-Marie Slaughter's more liberal arguments elsewhere about "transgovernmentalism" take a different tack. They specify mechanisms by which substate functional units (justice ministries, intelligence agencies, antinarcotics units) may coordinate and regulate transnationally through processes distinct from the apex-level state-to-state interaction envisioned by traditional notions of interstate agreement.[21]

Theorizing a role for nonstate actors raises important conceptual problems in IR and IL, however. For IR scholars, it raises questions about both ontology and logics of action. Ontologically, the standard "neo" theories (neorealism, neoliberalism) are theories of states and state action. We live in a world of states, according to these theories, and all of the other bits of furniture in the international system – international law, international tribunals, international organizations – are understood as epiphenomena of state action. There is no conceptual basis on which to ascribe agency or autonomy of any kind to nonstate actors. Thus, saying that "the UN does such and so" is theoretically meaningless, since only states have power, capability, and agency in most IR theory. State-centric theories would tell us, by assumption, that the five permanent members of the UN Security Council act, not the UN itself; the UN cannot act or behave at all, by theoretical axiom. For legal scholars, there are related questions about standing, sources of law, and hierarchies of law. Some of this has come through clearly here in our explorations of international criminal law and claims about universal jurisdiction.

Recent work in both IR and IL has also begun to push beyond these ontological claims of state-centrism by providing theoretical bases for attention to other types of actors. Scholars in IR have begun to theorize international organizations (IOs) in ways that would make them more than simple arenas in which states interact, as regimes theory posits. In this more recent view, IOs are autonomous actors with their own interests, capabilities, and agendas for action. They are authorities in their own right, able to make rules that bind states, individuals, NGOs, and others.[22] Scholars in IL have similarly begun to explore bodies of law that have more complex sources than just national legislation or interstate treaty. The emerging field of global administrative law, for example, explores the expansion of transnational regulation promulgated by transnational regulatory bodies, private business organizations, NGOs, international organizations, and informal groups in a host of functional areas.[23] In both lines of theory, complex policy challenges are being managed and regulated by actors other than states.

Efforts are also being made in IR to theorize NGOs as actors. Some of this work uses organization theory to explore the dynamics, incentives, and agendas of NGO actors. Alexander Cooley and James Ron have used the "new economics" literature and drawn on work by Oliver Williams and others to investigate the dynamics of NGO behavior.[24] This view treats NGOs as driven by resource needs and argues that NGO action is explained by the perpetual need to secure contracts from states and others who fund their work. This approach can be extremely helpful when analyzing NGOs that provide services. It is less clearly helpful in explaining many of the activists examined in this volume. Those NGOs are better treated by the strain of theorizing about NGOs, launched by Margaret Keck and Kathryn Sikkink, that emphasizes the principled motives driving NGO action. Intellectually, this line of argument has its roots in social movement theory, not institutional economics. It sees NGOs as highly strategic, but with an eye to maximizing impact on their principled agenda rather than securing resources. Following Sidney Tarrow and others in the social movement field, these scholars highlight the ways NGOs strategize to "frame" issues in favorable ways – for example, by reframing landmines as a humanitarian concern, rather than an arms control problem. NGOs manipulate more than costs and benefits; they also manipulate emotions and play on identity politics to achieve their goals.[25]

Policymaking and lawmaking by nonstate actors raises a host of questions, however. Among the most pressing of these are normative questions, particularly questions of accountability. In many ways, NGOs are a positive force for the kinds of ethical concerns raised by Clarence Dias in this volume. NGOs often advocate for the "have-nots" – those who have less international law and fewer legal protections from abuse by the powerful. We have seen this in our work on international criminal accountability and on IDPs, in particular. However, mechanisms of accountability for NGOs, themselves, are scarce. Accountability mechanisms for intergovernmental organizations are also problematic.[26] However, to be normatively defensible, approaches to IL and IR that recognize nonstate actors as sources of authority must offer some understanding of the ethical implications of such a move.

Conclusion

Opportunities for cross-disciplinary collaboration have never been more promising for IL and IR. Not only is there a wealth of pressing policy challenges that would benefit from a combination of legal and political remedies, but we now also have more shared intellectual tools than ever before. As both fields expand their inquiries beyond state action, beyond hard law and formal institutions, the overlap in our interests grows. The current focus on political and legal change in both disciplines is welcome as well. Not only does this enrich our theories, but it also brings us into deeper conversation with the practioners whose work we study.

Notes

1 Stephen D. Krasner, ed., *International Regimes* (Ithaca: Cornell University Press, 1983); Andreas Hasenclever, Peter Mayer, and Volker Rittberger, *Theories of International Regimes* (New York: Cambridge University Press, 1997).

2 The seminal and classic statement of neorealism is Kenneth Waltz, *Theory of International Politics* (New York: Random House, 1979). For neoliberal institutionalism, the seminal work is probably Robert O. Keohane, *After Hegemony: Cooperation and Discord in the World Political Economy* (Princeton: Princeton University Press, 1984).

3 Spiro, "Disaggregating US interests in International Law," Chapter 16 in this volume.

4 This grossly simplifies an extraordinarily rich literature on identity generally and on European identity and socialization specifically. Seminal works on identity in IR include Peter J. Katzenstein, ed., *The Culture of National Security* (New York: Columbia University Press, 1996), esp. chaps. 1–2; and Alexander Wendt, *Social Theory of International Politics* (New York: Cambridge University Press, 1999). For recent work on socialization in Europe, including citations to the wide-ranging socialization literature, see the special issue of *International Organization* edited by Jeffrey T. Checkel, "International Institutions and Socialization in Europe," vol. 59, no. 4 (Fall 2005), esp. Checkel's introductory essay, pp. 801–26.

5 Henry R. Nau, *At Home Abroad: Identity and Power in American Foreign Policy* (Ithaca: Cornell University Press, 2002); Christian Reus-Smit, *American Power and World Order* (Cambridge: Polity Press, 2004).

6 George W. Thomas, John W. Meyer, Francisco O. Ramirez, and John Boli, eds, *Institutional Structure: Constituting State, Society, and the Individual* (Newbury Park,

CA: Sage, 1987) is a cornerstone work for these scholars. For a review of this literature from an IR perspective, see Martha Finnemore, "Norms, Culture, and World Politics: Insights from Sociology's Institutionalism," *International Organization* vol. 50, no. 2 (Spring 1996), pp. 325–47.

7 John Boli and George Thomas, eds, *Constructing World Culture: International Nongovernmental Organizations Since 1875* (Stanford: Stanford University Press, 1999).

8 See, for example, John Boli, "Human Rights or State Expansion: Cross-National Definitions of Constitutional Rights, 1870–1970" and "World Polity Sources of Expanding State Authority and Organization, 1870–1970," both in Thomas *et al.*, *Institutional Structure*; Francisco Ramirez, Yasemin Soysal, and Suzanne Shanahan, "The Changing Logic of Political Citizenship: Cross-National Acquisition of Women's Suffrage Rights, 1890–1990," *American Sociological Review* vol. 62 (1997), pp. 735–45; Yasemin Soysal, *Limits of Citizenship: Migrants and Postnational Membership in Europe* (Chicago: University of Chicago Press, 1994).

9 These scholars would also argue that rational choice and instrumental calculations of costs and benefits are, themselves, cultural construct peculiar to "modernity." See, for example, John W. Meyer, John Boli, and George Thomas, "Ontology and Rationalization in the Western Cultural Account," in Thomas *et al.*, *Institutional Structure.*

10 For discussion of the many varieties of liberal theory, see Mark Zacher and Richard Matthews, "Liberal International Theory: Common Threads, Divergent Strands," in Charles Kegley, ed., *Controversies in International Relations Theory* (New York: St. Martin's Press, 1995); Robert O. Keohane, "International Liberalism Reconsidered," in John Dunn, ed., *Economic Limits to Modern Politics* (Cambridge: Cambridge University Press, 1990); Michael Doyle, *Ways of War and Peace* (New York: W. W. Norton, 1997).

11 Jean-Jacques Rousseau stresses similar processes in *Emile, or On Education* (New York: Basic Books, 1979).

12 The academic literature on activists has discussed this explicitly. See Margaret Keck and Kathryn Sikkink, *Activists Beyond Borders* (Ithaca: Cornell University Press, 1998); Thomas Risse, Stephen Ropp, and Kathryn Sikkink, eds, *The Power of Human Rights: International Norms and Domestic Change* (New York: Cambridge University Press, 1999). Note that a similar engagement of emotion is used by activists promoting other causes, for example environmental protection. See Paul Wapner, *Environmental Activism and World Civic Politics* (Albany: State University of New York Press, 1996).

13 Fareed Zakaria, "The Rise of Illiberal Democracy," *Foreign Affairs* vol. 76, no. 6 (November–December 1997), pp. 22ff.

14 For an extended discussion, see Michael Barnett and Martha Finnemore, *Rules for the World: International Organizations in Global Politics* (Ithaca: Cornell University Press, 2004), esp. chap. 2.

15 Thomas Franck, *The Power of Legitimacy Among Nations* (New York: Oxford University Press, 1990). For a more extended discussion of this problem, see Martha Finnemore and Stephen J. Toope, "Alternatives to 'Legalization': Richer Views of Law and Politics," *International Organization* vol. 55, no. 3 (Summer 2001), pp. 743–58.

16 Richard Price, "Reversing the Gunsights: Transnational Civil Society Targets Landmines," *International Organization* vol. 52, no. 3 (Summer 1998), pp. 613–44.

17 Deng, "The Guiding Principles on Internal Displacement and the Development of International Norms," Chapter 9 in this volume.

18 See, for example, Muggah, "Moving Forward?" Chapter 2 in this volume.

19 See, for example, Reno, "Small Arms, Violence, and the Course of Conflicts," and Koh, "A World Drowning in Guns," Chapters 3 and 4 in this volume.

20 Keck and Sikkink, *Activists Beyond Borders*, is the seminal work in this vein, but also see Paul Wapner's examination of environmental NGOs and arguments about a "world civic politics" and "politics beyond the state" in *Environmental Activism and World Civic Politics*.
21 Anne-Marie Slaughter, "The Real World Order," *Foreign Affairs* vol. 76, no. 5 (September–October 1997), pp. 183–97.
22 Barnett and Finnemore, *Rules for the World*.
23 Benedict Kingsbury, Nico Krisch, and Richard B. Stewart, "The Emergence of Global Administrative Law," *Law and Contemporary Problems* vol. 68, no. 3 (Summer 2005), pp. 15–61, available online at www.iilj.org/global_adlaw/documents/10120502_kingsburykrischstewart.pdf. Also see Jose E. Alvarez, *International Organizations as Law-Makers* (New York: Oxford University Press, 2005).
24 Alexander Cooley and James Ron, "The NGO Scramble," *International Security* vol. 27, no. 1 (Summer 2002), pp. 5–39.
25 On framing, see Robert D. Benford and David A. Snow, "Framing Processes and Social Movements: An Overview and Assessment," *Annual Review of Sociology* vol. 26 (2000), pp. 11–39; Sidney Tarrow, *Power in Movement: Social Movements and Contentious Politics* (New York: Cambridge University Press, 1998). For reviews of this literature, see Martha Finnemore and Kathyrn Sikkink, "International Norm Dynamics and Political Change," *International Organization* vol. 52, no. 4 (Autumn 1998), pp. 887–917; Martha Finnemore and Kathryn Sikkink, "Taking Stock: The Constructivist Research Program in International Relations and Comparative Politics," *Annual Review of Political Science* vol. 4 (2001), pp. 391–416.
26 Ruth Grant and Robert O. Keohane have offered some of the more probing analyses of this as a generic problem; see Ruth Grant and Robert O. Keohane, "Accountability and Abuses of Power in World Politics," *IILJ Working Paper* 2004/7, available online at www.iilj.org/papers/2004/2004.7%20grant%20keohane.pdf; Ruth Grant and Robert O. Keohane, "Accountability and Abuses of Power in World Politics," *APSR* vol. 99, no. 1 (February 2005), pp. 29–43. For a historical discussion, see Steve Charnowitz, "Accountability of Nongovernmental Organizations (NGOs) in Global Governance," *GWU Law School Public Law Research Paper* 145 (April 2005), available online at http://papers.ssrn.com/sol3/papers.cfm?abstract_id=716381.

18

INTERNATIONAL RELATIONS AND INTERNATIONAL LAW

From competition to complementarity

Clarence J. Dias

"And ne'er the twain shall meet"

In the world of theory, there are many dichotomies. In the real world, there are many divisions and divides. In the world of power, all too often, these divisions, divides, and dichotomies serve to maintain and reinforce existing imbalanced and skewed power relations between individuals, communities, governments, and nation-states. In the world of power, it is indeed *divide and rule.*

A long time ago, Rudyard Kipling asserted, "East is East and West is West and ne'er the twain shall meet." In the Cold War era, the term "East" assumed not so much a geographical, directional meaning, but rather an ideological one. In today's single superpower world, the divides are deepening and becoming ever-more divisive between North and South, East and West, and Haves and Have Nots. A quote commonly attributed to Philippine national hero Jose Rizal states, "Those who have less in life should have more in law." This chapter is propelled by the belief that those who have less in life should indeed have more in law, including international law. In order to make this a reality, rather than mere aspiration, it is necessary to understand the nature of the divide between the fields of international relations (IR) and international law (IL) and to find ways of bridging such divides.

The divide between international relations and international law is both tenuous and tendentious. Without international law, international relations theory and practice would amount to little more than a constant reaffirmation that *might is right.* Without international relations, we would not be able to expose instances when international law is an instrument of might or to advocate what needs to be done to reaffirm the principle *right not might.* Without international relations, our ability to succeed strategically in developing new international law, founded on the principle *right not might,* would be considerably limited.

This Social Science Research Council (SSRC) volume attempts to bridge the divide between international relations and international law. In this chapter, I examine the nature of this divide from the perspective of an international law practitioner and activist. I look particularly at two areas of international lawmaking covered by the SSRC project (small arms and international terrorism), while also making a short reference to the other two areas (internally displaced persons and international criminal accountability). I then put forward several challenges and crises that, in my view, currently confront international law. I end the chapter with some suggestions about bridging the divide in an effort to make international law more relevant and effective in addressing the challenge of providing more in law for those who have less in life.

A subjective view of the international relations–international law divide

How do the fields of IR and IL see concepts such as values, norms, the state and state sovereignty, law and particularly international law, and results? What are the main theoretical foundations of each of the two fields? Indeed how does each field view the interrelationship between theory and empiricism?

It is also important to stress that, though we talk of IR and IL as being "fields," there are many actors involved in each, and no one set of actors can lay claim to being the sole/authoritative spokesperson for their field. These actors include at a minimum: scholars and intellectuals involved in research, conceptualization, and theory construction; practitioners involved in rendering advice and professional services, negotiation, and representation to clients or beneficiaries, who in turn are also actors; and activists (social entrepreneurs) conducting advocacy and lobbying around policies and issues.

As the influential realist school has consistently maintained, IR theory is about states, their interests, and their power. The Cold War marked the dominance of state power, with two superpowers making it clear that they would not allow the establishment of an effective regime of international norms and law that significantly constrained state discretion and power to act. The realist school was dismissive of international law as being inconsequential in a world in which "rational self-interest and geopolitical capacities, not law, explained the global dynamic."[1] Realist IR theory is state-centered, embraces state sovereignty as a central concept, and under-appreciates the power of nonstate actors:

> The salience of nonstate actors is recognized, but only to the extent that that they either exercise political power within domestic structures (liberal IR theory) or seek to persuade states to adhere to particular norms (constructivist IR theory). State action remains the ultimate unit of analysis.[2]

Realist IR theory, adopting Austinian notions of law and power, did not consider international law to be law at all. In this respect, realist IR theorists shared common ground with legal theorists from the positivist school and from the realist school of jurisprudence.

Since the UN Charter, international law has been in the process of change. International human rights law, international labor law, and international environmental law place interests of individuals and groups above those of states. A large body of recent international law seeks to place constraints on the exercise of state sovereignty, even if such constraints are largely self-imposed by states. The individual rather than the state is argued to be the prime subject of such international law. Nonstate actors are recognized as wielding not only influence, but power as well. In a post-Cold War world, state action alone cannot remain the ultimate unit of analysis. Laws are implemented not only vertically (by top-down command of the sovereign), but also often horizontally, among formal equals (as the concept of sovereign equality of states adopted by the UN Charter indicates). Of course, as both the realist IR school and the growing critical legal studies movement emphasize, formal equality does not necessarily translate into equality on the ground. IR scholars accepted assymetries of power and capacity among states and the differences in the rights and privileges exercisable by some states as a result. IL is committed to the preservation of sovereign equality of all states. For IL, all states have equal rights and duties, even though they may have varying capacities to enforce such rights or discharge such duties.

In an increasingly globalized and interdependent world, international law is growing in importance not because of positivist justifications, but because a large range of activities and actors (transnational corporations, for example) are creating international consequences and necessitating international regulation and actions. The number and scope of international legal instruments, the variety of their nature (e.g. framework conventions, incorporating common but differentiated responsibilities), the attention that states pay to the negotiation, drafting, and application of such instruments, and the proliferation and prominence of international regimes and institutions, all point to an enhanced position of international law in today's world.[3] "After decades on the margins, international law is becoming a prominent force in virtually every area of domestic law."[4] This is a challenge that IR needs to address. As the conceptual and reality gap between IR and IL narrows, there is need for theoretical and practical response from IR, especially relating to nonstate actors both as a part of problems (e.g. violent nonstate actors) or as a part of possible solutions. International lawmaking processes have also been evolving, lending themselves to greater IR–IL interaction.

The key to understanding whether nations will obey international law is *transnational legal process*: the process by which public and private actors – namely nation-states, corporations, international organizations, and nongovernmental organizations (NGOs) – interact in a variety of forums to make, interpret, enforce, and ultimately internalize rules of international law.[5]

The key elements of this approach are interaction, interpretation, and internalization. For example, those seeking to create or embed human rights principles or environmental values into international and domestic law should promote transnational *interactions* that generate legal *interpretations* that can in turn be *internalized* into the domestic law of even skeptical nation-states.[6]

Applying such an approach to developing a global regulatory solution for any global problem can comprise five stages:

1 Understanding the nature of the global problem.
2 The creation of NGO and civil society networks to start to build a regime to address the problem.
3 Developing norms and recruiting committed individuals to promote such norms.
4 A "horizontal process" that occurs at an intergovernmental level, either formally or at informal state-to-state gatherings.
5 A "vertical process" whereby rules negotiated between governments at the horizontal level, and interpreted through the interactions of transnational actors in law-declaring forums, are internalized into the domestic law of each participating country, through domestic statute, executive practice, or judicial decision.

This is how international law becomes law that people actually obey: by moving from knowledge, to networks, to norms, to horizontal process, and to vertical process.[7]

Today, the divide between IR and IL is closing. Both fields embrace empiricism and realism in developing concepts and theories, to reduce the gap between rhetoric and practice (IR) and between the law on the books and the law in practice (IL). Both IR and IL are moving toward a common understanding of the definition and significance of norms.

There is broad consensus across the fields of international relations and international legal studies that a norm represents a shared standard of behavior for a given set of actors. Along these lines, norms have been variously described as standards of appropriate behavior, collective expressions of the proper behavior of given actors, shared (thus social) understandings of standards of behavior, and prescriptions for action in situations of choice carrying a sense of obligation, a sense that they *ought* to be followed.[8]

Norms spring from numerous sources, including religious, ethical, and cultural beliefs. But they derive fundamentally from "principled ideas" – "beliefs about right and wrong held by individuals."[9] Today, both IR and IL agree that norms may be embodied in laws, codes, guidelines, and other similar mechanisms, and that the absence of a formal and legally binding requirement (soft law) does not necessarily imply the absence of a norm. The important question as to how norms function "is at the heart of the battleground between various schools of thought within international relations and international legal theory."[10]

There are other areas of contention between IR and IL as well. The two disciplines are divided by different conceptions of sovereignty. IR views sovereignty as a prelegal phenomenon (capable of being constrained by legal norms, but apt to bypass these norms at times as well). IL conceives sovereignty as constituted by the framework of legal norms. IR remains essentially state-centered. IL is increasingly becoming people-centered; NGOs and civil society actors are often the prime drivers in IL processes (e.g. landmines, the International Criminal Court). Nonstate actors have still to be accorded the place they deserve in IR theory and practice. Pursuit or defense of state interests is usually the prime motivation of IR action. Promotion of human well-being and protection and promotion of human rights and the environment propel much of IL activism. Values of transparency and accountability are at the heart of IL. Expediency and impunity often figure unabashedly in IR.

These areas of contention can be bridged in mutually beneficial ways, however. In the past,

> IR theory has informed an important strain of international law scholarship. It provides a useful frame for situating international law as a matter of institutional interactions rather than as a matter of doctrine. "By situating legal rules and institutions in their political context, IR helps to reduce the abstraction and self-contained character of doctrinal analysis and to channel normative idealism in effective directions."[11]

Perhaps the time is ripe for IL jurisprudence to return the favor, and help reduce the state-centeredness and increase the people-centeredness of IR.

International relations and international law: two cases of constructive engagement?

I examine more closely here two of the four areas of international lawmaking covered by the SSRC project – small arms and international terrorism – as examples of "constructive engagement" that has taken place between IR and IL.

Small arms

Today there are an estimated 639 million documented small arms in the world: more than one for every 12 men, women, and children on the face of the earth. This figure does not include the millions of undocumented, privately held arms.

> [S]mall arms are implicated in 1,300 deaths a day, a toll that approaches the magnitude of the global AIDS crisis. Yet the costs of these weapons run far deeper than just the mortality, injury, and psychological trauma of people who are shot. In assessing the social costs of these weapons, one must also take account of the public health costs in terms of lost productivity; the crime costs in terms of increases in insurance and the costs of hiring private security firms; the humanitarian costs in terms of displaced persons and injuries to relief personnel; the militarization of refugee camps; and the development costs in terms of economic, social, and educational underdevelopment.[12]

Current international efforts to address the problem focus on the supply side, and seek to regulate the illicit manufacture, stockpiling, transfer, and trade of small arms. Such a supply-focused approach has been a product of conventional approaches to IR (state-centered and focusing on key arms controllers more familiar with supply-focused mechanisms) and to IL (as governing relations between states and relying on states to implement regulatory agreements). However, both IR and IL research has shown that such an approach has been largely ineffective, first because of lack of political will on the parts of states who resist attempts to examine the sources that drive demand for small arms (including their own weaknesses and failures). These states are the prime negotiators of the international regulatory regime – small wonder that regulatory efforts have been hampered. Second, efforts to frame the problem in terms of "illicit and criminal activity" draw on traditional biases and shortcomings in the arms control and law enforcement communities. They also appeal to governments that are reluctant to discuss the political dimensions of the small arms trade in international political forums.[13]

This has affected the design of the UN forums created to address the issue (the 2001 UN Programme of Action, which has no legally binding powers or authority), and the nature of the norm development (the UN Firearms Protocol, which focuses on supply-side control). In response to this situation, fortunately, NGO practice has begun to lead and drive the process. The International Action Network on Small Arms (IANSA) is a network of over 500 nongovernmental partners in over 100 countries. Through IANSA, an alternative approach is being advocated that focuses on (1) the demand for small arms from defense and security sectors by nonstate groups, including those in conflict with the state, and micro-level demand by individuals concerned about the security of themselves and their families; and (2) the direct and indirect humanitarian effects of small arms: on mortality and injury, public health costs, criminality, and poverty and development.[14] Jurists working at both the national and the international level face the challenge of articulating a lawmaking agenda to support an approach to dealing with small arms from a perspective that focuses on the demand side and on the direct and indirect effects of small arms.

Concrete interventions are taking place at country level by NGOs focusing on ameliorating the direct and indirect effects of small arms. Some of these have found their way into the UN Programme of Action, which lays out a number of indirect approaches to addressing such effects: disarmament, demobilization, and reintegration of former combatants; security sector reform; attending to the special needs and vulnerabilities of children and of women; focusing on problems related to human and sustainable development; encouraging education and public awareness programs; and promoting dialogue and a culture of peace. These programs have been inspired by, and often are implemented by, national and local NGOs. UN member states will have an opportunity to address inconsistencies and inadequacies in the UN Programme of Action when it is reopened for negotiation in 2006.

Efforts to frame the problem in terms of "illicit and criminal activity" have created an area of sensitivity related to demand and use of small arms by insurgent groups. If international law development automatically labels this type of demand in such terms, as a result of dominance of the state-centered paradigm, the very credibility of international law may be at stake. "If international law is applied against the interests of insurgents whom local people believe are their legitimate rulers, then they may come to see international law as a threat to their political aspirations."[15]

International terrorism

The field of international relations has traditionally been concerned with conflicts among state actors, rather than with the role nonstate actors may play regarding international security. The problem of international terrorism therefore poses a conceptual challenge. International terrorism is an international phenomenon, impacting on international security and stability, and therefore "falls squarely within the domain of what IR should be able to explain and understand."[16] It also falls squarely within the domain of what IL should be able to regulate and prevent.

Traditionally, IR has tended to focus on specific groups, particular ideologies, or even particular strategies or threats of terror or violence. The realist school of IR, refusing to admit that nonstate actors are endowed with independent agency or power in international politics, suggests that the way to formulate policy is to refocus on "rogue" states as the sponsors of violence through proxy nonstate actors. The liberal IR school suggests a regulatory response, with international organizations providing multilateral forums for coordinating state responses to international terrorism. IL has focused on criminalizing particular acts of terrorism (such as piracy or hijacking) and punishing those who commit such acts. It has been primarily a reactive and piecemeal approach. Only recently has IL begun trying to focus on prevention and the links between terrorist groups and transnational organized crime.

Given the limited success of the approaches discussed above, the case can be made for analyzing international terrorism not only as a security threat, but also as a political phenomenon. There is a common and identifiable pattern that nonstate actors adopt when mounting a violent challenge to the political status quo. This pattern of transnational political mobilization coexists with an international system of states. It is useful, therefore, to view the international system as a single political space in which both state and nonstate actors interact and respond to one another. Such an approach, which focuses on the processes of transnational political mobilization, emphasizes "the need to promote stronger institutional channels both within and beyond the state for nonstate actors to use to articulate political grievances."[17] By providing institutional channels and legitimate avenues for the articulation of grievances, nonstate actors can be dissuaded and prevented from taking recourse to violence. Such institutions, including strong regional court systems (such as the European Court of Human Rights) "provide a useful focus for a common research agenda that could be pursued by both international relations and international law scholars."[18]

The George W. Bush administration's doctrine of preemptive strike, as applied in Iraq, poses a fundamental challenge to both IR and IL. The doctrine, bluntly put, asserts America's right to strike first in combating the peril posed by terrorist networks and rogue states armed with weapons of mass destruction. "Whether the new US policy attempts to carve out an amendment to the existing rules that only applies to America, or indeed, whether the United States is seeking to move outside the legal framework altogether by excepting itself from these rules," the Bush Doctrine poses a serious threat to the existing international law regulating the use of force and needs to be addressed seriously by both IR and IL communities.[19]

In the two other areas of international lawmaking examined by the SSRC project, there is also evidence of constructive engagement between IR and IL. Both the process and outcome that led to the UN's Guiding Principles on Internal Displacement (1998) reveal a softening of the rigidities that keep the two disciplines apart. The process allowed for significant roles and contributions from nonstate actors. The outcome was deliberately and strategically embodied in the Guiding Principles – a "soft law" instrument.[20]

Similarly, NGOs played a significant, some would say dominant, role in the process that led to the adoption of the Rome Treaty, which created the International Criminal Court. But at the end of the day, it was states, 139 of them, that signed on to the treaty.

The establishment of the International Criminal Court represented a *constitutional moment* for international law, whereby notions about the legality and legitimacy (under international law) of the extraterritorial jurisdiction of states were transformed into principles governing the exercise of criminal jurisdiction by the international community as a whole.[21]

Concepts embodied in the Rome Treaty, including universal (*jus cogens*) crimes, universal jurisdiction, and complementarity, all challenge both IR and IL scholars to do some fundamental rethinking, preferably together.

Bridging the international relations–international law divide to confront current challenges and crises

Today international law is facing multiple crises:

- The global crisis of *erosion of the rule of law*. Some states, such as the Iraq war's so-called coalition of the willing, are flouting international law with impunity and are willing to attack the UN if it tries to hold them to their Charter obligations.
- The related crisis of *unilateralism and exceptionalism*.

- The crisis of *accountability*, especially in the case of certain transnational corporations and certain international organizations.
- The crisis of *effectiveness*, as a result of lack of implementation and inadequate enforcement of international law.
- The crisis of *relevance.* Increasing numbers of problems that are international in nature and therefore need international norms, standards, and responses (such as trafficking, transborder pollution, etc.) are just not covered, or are inadequately covered, by international law.
- The crisis of *unmet needs.* Indigenous people, minorities, internally displaced people, and the disabled all need international law to recognize their rights and international institutions to address their problems. Yet international lawmaking proceeds at a snail's pace.

Now is the time for the IR and IL communities to bridge their divide and address the multiple crises facing international law. Otherwise, not only will international law become redundant, but the IR and IL communities will face the threat of extinction as well. Now is not the time for staking and defending turf, or for entrenchment of attitudes. Now is the time for crossing lines, building bridges, and partnering. This SSRC project represents a promising start. But it needs to be built upon, through partnering in research, conceptualization, theory construction, lobbying, advocacy, and the spearheading of international lawmaking initiatives.

Notes

1 Spiro, "Disaggregating U.S. Interests in International Law: Sketching a Theory of Liberal Transnationalism," Chapter 16 in this volume.
2 Ibid.
3 A. Chayes and A. Chayes, *The New Sovereignty: Compliance with International Regulatory Agreements* (Cambridge: Harvard University Press, 1995).
4 Spiro, "Disaggregating U.S. Interests in International Law."
5 Koh, "A World Drowning in Guns," Chapter 4 in this volume.
6 Ibid.
7 Ibid.
8 Deng, "The Guiding Principles on Internal Displacement and the Development of International Norms," Chapter 9 in this volume.
9 T. Risse and K. Sikkink as cited in ibid.
10 Deng, "Guiding Principles on Internal Displacement."
11 Spiro, "Disaggregating U.S. Interests in International Law," (citing Kenneth Abbott).
12 Koh, "A World Drowning in Guns."
13 Muggah, "Moving Forward? Assessing Normative and Legal Progress in Dealing with Small Arms," Chapter 2 in this volume.
14 Ibid.
15 William Reno, "Small Arms, Violence, and the Course of Conflicts," Chapter 3 in this volume.
16 Adamson, "International Terrorism, Nonstate Actors, and Transnational Political Mobilization: A Perspective from International Relations," Chapter 5 in this volume.
17 Ibid.

18 Ibid.
19 Simpson and Wheeler, "Preemption and Exception: International Law and the Revolutionary Power," Chapter 7 in this volume.
20 Deng, "Guiding Principles on Internal Displacement," Chapter 9 in this volume.
21 Leila Sadat, "The International Criminal Court and Universal International Jurisdiction: A Return to First Principles," Chapter 11 in this volume.

SELECTED BIBLIOGRAPHY

Books

Adebajo, Adekeye and Ismail Rashid, eds. *West Africa's Security Challenges: Building Peace in a Troubled Region.* Boulder: Lynne Rienner, 2004.

Agamben, Giorgio. *State of Exception.* Translated by Kevin Attell. Chicago: University of Chicago Press, 2005.

Anonymous. *Imperial Hubris: Why the West Is Losing the War on Terror.* Dulles, VA: Brassey's, 2004.

Archibugi, Daniele, D. Held, and M. Kohler, eds. *Reimagining Political Community: Studies in Cosmopolitan Democracy.* Cambridge: Polity Press, 1999.

Austin, John. *The Province of Jurisprudence Determined.* Edited by H. L. A. Hart. New York: Noonday, 1954.

——. *The Province of Jurisprudence Determined.* Cambridge: Cambridge University Press, 1995.

Ballentine, Karen and Jake Sherman, eds. *The Political Economy of Armed Conflict: Beyond Greed and Grievance.* Boulder: Lynne Rienner, 2003.

Barber, Benjamin R. *Fear's Empire: War, Terrorism, and Democracy.* New York: Norton, 2003.

Barkey, Karen. *Bandits and Bureaucrats: The Ottoman Route to State Centralization.* Ithaca: Cornell University Press, 1994.

Barnett, Michael N. *Eyewitness to a Genocide: The United Nations and Rwanda.* Ithaca: Cornell University Press, 2002.

Bass, Gary Jonathan. *Stay the Hand of Vengeance: The Politics of War Crimes Tribunals.* Princeton: Princeton University Press, 2000.

Bassiouni, M. Cherif. *International Terrorism: Multilateral Conventions (1937–2001).* Ardsley, NY: Transnational, 2001.

——. *Introduction to International Criminal Law.* Ardsley, NY: Transnational, 2003.

Bassiouni, M. Cherif and Edward M. Wise. *Aut Dedere, Aut Judicare: The Duty to Extradite or Prosecute in International Law.* Dordrecht: Martinus Nijhoff, 1995.

Bates, Robert. *Prosperity and Violence: The Political Economy of Development.* New York: W. W. Norton, 2001.

Beck, Robert J., *et al.*, eds. *International Rules: Approaches from International Law and International Relations.* New York: Oxford University Press, 1996.

Beitz, Charles. *Political Theory and International Relations.* Princeton: Princeton University Press, 1979/1999.

Benedick, Richard. *Ozone Diplomacy*. Cambridge: Harvard University Press, 1998.

Benvenisti, Eyal and Moshe Hirsch, eds. *The Impact of International Law on International Cooperation: Theoretical Perspectives*. Cambridge: Cambridge University Press, 2004.

Bergesen, Albert, ed. *Studies of the Modern World-System*. New York: Academic Press, 1980.

Bickel, Alexander M. *The Least Dangerous Branch: The Supreme Court at the Bar of Politics*. 2nd edn. New Haven: Yale University Press, 1986.

Boli, John and George M. Thomas, eds. *Constructing World Culture: International Non-governmental Organizations Since 1875*. Stanford: Stanford University Press, 1999.

Booth, Ken and Timothy Dunne. *Worlds in Collision: Terror and the Future of Global Order*. London: Palgrave Macmillan, 2002.

Boutwell, Jeffrey, ed. *Lethal Commerce: The Global Trade in Small Arms and Light Weapons*. Cambridge, MA: American Academy of Arts and Sciences, 1995.

Boutwell, Jeffrey and Michael Klare. *Light Weapons and Civil Conflict: Controlling the Tools of Violence*. Boston: Rowman and Littlefield, 1999.

Brierly, J. L. *The Law of Nations*. 6th edn. Edited by Sir Humphrey Waldock. New York: Oxford University Press, 1963.

Bull, Hedley. *The Anarchical Society: A Study of Order in World Politics*. London: Palgrave Macmillan, 1971, 1977, 2002.

Byers, Michael, ed. *The Role of Law in International Politics: Essays in International Relations and International Law*. Oxford: Oxford University Press, 2001.

——. *War Law*. London: Atlantic Books, 2005.

Byman, Daniel, *et al*. *Trends in Outside Support for Insurgent Movements*. Santa Monica, CA: Rand, 2001.

Cameron, Maxwell, *et al*., eds. *To Walk Without Fear: The Global Movement to Ban Landmines*. Toronto: Oxford University Press, 1998.

Carlsnaes, Walter, Thomas Risse, and Beth A. Simmons. *Handbook of International Relations*. London: Sage, 2002.

Carr, E. H. *The Twenty Years' Crisis: An Introduction to the Study of International Relations*. London: Palgrave Macmillan, 2001.

Cassese, Antonio, ed. *The Current Legal Regulation of the Use of Force*. Dordrecht: Martinus Nijhoff, 1986.

Cassese, Antonio, *et al*., eds. *The Rome Statute of the International Criminal Court: A Commentary*. Oxford: Oxford University Press, 2001.

Chayes, Abram. *The Cuban Missile Crisis: International Crises and the Role of Law*. Oxford: Oxford University Press, 1974.

Chayes, Abram and Antonia Handler Chayes. *The New Sovereignty: Compliance with International Regulatory Agreements*. Cambridge: Harvard University Press, 1998.

Chikulo, Bornwell and Kempe Ronald Hope, eds. *Corruption and Development in Africa: Lessons from Country Case Studies*. New York: St. Martin's Press, 2000.

Cohen, Roberta and Francis Deng. *Masses in Flight: The Global Crisis of Internal Displacement*. Washington, DC: Brookings Institution, 1998.

Cohen, Roberta, Walter Kälin, and Erin Mooney, eds. "The Guiding Principles on Internal Displacement and the Law of the South Caucasus: Georgia, Armenia, Azerbaijan." *Studies in Transitional Legal Policy* no. 34 (2003). [Book-length report of the American Society of International Law.]

Collier, Paul and Nicholas Sambanis, eds. Special Issue, *Conflict Resolution: Understanding Civil Wars* vol. 46, no. 1 (February 2002).

Comerford, Richard Vincent. *The Fenians in Context: Irish Politics and Society: 1848–82.* Dublin: Wolfhound Press, 1985.

Commonwealth Human Rights Initiative. *In Pursuit of Justice: A Report on the Judiciary in Sierra Leone.* Freetown: Commonwealth Human Rights Initiative, 2002.

Cook, Phil. *Gun Violence: The Real Costs.* Oxford: Oxford University Press, 2000.

Cutler, A. Claire, *et al.*, eds. *Private Authority and International Affairs.* Albany: State University of New York Press, 1999.

Danilenko, Gennady M. *Law-Making in the International Community.* Boston: Martinus Nijhoff, 1993.

Detter, Ingrid. *Law of War.* 2nd edn. Cambridge: Cambridge University Press, 2000.

Dezalay, Yves and Bryant G. Garth, eds. *Global Prescriptions: The Production, Exportation, and Importation of a New Legal Orthodoxy.* Ann Arbor: University of Michigan Press, 2002.

DiMento, Joseph F. C. *The Global Environment and International Law.* Austin: University of Texas Press, 2003.

Dunne, Tim and Nicholas Wheeler, eds. *Human Rights in Global Politics.* Cambridge: Cambridge University Press, 1999.

Falk, Richard. *Revitalising International Law.* Ames: Iowa State University Press, 1989.

——. *On Humane Governance.* Cambridge: Polity Press, 1995.

Fijnaut, C., J. Wouters, and F. Naert, eds. *Legal Instruments in the Fight Against International Terrorism: Transatlantic Dialogue.* Leiden: Brill Publishing, 2004.

Finnemore, Martha. *National Interests in International Society.* Ithaca: Cornell University Press, 1996.

——. *The Purpose of Intervention: Changing Purposes of the Use of Force.* Ithaca: Cornell University Press, 2004.

Fischer, Horst, *et al.*, eds. *Krisensicherung und Humanitarer Schutz: Crisis Management and Humanitarian Protection.* Berlin: Berliner Wissenschafs-Verlag, 2004.

Fleck, Dieter, ed. *The Handbook of Humanitarian Law in Armed Conflict.* New York: Oxford University Press, 1995.

Franck, Thomas. *The Power of Legitimacy Among Nations.* Oxford: Oxford University Press, 1990.

——. *Fairness in International Law and Institutions.* Oxford: Oxford University Press, 1995.

Freeman, Michael, ed. *Current Legal Problems.* Vol. 56. New York: Oxford University Press, 2004.

Goertz, Gary. *Contexts of International Politics.* New York: Cambridge University Press, 1994.

Goldring, Nathalie. *Research Sources on the International Trade in Light Weapons.* London: BASIC, 1995.

Goldsmith, Jack L. and Eric A. Posner. *The Limits of International Law.* New York: Oxford University Press, 2004.

Goldstein, Judith L., Miles Kahler, Robert O. Keohane, and Anne-Marie Slaughter, eds. *Legalization and World Politics.* Cambridge: MIT Press, 2001. [Reprint of Special Issue, *International Organization* vol. 54, no. 3 (Summer 2000).]

Goldstein, Judith and Robert O. Keohane, eds. *Ideas and Foreign Policy.* Ithaca: Cornell University Press, 1993.

Graham, Senator Bob, with Jeff Nussbaum. *Intelligence Matters.* New York: Random House, 2004.

Greenberg, Karen J. and Joshua L. Dratel, eds. *The Torture Papers: The Road to Abu Graib*. Cambridge: Cambridge University Press, 2005.

Grotius, Hugo. *The Rights of War and Peace*. 3 vols. Indianapolis: Liberty Fund, 2005.

Haas, Ernst B. *When Knowledge Is Power*. Berkeley: University of California Press, 1990.

Hall, Rodney and Thomas Biersteker, eds. *The Emergence of Private Authority in Global Governance*. Cambridge: Cambridge University Press, 2002.

Hanioðlu, M. Şükrü. *The Young Turks in Opposition*. New York: Oxford University Press, 1995.

Hart, H. L. A. *The Concept of Law*. Oxford: Clarendon Press, 1961, 1994.

Hasenclever, Andreas, Peter Mayer, and Volker Rittberger. *Theories of International Regimes*. New York: Cambridge University Press, 1997.

Haveman, Robert and Bruce Zellner, eds. *Policy Studies Annual*. Beverly Hills: Sage, 1979.

Hayner, Priscilla B. *Unspeakable Truths: Confronting State Terror and Atrocity*. New York: Routledge, 2001.

Held, David. *Democracy and the Global Order: From the Modern State to Cosmopolitan Governance*. Cambridge: Polity Press, 1995.

Held, David and Mathias Koenig-Archibugi, eds, *Taming Globalization: Frontiers of Governance*. Cambridge: Polity Press, 2003.

Held, David, *et al*. *Global Transformations: Politics, Economics, and Culture*. Cambridge: Polity Press, 1999.

Henkin, Louis. *How Nations Behave: Law and Foreign Policy*. New York: Columbia University Press for the Council on Foreign Relations, 1979.

Hirsch, John. *Sierra Leone: Diamonds and the Struggle for Democracy*. Boulder: Lynne Rienner, 2001.

Hobsbawm, Eric. *The Age of Capital: 1848–1875*. New York: Vintage, 1996.

Hoffman, Bruce. *Inside Terrorism*. New York: Columbia University Press, 1998.

Huntington, Samuel P. *Political Order in Changing Societies*. New Haven: Yale University Press, 1968.

Ikenberry, G. John. *America Unrivaled: The Future of the Balance of Power*. Ithaca: Cornell University Press, 2002.

International Committee of the Red Cross. *Arms Availability and the Situation of Civilians in Armed Conflict*. Geneva, 1999.

International Crisis Group. *Sierra Leone: The State of Security and Governance*. Freetown, September 5, 2003.

International Development Research Centre. *The Responsibility to Protect: Report of the International Commission on Intervention and State Sovereignty*. Ottawa: International Development Research Centre, 2001.

Jackson, Robert. *Quasi-States: Sovereignty, International Relations, and the Third World*. New York: Cambridge University Press, 1990.

Jennings, Robert and Arthur Watts, eds. *Oppenheim's International Law*. 9th edn. Harlow: Longman, 1992.

Kaldor, Mary. *New and Old Wars: Organized Violence in a Global Era*. Stanford: Stanford University Press, 1999.

Kang, David. *Crony Capitalism: Corruption and Development in South Korea and the Philippines*. New York: Cambridge University Press, 2002.

Kaplan, Lawrence F. and William Kristol. *The War over Iraq: Saddam's Tyranny and America's Mission*. San Francisco: Encounter Books, 2003.

Katzenstein, Peter J., ed. *The Culture of National Security.* New York: Columbia University Press, 1996.

Kaufman, Natalie Hevener. *Human Rights Treaties and the Senate.* Chapel Hill: University of North Carolina Press, 1990.

Keck, Margaret and Kathryn Sikkink. *Activists Beyond Borders: Advocacy Networks in International Politics.* Ithaca: Cornell University Press, 1998.

Kelsen, Hans. *Principles of International Law.* New York: Rinehart, 1952.

Keohane, Robert. *After Hegemony: Cooperation and Discord in the World Political Economy.* Princeton: Princeton University Press, 1984.

——. *Power and Governance in a Partially Globalized World.* London: Routledge, 2002.

Kirchheimer, Otto. *Political Justice: The Use of Legal Procedures for Political Ends.* Princeton: Princeton University Press, 1961.

Kissinger, Henry. *A World Restored: The Politics of Conservatism in a Revolutionary Era.* London: Victor Gollancz, 1977.

Klotz, Audie. *Norms in International Relations: The Struggle Against Apartheid.* Ithaca: Cornell University Press, 1995.

Korey, William. *The Promises We Keep: Human Rights, the Helsinki Process, and American Foreign Policy.* New York: St. Martin's Press, 1993.

Krasner, Stephen D. *Sovereignty, Organized Hypocrisy.* Princeton: Princeton University Press, 1999.

Kratochwil, Friedrich. *Rules, Norms, and Decisions: On the Conditions of Practical and Legal Reasoning in International Relations and Domestic Affairs.* Cambridge: Cambridge University Press, 1989.

Kritz, Neil J., ed. *Transitional Justice: How Emerging Democracies Reckon with Former Regimes.* Washington, DC: US Institute of Peace, 1995.

Lumpe, Lora, ed. *Running Guns: The Global Black Market in Small Arms.* London: Zed Books, 2000.

Macedo, Stephen, ed. *Universal Jurisdiction: National Courts and the Prosecution of Serious Crimes Under International Law.* Philadelphia: University of Pennsylvania Press, 2003.

Macedo, Stephen and Allen Buchanan, eds. *NOMOS: Secession and Self-Determination.* Vol. 45. New York: New York University Press, 2003.

Malanczuk, Peter. *Akehurst's Modern Introduction to International Law.* London: Routledge, 1997.

Malone, David M. and Yuen Foong Khong, eds. *Unilateralism and U.S. Foreign Policy: International Perspectives.* Boulder: Lynne Rienner, 2003.

McAdam, Doug, Sidney G. Tarrow, and Charles Tilly. *Dynamics of Contention.* New York: Cambridge University Press, 2001.

McDougal, Myres, S., Harold D. Lasswell, and Lung-chu Chen. *Human Rights and World Public Order: The Basic Policies of an International Law of Human Dignity.* New Haven: Yale University Press, 1980.

Migdal, Joel. *Strong Societies and Weak States.* Princeton: Princeton University Press, 1988.

Minow, Martha. *Between Vengeance and Forgiveness: Facing History After Genocide and Mass Violence.* Boston: Beacon Press, 1998.

Morgenthau, Hans. J. *Politics Among Nations.* 3rd edn. New York: Knopf, 1960.

Muggah, Robert and Peter Batchelor. *Development Held Hostage: The Socio-Economic Impacts of Small Arms Availability and Misuse.* New York: United Nations Development Programme, 2004.

Muggah, Robert and Eric Berman. *Humanitarianism Under Threat: Small Arms and Humanitarian Action.* New York: Inter-Agency Standing Committee of the UN and Small Arms Survey, 2001.

Nacos, Brigitte. *Terrorism and the Media: From the Iran Hostage Crisis to the Oklahoma City Bombing.* New York: Columbia University Press, 1994.

Neier, Aryeh. *War Crimes: Brutality, Genocide, Terror, and the Struggle for Justice.* New York: Times Books, 1998.

Newmann, Iver B. and Ole Waever, eds. *The Future of International Relations: Masters in the Making?* New York: Routledge, 1997.

Nolan, Janne E., ed. *Global Engagement Cooperation and Security in the 21st Century.* Washington, DC: Brookings Institution, 1994.

Nye, Joseph S., Jr. *The Paradox of American Power.* Oxford: Oxford University Press, 2002.

——. *Soft Power: The Means to Success in World Politics.* New York: PublicAffairs, 2004.

O'Broin, Leon. *Revolutionary Underground: The Story of the Irish Republican Brotherhood, 1858–1924.* Dublin: Gill and Macmillan, 1976.

Olson, Mancur. *Power and Prosperity.* New York: Basic Books, 2000.

Osiel, Mark. *Mass Atrocity, Collective Memory, and the Law.* New Brunswick, NJ: Transaction, 1997.

Patrick, Stewart and Shepard Forman, eds. *Multilateralism and U.S. Foreign Policy: Ambivalent Engagement.* Boulder: Lynne Rienner, 2002.

Pollack, Mark A. and Gregory C. Shaffer, eds. *Transatlantic Governance in the Global Economy.* Lanham: Rowman and Littlefield, 2001.

Posner, Richard. *Cardozo: A Study in Reputation.* Chicago: University of Chicago Press, 1989.

Prestowitz, Clyde. *Rogue Nation: American Unilateralism and the Failure of Good Intentions.* New York: Basic Books, 2003.

Pugh, Michael and Neil Cooper with Jonathan Goodhand. *War Economies in Regional Context.* Boulder: Lynne Rienner, 2004.

Rana, Swadesh. *Small Arms and Intra-State Conflicts.* Geneva: United Nations Institute for Disarmament Research, 1995.

Reisman, Michael and Andrew R. Willard, eds. *International Incidents: The Law That Counts in World Politics.* Princeton: Princeton University Press, 1988.

Reus-Smit, Christian. *American Power and World Order.* Cambridge: Polity Press, 2004.

——. ed. *The Politics of International Law.* Cambridge: Cambridge University Press, 2004.

Riles, Annelise. *The Network Inside Out.* Ann Arbor: University of Michigan Press, 2000.

Risse, Thomas, Stephen C. Ropp, and Kathryn Sikkink, eds. *The Power of Human Rights: International Norms and Domestic Change.* Cambridge: Cambridge University Press, 1999.

Risse-Kappen, Thomas, ed. *Bringing Transnational Relations Back In: Non-State Actors, Domestic Structures, and International Institutions.* Cambridge: Cambridge University Press, 1995.

Roht-Arriaza, Naomi, ed. *Accountability for Human Rights Violations in International Law and Practice.* New York: Oxford University Press, 1995.

Roht-Arriaza, Naomi and Javier Mariezcurrena, eds. *Transitional Justice in the Twenty-First Century: Beyond Truth Versus Justice.* Cambridge: Cambridge University Press, forthcoming 2006.

Romano, Cesare P. R., André Nollkaemper, and Jann K. Kleffner, eds. *Internationalized Criminal Courts.* Oxford: Oxford University Press, 2004.

Ronit, Karsten and Volker Schneider, eds. *Private Organizations in Global Politics.* London: Routledge, 2000.

Sadat, Leila Nadya. *The International Criminal Court and the Transformation of International Law: Justice for the New Millennium.* Ardsley, NY: Transnational, 2002.

Sampson, Andrew. *The Arms Bazaar.* New York: Viking, 1977.

Sands, Phillippe. *Lawless World: America and the Making and Breaking of Global Rules.* New York: Viking, 2005.

Schacter, Oscar. *International Law in Theory and Practice.* Dordrecht: Martinus Nijhoff, 1991.

Schmitt, Carl. *The Concept of the Political.* Translation, Introduction, and Notes by George Schwab. Chicago: University of Chicago Press, 1996.

Schrage, Eliot J. *Promoting International Worker Rights Through Private Voluntary Initiatives: Public Relations or Public Policy?* Iowa City: University of Iowa Center for Human Rights, 2004.

Shain, Yossi. *The Frontier of Loyalty: Political Exiles in the Age of the Nation-State.* Middletown, CT: Wesleyan University Press, 1989.

Simpson, Gerry. *Great Powers and Outlaw States.* New York: Cambridge University Press, 2004.

Slaughter, Anne-Marie. *A New World Order.* Princeton: Princeton University Press, 2004.

Small Arms Survey. *Profiling the Problem.* Oxford: Oxford University Press, 2001.

——. *Counting the Human Costs.* Oxford: Oxford University Press, 2002.

——. *Development Denied.* Oxford: Oxford University Press, 2003.

——. *Rights at Risk.* Oxford: Oxford University Press, 2004.

Smith, Jackie, ed. *Transnational Social Movements and Global Politics: Solidarity Beyond the State.* Syracuse, NY: Syracuse University Press, 1997.

Sriram, Chandra Lekha. *Confronting Past Human Rights Violations: Justice vs. Peace in Times of Transition.* London: Frank Cass, 2004.

——. *Globalizing Justice for Mass Atrocities: A Revolution in Accountability.* London: Routledge, 2005.

Sriram, Chandra Lekha and Zoe Nielsen, eds. *Exploring Subregional Conflict: Opportunities for Conflict Prevention.* Boulder: Lynne Rienner, 2004.

Steiner, Henry J. and Phillip Alston. *International Human Rights in Context: Laws, Politics, Morals.* Oxford: Oxford University Press, 2000.

Stern, Jessica. *Terror in the Name of God.* New York: HarperCollins, 2003.

Stewart, Frances and Valpy Fitzgerald, eds. *War and Underdevelopment: The Economic and Social Consequences of Conflict.* Oxford: Oxford University Press, 2001.

Stockholm International Peace Research Institute (SIPRI). *SIPRI Yearbook: Armaments, Disarmament, and International Security.* Oxford: Oxford University Press, 2002.

Tarrow, Sidney. *Power and Movement: Social Movements and Contentious Politics.* Cambridge: Cambridge University Press, 1998.

Teitel, Ruti G. *Transitional Justice.* New York: Oxford University Press, 2000.

Thomas, Daniel C. *The Helsinki Effect: International Norms, Human Rights, and the Demise of Communism.* Princeton: Princeton University Press, 2001.

Thomas, George M., John W. Meyer, Francisco O. Ramirez, and John Boli. *Institutional Structure: Constituting State, Society, and the Individual.* Beverly Hills: Sage, 1987.
Tilly, Charles. *From Mobilization to Revolution.* Reading, MA: Addison-Wesley, 1978.
Tirman, John, ed. *The Maze of Fear: Security and Migration After 9/11.* New York: New Press, 2004.
Tushnet, Mark, ed. *The Constitution in Wartime.* Durham, NC: Duke University Press, 2005.
Walter, Barbara and Jack Snyder, eds. *Civil Wars, Insecurity, and Intervention.* New York: Columbia University Press, 1999.
Waltz, Kenneth. *Theory of International Politics.* New York: McGraw-Hill, 1979.
Walzer, Michael. *What It Means to Be an American.* New York: Marsilio, 1996.
Wapner, Paul. *Environmental Activism and World Civic Politics.* New York: State University of New York Press, 1996.
Weissbrodt, David, ed. *International Human Rights: Law, Policy, & Process.* 3rd edn. Cincinnati: Anderson, 2001.
Wendt, Alexander. *Social Theory of International Politics.* Cambridge: Cambridge University Press, 1999.
Wheeler, Nicholas J. *Saving Strangers: Humanitarian Intervention in International Society.* Oxford: Oxford University Press, 2000.
Wight, Martin. *International Theory: The Three Traditions.* London: Holmes and Meier, 1992.
Wolfers, Arnold. *Discord and Collaborations: Essays on International Politics.* Baltimore: Johns Hopkins University Press, 1962.
Woodward, Bob. *Bush at War.* New York: Simon and Schuster, 2002.
World Bank. *World Development Report 2003.* New York: Oxford University Press, 2003.
Yans-McLaughlin, Virginia, ed. *Immigration Reconsidered.* New York: Oxford University Press, 1990.

Articles, chapters, and papers

Abbott, Kenneth W. "Modern International Relations Theory: A Prospectus for International Lawyers." *Yale Journal of International Law* vol. 14, no. 2 (Summer 1989).
——. "International Relations Theory, International Law, and the Regime Governing Atrocities in International Conflicts." *American Journal of International Law* vol. 93 (1999).
Abbott, Kenneth W., Robert O. Keohane, Andrew Moravcsik, Anne-Marie Slaughter, and Duncan Snidal. "The Concept of Legalization." *International Organization* vol. 54 (2000).
Abbott, Kenneth W. and Duncan Snidal. "Hard and Soft Law in International Governance." *International Organization* vol. 54 (2000).
——. "International 'Standards' and International Governance." *Journal of European Public Policy* vol. 8 (2001).
"Agora: The United States Constitution and International Law." *American Journal of International Law* vol. 98 (2004).
Akhavam, Payam. "Justice in the Hague, Peace in the Former Yugoslavia?" *Human Rights Quarterly* vol. 20 (1999).

Amar, Akhil Reed. "The Second Amendment: A Case Study in Constitutional Interpretation." *Utah Law Review* vol. 2001 (2001).

Annacker, Claudia. "The Legal Régime of Erga Omnes Obligations in International Law." *Austrian Journal of Public International Law* vol. 46 (1993).

Axelrod, Robert. "An Evolutionary Approach to Norms." *American Political Science Review* vol. 80, no. 4 (December 1986).

Ayres, Ian and John J. Donohue III. "Shooting Down the More Guns, Less Crime Hypothesis." *Stanford Law Review* vol. 55 (2003).

Bagshaw, Simon. "Developing the Guiding Principles on Internal Displacement: The Role of a Global Public Policy Network." Available online at www.globalpublicpolicy.net/index.php?id=165.

Barnett, Randy E. and Don B. Kates. "Under Fire: The New Consensus on the Second Amendment." *Emory Law Journal* vol. 45 (1996).

Bassiouni, M. Cherif. "Universal Jurisdiction for International Crimes: Historical Perspectives and Contemporary Practice." *Virginia Journal of International Law* vol. 42, no. 1 (Fall 2001).

Berman, Nathaniel. "Privileging Combat? Contemporary Conflict and the Legal Construction of War." *Columbia Journal of Transnational Law* vol. 43, no. 1 (2004).

Bilder, Richard B. and Detlev F. Vagts. "Speaking Law to Power: Lawyers and Torture." *American Journal of International Law* vol. 98 (2004).

Bolton, John. "The Global Prosecutors: Hunting War Criminals in the Name of Utopia." *Foreign Affairs* (January–February 1999).

——. "Is There Really 'Law' in International Affairs?" *Transnational Law & Contemporary Problems* vol. 10, no. 1 (Spring 2000).

——. "The Risks and Weaknesses of the International Criminal Court from America's Perspective." *Virginia Journal of International Law* vol. 41 (2000).

Bradley, Curtis A. and Jack L. Goldsmith. "Customary International Law as Federal Common Law: A Critique of the Modern Position." *Harvard Law Review* vol. 110 (1997).

——. "Treaties, Human Rights, and Conditional Consent." *University of Pennsylvania Law Review* vol. 149 (2000).

——. "Congressional Authorization and the War on Terrorism." *Harvard Law Review* vol. 118 (2005).

Brown, Bartram S. "U.S. Objections to the Statute of the International Criminal Court: A Brief Response." *New York University Journal of International Law and Policy* vol. 3 (1999).

Brown Weiss, Edith. "Understanding Compliance with International Environmental Agreements: The Baker's Dozen Myths." *University of Richmond Law Review* vol. 32 (1999).

Chayes, Abram and Antonia Handler Chayes. "On Compliance." *International Organization* vol. 47 (1993).

Chemerinsky, Erwin. "Forward: The Vanishing Constitution." *Harvard Law Review* vol. 103 (1989).

Chinkin, C. M. "The Challenge of Soft Law: Development and Change in International Law." *International and Comparative Law Quarterly* vol. 38 (1989).

Choper, Jesse H. "The Supreme Court and the Political Branches: Democratic Theory and Practice." *University of Pennsylvania Law Review* vol. 122 (1974).

Cohen, Roberta. "The Guiding Principles on Internal Displacement: An Innovation in International Standard Setting." *Global Governance* vol. 10, no. 459 (2004).

Collier, Paul and Anke Hoeffler. "Greed and Grievance in Civil War." *World Bank Policy Research Working Paper*. Washington, DC: World Bank 2001.

Cover, Robert M. "Forward: *Nomos* and Narrative." *Harvard Law Review* vol. 97 (1983).

——. "Violence and the Word." *Yale Law Journal* vol. 95 (1986).

Crockett, Clyde. "Toward a Revision of the International Law of Piracy." *DePaul Law Review* vol. 26 (1976).

Cronin, Audrey Kurth. "Behind the Curve: Globalization and International Terrorism." *International Security* vol. 27, no. 3 (Winter 2002–3).

D'Amato, Anthony. "The Concept of Special Custom in International Law." *American Journal of International Law* vol. 63 (1969).

——. "It's a Bird, It's a Plane, It's Jus Cogens." *Connecticut Journal of International Law* vol. 6, no. 1 (Fall 1990).

Danilenko, Gennady M. "International Jus Cogens: Issues of Law-Making." *European Journal of International Law* vol. 2, no. 1 (1991).

Dennis, Michael J. "Human Rights in 2002: The Annual Sessions of the UN Commission on Human Rights and the Economics and Social Council." *American Journal of International Law* vol. 97, no. 17 (2003).

D'Souza, Frances. "Brief Background to the Johannesburg Principles." 1996. Available online at www.article23.org.hk/english/research/johan_and_lima_brief.doc.

Eskridge, William N., Jr. "Dynamic Statutory Interpretation." *University of Pennsylvania Law Review* vol. 135 (1987).

——. "Politics Without Romance: Implications of Public Choice Theory for Statutory Interpretation." *Virginia Law Review* vol. 74 (1988).

——. "Channeling: Identity-Based Social Movements and Public Law." *University of Pennsylvania Law Review* vol. 150 (2001).

Farer, Tom. "Problems of an International Law of Intervention." *Stanford Journal of International Studies* vol. 3 (1968).

Finnemore, Martha. "Norms, Culture, and World Politics: Insights From Sociology's Institutionalism." *International Organization* vol. 50, no. 2 (1996).

——. "Are Legal Norms Distinctive?" *NYU Journal of International Law and Politics* vol. 32 (2000).

Finnemore, Martha and Kathryn Sikkink. "International Norm Dynamics and Political Change." *International Organization* vol. 52, no. 4 (Autumn 1998).

Franck, Thomas. "The Emerging Right to Democratic Governance." *American Journal of International Law* vol. 86 (1992).

——. "Criminals, Combatants, or What? An Examination of the Role of Law in Responding to the Threat of Terror." *American Journal of International Law* vol. 98 (2004).

Friedman, Barry. "Dialogue and Judicial Review." *Michigan Law Review* vol. 91 (1993).

Fund for Peace. *Model Convention on the Registration of Arms Brokers and the Suppression of Unlicensed Arms Brokering*. 2001. Available online at www.fundforpeace.org.

Gathii, James Thuo. "Torture, Extraterritoriality, Terrorism and International Law." *Albany Law Review* vol. 67, no. 2 (December 2003).

Gereffi, Gary, *et al.* "The NGO-Industrial Complex." *Foreign Policy* (July–August 2001).

Global IDP Project. "Angola: While Large Numbers of IDPs Are Returning Home, Authorities Have Largely Ignored Minimum Standards." December 2002. Available online at www.idpproject.org.

Goldsmith, Jack and Stephen D. Krasner. "The Limits of Idealism." *Dædalus* (Winter 2003).

Goldsmith, Jack and Eric Posner. "A Theory of Customary International Law." *University of Chicago Law Review* vol. 66 (1999).

Gomez, Mario. "National Human Rights Commissions and Internally Displaced Persons." *Brookings Institution–SAIS Project on Internal Displacement Occasional Paper.* Washington, DC: Brookings Institution, 2002.

Graduate Institute of International Studies. "Small Arms Survey 2001 Executive Summary." Available online at www.smallarmssurvey. _en.pd

Graff, James. "Can France Put a Cork In It? With the U.S. Boycott Hurting Wine Sales, Chirac Quiets Down and Tries to Make Nice." *Time*, April 28, 2003.

Greenwood, Christopher. "War, Terrorism, and International Law." *Current Legal Problems* vol. 56 (February 2004).

Gruchalla-Wesierski, Tadeusz. "A Framework for Understanding 'Soft Law.'" *Revue de Droit de McGill* vol. 30 (1984).

Haas, Peter. "Introduction: Epistemic Communities and International Policy Coordination." *International Organization* vol. 46, no. 2 (Winter 1992).

Harris, Paul and Jason Burke. "Flirting with Armageddon: Welcome to a New Arms Race." *Observer*, February 20, 2005.

Hassner, Pierre. "Friendly Questions to America the Powerful." *The National Interest* (Fall 2002).

Hathaway, Oona A. "Do Human Rights Treaties Make a Difference?" *Yale Law Journal* vol. 111 (2002).

Head, John. "Supranational Law: How the Move Toward Multilateral Solutions Is Changing the Character of International Law." *Kansas Law Review* vol. 42 (1994).

Hedges, Chris. "Kosovo's Next Masters." *Foreign Affairs* vol. 78, no. 3 (May–June 1999).

Helfer, Laurence R. and Anne-Marie Slaughter. "Toward a Theory of Effective Supranational Adjudication." *Yale Law Journal* vol. 107 (1997).

Hendrickson, David C. "Toward Universal Empire: The Dangerous Quest for Absolute Security." *World Policy Journal* (Fall 2002).

Hoffman, Stanley. "The High and the Mighty: Bush's National Security Strategy and the New American Hubris." *American Prospect*, January 13, 2003.

Human Rights Watch. "UN: Programme of Inaction on Small Arms." *Human Rights News,* July 19, 2001.

——. "My Gun Was As Tall As Me: Child Soldiers in Burma." October 2002. Available online at www.hrw.org/reports/2002/burma.

Kälin, Walter. "How Hard Is Soft Law? The Guiding Principles on Internal Displacement and the Need for a Normative Framework." In *Recent Commentaries About the Nature and Application of the Guiding Principles on Internal Displacement.* Washington, DC: Brookings Institution, 2002.

Karp, Aaron. "Small Arms Control: The Need for Coordination." *Disarmament Forum* vol. 2 (2000).

——. "Laudable Failure: the UN Small Arms Conference." *SAIS Review* vol. 22, no. 1 (Winter–Spring 2002).

Keohane, Robert O. "Ironies of Sovereignty: The European Union and the United States." *Common Market Study* vol. 40 (2002).

Keohane, Robert and Lisa Martin. "The Promise of Institutionalist Theory." *International Security* vol. 20, no. 1 (Summer 1995).

Kissinger, Henry A. "The Pitfalls of Universal Jurisdiction." *Foreign Affairs* vol. 80, no. 4 (July–August 2001).

Koh, Harold Hongju. "Transnational Public Law Litigation." *Yale Law Journal* vol. 100 (1991).

——. "The 'Haiti Paradigm' in United States Human Rights Policy." *Yale Law Journal* vol. 103 (1994).

——. "Transnational Legal Process." *Nebraska Law Review* vol. 75 (1996).

——. "Why Do Nations Obey International Law?" *Yale Law Journal* vol. 106 (1997).

——. "Bringing International Law Home." *Houston Law Review* vol. 35 (1998).

——. "The 1998 Frankel Lecture: Bringing International Law Home." *Houston Law Review* vol. 35 (1998).

——. "How Is International Human Rights Law Enforced?" *Indiana Law Journal* vol. 74 (1999).

——. "The Case Against Military Commissions." *American Journal of International Law* vol. 96 (2002).

——. "American Exceptionalism." *Stanford Law Review* vol. 55 (2003).

Krasner, Stephen D. "Power Politics, Institutions, and Transnational Relations." In Thomas Risse-Kappen, ed., *Bringing Transnational Relations Back In: Non-State Actors, Domestic Structures, and International Institutions*. Cambridge: Cambridge University Press, 1995.

Krause, Keith. "Multilateral Diplomacy, Norm Building, and UN Conferences: The Case of Small Arms and Light Weapons." *Global Governance* vol. 8, no. 2 (2002).

Laurence, Edward. "Shaping Global Public Policy on Small Arms: After the UN Conference." *World Affairs* vol. 9, no. 1 (Spring 2002).

Laurence, Edward and Rachel Stohl. "Making Global Public Policy: The Case of Small Arms and Light Weapons." *Occasional Paper* 7. Geneva: Small Arms Survey, 2002.

Lavoyer, Jean-Philippe. "Guiding Principles on Internal Displacement: A Few Comments on the Contribution of International Humanitarian Law." *International Review of the Red Cross* no. 324 (September 30, 1998).

Levinson, Sanford. "The Embarrassing Second Amendment." *Yale Law Journal* vol. 99 (1989).

——. "Looking Abroad When Interpreting the Constitution: Some Reflections." *Texas International Law Journal* vol. 39 (2004).

L'Heureux-Dubé, Claire. "The Importance of Dialogue: Globalization and the International Impact of the Rehnquist Court." *Tulsa Law Journal* vol. 34 (1998).

Litvin, Daniel. "Needed: A Global Business Code of Conduct." *Foreign Policy* (November–December 2003).

Lutz, Ellen and Kathryn Sikkink. "International Human Rights Law and Practice in Latin America." *International Organization* vol. 54 (2000).

——. "The Justice Cascade: the Evolution and Impact of Foreign Human Rights Trials in Latin America." *Chicago Journal of International Law* vol. 2 (Spring 2001).

Macey, Jonathan R. "Regulatory Globalization as a Response to Regulatory Competition." *Emory Law Journal* vol. 52 (2003).

Marshall, Andrew. "Boycott Targets Friends of Bush." *Christian Science Monitor*, April 20, 2001.

Martin, Francisco Forrest. "Using International Human Rights Law for Establishing a Unified Use of Force Rule in the Law of Armed Conflict." *Saskatachewan Law Review* vol. 64 (2001).

Mathews, Jessica. “Power Shift” *Foreign Affairs* vol. 76 (January–February 1997).

McCorquodale, Robert. “An Inclusive International Legal System.” *Leiden Journal of International Law* vol. 17, no. 3 (September 2004).

McGowan, Patrick. “African Military Coups d’État, 1956–2001: Frequency, Trends, and Distribution.” *Journal of Modern African Studies* vol. 41, no. 3 (2004).

Meyer, John W., John Boli, George M. Thomas, and Francisco O. Ramirez. “World Society and the Nation-State.” *American Journal of Sociology* vol. 103, no. 1 (1997).

Moravcsik, Andrew. “Taking Preferences Seriously: A Liberal Theory of International Politics.” *International Organizations* vol. 51 (1997).

——. “The Origin of Human Rights Regimes: Democratic Delegation in postwar Europe.” *International Organization* vol. 54, no. 2 (Spring 2000).

Morris, Madeline. “The Disturbing Democratic Deficit of the ICC.” *Finnish Yearbook of International Law* vol. 12 (2001).

——. “Universal Jurisdiction in a Divided World: Conference Remarks.” *New England Law Review* vol. 35 (Winter 2001).

——. “Terrorism: The Politics of Prosecution.” *Chicago Journal of International Law* vol. 5 (Winter 2005).

Muggah, Robert. “Why Should We Have a Humanitarian Perspective on Small Arms?” *Humanitarian Practice Review* (2002).

——. “Diagnosing Demand: Assessing Motivations and Means for Small Arms in Solomon Islands and Papua New Guinea.” *Australia National University Occasional Paper* 15. Canberra: Australian National University, 2004.

——. “Small Arms – Big Bills.” *ID21 Insights: Development Research* vol. 50 (June 2004).

——. “No Magic Bullet: A Critical Perspective on DDR and Weapons Reduction in Post-Conflict Contexts.” *Journal of Contemporary Security Policy* (vol. 94, 2005).

Muggah, Robert and Peter Batchelor. “Development Held Hostage: Assessing the Effects of Small Arms on Human Development.” *Preliminary Study of the Socio-Economic Impacts and Development Linkages of Small Arms Proliferation, Availability, and Use.* New York: United Nations Development Programme, April 2002. Available online at www.undp.org/erd/smallarms/docs/development_held_hostage.pdf.

Muggah, Robert and Jurgen Brauer. “Diagnosing Demand: An Economic Framework to Assessing the Demand for Small Arms.” *Discussion Paper* 50. Cape Town: University of Cape Town, School of Economics and Management, 2004.

O’Connell, Mary Ellen. “Lawful Self-Defense to Terrorism.” *University of Pittsburgh Law Review* vol. 63 (2002).

——. “To Kill or Capture Terrorists in the Global War on Terror.” *Case Western Reserve Journal of International Law* vol. 35 (2003).

——. “Enhancing the Status of Non-State Actors Through a Global War on Terror.” *Columbia Journal of Transnational Law* vol. 43 (2005).

——. “Affirming the Ban on Coercive Interrogation.” *Ohio State Law Journal* vol. 66 (November 2005).

O’Connor, Michael P. and Celia M. Rumann. “Into the Fire: How to Avoid Getting Burned by the Same Mistakes Made Fighting Terrorism in Northern Ireland.” *Cardozo Law Review* vol. 24, no. 4 (2003).

O’Hanlon, Michael E., Susan E. Rice, and James B. Steinberg. “The National Security Strategy and Preemption.” *Policy Brief* 113. Washington, DC: Brookings Institution, December 2002.

Orentlicher, Diane F. "The Power of an Idea: The Impact of United States Human Rights Policy." *Transnational Law and Contemporary Problems* vol. 1 (1991).

——. "Settling Accounts: The Duty to Prosecute Human Rights Violations of a Prior Regime." *Yale Law Journal* vol. 100 (1991).

Paust, Jordan J. "The Right to Life: Human Rights Law and the Law of War." *Saskatchewan Law Review* vol. 65 (2002).

Pellet, Alain. "No, This Is Not War." *European Journal of International Law* (October 2001). Available online at www.ejil.org/forum_wtc/ny-pellet.html.

Price, Richard. "Reversing the Gun Sights: Transnational Civil Society Targets Land Mines." *International Organization* 52, no. 3 (Summer 1998).

PRIDE. "Ex-Combatant Views of the Truth and Reconciliation Commission and the Special Court in Sierra Leone." Freetown, September 12, 2002. Available online at www.ictj.org.

Randall, Kenneth C. "Universal Jurisdiction Under International Law." *Texas Law Review* vol. 66 (1988).

Rapoport, David C. "The Fourth Wave: September 11 and the History of Terrorism." *Current History* (December 2001).

Ratner, Steven R. "Does International Law Matter in Preventing Ethnic Conflict?" *New York University Journal of International Law and Politics* vol. 32 (2000).

Raustiala, Kal. "The Architecture of International Cooperation: Transgovernmental Networks and the Future of International Law." *Virginia Journal of International Law* vol. 43 (2002).

Reisman, W. Michael. "Editorial Comment: Sovereignty and Human Rights in Contemporary International Law." *American Journal of International Law* vol. 84 (1990).

"The Revival of Empire." Special Section, *Ethics in International Affairs* vol. 17 (2003).

Rice, Condoleezza. "Promoting the National Interest." *Foreign Affairs* vol. 79, no. 1 (January–February 2000).

Rieff, David. "Hope Is Not Enough." *Prospect* (October 2003).

Roberts, Anthea. "Traditional and Modern Approaches to Customary International Law: A Reconciliation." *American Journal of International Law* vol. 95 (2001).

Rosand, Eric. "Current Developments: The Security Council's Efforts to Monitor the Implementation of Al Qaeda/Taliban Sanctions." *American Journal of International Law* vol. 745, no. 63 (2004).

Roth, Brad and Chandra Lekha Sriram. "Externalization of Justice: What Does It Mean and What Is at Stake." *Finnish Yearbook of International Law* vol. 12 (2001).

Rudolph, Christopher. "Constructing an Atrocities Regime: The Politics of War Crimes Tribunals." *International Organization* vol. 55, no. 3 (Summer 2001).

Sadat, Leila Nadya. "The Proposed Permanent International Criminal Court: An Appraisal." *Cornell International Law Journal* vol. 29, no. 3 (1996).

——. "Redefining Universal Jurisdiction." *New England Law Review* vol. 35, no. 2 (Winter 2001).

——. "Terrorism and the Rule of Law." *Washington University Global Studies Law Review*, vol. 3 (2004).

Sadat, Leila Nadya and S. Richard Carden. "The New International Criminal Court: An Uneasy Revolution." *Georgetown Law Journal* vol. 88, no. 3 (March 2000).

Sassoli, Marco. "Use and Abuse of the Laws of War in the 'War on Terrorism.'" *Law and Inequality* vol. 12, no. 2 (Summer 2004).

Scalia, Antonin. "Commentary." *St. Louis Law Journal* vol. 40 (1996).

Schacter, Jane S. "Metademocracy: The Changing Structure of Legitimation in Statutory Interpretation." *Harvard Law Review* vol. 108 (1995).

Scharf, Michael P. "The ICC's Jurisdiction over the Nationals of Non-Party States: A Critique of the U.S. Position." *Law and Contemporary Problems* vol. 64, no. 1 (Winter 2001).

Schliefer, Andrei and Robert Vishny. "Corruption." *Quarterly Journal of Economics* vol. 108 (August 1993).

Schöri, Pierre. "Painful Partnership: The United States, the European Union, and Global Governance." *Global Governance* vol. 11, no. 3 (July–September 2005).

Shue, Henry. "Torture." *Philosophy and Public Affairs* vol. 7 (1978).

Slaughter, Anne-Marie. "International Law and International Relations Theory: A Dual Agenda." *American Journal of International Law* vol. 87 (1993).

——. "International Law in a World of Liberal States." *European Journal of International Law* vol. 6 (1995).

——. "Judicial Globalization." *Virginia Journal of International Law* vol. 40 (2000).

——. "The Global Community of Courts." *Harvard Journal of International Law* vol. 44 (2003).

Slaughter, Anne-Marie and William Burke-White. "An International Constitutional Moment." *Harvard Journal of International Law* vol. 43 (Winter 2002).

Slaughter, Anne-Marie, *et al.* "International Law and International Relations Theory: A New Generation of Interdisciplinary Scholarship." *American Journal of International Law* vol. 92 (July 1998).

Slaughter Burley, Anne-Marie. "International Law and International Relations Theory: A Dual Agenda." *American Journal of International Law* vol. 87, no. 2 (April 1993).

Smis, Stefaan and Kim van der Borght. "Belgian Law Concerning the Punishment of Grave Breaches of International Humanitarian Law: A Contested Law With Uncontested Objectives." *ASIL Insights* (July 2003). Available online at www.asil.org/insights.htm#2003.

Smith, Ron and Ali Tasiran. "The Demand for Arms Imports." *Journal of Peace Research* vol. 42, no. 2 (2005).

Smith, Steve. "Paradigm Dominance in International Relations: The Development of International Relations as a Social Science." *Millennium: Journal of International Studies* vol. 16, no. 2 (1987).

Snyder, Jack and Leslie Vinjamuri. "Trials and Errors: Principle and Pragmatism in Strategies of International Justice." *International Security* vol. 28, no. 3 (Winter 2003–4).

Sofaer, Abraham. "On the Necessity of Preemption." *European Journal of International Law* vol. 14, no. 2 (2003).

Spar, Debora L. and Lane T. LaMure. "The Power of Activism: Assessing the Impact of NGOs on Global Business." *California Management Review* vol. 45 (2003).

Spiro, Peter J. "New Global Potentates: Nongovernmental Organizations and the 'Unregulated' Marketplace." *Cardozo Law Review* vol. 18 (1996).

——. "Dual Nationality and the Meaning of Citizenship." *Emory Law Journal* vol. 46 (1997).

——. "Foreign Relations Federalism." *University of Colorado Law Review* vol. 70 (1999).

——. "Globalization, International Law, and the Academy." *New York University Journal of International Law and Politics* vol. 32 (2000).

——. "The New Sovereigntists." *Foreign Affairs* (November–December 2000).

——. "Globalization and the (Foreign Affairs) Constitution." *Ohio State Law Journal* vol. 63 (2002).

——. "Treaties, International Law, and Constitutional Rights." *Stanford Law Review* vol. 55 (2003).

Sriram, Chandra Lekha. "Book Review: *The Limits of International Law* and *The Politics of International Law*." *APSR-Perspectives on Politics* vol. 3, no. 3 (September 2005).

Sunstein, Cass R. "Interest Groups in American Public Law." *Stanford Law Review* vol. 38 (1985).

Tejan-Cole, Abdul. "The Special Court for Sierra Leone: Conceptual Concerns and Alternatives." *African Human Rights Law Journal* vol. 1 (2001).

Teson, Fernando. "The Kantian Theory of International Law." *Columbia Law Review* vol. 92 (1992).

Thakur, Ramesh. "Global Norms and International Humanitarian Law: An Asian Perspective." *International Review of the Red Cross* no. 841 (March 31, 2001).

Tonnesson, Stein. "A Global Civil War?" *Security Dialogue* vol. 33, no. 3 (2002).

Trimble, Philip R. "A Revisionist View of Customary International Law." *U.C.L.A. Law Review* vol. 33 (1985).

Tucker, Robert and David Hendrickson. "The Sources of American Legitimacy." *Foreign Affairs* (November–December 2004).

Tushnet, Mark. "The Possibilities of Comparative Constitutional Law." *Yale Law Journal* vol. 108 (1999).

Vagts, Detlev. "Hegemonic International Law." *American Journal of International Law* vol. 95 (2001).

Ward, Curtis A. "Building Capacity to Combat International Terrorism: The Role of the United Nations Security Council." *Journal of Conflict & Security Law* vol. 8, no. 2 (October 2003).

Weber, Max. "Politik als Beruf." *Gesammelte Politische Schriften.* Muenchen, 1921 (lecture).

Wedgwood, Ruth. "Combatants or Criminals? How Washington Should Handle Terrorists." *Foreign Affairs* (May–June 2004).

Weiler, J. H. H. "Does Europe Need a Constitution? Demos, Telos and the German Maastricht Decision." *European Law Journal* vol. 1 (1995).

Wendt, Alexander. "Anarchy Is What States Make of It: The Social Construction of Power Politics." *International Organization* vol. 46, no. 2 (Spring 1991).

Wheeler, Nicholas. "The Bush Doctrine: The Dangers of American Exceptionalism in a Revolutionary Age." *Asian Perspective* vol. 27, no. 3 (2004).

Wiessner, Siegfried and Andrew R. Willard. "Policy-Oriented Jurisprudence and Human Rights Abuses in Internal Conflict: Toward a World Public Order of Human Dignity." *American Journal of International Law* vol. 93 (1999).

Winter, Steven L. "An Upside/Down View of the Countermajoritarian Difficulty." *Texas Law Review* vol. 69 (1991).

Wohlforth, William C. "The Stability of a Unipolar World." *International Security* vol. 24, no. 1 (Summer 1999).

Young, Ernest A. "The Trouble with Global Constitutionalism." *Texas International Law Journal* vol. 38 (2003).

Treaties, United Nations documents, cases, and other legal materials

Abbasi v. *Secretary of State for Defence, Abbasi* v. *Secretary of State for Commonwealth and Foreign Affairs.* Available online at www.courtservice.gov.uk/judgmentsfiles/j1354/abassi_judgment.htm.

African Charter on Human and Peoples' Rights. Concluded at Banjul, June 26, 1981; entered into force October 21, 1986. OAU Doc. CAB/LEG/67/3 Rev. 5. reprinted in 21 I.L.M. 59 (1982).

American Convention on Human Rights. Concluded at San José, November 22, 1969; entered into force July 18, 1978. 1144 U.N.T.S. 123, O.A.S.T.S. No. 36.

American Servicemembers' Protection Act. 22 U.S.C. 7241.

Annan, Kofi. *In Larger Freedom: Towards Development, Security and Human Rights for All.* Report of the Secretary-General of the United Nations for Decision by Heads of State and Government. September 2005.

Belgium's Amendment to the Law of 15 June 1993 (as amended by the Law of 10 February 1999 and 23 April 2003) Concerning the Punishment of Grave Breaches of Humanitarian Law. Art. 18, unofficial translation. 42 I.L.M. 1258, 1267–68 (2003).

The Caroline Case (1837). 29 Brit & For St Papers 1137.

Case Concerning Certain Criminal Proceedings in France (Republic of the Congo v. *France).* 2003. Available online at www.icj-cij.org/icjwww/idocket/icof/icofframe.htm.

Case Concerning the Arrest Warrant of 11 April 2000 (Democratic Republic of the Congo v. *Belgium)* (*Yerodia* case). I.C.J. Order of December 14, 2002. General List No. 121. Available online at www.icj-cij.org/icjwww/idocket/icobe/icobeframe.htm.

Colombian Constitutional Court Decisions T-327 and SU-1150 (March 2001 and August 2000).

Compilation and analysis of legal norms. E/CN.4/1996/52/Add.2 (1996).

Convention Against Torture. S. Treaty Doc. No. 100-20. 1465 U.N.T.S. 113–22 (December 10, 1984).

Convention for the Protection of Cultural Property in the Event of an Armed Conflict (1954). 249 U.N.T.S. 240, Art. 4(3).

Convention Respecting the Laws and Customs of War on Land (1907 Hague Convention IV) (October 18, 1907). Annex, Art. 43, 36 Stat. 2277, T.S. No. 539, 1 Bevans 631.

Decision on Challenge to Jurisdiction: Lomé Accord Amnesty. Appeals Chamber of the Special Court of Sierra Leone. Case nos. SCSL-2004-15-AR72(E) and SCSL-2004-16-AR72(E) (March 13, 2004).

Declaration of Peter Bauer Filed in Support of Plaintiffs' Motion for Preliminary Injunction Against CACI International. Para. 9, *Saleh* v. *Titan.* Case No. 04 CV 1143 R (NLS) (S.D. Cal. 2004).

EU Joint Action of 17 December 1998, 1999/34 (1999). Adopted by the Council on the basis of Article J.3 of the Treaty on the European Union's Contribution to combating the destabilizing accumulation and spread of small arms and light weapons. Available online at www.iansa.org/documents/regional/eujoint.pdf.

European Union. *European Code of Conduct on Arms Exports* (June 8, 1998). UN Doc. A/CONF.192/PC/3 (March 13, 2000).

Geneva Convention [No. III] Relative to the Treatment of Prisoners of War (August 12, 1949). Art. 118.

Guiding Principles on Internal Displacement. UN Doc. E/CN.4/1998/53/Add.2.

Inter-American Convention Against the Illicit Manufacturing of and Trafficking in Firearms, Ammunition, Explosives, and Other Related Materials (November 1997). Available online at www.iansa.org/documents/regional/reg5.htm.

Interlaken Declaration of 5 November 2002 on the Kimberley Process Certification Scheme for Rough Diamonds (2002). Available online at www.kimberlyprocess.com:8080/site/www_docs/plenary_meetings9/interlaken_declaration.pdf.

International Covenant on Civil and Political Rights (December 16, 1966). S. Exec. Doc. 95-2, 999 U.N.T.S. 171.

International Symposium on the Mandate of the Representative of the UN Secretary-General on Internally Displaced Persons. "Taking Stock and Charting the Future." 2003.

"Introductory Note by the Representative of the Secretary-General on Internally Displaced Persons." Available online at www.unhchr.ch/html/menu2/7/b/principles_lang.htm.

Knight v. *Florida*. Case No. 98–9741, 528 U.S. (1999).

Military and Paramilitary Activities In and Against Nicaragua (Nicaragua v. *United States of America)*. 1986 I.C.J. Rep. 14 (June 27, 1986).

The National Security Strategy of the United States (September 20, 2002).

Office of the UN High Commissioner for Human Rights. *Basic Principles on the Use of Force and Firearms by Law Enforcement Officials*. Adopted by the Eighth United Nations Congress on the Prevention of Crime and the Treatment of Offenders, Havana, Cuba, August 27–September 7, 1990. Available online at http://193.194.138/html/menu3/b/h_comp43.htm.

Oil Platforms (Islamic Republic of Iran v. *United States of America)*. 2003 I.C.J. Reports (November 6, 2003).

Organization of African Unity. *Bamako Declaration on an African Common Position on the Illicit Proliferation, Circulation, and Trafficking of Small Arms and Light Weapons* (December 1, 2001).

Organization of American States. *Inter-American Convention Against the Illicit Manufacturing of and Trafficking in Firearms, Ammunition, Explosives, and Other Related Materials* (December 14, 1997).

Organization for Security Cooperation in Europe (OSCE). *OSCE Document on Small Arms and Light Weapons*. FSC.DOC/1/00 (November 24, 2000).

Prosecutor v. *Charles Ghankay Taylor*. Case No. SCSL-2003-01-I, decision (May 31, 2004).

Prosecutor v. *Furundzija*. Case No. IT-95-17/1-T, Judgment, para. 153 (December 10, 1998).

Prosecutor v. *Slodoban Milosevic, Decision on Preliminary Motions*. Case No. IT-02-54 (November 8, 2001). Available online at www.un.org/icty/ind-e.htm.

Prosecutor v. *Tadić, Decision on the Defense Motion for Interlocutory Appeal on Jurisdiction*. Case No. IT-94-1, para. 70 (October 2, 1995).

Protocol Additional to the Geneva Conventions of 12 August 1949, and Relating to the Protection of Victims of International Armed Conflicts, 8 June 1977. Art. 75(3). ["Prisoner's Convention"]

Protocol to the European Convention for the Protection of Human Rights and Fundamental Freedoms. As amended by Protocol No. 11. Signed at Paris, March 20, 1952; entered into force May 18, 1954. 213 U.N.T.S 262, E.T.S. 9.

Protocole Relatif a la Creation d'un Cadre Permanent de Concertation Pour la Protection des Personnes Deplacees (February 7, 2001).

Regina R. v. *Bow St. Metro. Stipendiary Magistrate, ex parte Pinochet Ugarte* (No. 3), [2000]. 1 A.C. 147, 198 (H.L. 1999). Reprinted in 38 I.L.M. 581, 589 (1999).

Republic of Somaliland. *Submission on Statehood and Recognition of the Republic of Somaliland.* Hargeisa, 1996.

Restatement (Third) of the Foreign Relations Law of the United States. Sec. 702 and comment n (1987).

Rome Statute of the International Criminal Court (July 17, 1998). UN Doc. A/CONF. 183/9.

South African Development Cooperation. *Protocol on the Control of Firearms, Ammunition, and Other Related Materials in the Southern African Development Community Region* (August 14, 2001).

Special Court Agreement, 2002, Ratification Act, 2002. In Supplement to *Sierra Leone Gazette* vol. 130, no. 2 (March 7, 2002).

Special Court for Sierra Leone. *Prosecutor of the Special Court* v. *Sam Hinga Norman, Moinina Fofana, Allieu Kondewa.* Case No. SCSL-04-14-T (June 3, 2004).

——. *Prosecutor* v. *Augustine Gbao.* Case No. SCSL-2004-15-AR72(E) (May 25, 2004).

——. *Prosecutor* v. *Charles Ghankay Taylor.* Case No. SCSL-2003-01-I, decision (May 31, 2004).

——. *Prosecutor* v. *Kallon and Kamara, Decision on Challenge to Jurisdiction: Lomé Accord Amnesty.* Case Nos. SCSL-2004-15-AR72(E), SCSL-2004-16-AR72(E), para. 25 (SCSL App. Ch., March 13, 2004).

United Nations. *Compilation and Analysis of Legal Norms.* Report of the Representative of the Secretary-General on Internally Displaced Persons. UN Doc. E/CN.4/1996/52/Add.2 (1995).

——. *Independent Study on Best Practices, Including Recommendations, to Assist States in Strengthening Their Domestic Capacity to Combat All Aspects of Impunity, by Professor Diane Orentlicher.* UN Doc. E/CN.4/2004/88 (February 27, 2004).

——. *International Law Commission Articles on the Draft Code of Crimes Against the Peace and Security of Mankind* (1996).

——. *Letter from the Charge d'Affaires of the United Kingdom to the President of the Security Council.* UN Doc. S/2001/947 (October 7, 2001).

——. *A More Secure World: Our Shared Responsibility.* Report of the Secretary-General's High-Level Panel on Threats, Challenges, and Change. 2004.

——. *Part II: Legal Aspects Relating to the Protection Against Arbitrary Displacement.* UN Doc. E/CN.4/1998/53/Add.1 (1998).

——. *Peace Agreement Between the Government of Sierra Leone and the Revolutionary United Front of Sierra Leone.* UN SCOR, annex. UN Doc. S/1999/777.

——. *Report of the International Law Commission.* UN GAOR, 49th Sess., Supp. No. 10. UN Doc. A/49/10 (1994).

——. *Report of the Panel of Experts Appointed Pursuant to Security Council Resolution 1395 (2002), Paragraph 4, in Relation to Liberia* (April 2002).

——. *Report of the Panel of Governmental Experts on Small Arms.* UN Doc. A/52/298 (August 27, 1997).

——. *Report of the Representative of the Secretary-General.* Mr. Francis M. Deng, submitted pursuant to Commission on Human Rights Resolution 1995/57.

——. *Report of the Representative of the Secretary-General.* Mr. Francis M. Deng, submitted pursuant to Commission on Human Rights Resolution 1997/39.

——. *Report of the Representative of the Secretary-General on Internally Displaced Persons.* Francis M. Deng, submitted pursuant to Commission on Human Rights Resolution 2002/56, E/CN.4/2003/86 (January 21, 2003).

——. *Report of the Secretary-General: The Rule of Law and Transitional Justice in Conflict and Post-Conflict Societies.* UN Doc. S/2004/616 (August 23, 2004).

——. *Report of the United Nations Conference on the Illicit Trade in Small Arms and Light Weapons in All Its Aspects* (July 9–20, 2001). Available online at http://disarmament.un.org/cab/smallarms/.

——. *Statute of the International Tribunal for Rwanda* (November 8, 1994). UN Doc. S/RES/955. 33 I.L.M. 1598 (1994). Available online at www.un.org/ictr/statute.html.

——. *Statute of the International Criminal Tribunal for the Former Yugoslavia.* UN Doc. S/25704 (as amended May 17, 2002). Available online at www.un.org/icty/basic/statut/stat2000.htm

——. *Supplement to an Agenda for Peace: Position Paper of the Secretary-General on the Occasion of the Fiftieth Anniversary of the United Nations.* UN Doc. A/50/60-2/1995/1 (January 3, 1995).

——. *U.N. Convention on the Laws of the Sea* (December 10, 1982). Art. 101, 102. UN Doc. A/CONF. 62/122, 21 I.L.M. 1261 (1982).

——. *Vienna Convention on the Law of Treaties.* UN Doc. A/CONF 39/28. U.K.T.S. 58 (1980), 8 I.L.M. 679.

United Nations Department for Disarmament Affairs. "Military Spending and Development." *DDA 2002* (April 29, 2002).

United Nations Development Programme. *Human Development Report 2003.* New York, 2003.

United Nations Economic and Social Council. *Basic Principles on the Use of Force and Firearms by Law Enforcement Officials.* Eighth UN Congress on the Prevention of Crime and the Treatment of Offenders, August 27–September 7, 1990.

——. *Use and Application of the Code of Conduct for Law Enforcement Officials, Together with the Basic Principles of the Use of Force and Firearms by Law Enforcement Officials.* Report of the Secretary-General. Addendum, UN Doc. E/CN.15/1996/16/Add.2 (March 28, 1996).

United Nations Flash Appeal for the Humanitarian Requirements of the Iraq Crisis. "Six Month Response" (March 28, 2003).

United Nations General Assembly. *Code of Conduct for Law Enforcement Officials.* UN Doc. A/RES/4/169 (December 17, 1979).

——. *The Illicit Trade in Small Arms and Light Weapons in All Its Aspects.* Resolution 56/24 (December 24, 2001).

——. *Programme of Action to Prevent, Combat, and Eradicate the Illicit Trade in Small Arms and Light Weapons in All Its Aspects* (UN Programme of Action). UN Doc. A/CONF.192/15 (July 20, 2001).

——. *Protocol Against the Illicit Manufacturing of and Trafficking in Firearms, Their Parts and Components, and Ammunition, Supplementing the United Nations Convention Against Transnational Organised Crime* (UN Firearms Protocol). A/RES/55/255 (June 8, 2001).

——. *Report of the Committee on International Criminal Jurisdiction.* UN GAOR, 7th Sess., Supp. No. 11. UN Doc. A/2136 (1952).

——. *Report of the 1953 Committee on International Criminal Jurisdiction.* UN GAOR, 9th Sess., Supp. No. 12. UN Doc. A/2638 (1954).

——. Resolution A/RES/59/290 (April 15, 2005). Adopting the *International Convention for the Suppression of Acts of Nuclear Terrorism.*

——. *United Nations Convention Against Trans-national Organised Crime.* A/RES/55/25 (January 8, 2000).

——. *Universal Declaration of Human Rights.* Resolution 217 A (III) (December 10, 1948).

United Nations High Commissioner for Refugees. "Phase One of the Action Plan for Accelerated Resettlement Programme in Jaffna District Begins: Government, LTTE, and UNHCR Teams Start Work" (January 28, 2003). Press release.

——. *The State of the World's Refugees: A Humanitarian Agenda.* New York, 1998.

——. *UNHCR Global Report 2002.* New York, 2003.

United Nations Mission in Sierra Leone mandate. UN Doc. S/RES/1270 (October 22, 1999).

United Nations Security Council. *Report of the Panel of Experts on Somalia Pursuant to Security Council Resolution 1425 (2002)* (March 25, 2003).

——. *Report of the Team of Experts Appointed Pursuant to Security Council Resolution 1407 (2002), Paragraph 1, Concerning Somalia* (July 3, 2002).

——. Resolution 1315. UN Doc. S/Res/1315 (August 14, 2000).

——. *Resolution 1325 on Women, Peace, and Security.* UN Doc. S/RES/1325 (October 31, 2000).

——. Resolution 1441.UN Doc. S/RES/1441 (November 8, 2002).

United States v. *Verdugo-Urquidez.* 494 U.S. 259 (1990).

Universal Declaration of Human Rights. General Assembly Resolution 217A. UN GAOR, 3rd Sess., Pt. 1, 183rd plenary meeting, at 75. UN Doc. A/810 (1948).

US Congress. "Hearing Before the Subcommittee on International Operations of the Senate Committee on Foreign Relations of the United States Senate. July 23, 1998. 105th Cong., 2nd Sess., S. Rep. No. 105724.

White House. *Presidential Directive No. 6* (2001).

World Health Organization. "Internally Displaced Persons, Health, and WHO." Paper presented at the humanitarian affairs segment of the substantive session of the Economic and Social Council for 2000.

——. *Small Arms and Global Health.* Geneva, 2001.

——. *World Report on Violence and Health.* Geneva: Oxford University Press, 2002.

INDEX